THE HUMP

Number 134:
Williams-Ford Texas A&M University Military History Series

THE HUMP

America's Strategy for Keeping China
in World War II

JOHN D. PLATING

Texas A&M University Press
College Station

This paper meets the requirements of ANSI/NISO Z39.48-1992 (Permanence of Paper).

Binding materials have been chosen for durability.

Library of Congress Cataloging-in-Publication Data

Plating, John D. (John David), 1967–

   The Hump : America's strategy for keeping China in World War II / John D. Plating. – 1st ed.

     p. cm. – (Williams-Ford Texas A&M University military history series ; no. 134)

   Includes bibliographical references and index.

   ISBN-13: 978-1-60344-237-4 (cloth : alk. paper)

   ISBN-10: 1-60344-237-5 (cloth : alk. paper)

   ISBN-13: 978-1-60344-238-1 (e-book)

   ISBN-10: 1-60344-238-3 (e-book)

   1. World War, 1939–1945–Aerial operations, American. 2. World War, 1939–1945–China.

3. World War, 1939– 1945–Himalaya Mountains. 4. Airlift, Military–United States–History–20th

century. 5. United States. Army Air Forces–Transport service–History. 6. United States–Foreign

relations–1933–1945. 7. Military doctrine–United States–History–20th century. I. Title. II. Series:

Williams-Ford Texas A&M University military history series ; no. 134.

D790.2.P59 2011

940.54′49730951–dc22

                                       2010034329

To the aircrews who flew the Hump

CONTENTS

LIST OF ILLUSTRATIONS

ACKNOWLEDGMENTS

Many people have helped make this project a reality. First, I want to thank Jerry White for his casual remark to me in 2003 when he expressed that no one had yet subjected the Hump airlift to academic scrutiny. A quick survey of the literature on the operation proved the truth of his point, prompting me to see what I might contribute to this void in airpower history.

Jay Vinyard and the generous members of the Hump Pilots Association (HPA) made my job much easier by sharing many hours of war stories and anecdotes that raised my appreciation for the Hump's challenges. As the president of the HPA in its final year of formal existence (it disbanded in December 2005), Jay was always willing to share his assessment of the airlift with an uncommon degree of lucidity and candor. He brought a unique blend of professionalism and warmth to the leadership of that organization and was always prepared to lend me an ear and give me his time as I sought to get "inside" the Hump some six decades after it happened.

I would also like to thank the research assistants at the Air Force Historical Research Agency (AFHRA), the Air Mobility Command History Office (AMC/HO), and the National Museum of the U.S. Air Force for their help. Toni Petito at AFHRA was always willing to go out of her way to lend a hand or mail off a specially requested document, and Mark Morgan was kind enough to feed me a constant supply of Air Transport Command files during my visit to Scott Air Force Base; Brett Stolle was also very helpful in digging for documents at the Air Force's museum in Dayton, Ohio.

I would also like to thank Don Bishop for his encouragement in prodding me to make a research trip to China in 2005. He and his staff at the U.S. Embassy made the excursion a worthwhile endeavor that will not soon be forgotten. I also want to extend my special thanks to Zou Guihu and Lan Xi for their indispensable translation help, without which I would have been sorely lost. Thanks should also go to Professor Wang Jianlang (deputy director of the Institute of Modern History at the Chinese Academy of Social Sciences), Liu Xiatong, and Li Xiaowei for their help in sharing with me the Chinese perspective of the Anti-Japanese War and the place of the Hump in that history. I also want to extend my thanks for the rich hospitality and generosity of Fan Jianchuan, the owner of the Jian- chuan Museum in Dayi County, Sichuan Province.

I especially want to thank Professor Joe Guilmartin for his timely pep talks and constant encouragement as my advisor on this project. He never failed to provide me needed chiding when I found myself questioning the focus of this project, while also giving me constant reminders that history often turns on very narrow details. He perhaps helped me most by trusting that I could pull this off, even when I had serious doubts. I also want to thank Professor Allan Millett for his encouragement and insight that helped to keep this study on track. I am also greatly indebted to Professor Chris Reed for the level of academic rigor he required of me, one that forced me to grapple with this topic from both American and Chinese perspectives. Dennis Showalter also deserves my thanks for taking the time to plow through my manuscript to offer his vote of confidence.

I also want to thank Dr. Roger Miller of the Air Force Historical Studies Office for his insights on the revolutionary impact of airlifts on World War II, not- ing that air transport deserves as much visibility as strategic bombing and tactical aviation in the larger rubric of airpower studies. I am also indebted to Ed Kaplan, a friend and comrade whose technical expertise helped to make my life as a researcher infinitely easier. Additionally, I want to express my thanks to Mary Lenn Dixon and Thom Lemmons at Texas A&M University Press for the pro- fessional support offered in this work's publication. Lastly–but surely not least–I want to thank my wife Paula, who tirelessly nurtured and cared for our five chil- dren in my absence and who served–at the same time–as my keenest critic and biggest fan. Without her support none of this would have been possible.

THE HUMP

INTRODUCTION

The trans-Himalayan airlift of World War II, better known as the "Hump,"[1] is recognized among specialists as the first sustained and most ambitious combat airlift operation in modern history, though its full impact has received little attention. Cobbled together with only a handful of airplanes and aircrews in early 1942, the operation grew to become the best tangible expression of the U.S. government's commitment to China, in the end delivering nearly 740,000 tons of cargo and dwarfing the supplies delivered to China by land over the Burma and Ledo Roads.[2] This airlift operation was carried out in what is arguably the world's worst weather system and over its most rugged terrain, all the while under the constant threat of enemy attack. Despite its reputation, the Hump has never been the topic of a concentrated study; existing books on the airlift are either memoirs of participants or short popular histories.[3] Typically the airlift operation is cast as an appendage to the larger story of the China-Burma-India (CBI) theater, though no historical inquiry has yet to objectively explore the operation in detail with an eye toward the Hump's central place in the CBI narrative.

This monograph argues that the Hump airlift was initially undertaken to serve as a display of U.S. support for its Chinese ally, which had been at war with Japan since 1937. However, by the start of 1944, with the airlift's capability gaining momentum, U.S. strategists set aside concerns for the ephemeral goal of bolstering Chinese national will and instead used the airlift as the chief means of supplying U.S. forces in China in preparation for their final assault on Japan. From the standpoint of war matériel, it comes as no surprise that the airlift was *the* precondition that had to be met to make possible all other Allied military[1] action, as it was an enabling force in the theater. It dictated the level of effort the Americans could bring to bear against the Japanese, being the sole route to China until the end of 1944, when the newly built Ledo Road connected with the older

1

[1] All other mil action? Seems like a stretch given the two other larger theater pushes.∴

Burma Road to form the Stilwell Road. Other routes of supply were discussed and attempted, but in the end the best way for supplies to get into China was over the Himalayas. The airlift was also consistent with the broader airpower orientation of the theater. Difficult terrain, extreme weather, and primitive roads all combined to make the CBI a theater best traversed by air. It was in the CBI, and only in the CBI, that Allied troops were most commonly inserted, supplied, and extracted by air. And because decision makers deemed the CBI theater of lesser importance than Europe or the Pacific, it got fewer supplies and its manpower base was only a fraction of these other theaters. This meant that fewer Americans (and other Allies) would be deployed here, making airpower the best means of getting the most return for the Allied investment.

In the European theater the primary expression of airpower came in the form of strategic bombing, as the Anglo-U.S. Combined Bomber Offensive sought to constitute an aerial front in Western Europe until such a time as a land invasion could take place. In the Pacific the primary use of airpower came first in the form of carrier aviation, then later in the form of strategic bombardment culminating with the first-ever use of atomic weapons. But in the CBI airpower was expressed in a wide array of forms to include strategic bombardment (seen in Operation Matterhorn, the first B-29 attacks on Japan, launched from China), fighter aviation (with Claire Chennault's Fourteenth Air Force maintaining air superiority over Japanese forces in China), and, most important, in the form of air transport—transport to companies of troops trapped behind Japanese lines, transport of special forces–type "long-range penetration groups" that worked to wreak havoc deep in enemy territory, or transport on the grand scale, like the Hump. But this airlift was not simply a means of supply with implications for military strategy in the CBI. It had a powerful political component as well.

Within days of the Japanese attack on Pearl Harbor, Roosevelt pushed for the creation of the China Theater of operations (CT). Churchill, who was more concerned with maintaining Britain's Asian colonial holdings, viewed an alliance with China as potentially dangerous vis-à-vis the growing Indian independence movement, but he went along with the decision, if only to humor his U.S. counterpart. Generalissimo Chiang Kaishek, the head of the Nationalist (in Chinese, Guomindang or GMD) government, was designated as that theater's supreme commander.[4] The declaration was really a matter of expedience, though, as the

Chinese had been at war with Japan since the summer of 1937 and it was in the Allies' best interest to keep China a strong fighting force in an effort to tie down the nearly one million Japanese soldiers on Chinese soil. Chiang was not fooled by the Anglo-U.S. rhetoric, though, as he knew full well if he–together with Stalin–was to be considered one of the so-called "Big Four," it was in name only. The weight of the war's effort was being dedicated to Europe–something Roosevelt and Churchill agreed upon at the Arcadia Conference in January 1942–such that any Chinese solicitations for wartime aid would have to compete from a disadvantaged position with the Allies' broader wartime strategy.

THE HUMP AND WARTIME STRATEGY

What ensued was a series of diplomatic maneuvers between Roosevelt and Chiang, with the Hump used as a bargaining chip. U.S. rhetoric elevated the importance of China, calling it a major theater of war, but only a few U.S. combat soldiers were deployed there, no ground offensives were to be planned or executed against the Japanese except for the recapture of Burma in 1944 (but, as will be discussed later, even this objective had mixed motives), and the only dedicated U.S. air component in China was Chennault's Fourteenth Air Force–the smallest of all U.S. "numbered" air forces. Chiang suspected that China was only marginally important to the United States, but he also knew he could use U.S. claims of China's supposed importance against Roosevelt–something that allowed the generalissimo to make frequent demands of the United States, usually in the form of increased Hump tonnage.[5]

On the other side of the table, Roosevelt could point to a number of things to show his commitment to his Chinese ally; but at the end of the day, the Hump's haul, expressed in tons per month, became the most expedient gauge of U.S. allegiance to China. Over time, U.S. success could be measured in tons, as in December 1943, when the presidentially mandated (and long past due) goal of ten thousand tons per month was finally reached. In modern managerial parlance, the number of tons per month delivered to China became the "metric" by which Chiang was supposed to feel the weight of U.S. commitment. It was a firm quantity that could be measured and marked. This monthly figure became so important that it was often under the scrutiny of either Roosevelt or Marshall, becoming something of a fetish in the War Department because it was a quantitative reflection of the United States' alliance with China. As the war progressed, Hump tonnage reporting was honed to a science as statisticians meticulously tracked the airlift's deliveries, projected monthly outcomes, and quickly notified senior commanders (and even the president) of operations that might divert missions from the raw tonnage transported from India to China—even if those "distractions" were fundamental to the well-being of the airlift itself.[6] Thus, by the end of the war, with Air Transport Command (ATC) delivering over 71,000 tons in July 1945 (a twenty-fold increase from two years earlier), U.S. political and military leaders could look with satisfaction on the fact that they had lived up to their wartime commitment to China.

Roosevelt's push to have China regarded as a major theater of the war—despite Churchill's antipathy toward the idea—was not pulled out of thin air. FDR time and again showed a predisposition to look past the war, seeing China through eyes that blended romantic and pragmatic elements. During his first year in office he remarked, "I have always had the deepest sympathy for the Chinese," a sentiment likely shaped by his family's years of trade with China.[7] But he also considered a strong China to be a stabilizing force in Asia, especially because he anticipated the demise of British, French, and Dutch colonial holdings and feared that once the Japanese were vanquished, the power vacuum might be filled by the Soviets.[8] China's reemergence as an Asian power—and U.S. ally—was a solution to this eventuality, and there was plenty of U.S. popular sentiment to go along with Roosevelt's vision. In his State of the Union address to Congress just a month after the attack on Pearl Harbor, he praised the "brave people of China . . . who for four and a half years have withstood the bombs and starvation and have whipped the invaders time and again," a declaration that provoked the speech's loudest applause. FDR was not speaking to the wind, either. Polls taken in 1942 showed that between 80 and 86 percent of respondents believed that China could be depended on as an ally both during and after the war; two years later nearly two-thirds of those polled felt that China, along with Great Britain, the Soviet Union, and the United States, should have the most influence in an international body like the postwar United Nations.[9] By way of exposure, well-known missionaries like Pearl Buck served as cultural conduits between China and the U.S. public. Perhaps the most influential of these was not a missionary but rather a missionary's son, Henry R. Luce. Luce's *Time* magazine made

4

China regular fare for the reading public, featuring Chiang Kaishek on the cover eight times between 1927 and the end of 1941.[10] Additionally, the China Lobby enjoyed tremendous political influence and succeeded in helping Madame Chiang become the first Asian and second woman ever to address the U.S. Congress. Indeed, the United States had a clear inclination toward China as December 1941 approached, though not all sentiment was altruistic.

It was also strategically expedient for the United States to place Chiang on equal terms with Churchill and Stalin. The cornerstone of U.S. strategy toward China was twofold: its geographic proximity to Japan made it useful as a potential staging base for both strategic bombing attacks and a land invasion of the Japanese home islands, and it was in the best interest of the United States to keep the occupational force of nearly one million Japanese soldiers tied up in China and not fighting to defend Japanese holdings elsewhere in the Pacific. The Americans adopted a "Europe first" strategy in the weeks following Pearl Harbor, and if they were unable or unwilling to go on the offensive against the Japanese, at least they could work to sustain the Chinese, who had been at war with Japan for the past four years. China had been a recipient of U.S. aid–through the Lend-Lease program–in the summer of 1941 and had played host to a U.S. military mission in Chongqing dedicated to overseeing that flow of supplies. This mission was expanded significantly in February 1942, when Roosevelt sent Lt. Gen. Joseph W. Stilwell to China to serve in a dual-purpose capacity as both the commander of all U.S. forces in the theater (of which there were only a handful) and as Chiang's chief of staff. The United States would eventually deal directly with the Japanese, but for the time being the Chinese would have to serve as a proxy for the United States.

WORLD WAR II IN CHINA: THREE WARS IN ONE

This role, of course, assumes that the Chinese were willing to adopt the U.S. strategy while also receiving U.S. aid. But the way the Americans viewed the war in China was incongruous with the Chinese perspective, a difference that grew into the greatest source of discord between the two nations. While the war on the mainland was seen by the United States as an extension of a larger Pacific war against Japan, with China serving as the "western front" of that war, Chiang saw the war as three wars in one. First, and perhaps most important, there was his ongoing war against the Chinese Communists; it was this on-again, off-again civil war that in his mind—and, in retrospect, in reality—trumped all other conflicts on the mainland. Despite the facade of a Nationalist-Communist "united front" (which ended before the United States entered the war), Chiang was serious when he famously said that he regarded the Japanese as only a "disease of the skin," while the Communists were a "disease of the heart."[11]

Second, there was the War of Resistance against Japanese Aggression, or "War of Resistance" for short. This war was rooted in events of 1931, when the Japanese invaded and annexed Manchuria, renaming it Manchukuo and establishing a puppet Chinese government in the province. Tensions grew until the outbreak of a full-scale war in the summer of 1937, with the Nationalist government moving from Nanjing to Chongqing in China's southwestern Sichuan Province and adopting a strategy that traded space for time.

The third war the Nationalists were involved in—yet only by way of alliance—was World War II in the Pacific. Chiang's role as supreme commander of the China Theater gave him great international esteem (as well as a fair amount of domestic stature), but it also meant that his allies expected him to commit his troops to the defense of India and the reconquest of Burma—no small feat, as Chinese nationalism was diametrically opposed to British imperialism. So while the Allies expected Chiang to see the Japanese as his chief opponent in a larger Asian war, Chiang saw the Communists as his fundamental rivals in China, with the Japanese presence only exacerbating that problem. The best Chiang could do was to employ the art of *yiwu*, or "barbarian management," an ancient Chinese skill that blended diplomacy and military strategy in pitting one "barbarian" (the Americans) against another (the Japanese).[12] His was not a position of power. China was militarily weak at the end of 1941, its economy was in shambles, and its government's authority was questionable, but the infusion of U.S. aid coming as it did from India over the Himalayas meant Chiang could protect his power base in Chongqing, continue a small-scale campaign against the Japanese, all the while preparing to confront his real opponent, the Communists.

AIRLIFT AS AIRPOWER

Five themes weave their way through my discussions of the interaction of airpower, logistics, and strategy in the context of the Hump airlift. These include:

airlift as an expression of airpower; the Hump as a dramatic feat of aerial logistics; the impact of the Hump in both theater and global war strategy; airlift as an expression of the "national-ness" of airpower; and airlift as facilitating a paradigm shift in global logistics.

First, in considering airlift as an expression of airpower, it is important to recognize that the broader topic of airpower still suffers from the fact that it is largely understood in terms of land and sea warfare. Put geometrically, airpower is still studied in two dimensions rather than three. Early airpower advocates complained that their land and seaborne peers were not "air minded" enough to conceptually grasp the nuances of airpower thinking, thus arguing that only airmen should employ and control airpower. One contributing factor here was that these early airmen really *did* understand aerial warfare infinitely better than their land and naval counterparts, but their understanding was intuitive—coming from practical experience—as they were first men of action, not of words. This argument eventually led to the formation of a separate service in the United States, but airmen have still yet to produce their "Clausewitz" in constructing a systematic understanding of air war. Air transport especially suffers in this regard, as it is usually viewed as a subcategory of logistics, even though air transport's speed, range, and geographic indifference make it unique among other forms of logistics. The Hump serves as an example of a strategically vital airlift campaign that will allow the "airpower-ness" of airlift to be explored in fuller detail, allowing us to see airlift *as* airpower, not something that merely *supports* airpower.

THE HUMP AS A FEAT OF AERIAL LOGISTICS

In the summer of 2006 I made a nonstop flight from Beijing to Chicago. Thanks to a courtesy upgrade from the airline, I was sitting in business class in a Boeing 747–400, complete with personal flight attendant service (who never let my glass of pinot noir go empty), my own television screen on which I could watch any number of first-run Hollywood films, and a seat that reclined to a near-horizontal position. I was warm, well fed, and entertained beyond imagination—and my experience at 39,000 feet crossing over northern Siberia could not have been farther from that of the men who crossed the Himalayas some six decades earlier. Mine was ridiculously comfortable, and except for the amount of leg room, choice of movies to watch, or amount (and quality) of food and drink I enjoyed, my experience during that fourteen-hour flight is not too fundamentally different from that of most who have experienced air travel over the past forty years. In short, contemporary jet travel—which has changed little since the proliferation of Boeing's 707 in the 1960s—bears scant resemblance to a wartime flight over the Himalayas, though it is tempting for today's reader to interpret Hump flights through the lens of their own air travel experiences. As a pilot with flight experience in modern military transports, I can say that my own experience only slightly resembles that of the Hump's flyers, but when one considers the environment in which they flew, the planes they operated, and the loads they carried, it becomes evident that a great chasm separates today's air travelers with those who flew the Hump.

In light of the stark difference between contemporary jet aviation and World War II–era flight, the next theme of this work considers the Hump airlift as a dramatic feat of aerial logistics. What I have outlined above addresses the personal experiences of those who flew the missions, but the unusual nature of the Hump as an artifact of aviation prowess *is the fact that it was contemplated and tried in the first place.* Airlift was not a novel concept at the beginning of World War II, but what was novel was that the United States was both willing and able to deliver such a large amount of supplies by air, especially considering the numerous obstacles. It is for this reason that those veterans of the Hump still puff out their chests and recount their favorite Hump stories with rich bravado. In some ways they are no different from any other war veteran, but their stories differ from those of their bomber-crew peers or fighter-pilot buddies in one key respect: the Hump pilot's victory was over the weather and the terrain, impersonal foes that were no less deadly or predictable than enemy fighters or flak.

THE HUMP'S IMPACT ON WARTIME STRATEGY

The impact of the Hump airlift was felt both materially and symbolically. Because the Allies' main objective was to keep China in the war and because the Hump was the main method of accomplishing this, the operation really deserves to be viewed as central to the Allied strategy in the CBI, not simply an ancillary logistical mission. Throughout the war Hump deliveries were parsed out to one of three places: they contributed to Stilwell's effort to equip and train nearly 30,000 Chinese troops, they supported Chennault's China-based U.S. Air Force component, or they went directly to the Chinese government. The first two recipients got the lion's share of the supplies, and that created a strategic conflict all its own, as Stilwell and Chennault constantly bickered over who should be allowed to get the most tonnage. On its face, it would seem that Stilwell, the overall U.S. commander in the CBI, could have done as he pleased, but such was not the case, as Roosevelt was enamored of Chennault's claims that China-based airpower could do great harm to the Japanese—perhaps even defeating them—without the unnecessary trappings of a slow-moving ground component. Regardless of the wrangling between Stilwell and Chennault, it was still the Hump that made possible their actions. Stepping back, it is also important to note that the Hump airlift was a strategic choice that had implications in other theaters, as a significant proportion of the transport capability of the U.S. Army Air Forces (AAF) was sent to India and not to North Africa, Italy, or the Southwest Pacific.

As mentioned earlier, the Hump airlift was also important as a symbol of U.S. support for the Chinese government. The Sino-U.S. relationship, which predated the 1911 revolution, was one that reached its fullest maturity by 1941 with the U.S. pledge of Lend-Lease aid to the Chinese as well as to the British and Soviets. It is important to bear in mind that, in the ups and downs of this wartime relationship, the Hump airlift was the ever-present reminder of the U.S. government's commitment to China. Thus, the visible manifestation of the U.S. slogan to "keep China in the war" was first expressed with the Hump airlift. The following study will investigate both the material and symbolic components of the airlift with an eye toward discovering whether the airlift really *did* keep the Chinese from surrendering to the Japanese before August 1945.

AIRLIFT AND THE "NATIONAL-NESS" OF AIRPOWER

Among the different forms of airpower, air transport is unique because it has a nonmilitary parallel in the form of commercial aviation. In fact, within the context of a market economy, the commercial side of air transport before the war operated on a larger scale and with more efficiency and expertise than its military cousin. Immediately following the United States' entry in the war, the air transport fleet of the U.S. Army Air Corps numbered only 254 airplanes, a mere 2 percent of its total inventory of 12,297 airplanes.[13] Recognizing this shortfall, Henry "Hap" Arnold, the Air Corps' top general, began wooing airline executives to come work for him as commissioned officers.[14] The most celebrated of these officers was C. R. Smith, the man who led American Airlines for over thirty years, building that airline into one of the world's largest until he retired in 1968. Smith was among the dozens of executives "hired" by Arnold in early 1942 after the Air Corps commander recognized that the force lacked any expertise in organizing, maintaining, and equipping an air transport component. Fortunately, this expertise was resident in spades in civil aviation, with Arnold's affability wooing many of these executives to don an Air Corps uniform during the war.[15] Air transport involves much more than pilots and planes; it includes an equally important emphasis on flight scheduling, route organization, aircraft maintenance, the on-loading and off-loading of cargo, and mission planning. C. R. Smith and his civilian colleagues would be just the cohort of expertise Arnold needed to build what became—by the end of the war—the world's largest airline.

As an aside, this brings up an important point in the broader study of society and warfare—the role of permeability between civil and military spheres in fields where a specific technology clearly overlaps both realms. In most cases, the society that allows a free flow of ideas between these two areas is the one to see the most effective use of a specific technological tool, and this is clearly borne out with the United States' military air transport service in World War II, as military leaders were wise enough to recruit experts from outside their ranks, men who at the time were managing the world's most robust commercial airline companies.[16]

AIRLIFT AS A PARADIGM SHIFT IN GLOBAL LOGISTICS

The fifth theme has to do with the way the Hump reveals what is arguably the most overlooked or underrated airpower revolution of World War II, that of global air transport.[17] Much of the focus in airpower studies during the war is fixed on strategic bombing, a natural response, given the destruction wrought by the Allied bombing campaign over Germany and the U.S. atomic attacks on Japan, with these discussions usually distilling to a debate over the efficacy or morality of the bombings. But strategic bombing was not new in World War II; it was employed in the German Zeppelin and Gotha raids over England and the Allied bomber attacks on Germany in World War I. Strategic bombing did bring a revolutionary dimension to warfare, but it did so much earlier than 1939. The only truly new aspect of airpower to manifest itself in World War II was in the arena of air transport, as it allowed logistics–the "lifeblood of war"–to become a three-dimensional affair.

Airlift, like airpower in general, tends to blur the distinctions between *tactical* and *strategic* aspects of warfare. Tactics is traditionally understood as those means employed to achieve an end in battle, while strategy is concerned with the larger context, with Clausewitz defining it as "the employment of battles to gain the end of war." Logistics–the supply of armies–is wedded to tactics and strategy and is typically viewed in terms of either tactical logistics (the supply of an army on the battlefield) or strategic logistics (the positioning of supplies in preparation for a campaign). But the speed and range of air transport obscures this distinction, as witnessed in the summer of 1942 during Rommel's push toward Cairo. On the evening of July 2, a Royal Air Force (RAF) liaison officer to the British Army notified his contacts at Heliopolis Field (near Cairo) that they had no more antitank shell fuses, a desperate circumstance as a German attack was imminent. Heliopolis contacted the port at Lagos (in Nigeria), some 3,100 miles away, where a shipload of fuses was being off-loaded. The airfield at Accra (in modern-day Ghana) was phoned and crews were scrambled to pick up the fuses and fly them to Egypt as soon as possible. The first planeload of fuses landed in Heliopolis less than forty-eight hours from the first phone call and were delivered to the front as the Germans were moving into position for the attack–an attack that was blunted.[18] Airpower altered war's geometry by facilitating war in the third dimension, but air transport enhanced this alteration by accelerating the category of time and expanding the category of distance, connecting theaters of war into an integrated whole. In this sense air transport mutes earlier geographic limitations on warfare. The ability to deliver soldiers and supplies anywhere in the world in a matter of hours has paradigmatically altered the shape of modern warfare; just as Pax Britannica of the nineteenth century was facilitated by British sea power, so today's so-called Pax Americana has been facilitated by airpower–airpower in both its lethal and nonlethal forms.

THE THREE STAGES OF THE HUMP

The history of the Hump airlift naturally divides into three phases,[19] which is the general pattern this work follows, with the exception of a chapter devoted to weather, terrain, pilots, and planes. The first phase is called the "barnstorming" period, from the airlift's conception in early 1942 to what I refer to as FDR's "institutionalization" of the Hump in May 1943. During this first phase the airlift witnessed a time of ad hoc organization, few airplanes and crews, and little coordination resulting from a "catch-as-catch-can" attitude. Military aviators would refer to this early airlift as a "flying club," as individual pilots decided whether they wanted to fly, served as their own weather forecasters, and chose their own routes of flight. With U.S. strategy in Asia in general disarray, it is no surprise that the Hump bore the same marks. Those who were skeptical of the airlift's potential, such as Brig. Gen. Clayton Bissell, continually pointed to this first year as an example of how little could be delivered to China by air. The beginning of the end of this first phase came in December 1942, when the airlift was made part of the Air Corps' Air Transport Command, an organizational move that began to transform the airlift into a deliberate air transport effort.

The Hump's second phase covers the thirteen months from May 1943 to May 1944, the most important period in the Hump's history. It began with the AAF's furious effort to carry out Roosevelt's taxing order to expand the airlift so that it could first double, then triple, its delivered tonnage in less than four months. It is no surprise that the Hump was three months late in meeting FDR's goal, but it *was* a great surprise that the goal was met *only* three months late. This was also the most dangerous time to fly the Hump; routes were still undefined, weather reporting was accomplished pilot-to-pilot, ground-based navigation aids were still only an idea, and enemy fighters began their own "anti-Hump" effort, deliberately targeting transports in flight and on the ground. Strong leadership was the key to the success of this period; Col. Thomas Hardin, a former TWA executive, demanded more of the Hump's planes and pilots than anyone else thought possible. His hard-charging style brought the airlift through its most difficult and most important time of growth. This second phase came to an end with the capture of Myitkyina, a Japanese stronghold in north Burma, allowing the airlift to fly a more southerly, direct route to China over lower terrain.

The Hump's third phase covered the period from May 1944 until the airlift's end in November 1945. This was the so-called heyday of the airlift campaign, with monthly tonnage increases taking on an exponential dimension. Brig. Gen. William Tunner—the man who would later be best known for leading the Berlin Airlift—built off of Hardin's work and made the operation a booming success, as the airlift's best delivery month, July 1945, hauled thirty-five times more cargo than the same month just three years earlier. This was the period of "big business," with the airlift bearing all the marks of an efficient commercial airline, complete with refined organization, innovative aircraft maintenance procedures, and choreographed routes of flight. Ironically, it was also during this period that China's importance in the United States' strategic calculus was on the decline.

As we shall see, the Hump's legacy is far-reaching. It became the example and prototype for the Berlin Airlift—the first air battle of the Cold War. It also bore significantly on the initial moves of the Chinese Civil War, when Air Transport Command aircraft moved entire armies of Nationalist troops hundreds of miles in a matter of days to be in position to keep Zhu De's Communist forces from accepting the Japanese surrender—a noteworthy accomplishment, especially because the United States was committed to a position of neutrality between Chiang and Mao. Lastly, the Hump sheds some light on the manner in which diplomatic alliances are nourished and maintained, seen in the way the China Theater was sustained as much by the matériel delivered by Hump aircraft as it was by the way that airlift displayed the United States' moral commitment to its Chinese ally.

FROM THE MARCO POLO BRIDGE
TO ABC FERRY COMMAND

JULY 1937 TO MARCH 1942

On the muggy evening of July 7, 1937, Japanese soldiers from the North China Garrison Army were on maneuvers on the banks of the Yanting River southwest of Beijing. The Boxer indemnity protocols allowed them to conduct military exercises, even though such actions did little to assuage mounting friction between Chinese and Japanese. Then, just before midnight while the troops were taking a break, they claimed they were fired upon. A brief skirmish ensued, and when the Japanese roll was called, one soldier, Private Kikujiro Shimura, was missing. Assuming the shots were fired by Chinese Nationalists, the Japanese demanded that they be allowed to search for the private in the nearby town of Wanping. Local Chinese officers refused to allow the search, and so the Japanese opened fire and assaulted the town, an attack that was repelled by the Chinese Twenty-ninth Army the next day.

To this day, both parties accuse the other of firing the first shots that night, and though precise culpability might be difficult to ascribe, clearly this incident at the Marco Polo Bridge (Lugouqiao in Chinese sources) was merely the spark that ignited the tinderbox of Sino-Japanese tension. Claiming that China was the "sick man of Asia," the Japanese government was most concerned with checking the on-again, off-again revolution on the mainland, fearing the Soviets would take advantage of Chinese weakness. Occupying Manchuria in 1931 and imposing puppet rule the next year, the Japanese forced the Soviets to sell them the China Eastern Railway four years later. Ever wary of the growing warmth between Moscow and Nanjing, the capital of Nationalist China, the Japanese quickly recognized that the events that night at the Marco Polo Bridge needed a stout response and immediately mobilized five divisions of the Guandong Army to begin pouring troops into the area. China's Generalissimo Chiang Kaishek had been forcibly goaded into a so-called United Front with the Chinese Communists after the dramatic episode at Xian six months earlier, and he was now emboldened to meet Japanese aggression with Chinese force, declaring "the limits of endurance had been reached."[1]

Japanese commanders anticipated a quick war, predicting that it would take only three months to subdue the Chinese; such thinking was wishful, considering it took sixteen months to reach some sort of strategic stalemate, with the war never ending on pro-Japanese terms.[2] The war comprised two major fronts: one in the north that stretched west and south from the Tianjin-Beijing area, and the other in central China, spreading west and south from Shanghai. The Japanese path of advance was no secret, as it followed either the major rivers or railroads of China. Both the Yellow and Yangzi Rivers were followed inland for roughly five hundred miles, while the two key north-south railroads—the Tianjin-Nanjing and Beijing-Hankou lines—were captured and controlled by the Japanese to serve as their main arteries of internal supply. In addition, Japanese soldiers were better equipped and better led, and they won nearly every battle on their way to sealing off China's coast, while also killing thousands of civilians along the way. The cost was high, though, as the Chinese bravely held for three months before retreating at Shanghai in the fall of 1937, winning a stunning victory at Tai'erzhuang the following spring.[3] In the words of Edward Drea, the war had become a "meat-grinder," with the China Expeditionary Army (CEA) of the Imperial Japanese Army (IJA) deploying some 700,000 troops to China in the first six months of the war, with twenty-three divisions in place by July 1938. This commitment was especially troublesome in light of the fact that Japan's main strategic concern was the Soviet Union, with the IJA having only nine divisions deployed to Manchuria and Korea. Japanese casualties numbered 600,000 by December 1941—Chinese military and civilian deaths probably numbered in the millions—but still the

Nationalists did not capitulate, moving their capital to Chongqing, deep into the heart of western China. Japanese military strategy held that the best way to defeat the Chinese was by sealing off all paths of supply, or "lines of communication" in military parlance. If China had no external aid, it would then surrender.[4] What followed was a logistical war, with the Japanese working to close off all established means of supply faster than the Chinese could acquire new ones.

ROUTES OF SUPPLY AND STRATEGIC STRANGULATION

From the beginning of the Sino-Japanese War in July 1937 until the Japanese capture of northern Burma five years later, there were four main arteries of supply for the Nationalist government. Listed in the order in which they were eventually blocked by either direct Japanese military intervention or diplomatic pressure, these included shipping that entered through Hong Kong to the port at Guangzhou, shipping that entered through the port at Haiphong in Indochina, the overland route from Soviet Kazakhstan along the ancient Silk Road, and the overland route along the Burma Road. Each route had its own challenges—both for the Chinese who used them and for the Japanese who worked to seal them off—but it is important to bear in mind that they were considered by both belligerents to be the keys to the war. Japanese strategy, not just in China, but in greater Southeast Asia, was driven in large part by a desire to seal China's borders and achieve victory by imposing logistical starvation, ending a war that by 1940 had dragged on too long (see figure 1).

The first route of supply was the port of Hong Kong (nearby Guangzhou) on China's southeastern coast, which was the most substantial for the Chinese but also the easiest for the Japanese to secure. The Imperial Japanese Navy (IJN) declared the entire coast of China closed on August 25, 1937, just seven weeks after hostilities began, a testimony to the absence of a Chinese navy. One flaw in the blockade was the fact that the Japanese could exercise jurisdiction only over Chinese vessels, as foreign ships were free to enter ports unchallenged by Japanese soldiers of the CEA. That left Guangzhou opened, which was a boon for Chiang Kaishek as roughly 80 percent of all military aid had flowed through this port before the war began. Nearly as important was the fact that regular trade was conducted through Guangzhou as well; 55 percent of all foreign imports entered China here in the third quarter of 1937.[5] This situation changed in the fall of 1938

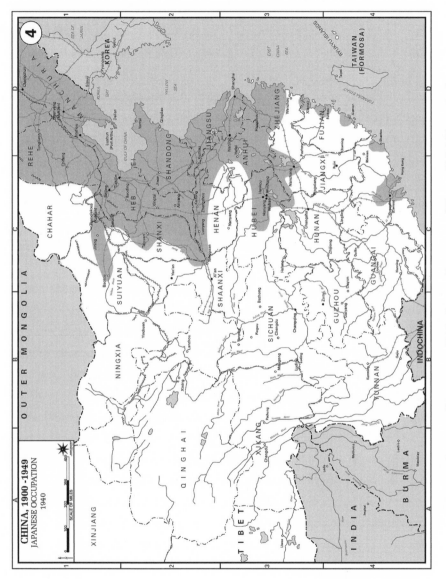

FIGURE 1. Japanese Occupation, 1940. *Courtesy Department of History, U.S. Military Academy.*

when the CEA launched an offensive directed against this supply route, first by attacking Wuhan in the interior to secure the rail line to Guangzhou, then by attacking the port city itself. Guangzhou was sealed off from foreign shipping by the end of October 1939, delivering a tough blow to the Nationalists, though one that would be softened by the opening of the Burma Road two months later. With the flow of supplies cut from southeastern China, the Japanese next turned their attention to closing Haiphong Harbor, nearly five hundred miles to the west.

The Japanese effort to close the supply route from Indochina began as a diplomatic problem, not a military one. As early as September 1937, the Japanese consul in Paris, Uchiyama Iwatoro, began negotiating with Henry Hoppenot, the head of France's Foreign Ministry (Asian Division) to try to persuade the latter to stop the delivery of an estimated 10,000 to 15,000 metric tons of goods that monthly flowed into Haiphong harbor, were hauled to Hanoi, and carried into China on the Yunnan railroad.[6] The French government in Indochina would not yield, primarily because of the revenue that came from the steady flow of arms along the railroad, but also because the United States and Britain both had condemned the "China Incident," and it was in Paris' best interest to stay in the good graces of Washington and London.

With diplomacy failing, the Japanese tried to pressure the French by seizing Hainan Island in the spring of 1939, a move that placed Japanese bombers within range of Hanoi (on the Indochina supply route) and the Burma Road. Pressure via airpower was convenient for Tokyo because the twenty-four Japanese divisions already in China were having a tough enough time staying resupplied with logistical lines now stretching more than 1,100 miles from Beijing to Guangzhou. Additionally, in May of that year 30,000 Japanese troops were involved in an undeclared war with the Soviets near the Manchurian-Mongolian border town of Nomonhan. For the time being the Japanese would have to be content to pressure the French with only the threat of air attack from Hainan, but this would soon change.

The German invasion of Poland in September 1939 altered the strategic calculus in Asia in favor of the Japanese. With Western attention fixed on Europe, the Japanese launched an offensive to capture Nanning, an important junction of the supply route from Hanoi to Chongqing. The Chinese rerouted the supply line, so the Japanese began bombing the Yunnan railroad in China that December, still being careful to respect French territorial integrity. Tensions grew to a boil the following February when a Japanese bomber accidentally struck a passenger train full of French civilians, but once the Germans defeated metropolitan France in June 1940, the French in Indochina had little negotiating room The Japanese government was permitted to send the IJA's 5th Division (with light bomber aircraft to interdict the Burma Road to Kunming) to occupy positions north of the Red River at the end of September to finally halt this flow of supplies from Hanoi to the Nationalists.[7]

The Japanese advance into Indochina is typically viewed as a harbinger of Asian expansionism run amok, but to see it exclusively in these terms is to forget that Japan was working hard to extricate itself from the quagmire that had become the China Incident, with the move to Indochina simply serving as another step along the road to end that costly war. Put differently, where Asian domination may have been Japan's distant concern, resolving the China Incident was its immediate concern. Gen. Hattori Takushiro, the chief of the Operations Division of the army section of the Imperial General Staff records of the move into Indochina: "Although the sending of troops into northern French Indochina was intended primarily for an early termination of the China incident, it was an undeniable fact that some quarters in the Supreme Command desired to make it the initial step in the southward expansion."[8] Even after December 1941, China played a central role in Japanese planning, as it tied up so many men and so much matériel. As one Japanese military history states, recorded soon after the war ended:

> *The outbreak of the Pacific War did not alter the main objective of the Japanese operations against China, which was the overthrow of the Chiang Kaishek regime. It was hoped by exploiting the gains in battle in the Southern Area [a reference to Southeast Asia] to bring greater pressure on the Chinese and, although part of the Japanese forces would have to be withdrawn from China to be used in the south, all important areas in China would continue to be occupied. Hong Kong would be captured and all enemy foreign influence would be forced out of China by the confisca-*

tion of their concession, rights, and interests. Furthermore, it was felt that if military successes were followed by adequate political and administrative measures, the Chiang Kaishek regime would ultimately surrender.[9]

With supply routes from Guangzhou and Hanoi closed, the Japanese had to contend with the third and lengthiest line of supply, the Silk Road. Within months of the start of the Sino-Japanese War, Chiang Kaishek had brokered a deal with the Soviets to deliver thousands of tons of military goods using this historic route. Most supplies were initially shipped from the Black Sea port of Odessa, but with Guangzhou and Haiphong closed, supplies were forced to take the 1,800-mile road from the railhead near Alma Ata (Almaty) on the Turkistan-Siberia railroad to Lanzhou, the capital of Gansu Province. Between October 1937 and February 1939, over 5,000 trucks were used to move supplies through China's barren Xinjiang Province while thousands of laborers worked to improve the road, shovel snow in the winter, and lead camel caravans that took up the slack when motor transport broke down.[10]

The Soviet motive for supplying the Chinese in the late 1930s was similar to that of the United States in the early 1940s, namely to block Japanese military power with Chinese blood. As one Russian historian notes, "Soviet aid to China therefore was designed to keep China in the war against Japan and the Soviet Union itself out of such a war."[11] Following their strategy of logistical strangulation, the Japanese again took strides to block this overland route; in November 1937 Japanese naval G3M bombers flew the 1,500-mile round-trip missions from bases near Beijing to the road's terminus at Lanzhou in an attempt to interdict the flow of supplies. The naval aviators were ill prepared for the attack and were forced to rely on a map of the city cut out of a popular boys' magazine, failing to realize that high terrain meant they had to fly to their target between 13,000 and 15,000 feet—a difficult task for pilots without any supplemental oxygen to breathe. They arrived over the city nauseated and with bad headaches and were then forced to contend with Chinese fighters (probably piloted by Soviets), who were defending the skies over the city. This was to be the first of many arduous missions to Lanzhou.[12]

The Japanese also tried to interdict the Silk Road with ground forces deployed to Inner Mongolia to threaten the route. As tensions mounted, the Soviets moved an armor division and a squadron of bombers into Xinjiang to protect the route.[13] Border friction had been a regular feature of Russo-Japanese relations since the annexation of Manchuria, with over five hundred incidents recorded between 1932 and 1936.[14] And while the larger battles at Lake Khasan (also called the Changkufeng incident) in 1938 and at Khalkhin Gol (the Nomonhan incident) in 1939 were not directly related to interdicting the flow of supplies, Soviet aid to China undoubtedly exacerbated the already strained relationship between Japan and the Soviet Union.[15]

Four factors combined to stop Soviet aid to China by 1942, aid that by then totaled $191 million. The first was a general lack of satisfaction by Moscow that the Nationalists were living up to their end of the agreement. Soviet aid was meant to be repaid in agricultural goods like tea, animal hides, and pig bristles as well as strategic minerals like tungsten, tin, and antimony.[16] China had been shipping tungsten to Germany in exchange for military aid and advice in the mid-1930s, but this agreement formally ended in 1937. Nevertheless, China still sold 4,000 tons of tungsten to Germany in 1939 when its obligation was really to the Soviets (even in 1938 and 1939, well after the end of formal Sino-German relations, China still delivered twice as much tungsten to the Germans as the Russians). Moscow undoubtedly felt snubbed by the lack of commitment on the part of the Nationalist government to live up to its end of the bargain.[17]

The second factor that cooled Sino-Soviet relations was the New Fourth Army incident in January 1941. Relations between Moscow and Chongqing were predicated on the assumption that the Nationalists would deal equitably with the Chinese Communist Party (CCP), but when Chiang ordered his troops in southern Anhui Province to attack CCP soldiers of the New Fourth Army for failing to retreat north of the Yangtze River, killing thousands of Communist soldiers, this put further strain on Sino-Soviet relations. Such problems were reciprocated by the Soviets when they signed the Soviet-Japanese Neutrality Pact in April 1941, as Stalin had Molotov broker the agreement for fear of being caught in a two-front war with both Germany and Japan. This five-year pact stunned the Nationalists, with Moscow's chief military advisor to China recording that his hosts "reacted with alarm, bordering on panic," with Chiang himself giving the "impression of being at sea."[18]

Soviet aid to China was forbidden by the agreement, but it continued nonetheless for eight more months—until the Japanese attacked Pearl Harbor. The day after the attack Chiang met with the Soviet, British, and U.S. ambassadors at his home to persuade them to combine forces to mobilize against Japan. Four days later Stalin replied that while he sympathized with Chiang, his attention was fixed in the west where his armies were engaged with the Germans less than a hundred miles from Moscow. This ended Soviet aid to China and dried up the Silk Road supply route, with Stalin seeking to avoid a war with Japan until his war against Germany was finished.[19] With Guangzhou, Haiphong, and the Silk Road closed as routes of supply, there was only one remaining way for aid to enter Nationalist China—along the Burma Road.

Commissioned by the generalissimo at the start of his war with Japan, the Burma Road was a 715-mile route from Lashio, Burma (modern-day Myanmar) to Kunming, China. The ruggedness of the route is seen in the simple fact that Lashio is only 350 statute miles (by air) from Kunming, but constant switchbacks over rough terrain meant that any truck using the road would travel over twice that distance to deliver supplies. The road's construction was really a joint venture between the Chinese and Burmese governments, as Burma, a British colony, stood to gain financially from tariffs and toll fees charged for the supplies that had first to enter the port at Rangoon, be transferred from oceangoing vessels to river barges for shipment up the Irrawaddy, off-loaded at Bhamo, and hauled to Lashio and on to Kunming in China's southwest Yunnan Province. The amount of time it took for supplies to get from Rangoon to Kunming depended on the weather and the reliability of the help that hauled the goods—help that included drivers, mechanics, road workers, supply depot officials, and local bureaucrats who occasionally levied their own personal tariffs for freight passage; an efficient trip from Rangoon to Kunming could potentially take only month, but it usually took three to four times this long.

The road itself was cut by thousands of Burmese and Chinese, the former working for pay, the latter accomplishing the job as a form of taxation. (Chinese laborers received no pay or food for their work, only the forgiving of their "tax debt.") Because of this, a large number of Yunnanese immigrated to Burma to avoid the tax and receive some remuneration for their work. Sufficient labor for the road would be a constant problem because most workers were farmers who needed to tend their crops in the summertime—the season that required the most maintenance on the road, as monsoonal rains could wash out entire sections with floodlike damage even at elevations of 6,000 feet.

The road crossed twenty-two mountain passes, the highest being at 8,600 feet. In December 1938 the U.S. naval attaché to China drove the length of the road in his 1935 Ford V-8 sedan, a trip that took ten days. His report claimed that, because large sections of the road were hewn from talus and detritus rock, it was "as though the road had been cut out along the slopes of a mound of granulated sugar which constantly melts or slips from under it." Elevation changes could be extreme: one section of the road dropped 2,000 feet in elevation, with twenty-five switchbacks covering only a three-kilometer span, an overall 20 percent grade. Once the descent was over, the road then climbed 2,300 feet over a five-kilometer span (overall a 14 percent grade), requiring full power in low gear; much of the road had to be covered in a lower gear, either for ascents or descents. Some sections of the road were smooth, flat, and well maintained, but according to a 1938 report, its overall condition depended on bureaucratic control, as "only constant supervision such as has been exercised for years in the Panama Canal will keep the road open."[20]

It is difficult to assess the tonnage of material hauled over the Burma Road. In August 1941 Chinese foreign minister T. V. Soong felt that the port at Rangoon could handle 40,000 tons per month and the river port at Lashio could process 30,000 tons during the same period, but the best Chinese estimates put the monthly tonnage over the road at somewhere around 3,000 tons. Reports also speak of the thousands of tons of weapons and supplies that were cached away in caves along the road between the Burmese border and Kunming, whether by national or provincial officials. Furthermore, tonnages hauled usually included the fuel, food, and parts needed to make the passage, which meant that for every 14,000 tons that left Lashio, only 5,000 tons arrived in Kunming; all told, it is likely that the road never delivered more than 5,000 tons per month to Kunming.[21] But despite this meager amount of tonnage—something slightly larger than a trickle (a single U.S. Army infantry division at the time needed approximately 200 tons of supplies per day while on campaign, translating to 6,000 tons per month[22])—the Burma Road was important as a symbol, representing as it did China's last link to the outside world, a link that was given almost mythic status in the Chinese quest to gather as much military aid as possible.

Despite all of the Burma Road's inadequacies, Japanese leaders understood its moral influence as China's only link with the outside world, and as in the case of the supply route through Indochina, the Japanese first employed diplomacy in an effort to close it. Taking advantage of the fact that Britain was embroiled in an air battle with the Germans in the summer of 1940, Japanese foreign vice minister Ohashi Chuichi extended what he called a "friendly communication" to Whitehall intended to halt the British flow of supplies to China. Sir Alexander Cadogan of the Foreign Office countered with a display of concern for Britain's international reputation, stating that onlookers would think, "The English are beat anyhow, and we don't want that," and so rebuffed the Japanese missive. Churchill's choleric reply, though, was that the British "could not afford the Japanese navy being added to the German and Italian." Detractors thought the Japanese were bluffing, but as Neville Chamberlain wrote, "If they [the British detractors] were mistaken—and we have not to deal with the Foreign Office but the truculent and ignorant army officers who think we are going to be beaten by the Germans—we have not the forces to fight the Japs, Germans and Italians at once."[23]

The British closed the road in July 1940, justifying their decision with the claim that not much matériel could make it to Kunming during the summer's rainy season anyhow. Switching courses three months later, they reopened the road, partly to give the Chinese "moral encouragement," but also to "encourage the Americans on the right path" by exemplifying something of British national bravado in the face of danger.[24] The reopening of the road was not done without caution, though, as Churchill asked Roosevelt, "Would it be possible to send an American [naval] squadron to Singapore?" His motive for the request was that it "would have a marked deterrent effect upon a Japanese declaration of war upon us over the Burma Road opening."[25] Now the only remaining course for the Japanese finally to close the road was by military invasion, which meant a much wider war in Asia. As General Hattori records, "Strategically, Burma was so important that it had to be secured for the northern stronghold [shorthand for China] of the Southern Area [Southeast Asia] in order to conduct protracted operations [a euphemism for the logistical strangulation of China] after the conclusion of the invasion operations. Moreover, the occupation of Burma was necessary for cutting off Chiang's aid route."[26] Even after the Pacific war started, the Japanese Imperial General Headquarters (IGHQ) viewed Burma as a key to ending the

China Incident, not just because it kept foreign arms out of the hands of Chinese soldiers but also because it was a political weapon that could erode Chiang's government. In March 1940 the Japanese set up a puppet government in Nanjing under Wang Jingwei. By cutting the Burma Road, the Japanese hoped to stop the flow of commercial commodities going to local and provincial warlords, tempting them to switch their allegiance from Chiang to Wang, thus crumbling the generalissimo's already tenuous hold on Nationalist China.[27]

U.S. MILITARY AID TO CHINA

Once reopened by the British in October 1940, the Burma Road was in operation for the next year and a half, serving as the sole route for U.S. military aid to the Nationalists. The Americans were quickly becoming Chiang's supply source of choice. The war in Europe had evaporated any German support, and Soviet help was clearly waning following the settlement of the Soviet-Japanese Neutrality Pact earlier that spring; it was only a matter of time until all Russian advisors were recalled home.[28] As with the Germans and Soviets, U.S. aid came in the form of fiscal support, credits, and military hardware.[29] And as with the Germans and Soviets before, military aid was accompanied with advisors sent to ensure that hardware was used for its intended purpose. The heyday of German aid was between 1933 and 1937 when Hans von Seekt and Alexander von Falkenhausen labored to help the GMD build an elite army of thirty divisions fashioned after the best Prussian model.[30] The Germans were not alone in sending prominent commanders to China; Soviet advisors included Georgi Zhukov, a man soon to become the most senior commander in the Soviet army. This aid also included a robust aviation contingent; between two hundred and three hundred Russian pilots were in China at any one time, many of them coming directly from the Spanish Civil War and rotating back to the USSR after six months in Asia.[31] Like Soviet aid, U.S. airpower aid to China in the days leading up to Pearl Harbor followed a similar pattern.

The end of China's "warlord period" came in 1927 with the establishment of Chiang Kaishek's government in Nanking; this had once again made China attractive to foreign investors, including those businessmen in the fledgling aviation industry. It was under these auspices that retired U.S. Air Corps colonel John H. "Jack" Jouett arrived in China in July 1932, tasked to help the Chinese build an air force. Because of the United States' neutral posture toward Japan's annexation of Manchukuo, Jouett's work could be done only under the rubric of a business contract as a private U.S. citizen, even though the U.S. Department of Commerce clearly welcomed the mission. Nevertheless, congressional pressure threatened to revoke the citizenship of any Americans found working for the GMD. During his two-year tenure Jouett organized a flying school at Hangzhou that later moved to Luoyang in Henan Province and produced three hundred pilots. In all, nearly forty U.S. pilots worked in China during the mid-1930s, including such notables as Jimmy Doolittle and Claire Chennault, leaving a template for future U.S. military aviation interests in China.[32]

Claire Lee Chennault arrived in China in 1937. Born in Texas but raised in Louisiana, Chennault first saw army service in 1917 in World War I and gained entry to flight school after the war, earning his wings in 1919. He took a variety of assignments in the 1920s and ended up in 1931 as an instructor at the Air Corps Tactical School (ACTS), where he earned his reputation as a fierce supporter of pursuit (fighter) aviation, advocating teamwork and tactics in aerial combat in a day when nearly all of his contemporaries championed bomber aviation. He was a skilled pilot, forming the Air Corps' first aerial demonstration team ("Three Men on a Flying Trapeze"), but he was clearly out of step with the mood of his service, and in the spring of 1937 a personnel board recommended his early retirement at the permanent rank of captain on medical grounds (he suffered from chronic bronchitis and had substantial hearing loss). Confronted with the challenge of supporting his wife and eight children, Chennault accepted an offer by the Chinese to serve as an air advisor—a role patterned by Jouett—arriving in China two months before the start of China's war with Japan.[33]

Chennault worked with the understrength and poorly trained and equipped Chinese in the early days of the war until Chiang asked him to look for ways to replace the departing Soviet pilots with U.S. flyers. To do so, Chennault spent the winter of 1940–41 in Washington, D.C., with Maj. Gen. Mao Bangchu (Peter T. Mao), the director of operations for the Chinese Air Force (CAF), soliciting the U.S. government for planes and pilots. After a good deal of diplomatic wrangling, the planes were secured from an order of obsolescent Curtiss P-40B fighters, originally reserved for the British, who consented to let the Chinese have them, provided the United States let the British have the priority rights to a future order of later-model fighters. Just over a hundred pilots were recruited from the U.S. Navy, Marine Corps, and Army Air Corps and were allowed to resign from their respective services to travel to China as "tourists" in the summer of 1941. Charged with countering a well-trained Japanese air component in the defense of the Burma Road, the American Volunteer Group (AVG)—later dubbed the "Flying Tigers"—saw their first combat in December 1941 in the skies over Kunming.

Chennault and the AVG supplied badly needed help to the faltering CAF, though perhaps not up to the mythic proportions of their contemporary reputation; even so, the Flying Tigers did not represent official U.S. aid by virtue of the fact that they were organized under the auspices of a diplomatic "wink and a nod." Formal aid came by way of Lend-Lease legislation signed by FDR in March 1940—originally intended to bolster the British and Soviets, with the Chinese capturing only a small portion of the larger aid package. To get an accurate assessment of the Nationalists' needs, Roosevelt sent Dr. Lauchlin Currie, one of his administrative assistants, to China to meet with the generalissimo. Currie, an economist by training, discussed the details of Chinese needs while also offering suggestions for how the Nationalists might generate more revenue through land taxation.[34] In the end, Currie's six-week visit to China was of greater political consequence than anything else, as it left Roosevelt with the taste that U.S. aid could be the vehicle through which China could feel the influence of American liberalism.[35]

When Currie returned to Washington in April, he advocated sending to China a group of experts from an array of fields—to include economics, politics, and transportation—to manage the flow of aid. These advisors would then work alongside Chinese counterparts, who were reported to be steeped in corruption, something regarded within U.S. government circles as a dominant characteristic of Chinese bureaucracy. To head this team, Currie recommended that FDR appoint a "liberal advisor" who might, as Michael Schaller points out, "assist Chiang's political judgment" and help China become "a far more attractive postwar economic partner for the United States."[36] Currie's nominee for the job was Owen Lattimore, the acclaimed Asia scholar and British national who would be able to provide a "New Deal-esque" liberalizing influence at Chiang's side. Roosevelt agreed and made the appointment, which Chiang must have only accepted grudgingly, since the Lend-Lease law meant that the president was the executive agent for dispensing aid. Lattimore arrived in China in 1941, and in the end his mission was a disappointment. Chiang put up with the academic for less than a year until he sent him back to Washington, asking that he please lobby the president for more Chinese aid.[37]

Two War Department aid packages were authorized in the spring of 1940—one valued at $45 million and the other at $100 million. Given the fact that George Marshall, the U.S. Army chief of staff, was unconvinced that the Chinese knew how to distribute the aid, he urged Roosevelt to approve a military oversight body called the American Military Mission to China (AMMISCA), headed by an officer with much experience in China, Brig. Gen. John Magruder.[38] Marshall's motive for the creation of AMMISCA was twofold. First, he was convinced that the Chinese had little clue of what they were actually requesting (one example is seen in the Chinese request for four-ton trucks, when very few roads in China could handle such a vehicle), so he wanted an army staff in place to broker such requests. Second, Marshall was probably concerned that Chinese requests would be rubber-stamped by the president; by imposing a body like AMMISCA, Marshall was able to retain some say in the acquisition and dispensing of such aid.[39]

The creation of AMMISCA caused some friction with Currie and the China Defense Supply Company (CDS). This GMD liaison organ in Washington, headed by T. V. Soong, coordinated the receipt of all aid and suspected that the War Department was trying to derail the direct link between Chongqing and the White House. Chennault even warned Madame Chiang Kaishek that it was Magruder's job to spoil the supply relationship between Roosevelt and Chiang, an exaggeration, though not one that was unfounded, with most U.S. concern focused on the war in Europe. In fact, Magruder's resistance to Chinese requests for aid was motivated primarily by the fact that the U.S. was *not* at war with Japan in August 1941, and it is likely that Marshall directed Magruder to see that an overly generous White House did not provoke a war with the Japanese by offering too much U.S. weaponry to the Chinese.[40]

Trading Soviet aid for U.S. aid in 1940 and 1941 was a boon for Chiang. With the Soviets he had to operate with a degree of political deftness toward his real nemesis, the Chinese Communists, because of the limited patience of the Comintern and Stalin. The Soviets were faithful suppliers for Chiang, though, at least until such a time as they no longer needed a Chinese buffer against Japan. On the other hand, with the Americans Chiang could have his proverbial cake and eat it, too. He could exercise due diligence against the Communists and still stay in good graces with the United States, thanks to the seemingly inherent linkage between Soviets, the Comintern, and the Chinese Communists in the minds of many U.S. policy makers. Such sentiment is seen in a telegram sent by Sumner Welles of the State Department to the U.S. consul in Hangzhou, asking him to collect CCP propaganda for study and warning him that that the Communist Party was actively seeking "united front" normalized relations with the GMD (and even inclusion into the Nationalist government) "as merely a step in the direction of their ultimate goal: a Soviet Government of China."[41]

One similarity between Chiang's relationship with the Soviets and the Americans is seen in the way he used similar rhetoric in making his pleas for help. Six months after the start of the Sino-Japanese War, Chiang conducted an interview with a Russian journalist who published in newspapers meant for foreign consumption. In it he claimed, "In one year of war China has lost more than 500,000 killed and wounded. . . . The economy is undermined . . . China must receive support in its struggle from other states. . . . The Chinese people are patient and they show courage. Unity strengthens them."[42] Now with his hope set fully on the United States four years later, Chiang's language became shriller by threatening not only the capitulation of China to the Japanese but the utter defeat of any hopes for Asian democracy. Referencing his concern that the Americans might loosen their oil embargo against Japan in the summer of 1941, Chiang declared:

> *If, therefore, there is any relaxation of the embargo or freezing regulation, or if a belief of that gains ground, then the Chinese people would consider that China has been completely sacrificed by the United States. The morale of the entire people will collapse and every Asiatic nation will lose faith, and indeed suffer such a shock in their faith in democracy that a most tragic epoch in the world will be opened. The Chinese Army will collapse, and even the Japanese will be enabled to carry through their plans, so that even if in the future America would come to our rescue the situation would be already hopeless. Such a loss would not be to China alone.*[43]

On the eve of the Pacific War, the United States had completely succumbed to Chiang's repeated calls for aid. Of particular interest, though, is the fact that aid was becoming detached from actual military performance and instead was set forth as a tool to bolster a supposedly flagging Chinese national morale. This transition is seen in a telegram sent by James McHugh, the U.S. naval attaché to Chongqing from 1940 to 1943. McHugh was truly an "insider" in both GMD and Washington circles, spending time regularly with the Chiangs and making use of his direct line to Frank Knox, the secretary of the navy. McHugh's detailed reports were often insightful (he had a keen understanding of Chinese culture and spoke Mandarin fluently, publishing a dictionary and textbook to instruct other foreign service officers in Chinese), and they were often read with interest even by Roosevelt. In all, he spent twenty years in China and serves as a useful lens through which to view the inner workings of Sino-U.S. relations. He was also good friends with Lauchlin Currie, and in one private letter from April 1941 McHugh writes to "Lauch":

> *I have mentioned in past reports, and I am more certain than ever that this question of aid to China is far more a psychological one than it is physical. In other words, I believe that if you could dump a hundred planes and fifty million dollars in their laps tomorrow it would come far closer to serving our own ends through the boost in their morale, even though it all went down the drain in actual use, than work out a carefully established scheme and sent out a well trained force to fly their planes. The latter can follow in due course, but I firmly believe we ought to give them planes to crack up* immediately *[underlined in the original], ask no questions and merely say "we are with you to the bitter end, go to it." We cannot run their country for them, and cannot fight their war for them, but we can keep their heads up and let them do the job in their own way.*[44]

McHugh's assessment of the situation was only confirmed by the suspicions of Marshal Vasili Chuikov, Chiang's chief military advisor in 1941 (and future hero of the Battle of Stalingrad), when he objectively remarked—bearing no malice toward the United States—that "American military assistance . . . was intended to symbolize American good relations with China."[45]

Thus, on the eve of the Pacific War, four important pieces were in place that directed the course of U.S. involvement in China until the war's end. First was the assumption that China needed foreign supplies to survive the war; without those supplies it would collapse, something that would have dire consequences, vis-à-vis Japanese aggression, for the hope of democracy throughout all Asia. The second piece was the infrastructure to assess, regulate, and dispense aid that involved a relationship between the White House, the CDS, and the War Department's AMMISCA. The third had to do with the strategic route of supply, coming as it did through Burma. The Burma Road was regarded as China's umbilical cord and the key to China's life or death. The last piece of this collage was the presence of U.S. airpower in the theater. Chennault's Flying Tigers—most of whom were talented aviators who had gotten their training with either the army or navy—nonetheless constituted an unofficial venture to aid China while also representing a conceptual starting point for military commanders as they imagined the possibilities what airpower could do in this faraway theater.

FROM PEARL HARBOR TO THE FALL OF RANGOON

The Japanese attack on Pearl Harbor did little to alter this fundamental framework. What it did do, though, was give Chiang more bargaining power with the Americans by virtue of the fact that he alone was keeping the Japanese fixed in the east until such a time as U.S. naval power could engage the Japanese in the west. The United States' cultural link with China—a sort of Sino-U.S. brotherhood—offered Roosevelt the opportunity for Americans to begin immediately fighting the Japanese with U.S. arms and Chinese soldiers. To do this, the president created the China Theater (CT) of the war (which also included the portions of Thailand and Indochina still in friendly hands) at the end of December 1941 with Chiang as its commander. And because Magruder's AMMISCA lacked the gravity to display the full extent of U.S. sentiment toward China, FDR needed to appoint a more renowned and senior army officer to represent U.S. interests in the theater.

Maj. Gen. Joseph Warren Stilwell was one of over two dozen army officers who had experience serving in China. He spent almost nine years there on three separate assignments (1921–1923 at the U.S. legation in Beijing, 1926–1929 with the U.S. Fifteenth Infantry at Tianjin, and 1935–1939 as military attaché), traveled widely, and spoke the language with fair fluency.[46] Raised in Yonkers, New York, Stilwell's no-nonsense New England demeanor was borderline caustic at times, earning him the nickname "Vinegar Joe" among some of his students while teaching at the army's infantry school at Fort Benning, Georgia.[47] He was also close to George Marshall, serving with him in Tianjin and working for him at Fort Benning; so when Roosevelt asked for nominees to head the U.S. force in the China Theater, Stilwell's name naturally came up—though it was not the name at the top of the list. That distinction belonged to Hugh Drum.

Lt. Gen. Hugh A. Drum was Marshall's chief rival to replace Gen. Malin Craig as the chief of staff of the army in September 1939, Drum having served as a two-star general for almost eight years longer than Marshall. Drum's seniority alone was sure to communicate the depth of the United States' commitment to China should he be sent as the U.S. representative to the generalissimo. Drum was first made aware of the China mission by Marshall and Secretary of War Henry Stimson on January 2, 1942; caught unprepared for the meeting, Drum asked for a few days to do his own research on the proposal, promising a prompt reply. He consulted with various War Department officials on the subject of China who provided their appraisal in the form of a memo listing the many pitfalls that an officer of Drum's stature was likely to encounter should he accept the job in China.[48] Armed with that information, Drum then crafted his formal refusal to accept the position based on a series of concerns.

First, there was the matter of "face." Drum claimed he would have to tiptoe around the generalissimo's renowned ego because the creation of the China Theater (something that had happened only a few days earlier, on December 29) was done primarily because of "the well-known value of face to the Oriental," further stating that Chiang was designated CT commander simply so that "it would not injure his prestige with his own people or with the world."[49] Next, there was the matter of regulating Lend-Lease aid as the senior U.S. officer in China; Magruder was immensely popular with the Chinese, and any officer who appeared to be superimposing his authority on AMMISCA would be viewed with suspicion. Additionally, any senior army officer sent to China would also have to contend with Chennault (technically a private U.S. citizen working in China), a man whose "procedure has been established . . . and is in accordance with Chinese methods." The politics of the job were sure to be a challenge as well. "The Chinese don't trust the British, the British don't trust the Chinese, and the Burmese don't trust either of them." This was of particular importance because "the Burmese-French Indochina Peninsula is the key to the Chinese logistical problem" and "Little or nothing can be done for China if the Burma Road is blocked by the Japs." Drum's final conclusion to Marshall and Stimson's job offer was that it was "nebulous" and that "if a group representing the United States Government should be sent into China at this time, that it be a group diplomatic in nature."[50] He declined the position, opening the way to Marshall's second choice for the position.

Marshall also met with Stilwell on January 2 and told him that the president was looking for a senior officer to send to China. Stilwell knew that Drum was being considered for the job and—showing the low opinion he had of his rival—quipped, "The G-mo's a stuffed shirt; let's send him the biggest stuffed shirt we have."[51] Drum had a reputation for being pompous, as he and Marshall had had run-ins on at least one occasion. With Drum refusing the job three days later, Marshall pressed Stilwell, who continued to drag his heels on the idea ("Me? No thank you. They remember me as a small-fry colonel that they kicked around"[52]). But in the end, like a good soldier, he consented to the position, one that made him commander of all U.S. forces in the theater (which came to consist primarily of aviation assets and army engineers and eventually a regiment of soldiers) as well as Chiang's chief of staff, making Stilwell the head Allied advisor to a man he barely respected and privately referred to as "the Peanut."[53] Stilwell arrived in China a month later, on February 24, with the war in Asia well under way. In the Philippines the situation had deteriorated to the point that Roosevelt ordered MacArthur's departure; for the British, Hong Kong and Singapore had both fallen, and the battle cruiser *Repulse* and fast battleship *Prince of Wales* had both been sunk in Asian waters by Japanese aircraft. It was also in February that Burma became a formal target in Japan's war plans.

The Japanese Supreme Headquarters had long recognized the strategic importance of Burma but had never thought there would be adequate manpower to secure much of the country any farther north than Rangoon. The original war plan of the Japanese Fifteenth Army, published on December 11, called for only the seizure of Moulmein and the mouth of the nearby Salween River as a means of protecting the western flank of the IJA in Thailand. From here Japanese air and naval assets would be able to seal off the port of Rangoon with air attack and cut any supplies flowing from here up the Irrawaddy to be transferred to the Burma Road for delivery to Kunming.[54] Following this general plan, the Japanese took Moulmein (on the Burmese coast) in mid-December and began bombing Rangoon on December 23, causing general havoc in the city and virtually halting all work done by dock laborers when Burmese began fleeing the city.[55] The Japanese stayed with this general plan for Burma, preferring to hold key defensive positions and foment a Burmese independence movement, until the Fifteenth Army was given new orders on February 9 to occupy "important cities in central Burma" in concert with the IJN, including the cities of Rangoon in the south and Toungoo, Mandalay, and the oil fields at Yenangyaung in the north. In sum, the decision to venture into northern Burma was motivated by the success of the Japanese everywhere, by the opportunity to capture Burmese rice and oil fields, and also as a means to finally cut the Burma Road.

Not surprisingly, the Japanese advance into Burma created a panic in China, as Chiang feared they would not stop at the border but press into Yunnan Province and take Kunming. Even before the attack on Pearl Harbor, Chiang was concerned for the safety of Kunming, especially after the Japanese took Indochina in September 1940. He negotiated with Long Yun, Yunnan's provincial leader, who consented to allow Chiang to send the Sixtieth Army (consisting of two divisions and three independent brigades) to protect Kunming, the provincial capital, and the towns of Kaiyuan and Jianshi on Yunnan's border. Long was uncomfortable with the presence of so much GMD military might in his province, so Chiang promised not to meddle in local affairs. Long agreed, and both set about then to build fortifications to defend the Burma Road from paratroop attack.[56]

Chiang was not alone in his concern that the Japanese might advance into China and capture Kunming. The U.S. Army Air Forces released a study before the Pacific War began, acknowledging the fact that both Kunming and the supplies delivered on the Burma Road were subject to a possible Japanese attack from Indochina and that these supplies were critical to China's welfare, the stoppage of which would, as the report claims, "cause the collapse of China." Given the fact that air force assets were stretched thin, though, the report concludes that "the United States can do the most by deterring Japan from offensive ground operations against Kunming by building up to the present minimum strength [of heavy bombers] contemplated in the Philippine Islands and conducting operations from there." There were thirty-five B-17s on the Philippines on the day the report was released, with another ninety-five scheduled to arrive over the next two months. That day was December 1, 1941. One week later Japanese bombers based on Formosa destroyed over half of those B-17s on the ground in an attack referred to by one historian as "MacArthur's Pearl Harbor," forcing the rest into a fighting retreat through Java to Australia, dissolving the United States' "deterring" force protecting Kunming.[57]

The Japanese had sealed off Rangoon from seaborne supplies by February 1942, and the Chinese began looking furiously for a way to circumvent this stoppage of aid. Just as problematic as the loss of Rangoon was the absence of British or U.S. naval power in the Bay of Bengal. The loss of the *Repulse* and *Prince of Wales* within days of the attack on Pearl Harbor meant that the IJN was able to roam unthreatened off the western coast of India. But the Japanese Navy, encumbered by other commitments in the southwest Pacific, chose not to press farther west into the Arabian Sea, off the west coast of India, which meant supplies could be off-loaded at the port of Karachi, moved by train across the width of India to the railhead at Sadiya on the eastern edge of the Brahmaputra River, and flown two hundred miles by militarized DC-3 twin-engine transports over rugged mountains to Myitkyina (pronounced "Mitchinaw" and called "Mitch" by most U.S. soldiers), a small airfield in north Burma that was near the northern end of the Irrawaddy River. From Myitkyina the supplies were off-loaded from the planes, loaded onto barges, and floated a hundred miles downriver to Bhamo, where they were then transferred to trucks, then hauled to Kunming along the Burma Road. It was hoped that seventy-five transport planes could deliver 7,500 tons per month to north Burma for movement to China by that coming summer, a hope that was altogether unrealistic.

This cumbersome route was more contemplated than used, and it was shot down as an idea at the beginning of May when Myitkyina fell to advance units of the Fifteenth Army. Nevertheless, it was the first introduction of a formalized air-lift plan to keep China supplied, a move that stemmed from a directive by FDR. The first meeting of the Combined Chiefs of Staff (a body that included the senior military commanders from all the services in the United States and Great Britain) was on December 23, 1941, in the Oval Office. It was here that Roosevelt reiterated the fact that the Chinese must be supplied to "keep them in the war." The

Army Air Forces chief of staff, Lt. Gen. Henry "Hap" Arnold, recorded, "The President agreed with me that we must establish air bases in China for our bombers [to strike Japan] and transports, and that we must get more transports over there at once. He also realized that supplies for China would have to be taken by air. This was the real start of the 'Hump' operation."[58] Throughout the winter and into the spring, Roosevelt would continue to reiterate to his air chief that the main objective of the India-Burma Theater was to open and maintain an air route to China.[59]

CHINA NATIONAL AVIATION COMPANY

Fortunately for Arnold, he did not have to devise this air route from scratch, thanks to the efforts of the China National Aviation Company (CNAC), a commercial airline jointly owned by Pan American airlines and the Chinese government. CNAC's history went back to 1930, when Chiang Kaishek's government was looking at expanding its domestic aviation interests. Contracts were let to both the Curtiss-Wright company and Lufthansa, the former creating CNAC, the latter forming the Eurasia Aviation Corporation (EAC).[60] Pan Am took over the U.S. interest in CNAC three years later, controlling 45 percent of the company, the Chinese government controlling the other 55 percent. CNAC's mixed ownership was reflected in its personnel, consisting of both Chinese and U.S. managers and operators; a significant portion of the pilot manning consisted of Americans of Chinese descent, Chinese who had recently immigrated to the United States, and native Chinese. CNAC continued to do a good amount of business after the war began in 1937, adapting to the Japanese threat and moving to Chongqing with the Nationalist government. CNAC's purely commercial status should have rendered it immune from Japanese attack, but in one famous incident in August 1938 enemy fighters forced one of its DC-2s to land, after which it was strafed, killing nearly all of those on board. The episode was reminiscent of the *Panay* gunboat incident of that previous December and marked the first instance in aviation history that a commercial airliner was lost to enemy attack.[61]

Typical of most commercial airlines of the time, CNAC turned most of its revenue carrying passengers rather than cargo. In 1940, though, the organization began regularly scheduled freight operations, an important transition considering the part it would play in pioneering the Hump route of flight.[62] Anticipating the fact that China might one day be isolated from supplies delivered from Burma, William Langhorne Bond, the company's operations manager, began exploring options to keep China connected with Rangoon. Bond was fiercely committed to China's welfare; technically in China as a Pan Am employee, he resigned from the U.S. half of the company in 1937 and became a full employee of the Chinese part of CNAC to alleviate neutrality concerns with the Japanese.[63] When the British temporarily closed the Burma Road in the summer of 1940, Bond lobbied for the U.S. government to release more transport aircraft to CNAC under the provisions of Lend-Lease.[64] When Lauchlin Currie came to China the following spring, Bond persuaded him to advocate this request forcefully, though there were not enough transports to go around in the U.S. inventory.[65] Remaining undeterred, it was Bond who energized CNAC to search for a way to circumvent a closed Burma Road.

CNAC had been flying regularly scheduled passenger service from Lashio to Kunming as part of its service between Chongqing and Rangoon. Bond feared that Lashio was too vulnerable to Japanese fighters now in Indochina, so in November 1940 he traveled by car from Mandalay to Lashio, then by train to Myitkyina, the northernmost stop on the rail line from Rangoon. There was no airport at "Mitch," a problem he would persuade the British Burmese governor, Sir Alexander Cochrane, to solve. He then returned to Lashio and boarded a CNAC plane piloted by the company's chief pilot, Hugh Woods. He and Woods then flew back north, surveying the prospective airfield site at Myitkyina from the air, then arced northeast to Putao (called Fort Hertz by the British) on a track that notionally kept them clear of Japanese fighters, turning southeast over Dali Mountain, Chikiang, and Suifu and landing in Chongqing. Woods and Bond's route was over poorly charted terrain with many mismarked mountains listed with inaccurate elevations. Flying in mostly clear conditions, just above low wintertime clouds, they were able to cover the route at 14,800 feet and stay clear of mountain peaks. Bond's overall assessment was that "Little of definite value could be told from one flight. We know the country is high but if the weather should be much worse, with bad cross winds or bad icing conditions, or if the tops of the clouds should be higher than we saw, then it would be extremely dangerous and costly and very near impractical."[66]

Other CNAC pilots would try Woods's route, exploring better paths over the difficult terrain. In early 1941 Wu Shi flew the route from Lashio up the Irrawaddy to Fort Hertz, then headed east to along a similar track to Lijiang, Dali, Xichang, and Xufu (Yibin). Landing at Chongqing's Baishiyi Airport, Wu's experience mimicked Woods's with the Chinese pilot being struck by just how dangerously inaccurate the terrain elevations were on his flight charts. In anticipation that one day the Hump flights might not be able to depart from Burma, CNAC had Chinese pilot Xia Pu fly from Dinjan (a British military airfield in India's far eastern Assam Province) to Kunming in November 1941 in the first recorded flight across what later became the Hump route.[67] Xia's flight was undoubtedly one of several that CNAC was making to chart the most ideal route between India and China, and these trial flights allowed Bond's political influence to outstrip his position as simply the director of operations for a smallish Chinese airline. In the summer of 1942, when almost all of the military leadership in the theater—including Army Air Forces (AAF) leadership[68]—was pessimistic about the prospects of flying supplies from India to China, it was Bond's CNAC that had shown that such an operation was possible. Stanley K. Hornbeck, the State Department's influential advisor for Far Eastern affairs, wrote in May 1942 that "defeatist pronouncements . . . originate for the most part with people who sit in headquarters and make estimates, in contrast with which we have the opinion of Mr. Bond, who, on the basis of practical experience, firmly believes that the thing *can* be done and, while admitting that it may be proven impossible takes the position that he would not admit it to be impossible until it had been so proven by actual trial, trial for the making of which he has volunteered his own services, and those of the seasoned organization he directs."[69]

U.S. MILITARY AIR TRANSPORT

The "defeatist pronouncements" that Hornbeck referred to were probably not the complaints of just one man but a general consensus of those U.S. military leaders sent to India and China just weeks after Pearl Harbor, charged with carrying out Roosevelt and Arnold's directive to keep China supplied by air. It is easy to judge these naysayers as too nearsighted and pessimistic as to the capabilities of air transport, but this would be unfair considering the conditions. Existing airfields were few, and the prospects of using local labor in India to build more were being hurt by Gandhi's nationalist "Quit India" campaign; though directed at the British, their alliance with the United States made for the perception that both were to be resisted, diminishing the pool of available local labor. Next, the terrain was rightly considered the most rugged in the world, and the AAF had no prior expertise operating in the theater. Lastly, there was really no broader institution within the AAF charged primarily with airlift operations—Air Transport Command did not yet exist.

When the Pacific War began, the AAF had two organizations that conducted air transport duties. The first was the Fiftieth Transport Wing, a unit that carried supplies for the Air Corps' four main supply depots at Sacramento, San Antonio, Fairfield (Ohio), and Middletown (Pennsylvania), because it was cheaper for the Air Corps to haul these supplies than to pay to have them carried by rail. Because, as mentioned earlier, most commercial airlines carried passengers, the Fiftieth carried more cargo in the first half of 1941 than all other commercial airlines combined, a fact that made it the primary operator of the 250-plus transport aircraft in the Air Corps' inventory in December 1941. Despite this fact, Air Transport Command—an organization that grew to become essentially the largest airline in the world by the end of World War II—did not originate from the Fiftieth Transport Wing but rather from the unit charged with delivering Lend-Lease airplanes to the British.[70]

The second arm that conducted transport duties was Ferry Command, formed in May 1941 when Churchill asked for help delivering Lend-Lease planes to Britain.

Arnold knew that his pilots needed as much flying experience as possible, so he offered to have Americans fly the new planes from factories to ports of debarkation for transport across the Atlantic. Run by Brig. Gen. Robert Olds, Ferry Command (the name coming from the traditional British term for the relocation of aircraft) grew along with Lend-Lease, such that when Arnold was looking for an outfit within his AAF that most closely mimicked his vision for a worldwide transport operation, Ferry Command was the most proximate due to its work in pioneering transatlantic routes of flight. In time, Air Transport Command (ATC) became the organization that overcame the obstacles that made an airlift effort over the Himalayas seem so daunting in the spring of 1942. Even

FIGURE 2. Indian Airfield Construction, ca. 1943. *Courtesy McGraw-Hill.*

so, ATC did not officially exists until May 29, 1942, and it did not take over the Hump airlift until the end of that year; nevertheless, two key events took place between December 1941 and March 1942 that where pivotal to the Hump's future success.

The first was Roosevelt's decision to annex control of the nation's commercial air fleet, but to do so without formally militarizing the airlines. On December 15 the president signed Executive Order 8974, Control of Civil Aviation, allowing the secretary of war to "to take possession and assume control of any civil aviation system, or systems, or any part thereof, to the extent necessary for the successful prosecution of the war," a move intended to serve as an immediate remedy to the shortage of military transports and pilots.[71] And though the order gave Secretary of War Henry Stimson wide latitude in the military use of commercial air, what essentially happened was that each of the airlines in question kept its own internal composition while now serving the U.S. military under government contract. Thus, the only substantive result of Roosevelt's order was to shift the customer focus of the various private airlines from the general public to the War Department. In addition, Ferry Command was now given authority to execute all contracts with civil carriers, giving that organization tremendous authority in the formation of what would later become the AAF's Air Transport Command.

The key ingredient that made this system work was the steady flow of airline executives and managers who kept their airline jobs but also donned military uniforms, serving as conduits of expertise between the two organizations. As C. R. Smith later stated, "The whole damned Transport Section [of Air Transport Command] was . . . airline people. We never could have set up the Air Transport Command without the people we got from the airlines. We got them from all of them [the different airline companies], but we had quite a reputation among the British. I'm sure, a bunch of amateur airline operators trying to pose as military experts." Smith would later comment on his entry into the army, "I came into the Air Force a complete 100 percent civilian, I knew nothing about the Army. I didn't know how to march, and didn't know how to salute. Very few people in Air Transport Command did."[72] Roosevelt's executive order may have technically nationalized the airlines, but civil-military relations between corporate and AAF leaders was such that military air transport could grow with the infusion of commercial expertise, all the while maintaining the corporate identity of the individual airlines.

This arrangement led to the placement of key individuals in important positions in the army's air transport structure. In March 1942 Col. Robert Olds, the head of Ferry Command, was hospitalized by a heart attack. His health was already failing when Arnold began planning on transforming Ferry Command into ATC; to fill Olds's spot he asked Col. Harold "Hal" George–the chief of the AAF's War Plans Division–to take the position. George resisted. As one of the AAF's key advocates for strategic bombing, he wanted to be involved in the war-making business of the service, not the seemingly benign transport part of it. Arnold pressed him, and eventually George relented but claimed he knew nothing about air transport. To fix this, Arnold hired C. R. Smith, the well-respected president of American Airlines, to serve as George's director of operations, making Smith a colonel in the AAF. Arnold and Smith knew little of each other, but they had a mutual friend, Don Douglas (the owner of Douglas Aircraft), and an afternoon together on Douglas's fishing yacht convinced Arnold that Smith was the right man to manage his service's transport component as George's director of operations.[73] Time would come to prove Smith's pivotal role in the success of both ATC and the Hump. He was perhaps the best "connected" airline executive among the group at the time, playing a key part in seeing that ATC hired such talented executives as Fred Atkinson (the chief of personnel for Macy's department store), Louis Gimbel (the president of Gimbel's department store), and Jim Douglas (who would later serve as the secretary of the air force in the 1950s).[74] Smith was not intimidated by military rank or procedure in the least—in fact, his direct managerial style fit well with the AAF, having as he did a good sense of when to strictly follow (the sometimes) cumbersome regulations and when it was best to disregard those regulations to slice through military bureaucracy and get things done. His real skill was in business, having worked since his youth as an office boy for a wealthy Texas rancher to help support his abandoned mother and six younger siblings and later as a bookkeeper before graduating with a business degree from the University of Texas in 1924. He worked his way up in the industry over the next decade and was the president of the newly organized American Airlines by the time he was thirty-five years old.[75] He and George made an effective pair, blending the business acumen to organize a worldwide airline with the military stature and command to make it a reality.

The second event that ensured the future success of the Hump was Roosevelt's creation of the Assam-Burma-China (ABC) Ferry Command on March 20, 1942. The ABC Ferry Command would eventually become ATC's air transport complement for the Hump, but what was most important was the manner in which the organization was arranged as part of the AAF's Tenth Air Force, charged with flying and protecting the Hump route.[76] The Tenth's commander was Maj. Gen. Lewis Brereton, the man recently (and unjustly) criticized by MacArthur in the Philippines for supposedly not taking adequate measures to protect his bombers from the Japanese attack that came just hours after Pearl Harbor.[77] Reassigned to India, Brereton was headquartered in New Delhi, but it was his chief of staff—a subordinate, Brig. Earl Naiden—who was given separate command of the air transport operation.[78] The motive behind this arrangement, one that peeved Brereton to no end, was to ensure that air transports would be used only for the airlift to China and not for other matters that Brereton might deem necessary in his theater. Brereton was not happy, telling George Marshall, "This is unacceptable. As Air Force commander, it is essential that responsibility for and direct control of all air activities in my theater be vested in me."[79] Marshall's reply was "Policies relating to the movement and supply of planes will be administered throughout the ferry system operated by a central office in Washington." The airlift of supplies to China, though miniscule in early 1942, would nonetheless be directed from Washington due to the airlift's political importance. The War Department did budge slightly: "Control of ferry operations insofar as they are affected by military operations in India will be exercised by you [Brereton]."[80] The die was cast nonetheless. The importance of the China resupply mission was such that the War Department knew that local commanders like Brereton would put the needs of their theaters above the broader national policy aims of the president and the Combined Chiefs of Staff. To prevent this, air supply to China was to be directed first from Washington and not from New Delhi, an arrangement that was the source of constant friction for the war's duration.

By April 1942 the idea of keeping China supplied by air was fixed in the minds of decision makers in Washington. Roosevelt, ever an advocate for the use of aircraft (he was the first sitting president to fly in an airplane, doing so in 1943), took for granted the idea that the AAF could move supplies just as easily as the army, thinking all it needed was enough planes and pilots. George Marshall was committed to the early notion of keeping China supplied by air—seen in his insistence that U.S. air transports in India were to be earmarked exclusively for that mission—but did not imagine such an airlift could ever provide more than a token amount of supplies. Hap Arnold pushed for the airlift but, as an airman, was aware of its limitations, caused by the lack of airplanes, airfields, and airmen needed to make it a reality. Nevertheless, the idea that U.S. supplies were needed to "keep China in the war" was now the orthodox mantra, and the only way to deliver those supplies—with the Japanese driving into northern Burma—was by air. For the remainder of 1942, though, Washington's optimism for the airlift's success was more than matched by the pessimism of AAF commanders in India, as only a handful of pilots with varying degrees of experience were available to fly over poorly charted mountains during the region's worst season of weather, and all this in underpowered airplanes poorly suited for the task at hand.

TERRAIN, WEATHER, PILOTS, AND PLANES

Before studying the chronological history of the Hump as it would begin to unfold after March 1942, it is worthwhile to pause and spend a chapter looking specifically at the environment in which the airlift took place as well as at the pilots and planes that flew there. Looking at a simple planiform map of the supply-mission's route might leave someone unimpressed, the flight being relatively short by air transport standards. Depending on the points of departure and arrival, the flights back and forth from India and China usually averaged only five hundred miles, whereas the trip from Natal, Brazil to Accra, Ghana, covered five times that distance. When matched with all of the regularly scheduled routes flown by AAF transports, the Hump route was among the shortest; yet to this day it is remembered as the most difficult of them all. For over sixty years a veterans' organization existed–the Hump Pilots Association (HPA)–with its members knitted together by one common experience, that of flying over the Himalayan "Hump." This was no back-alley organization, either, as its members, over time, garnered the respect of national leaders of both U.S. and Chinese stripes. In 1978 President Gerald Ford was the distinguished visitor at an annual HPA reunion in Vail, Colorado, where he extolled the heroics of the Hump's flyers.[1] The Republic of China also publicly recognized the efforts of the Hump pilots by awarding them the Chinese Commendation Medal, commemorating their "celebration of victory together."[2] In 2005 a group of approximately thirty former Hump fliers traveled to the People's Republic of China, where they were met by adoring crowds and addressed personally by President Hu Jintao, who hosted them at a state dinner held in Beijing at the Great Hall of the People near Tiananmen Square, honoring the memory of what they did during China's "Anti-Fascist" war.[3] To better understand the motivation behind such an outpouring of gratitude, it is necessary to appreciate the makeup of the Hump route; current Sino-U.S. sentiment recognizes the airlift not simply because it delivered supplies to "keep China in the war," but because of its demanding environment.

One qualification is necessary before going further, that having to do with the temptation to succumb too easily to the Hump's heroics. Joseph A. McKeown, a Northwest Airlines pilot before the war, recognized this tendency to overstate the airlift's dangers, reporting it in a letter written to his company's "tough and ambitious" president, Croil Hunter, on September 18, 1942.[4] McKeown was among the first batch of airline pilots commissioned by the AAF earlier that spring to serve as an initial cadre of aviators sent to fly supplies to China. Responding to a news article written by a reporter who flew with him on a flight over the Hump earlier that summer, McKeown wrote that he "saw an article from a U.S. newspaper about me flying the Burma road that was full of blood and thunder and malarkey," prompting him to "write and put you [Hunter] straight so you won't think I'm a scatterbrained nitwit instead of a sample of airline piloting technique." McKeown goes on to write, "On the aerial Burma road run the minimum instrument altitude is 17,000 feet with the mountains some 23,000 to the side of the course,"[5] adding, "We do not fly on instruments all iced up through narrow passes at 18,000 feet with no radio bearings [for navigation] as the newspaper stated." Perhaps in an effort to excuse the reporter's exaggerations, McKeown offers, "The particular trip that seemed so hair raising was only so because one of my engines was cutting out while on instruments," leading to this explanation: "We naturally have to take risks to get the job done, but we are not foolish enough to [as the article alleged] chase through passes blindly and take on ice at altitudes where the overloaded airplane is already mushing with full power and 2,459 rpm."[6]

Surprisingly, McKeown did claim there were hazards in flying the Hump—

not because it was too challenging to fly, but because at the time it was *not chal-lenging enough,* asserting that Hump flying was not difficult enough to hone the skills of newly trained pilots coming to the theater. He states, "The copilots that we brought over here were fresh out of flying school and they have been checked out and are flying along with us doing as good a job as we can do because there is no instrument, weather, or radio navigation required. In short since the monsoon has ended [at the end of the summer] the airline pilots are wasting their time over here"; in his opinion, they could be used with more effectiveness elsewhere and keep their weather-flying skills honed at the same time. McKeown goes on to complain about the blandness of Hump flying: "I have not done any instrument flying for a month except for a few hours under the hood and as we have practically no radio facilities our technique will deteriorate if our training is not utilized. Furthermore we have not done any night flying for months and when we realize how much good we could do this winter elsewhere we wonder why something isn't done about it."[7]

One needs to remember two things concerning McKeown's remarks. First, he was an experienced and seasoned airline pilot who flew for Northwest, an airline with the unique reputation for flying routes over mountainous terrain and in bad weather. Furthermore, immediately after the war he became a senior test pilot with Lockheed Aircraft and broke the flight-time record for a trip from Burbank, California, to Miami, Florida, a distance of 2,355 miles that he and his crew flew in 7 hours and 53 minutes in the new C-59 Constellation, breaking the old record by 2 hours and 17 minutes. As will be discussed later, McKeown's flying expertise was clearly above that of his peers who flew the Hump in 1942; things that were difficult for others were not so for him. Second, McKeown's recollections are just that—the observations of one man during what was probably no more than six months of Hump flying (the first group of airline pilots were commissioned into the service and arrived in India in April 1942). Was the weather unusually good during his tenure? Formal weather forecasting for Hump pilots by trained weathermen did not become a fixture on the Hump until 1944, but his service during the wet monsoon of 1942 was probably no cakewalk.[8] Were the airplanes he flew any more reliable than those that flew the Hump after he wrote this letter? Probably not, though factory-delivered C-46s arriving in India in the late spring of 1943 were riddled with mechanical problems inherent in any plane rushed to production under wartime conditions. Were Japanese fighters less of a threat in September 1942 than later in the operation? Perhaps, due to the fact that the Japanese Fifth Air Army was still getting settled in Burma in the summer of 1942 and did little flying during the wet monsoon. All in all, though, McKeown's recollections are his own and need to be treated as such, but they are also worthy of attention because they challenge the conventional narrative of the airlift, one susceptible to exaggeration under the romantic influence of nostalgia. This is in no way intended to take away anything from those who flew the Hump. As Dr. Dik Daso, curator for modern military aircraft at the Smithsonian National Air and Space Museum in Washington, D.C., recalls of the Hump's flyers, "They didn't have radar altimeters, so they never knew how high above the terrain they were. They flew dead reckonings [flying with the use of only a compass heading] through mountain passes using sometimes inaccurate charts. The weather was unpredictable: thunderstorms, hail, and icing could get you at any time. It was seat-of-the-pants flying in the most basic sense. And yet the whole idea of an airlift as a show of airpower came from that effort."[9] Flying the Hump was often a perilous trip with its chief obstacle coming not in the form of enemy fighters but rather in the form of the physiographical makeup of the place crews flew. What follows is a description of that physiography and of those who worked in it, in an effort to reconcile McKeown's and Daso's characterizations of that environment.

THE TERRAIN

Because weather has a direct correlation with geography, the first place to begin a discussion of the Hump's physiography is in a look at its geographical features. The airlift's western base was in India's Assam Province; its eastern terminus was in one of a handful of airfields in China's Yunnan Province, Kunming being the foremost. While not technically part of the Himalayas (or any of its lesser divisions found in four main groups of parallel belts: the Outer Himalayas, Lesser Himalayas, Great Himalayas, and Tibetan Himalayas), the route's proximity to this geographical phenomenon—rightly called the "roof of the world"—bears directly on the surrounding topographical features of eastern India, northern Burma, and southwestern China. Serving as the main topographical division between the Indian subcontinent and the Tibetan Plateau, the Himalayas are the causal factor behind the wide climatological variations in this part of Asia, with the Tibetan

FIGURE 3. An Air Transport Command C-46 with gear down for landing, coming in low over a Chinese donkey cart. These two modes of transportation—one ancient and one modern—portray some of the challenges and the character of the Hump. *Courtesy U.S. Army Center of Military History.*

Plateau being the largest and highest highland in the world. As an example of the topography's effect on climate, the Tibetan Plateau's mean elevation is 13,100 feet, which blocks or disrupts climactic circulation in the lower third of the troposphere and, in so doing, prevents moisture from the Indian Ocean and Mediterranean Sea from getting into North Asia, leading to the formation of such features as the Gobi Desert and producing drastic monsoonal weather.[10] And even though the airlift's Indian bases were located mostly in the Brahmaputra River valley and were over one hundred miles south of the mountain range (Sookerating, the airlift's most northeast airbase was 140 miles south of Namcha Barwa, the western anchor of the Himalayan chain sitting at 25,445 feet and located at 29°37′50″N, 95°03′19″E), the fact that the airlift was flown in the neighborhood of the Himalayas meant that nearby topographical and climatological characteristics would be equally severe.

While the larger contours of south-central Asian climatology are shaped by the Himalayas, the topography of the Hump route was more pressing in the minds of its pilots, with the flight path traversing a number of lesser mountain ranges that reached just below 15,000 feet. Starting from Lalmanir Hat, a westerly base in Assam, aircrews flew east along the Brahmaputra River and would first see rising terrain off their right wing (to the south) in the Khasi Hills (where Shillong and Cherrapunji are located); then, flying further to the east, they would see the Naga Hills to the south, the home of a legendary tribe of headhunters. The crew would then encounter the first rise in terrain on their flight path at the Patkai Range, with tops approaching 10,000 feet and located along the India-Burma border. After crossing the Upper Chidwin River valley, the first range of mountains with peaks over 14,000 feet was met in the Kumon Mountains. After passing the Kumon ridge the crew came to the West Irrawaddy (Mali Hka) River, which gave way to the broad valley where Fort Hertz (Putao) was located. Passing Fort Hertz, the crew then had to cross a series of ranges between 14,000 and 15,000 feet, mountains that were impressive in that there was often over 10,000 feet of relief between mountaintops and valley floor. These ridges were carved by the East Irrawaddy, the Salween (on the border between Burma and China), and Mekong Rivers, with the main "Hump" being the Sanstung Mountains (Nu Shan in Chinese, also called the Kaolikung Range in some AAF documentation), a 14,000-plus foot range that sat astride the two.[11] Once the Mekong River was passed, the terrain gradually became less rugged, giving way to rolling hills after the last vestiges of the Henduan Mountains were crossed. This made landmarks like Mount Dali, Erhai Lake (located just east of Dali), the L-shaped bend in the Yangtze River, and Lijiang Mountain easy to locate. From here the difficult part of the flight was over, and navigation to Kunming's airport, located at an elevation of 6,240 feet, was comparatively easy (see figure 4; see also figure 5 for a sketch of the route).[12]

Along the entire route from India to China there were no peaks over 20,000 feet, with the closest mountain to that elevation being Hkakabo Razi at 19,294 feet in northern Burma (coordinates 28°19′59″N, 97°28′00″E), the highest mountain in Southeast Asia, located sixty-five miles north of Fort Hertz. If an aircrew stayed within ten miles of the northerly "Able" route from Sookerating (India) to Fort Hertz (Burma) to Lijiang and Kunming (China), they would not encounter any terrain over 15,000 feet. When the weather was clear, it was possible for a crew

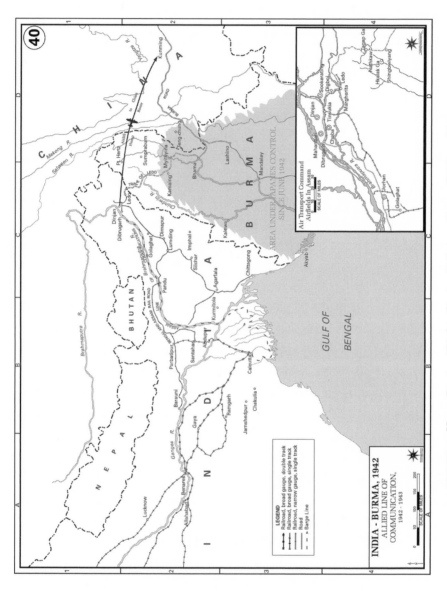

FIGURE 4. Hump Route of Flight. *Courtesy U.S. Army Center of Military History.*

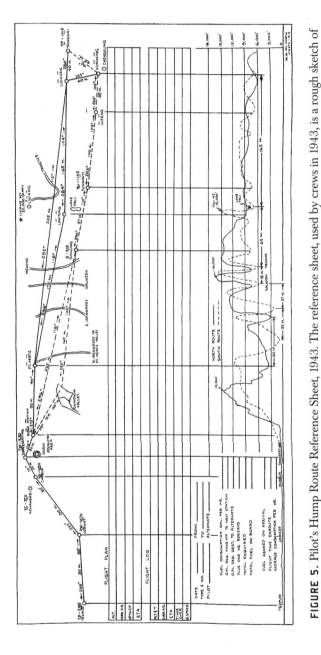

FIGURE 5. Pilot's Hump Route Reference Sheet, 1943. The reference sheet, used by crews in 1943, is a rough sketch of the overhead of the route (top portion of figure) as well as the terrain contours (bottom portion). *Source:* USAAF, ATC, Historical Officer, *Air Transportation to China under the 10th Air Force. Courtesy AFHRA.*

to fly much lower; in the case of one trip from Kunming to Chabua (one of the main bases in Assam, India) at 11,000 feet, made by a B-25 crew with C. R. Smith on board, flying at 100 feet above the ground![13] This was by far the exception, though, as no cargo-laden transport had enough power or performance to fly the route at such altitudes. Using 15,000 feet as a baseline, then, crews would normally add 2,000 feet of extra altitude to remain well clear of the terrain (this standard is used even today when airplanes are flying under instrument conditions), which is why Joseph McKeown, the experienced Northwest pilot, remarked that 17,000 feet was the minimum instrument altitude to cross the Hump.

Frequently in official 1940s correspondence the mountains that constituted the Hump were listed as being higher than they actually were. For example, Brig. Gen. Harold Alexander, the airlift's commander for most of 1943, remarked that "the minimum safe altitude for continuous operation over part of the route is 18,000 feet,"[14] a higher altitude that may have been chosen to compensate for the inaccuracies of flight charts, as a "War Zone Familiarization Guide" published in August 1944 claimed that some charts still had extreme errors of 3,000 feet.[15] But that same guide—written for pilots and navigators who flew in the CBI—stated in describing the Hump, "Many mountain ranges running in a northerly and southerly direction with altitudes varying from 8,500 feet in the south to 16,000 feet on the direct route from India to Southern China, to 25,000 in the north."[16] As mentioned earlier, there was no terrain above 15,000 feet within ten statute miles of the route of flight, though some pilots would have flown farther north on some occasions to remain clear of Japanese fighters. Even with such a deviation, the nearest peak over 16,000 feet was over fifty miles north of Fort Hertz (coordinates 28°04′N, 97°13′E), not "on the direct route," as the guide suggests. Additionally, the 25,000-foot peak mentioned in the guide must have been a reference to Namcha Barwa, the easternmost Himalayan peak that was 140 statute miles due north of the air bases in India, in terrain that only a very lost Hump pilot would pass through.

Nor is memoir literature immune from remembering the mountains as being higher than they actually were. Winton R. Close, a B-29 pilot (and retired air force major general) recalled that in flying bombing missions from Calcutta to Japan, "We could not get below the weather because the minimum instrument altitude over the Hump was 24,000 feet."[17] Why the frequent terrain elevation discrepancies? First of all, in a day before satellite mapping, flight charts were rife with altitude errors, especially in a part of the world that was so difficult to chart using the aircraft of the day. One example of a gross elevation error is seen in the Lijiang fix on the northerly "Able" route, about fifty miles due north of Mount Dali: a pilot's 1943 flight chart notes a 23,000-foot-high mountain fifteen miles north of this fix (Lijiang is located over the town of Dayan in central Yunnan Province), but charts published since the 1980s—renowned for their accuracy—list the same peak at 18,074 feet, almost 5,000 feet less than the Hump route chart. This discrepancy is particularly puzzling because crews routinely flew this route throughout 1943 and 1944 and would have been able to clearly recognize the difference between an 18,000-foot peak and one 5,000 feet higher.[18] The best explanation for such an altitude exaggeration is that the original charts—those that predated the war—had sizable errors that persisted because charts were seldom revised and republished. As an example of this, the AAF did not send an aircraft mapping squadron to the theater until November 1943 to map the 54,000 linear miles required for the ATC routes; the unit returned four months later to process a chart update.[19] As such, planners were content to allow the chart discrepancies to remain, especially as instrument navigation was more an art than a science, so long as the errors showed the mountains as being higher—not lower—than they were in actuality. Unwittingly, though, such persistent errors led to the perception that the Hump's mountains were actually more ominous than they really were.

None of this is mentioned to minimize the dangers of the Hump's terrain. Instrument navigation was performed via "dead reckoning," a technique whereby the pilot, knowing his point of departure, flew a specific heading (using a very imprecise compass) for a specific amount of time (based on his airspeed) and made turns along the course based on the amount of time elapsed. Of course, such a technique was prone to error if winds were not as planned, winds that the pilot had to take into account in calculating ground speed or heading drift corrections. As the airlift grew, radio beacons were placed along the route so pilots could update their positions along the way, but these short-range beacons could also be unreliable, with one source recording an instance in which the Japanese found—and moved—one such beacon so as to spoil navigation solutions and force airplane crashes.[20] Thus, it is not surprising that crews believed mountains to be taller than they actually were, as "altitude above you" is colloquially considered one of the two things worthless to a pilot.[21]

The high mountains and rugged terrain are worth discussion not just because of the fact that they dictated safe flight altitudes but because they also constituted a danger to crews that had to perform a crash landing. When a plane lost power and was unable to maintain a safe altitude above the ground, a forced landing was necessary, but only the most uncommonly gifted—or lucky—pilot could "dead-stick" his transport safely to a power-off landing on such rugged terrain. It was too easy for planners back in Washington to simply look at a map (one that probably had gross inaccuracies in the early 1940s) and dismiss any problems the Hump's altitude might pose, as in the case of a letter sent by Col. Harold R. Harris, the assistant chief of staff of Air Transport Command in November 1943 to Brig. Gen. Earl Hoag, the airlift's commander at the time. Regarding the terrain, Harris stated, "Many reports have mentioned that flight personnel operating over this route have a preconceived notion that the terrain traversed is an almost insuperable obstacle to the successful operation of this vital supply route. The terrain is admittedly rugged and the altitude extreme but this is in no way a limiting factor to the success of the operation." Harris goes on to compare Hump flying with stateside parallels, claiming that "there are many places in the world, such as the western part of the United States, Central America, etc., etc., where terrain exists which is equally rugged, though not so high, and where severe flight conditions are also encountered aloft, yet air operations over and through such areas are considered successful and not overly difficult." To Harris, the problem was not the terrain but the mindset of the flyers. He then continued, "It seems to me a constant campaign must be waged to educate flight personnel that the terrain is not the 'bugaboo' they believe it to be but merely another piece of ground over which aircraft can and must operate." To counter the "bugaboo" that was the Hump's terrain, Harris proposed a mountain-flying training program, later established in Reno, Nevada, where pilots could become comfortable with the idiosyncrasies of mountain flying. For the time being, though, he encouraged Hoag to first confront the problem with "the proper mental approach" so that "the practice of old pilots, who have been in the Wing some time" would not discourage "newly arrived pilots with exaggerated accounts of the hardships and difficulties." Harris hoped that if Hoag downplayed the Hump's dangers, this would in turn "give way to a feeling of conviction on the part of all concerned that this operation is no more difficult than many others throughout the world."[22]

Harris himself was an experienced flyer, serving as a test pilot during the interwar years and at one time in 1926 holding thirteen world flying records; he was also familiar with mountain flying in South America, helping to found Peruvian Airlines in 1928. This said, though, the answer to the airlift's terrain challenges was probably not to be found in merely a mindset that advanced a "proper mental attitude." Like McKeown, Harris was an experienced pilot reacting to a spate of Hump "lore" by encouraging a different attitude, something more easily done from a desk in Washington than a cockpit over China. Still, despite his brusqueness toward pilot opinion, he may have been partially correct, as seen in Hoag's reply the following month in which the Hump commander agreed with Harris: "Every effort has and is being made to minimize the Hollywood attitude toward this run." He went on, saying that he was working to see that the word "Hill" replaced the word "Hump" in both casual conversation and official correspondence in an effort to confront what he saw as a "distinct psychological attitude" that overstated the route's dangers. Part of the problem, as Hoag saw it, was that he had extra pilots in the fall of 1943, and so there was plenty of "idle time for those who made trips to sit around and magnify the achievement they had just performed when they were lucky enough to be assigned to an airplane."[23] As will be covered later, Hoag's understanding of the airlift's operational and tactical details was poor, as he spent much of his time dealing with bureaucratic paperwork. One thing is clear, though—his requirement for his pilots to refer to the Hump as the "Hill" never stuck. It is true that terrain elevations were sometimes inflated, owing perhaps to the twin problems of inaccurate charts and a "Hollywood attitude." But when crews—of varying experience—were forced to fly over that terrain in rough weather and in unreliable aircraft, it comes as no surprise that the mountain range over which they flew would serve to add to the very real mystique of the airlift.

THE WEATHER

The greatest obstacle to successful Hump operations was the weather. As the airlift matured toward the end of 1943, one pilot recalled, "Flying weather on instruments continued to be the most threatening ordeal for Hump pilots. Piloting a plane through the angry limbo of clouds was strange and frightening–flying twenty-five tons of metal, gasoline, high explosives, and humanity at 250 miles per hour through an unknown sky. 'Flying on instruments' sounded simple–so precise and scientific. In actual flight, instrument flying in bad weather was the most stressful and agonizing part of the mission."[24] Like the terrain that spanned the Hump's route, its weather was equally foreboding. What follows is a general description of weather along the route, followed by a more detailed discussion of the four weather phenomena that posed the greatest challenges for pilots, namely wind, turbulence, rain, and icing.

The weather over the Hump was, broadly speaking, the merger of weather from Siberia, the Bay of Bengal, and the South China Sea. As previously mentioned, the high Himalayas usually served as a physical barrier between the Indian subcontinent and greater central Asia, which meant that for the Hump, weather patterns in India were usually distinct from those of southwest China, as Siberian highs influenced China and Bengali lows influenced Assam. For troops on the ground, this usually meant that India was hot and either dry or wet (depending on the time of year), while southern Yunnan Province was cool and temperate (Kunming's high elevation made its climate cooler than that of most places in southwest China). But this did not mean that the two weather systems were completely distinct, as the prevailing current of winds was from west to east (referred to as "westerly," as compass directions denote the current's origin when applied to winds and fronts; thus, a New England "nor'easter" is a weather front that moves from the northeast, off the Atlantic coast, to the southwest), which meant that one day's bad weather in Assam was a sure sign of bad weather in Kunming thirty-six to forty-eight hours later.[25]

Hump weather–covering Assam and most of the route of flight–can be divided into four seasons of varying length: spring (February through April), summer (May through September), fall (October and November), and winter (December and January), with the best weather coming in the fall and the worst in the spring and summer. On a daily basis, the weather was generally best between midnight and daybreak and worst between noon and late evening. Weather in southwest China can be divided into two seasons, summer and winter, with May marking the start of summer and October the start of winter.

The weather in Assam and along the route was worst in spring (February–

April), with strong southwest winds and considerable thunderstorm activity, the tops of those storms averaging over 20,000 feet (roughly speaking, the strength of a thunderstorm can be quantified by the measure in its height and taking into account its geographic latitude; a storm of this height and location during this time of year was quite respectable). The icing level was usually 15,000 feet–the elevation of the route's highest terrain–which meant that if there was adequate moisture in the air, ice would be a problem during the flight. Severe icing was not uncommon in the spring,[26] though it was often localized and could be avoided. Strong westerly winds of up to 100 nautical miles per hour, or knots,[27] were not unusual, producing updrafts on the near side of mountains and downdrafts on the lee, or far side. March usually saw the highest winds along the route; thunderstorms reached up to 30,000 feet in the Brahmaputra Valley, where most of the India-based airfields were located. Additionally, thunderstorms usually got worse as spring gave way to summer.

The wet monsoon was the dominant weather phenomenon of the summer (May–September), as prevailing winds from the southwest brought with them much of the year's rainfall in a single season. Warmer temperatures usually meant that icing was not a problem, and westerly winds were usually calm; the warmer weather also brought with it increased thunderstorm activity with accompanying turbulence. On an average day it could rain for seven to eight hours, bringing low ceilings and poor visibility, not just at the airfields (which needed decent weather for arriving aircraft) but along the route as well. Stratus and cumulus clouds formed at low levels as early as nine o'clock in the morning, their tops growing to between 20,000 and 30,000 feet–meaning an entire flight had to be flown on instruments. The prevailing clouds also obscured the location of thunderstorms and made them difficult for crews to avoid.

By fall (October–November) the weather began to improve, with clearing skies and prevailing westerly winds of 30 to 40 knots. Cooler and dryer weather meant that turbulence was usually less than moderate (though the area around Mt. Dali was known for having bad turbulence in the fall), and icing was usually not problematic. As fall gave way to winter (December–January), winds began to pick back up to 100 knots, bringing accompanying turbulence. January was notorious for cloudy skies (the first few weeks of January were usually the cloudiest of the year), bringing a sharp increase in icing (which could be encountered as low as 11,000 feet), turbulence, and snowfall. Fog also became a problem for the air-fields along the Brahmaputra Valley, sometimes not clearing until ten o'clock in the morning.

Compared with that in India and along the Hump route, weather in China was usually milder. Summer (May–September) in Kunming and Yunnanyi saw a 60 percent increase in rainfall, tapering off by the end of the season. This rain was not a product of the Indian monsoon but rather the result of lows in southwest China that drew moisture from the South China Sea; as a rule, Kunming received about half as much rain as the Assam valley airfields. Winter (October–April) weather near Kunming was fairly benign, with four to five rainy days a month, good visibility, and occasional fog produced by Lake Dien Chi, located immediately south of the city.[28]

Besides the general problem of having to fly in continuously cloudy weather—what pilots today call "instrument meteorological conditions," or IMC—the four weather phenomena that caused the biggest problems for Hump fliers (wind, turbulence, rain, and icing) each had seasonal characteristics. In-flight winds were strongest in the winter and spring, with speeds measuring 130 knots in some of these westerlies, making for a quick flight to China and a slow flight back to India. Wind speeds at altitude were usually determined by comparing an aircraft's known airspeed with its actual speed across the ground (determined by the time it took to travel between two fixed landmarks), but as a rule of thumb, aviators knew that high surface winds—in excess of 25 knots—meant that winds at 20,000 feet were probably over 100 knots.[29] The strong winds aloft were caused by a south Asian subtropical jet stream, a continuous current of westerly air that had an average speed of 75 knots at 39,000 feet; while no airplanes flew at that altitude, this prevailing current, when mixed with lower-altitude winds or a frontal passage, made for an impressive feature.[30] Strong winds at altitude caused two problems. First, they complicated a crew's navigation solution, dictating the need, in some cases, to fly an extra twenty-five degrees into the wind just to keep an aircraft on course.[31] Second, strong winds at altitude caused severe updrafts and downdrafts in the mountains, leading to heavy turbulence, the second phenomenon that frequently caused problems.

What is today called "mountain wave turbulence" was common during windy periods, as westerlies would produce an updraft on the westward side of mountains and equally powerful downdrafts on the eastward, down slope, usually measured at speeds of 30 to 40 knots but found to be near 100 knots on rare occasions. On March 13, 1943, a pilot reported gaining 8,000 feet in about one minute when crossing the first ridge to China, the result of extreme mountain wave turbulence. Usually crews would "ride" the turbulence when flying east, as they would then experience strong downdrafts after crossing a ridgeline.[32] Violent updrafts and downdrafts wreaked havoc on a plane's structural integrity, but also caused problems with securing the airplane's cargo. One CNAC pilot recalls carrying a load of fifty-five-gallon drums of aviation fuel (fuel was the most common load carried over the Hump) when extreme turbulence caused the drums to break free from their moorings and violently roll about the cargo compartment, spilling much of their contents. The hardest part of getting the drums back upright was doing so without passing out from the fumes.[33] This was not an isolated incident; in the fall of 1944 ATC considered using lightweight aluminum barrels to haul fuel over the Hump, and one of the chief concerns was their strength in the face of heavy turbulence.[34]

While wind and turbulence often went hand in hand, rain and icing were not necessarily directly related. Rains in the CBI were legendary, especially during the summer's wet monsoon. In one of Hap Arnold's early briefings on the Hump that he delivered to China's foreign minister, T. V. Soong, and a mixed gallery of AAF leaders, Arnold claimed that parts of India witnessed 500 inches of rain annually. He was not exaggerating. Cherrapunji, a city 180 miles southwest of the Hump airfield at Jorhat, averaged 641 inches of rain a year and 366 inches in the month of July *alone,* claiming the title of being "the wettest place on earth."[35] While Cherrapunji is an extreme example, most of the India-based Hump airfields got a much more modest amount of rain, with Tezpur averaging 73 inches a year, and 12 inches a month between May and August.[36] Monsoonal rains accounted for months of poor Hump tonnage totals, dictated the campaigning season for ground offensives, prevented airfield construction in 1943, and even persuaded the Japanese to recall their fighters to other parts of the Pacific where they could be used more effectively until the season was over.[37]

The last weather phenomenon was icing. Worse in the winter and spring, low icing levels meant that a crew could not stay low enough (in warmer air) to remain clear of the terrain. Icing was a threefold problem. First, it added obvious weight to an already heavy airplane, making it difficult to maintain altitude; in some extreme cases, a crew would have to dump its cargo to lighten the aircraft just to remain clear of terrain when the airplane's deicing and anti-icing equipment did not keep it adequately free of ice. Second, when ice formed on the wings, it reduced the aerodynamic effectiveness of the aircraft and threatened a loss of altitude. Lastly, ice could form in the plane's carburetors, causing engines to choke and lose power or quit altogether. Transports like the Curtiss C-46 had deicing and anti-icing equipment like heated propellers, windshield deicing fluid, and wing deicing "boots," but the effectiveness of this equipment was often questionable when conditions were severe.[38] Making matters worse was the absence of institutionalized weather forecasting and reporting by trained meteorologists until 1944; before this time departing pilots normally got weather reports only from those who had just landed. But this method was prone to errors as several hours could elapse between the arrival and departure of crews, increasing the likelihood that weather conditions had changed.

THE PILOTS

Any general discussion of the pilots who flew the Hump is bound to be in error on points of detail; thousands of men piloted aircraft from India to China and to group them all together in an effort to make a universal claim as to their skills, frustrations, challenges, and victories is sheer folly. Nevertheless, it is still worthwhile to attempt to describe these transport pilots, especially as they compared with their peers who flew fighters and bombers, to get a general sense of their challenges, successes, and failures. This section will focus on piloting skill—especially as a function of training—to provide a snapshot of the nature and quality of the flyers who flew the Hump.

Where did the pilots come from who flew the airlift? As previously mentioned, Ferry Command, which was responsible for delivering airplanes from their factories for shipment abroad, would become Air Transport Command at the end of 1942 and would likewise be the first formal military airlift unit to fly the Hump under the auspices of the newly minted Assam-Burma Ferry Command. Before the United States entered the war, most Ferry Command pilots were on loan from fighter and bomber units in the Air Force Combat Command (AFCC), as ferrying aircraft was an easy way for pilots of any stripe to gain general flight experience. Once the war began, AFCC recalled all its pilots, leaving Ferry Command severely short of manpower. To fill this void, the command hired available civilian pilots from varied backgrounds—crop dusters, stunt pilots, test pilots, barnstormers, those who had experience flying their own private airplanes, and small "feeder-line" commercial airline pilots, this last category constituting the largest group. The pilots were hired for a probationary period of thirty to ninety days, based on their experience level. Once probation was over, they were either commissioned as officers (and given rank commensurate with their age and flying experience), or they were released. Even today, pilot experience is quantified in flying-hours, and these earliest hires needed 500 hours to qualify for the program. The pilot shortage became so acute in the summer of 1943 that this requirement was relaxed to 200 hours, but then increased to 300 hours by September 1943. The shortage was all but erased by 1944, when a civilian hire had to have 1,000 hours to qualify for the transition program.[39]

The recruitment of civilian pilots witnessed heavy growth in 1942, with 343 civilians joining Ferry Command by the end of January—less than two months after the program began—with this number growing to 800 by the end of March, a time when there were only 315 military pilots in the command. By the end of the year 1,730 civilians had been recruited, with nearly 80 percent of them being commissioned, a significant proportion as they accounted for roughly 20 percent of all the officers in Air Transport Command.[40] With the AAF's Training Command adding only just over 500 new transport pilots to the pool, the immediate relief provided by the "militarized" civilian pilots was also a significant help.[41] Incidentally, it was also this civilian recruitment program that gave birth to the Women's Air Ferry Service (WAFS), becoming the Women's Airforce Service Pilots (WASP) in August 1943.[42]

Many of the civilian hires had previous experience as military pilots and were military reservists, but the AAF had to be judicious in exercising its right to call them to service because it was reliant on commercial airlines to do most of its flying; in 1942 commercial companies under contract did 88 percent of all ATC work.[43] This percentage dropped off drastically as time passed, but among the first batch of seasoned reservists called to duty were the members of the 1st Ferry Group that gathered at Morrison Field in West Palm Beach, Florida, and headed to China in March 1942 to become the first military unit tasked to fly the Hump.

Following this course, the experience of Robert T. Rose was typical: enlisting in the Air Corps as an airplane mechanic in Rantoul, Illinois, in 1936, Rose attended Woodrow Wilson College, earned his degree, was commissioned, and finished AAF pilot training in 1940, after which he flew P-38s. Less than a year after finishing pilot training he was placed on reserve status and took a job with Eastern Airlines in Atlanta but came back on active duty in March 1942, being assigned to the 1st Ferry Group and flying missions over the Hump for the next twenty months.[44] Rose was among a uniquely qualified core of pilots whose flying experience ranged from 1,800 to more than 10,000 hours.[45]

In contrast to this core of experienced reservists were those newly trained pilots who were completing the AAF's twenty-seven-week training program in 1942 and receiving assignments as transport pilots, eventually constituting 35 percent of ATC's pilots by the end of the year.[46] These young flyers were qualified for their jobs, but they lacked the experience of the reservist transport pilots; they also caused something of a morale problem, being generally disgruntled with having to fly transports rather than combat aircraft like fighters or bombers. Assignments were usually doled out in order of one's class ranking from pilot training (with occasional exceptions to this policy), which meant that combat assignments were selected by those who graduated near the top of their class, and transport, training, and reconnaissance assignments went to those who finished in the bottom half of a class. Added to this was the lack of excitement inherent in ferry work. As historian John Carter aptly puts it:

> *The work, moreover, often seemed dull. Ferrying and transport work, where the emphasis was on safety and economy, might be satisfactory enough for the average civilian pilot turned military, who as often as not was approaching middle age. But to many of the adventurous and ambitious young men who had completed their training in a military flying school and found themselves assigned through no choice of their own to ATC, the prospect of guiding "boxcars" from here to there and back again came as a distinct disappointment. They found neither glamour nor hope of fame and advancement in the hauling of freight or in the delivery of aircraft from factory to air base. Many of them soon caught some glimpse of the larger mission they served, but in other cases the problem remained.[47]*

This lack of esteem among young transport pilots was not only a U.S. problem. Prior to 1936 the German Luftwaffe used the Ju 52 as a bomber until the experience of the Spanish Civil War made it clear that the aircraft was too slow (and vulnerable) for that mission. When the IV Group of the Hindenburg Wing at Fuestenwalde—a Ju 52 bombardment unit—was designated a transport unit in October 1937, it was officially dubbed a "bombardment group for special employment." This was done to keep the unit's personnel from "feeling that their mission was one of secondary importance," for at that time, transport pilots could not boast "a tradition of heroic service," attesting to the fact that ego in aviation has little respect for national boundaries.[48] Even more than just wanting to fly combat aircraft, most trainees regarded being a fighter pilot as the epitome of their aspirations, seen in a comment by one Marine Corps fighter pilot who remarked, "To choose any course except single-engine planes . . . would have seemed cautious, unromantic, almost middle-aged, like wearing your rubbers or voting Republican."[49]

As will be detailed later, the mixture of seasoned and novice flyers was a great help to the airlift's success; recent graduates from training were able to learn about the peculiarities of flying in the Hump's difficult environment from veterans with a wealth of flight experience. But as the mission grew in size and scope, more pilots were added who were fresh from the controlled environs of pilot training, reducing the overall aptitude of the piloting force. By the summer of 1943 Hump pilot inexperience had become standard fare in official correspondence. In a memo from the army chief of staff to Roosevelt on July 15, Marshall remarked, "Due to the operational requirements of the Army Air Forces in other theaters, the experience level of pilots and navigators is not as high as desired [among those flying the Hump]."[50] Marshall was probably referring specifically to the fact that many newly minted pilots were arriving in India with only the minimum qualifications for flight duties, the AAF training establishment being stretched by the war's requirement for thousands of pilots of all types. Nearly a third of the new transport pilots rushed to the CBI in the spring of 1943 were qualified in only single-engine aircraft and lacked even the minimum training in a multi-engine airplane, let alone the type of transport they would have to fly over the Hump.[51] Arnold sent a special representative to the India-China Wing to discreetly provide an independent assessment of problems with the airlift; the report came back that 75 percent of all accidents in the spring and summer of 1943 were caused by inexperienced flight personnel.[52]

The problem did not improve with time. At the end of 1943 the ATC commander, Maj. Gen. Hal George, sent C. R. Smith to the India-China Wing for two months to make a careful study of the unit. Among Smith's detailed observations was the recurring theme of pilot inexperience: "Most of the pilots are simply 'flying over their heads'; flying at night and under other adverse conditions for which they have not the experience. This has resulted in accidents and deaths but, with the men available, there is nothing else to do."[53] Smith was being neither hyperbolic nor dramatic; the India-China Wing accounted for a third of all ATC fatalities in July and August 1943 while flying only 15 percent of that command's miles. And while some pointed to the lack of good leadership as a contributing factor in the wing's high fatality rate, clearly the problem was more endemic, stemming back to deficiencies in the training provided to new pilots arriving in the theater.[54]

The nature of flying over the Hump required, perhaps more than any other skill, strong proficiency in instrument flying, something the AAF was weak in until midway through the war. Instrument training got short shrift when compared with visual "contact" training, as a pilot candidate had to master the latter skill before learning the former. Additionally, the AAF continued to train pilots on only the most rudimentary instruments, those being a rate-of-turn indicator, bank indicator, and airspeed indicator; training did not incorporate the use of a gyroscopic "artificial horizon" until the second half of 1943. Even then, some instructors were suspicious of the reliability of instruments, as recalled by C. V. Glines in one telling anecdote. While he was going through training, he asked one of his instructors about the gyroscopically driven instruments on his flight panel. "'Sir, what are these two instruments that we're supposed to keep caged all the time?'[55] One looked like a compass, and the other had a small airplane on it. 'Don't mess with those things, Glines! Keep those gyros caged. They're for airline pilots.'"[56] With the heavy emphasis on combat aviation skills like aerial gunnery and bombing, the more mundane matters of instrument flying took a back seat. In addition, nearly all training was done in single-engine aircraft due to a lack of twin-engine airplanes in Training Command; in September 1943, 75 percent of all AAF cockpits were in multi-engine airplanes, yet it took time for the training establishment to catch up with this need in delivering a proficient multi-engine pilot-trainee.[57]

Pilot proficiency did not improve overnight and continued to be a problem into the summer of 1944, when one pilot wrote home about how poor his peers were at basic instrument navigation, saying that many flew "lost or 'confused' and since they have had limited training in dead reckoning, appearing not to trust the compass, which results in milling around in search of check points instead of striking out on a course in an effort to work a time-distance problem."[58] A year later, the Hump's commander continued to cite pilot inexperience as first in a list of causal factors contributing to the surfeit of fatalities in the spring of 1945, a problem that he intended to remedy by emphasizing flight safety as being "of paramount importance *even over tonnage to China* [original underlined]," a seemingly innocuous yet important statement.[59] The weight placed on the airlift's success was something that emanated from the highest levels of leadership, even the president's office. FDR's penchant to "keep China in the war" via the Hump airlift translated into the influx of hundreds of poorly prepared pilots being sent to India to operate in airplanes they were ill equipped to fly, through weather they had little practice simulating, and over terrain they were not prepared to navigate. Even skilled pilots who had little practice with instrument flying found the route tough, as in the case of a B-25 squadron that was commissioned to augment the transports in July 1945 and that lost more men and airplanes in one month of Hump duty than in five months of combat duty in the theater.[60] As stated at the outset, this is a generalization, as there were most surely those pilots who learned quicker and were more skilled at their jobs. But in commenting on the Hump fliers as a whole, especially from the middle of 1943 to the middle of 1945, the combination of inadequate training and duty in one of the world's toughest spots was a deadly one indeed. All told, the official number of aircrew fatalities for the Hump's duration stands at 910, with 594 lost aircraft.[61] All things considered, rather than asking why there were so many deaths, perhaps it would be more appropriate to ask why there were so few.

THE PLANES

What were the aircraft like that flew the Hump and what characteristics made one airframe more desirable than another? An exhaustive discussion of the technical specifications of the many aircraft that flew supplies from India to China would take volumes, but four separate types were used with regularity: the Douglas-built C-47 and C-54, the Curtiss C-46, and the Consolidated C-87.[62] Of these four, the C-87 was the only one not originally designed as a transport, being a B-24 Liberator that was converted to the airlift mission to make up for the paucity of sizable transports in the early years of the war. Lauded for its reliability and ease of use—its close-to-the-ground profile made it easy to load and unload—the C-87 was nonetheless a stopgap measure on the Hump and was used there only sparsely into 1944. In focusing on the remaining three, each in turn saw service during the three periods that chronologically divide the airlift: the C-47 during the early "barnstorming" days, the C-46 during the period of most significant growth, and the C-54 during the heyday of "big business."

The C-47 was brought into service in 1940 as a militarized version of the DC-3, perhaps the most ubiquitous transport in the history of aviation; when the war began, it was being used by twenty-one foreign airlines in fifty-seven countries and had logged over 300 million miles in domestic service in the United States.[63] The civilian DC-3 was first conceived as an upgrade to its predecessor, the DC-2, when the company's founder, Donald Wills Douglas, was prodded by American Airlines president C. R. Smith in 1934 to increase the carrying capacity and range of its airliner. Smith wanted Douglas to build an aircraft that could not only fly from New York to Chicago without a refueling stop but also accommodate passenger sleeping berths on either side of a center aisle. In having Douglas make these improvements, Smith hoped to have an airplane that would carry more passengers without an appreciable increase in the cost of operating the airplane, thus maximizing his seat-to-mile profit without much of a boost in his airplane-to-mile expenses.[64] The product a year later was an airplane so successful that Eisenhower would number it alongside the bulldozer, jeep, two-and-a-half-ton truck, and DUKW as one the five most valuable pieces of equipment of the war.[65]

Despite the aircraft's huge success as an airliner before the war and as a transport during the war, the fact that it was nearly discarded by military planners on the eve of war is often overlooked. The DC-3 was judged too old and too ill suited as a cargo transport in 1939, with the AAF requiring Douglas to strengthen the floor of the cargo compartment, widen the cargo door, strengthen the fuselage, and boost the plane's horsepower with better engines before it would commit to order any of the transports, renaming it the C-47. With the adjustments made the following year, the AAF placed large orders for the aircraft in preparation for a possible war; it was viewed as outdated, but its reputation for easy maintainability and its forgiving flight characteristics overshadowed its small size and cumbersome loading qualities.

The C-47 was the first AAF transport to fly the Hump, a job for which it was poorly suited. Its range was sufficient for the comparatively short flight, but it lacked the cargo space to haul sizable payloads in a single hop. Furthermore, the high elevation of the airfield at Kunming could make takeoffs difficult in the summer if the plane was heavily loaded. Under normal conditions the airplane could carry 5,000 pounds of cargo or twenty-eight passengers in addition to its normal crew of three (pilot, copilot, and radio operator), though these limits were routinely stretched. As a testament to the C-47's heartiness, initial structural tests indicated that the airframe tolerated a load well in excess of 10,000 pounds before overstressing occurred. The airplane is also reported to have carried seventy-four passengers (most of them wounded) on an evacuation flight from Myitkyina to India during the fall of Burma in April 1942.[66] Even so, such heavy loads required the engines to operate at high RPMs, which forced frequent mechanical repairs and markedly reduced their usable life. Under ideal conditions with no maintenance problems—a rarity in the CBI—a normal C-47 was able to climb to high-enough altitudes for the Hump; it was capable of attaining a service ceiling of about 23,000 feet with a normal, full load (and well over 28,000 when lightweight), but if it lost one of its two engines, it was not able to maintain an altitude of 15,000 feet, even if it had no cargo on board. This meant that crews had to be prepared to toss their cargo overboard (provided their cargo was not a load of passengers) to remain just clear of mountain peaks if they lost power or lost their second engine altogether, as Fort Hertz (about midway along the route) was the only safe runway for a plane to land between the first and last ridges between India and China.[67] Also noteworthy was the fact that the C-47 did not have a pressurized cabin or a centralized oxygen supply system for its passengers; even if oxygen equipment was available for passengers, oxygen generation facilities were not available in the earliest days of the airlift, so crews would try to fly low enough to keep their passengers from passing out from hypoxia (a lack of oxygen at altitude). It was not until 1944 that passengers would have routine access to oxygen. The pilots would depend on oxygen supplied either by a supplemental bottle or the aircraft's oxygen system (on later models), consisting of a hose held up to the mouth or by a face mask. Though serving an obvious purpose, masks were uncomfortable, and pilots usually disliked wearing them, as they made it difficult to talk over the radio (which usually had a handheld microphone) or got in the way of enjoying a cigarette.[68] Weather might force a crew to fly higher, as in the case of icing at lower altitudes, which meant an entire load of passengers might pass out until the airplane descended to a more "breathable" altitude. *New York Times* correspondent Herbert Matthews reported a flight he took from India to China in December 1942 during which the pilot had to conduct an "altitude test" on the aircraft to see how high it could climb. The flight took off from India and headed north to the Nepalese-Indian border, coming within ten miles of Kanchenjunga, the third-highest mountain in the world, standing at over 28,000 feet. Matthews was able to remain conscious to 20,300 feet, struggling to fight off the "dangerous sleepiness, swallowing hard every few seconds while our lungs gasped for breath and our hearts pounded until they hurt."[69] Passengers could normally endure a loss of consciousness for short periods of time, but if they persisted too long, they ran the risk of dying from anoxia.

As a commercial airline, CNAC used DC-3s and C-47s for the duration of the war, but the AAF quickly realized that the plane's small cargo capacity made it inadequate for the task at hand. Hap Arnold recognized this in the summer of 1940 and let a contract to Curtiss-Wright for the production of a military version of its CW-20, later dubbed the C-46 by the AAF. The CW-20 was first designed by Curtiss as a commercial airliner to compete with the growing popularity of the DC-3 by offering a plane with larger passenger (and cargo) capacity and greater range. In designing the plane Curtiss also took pains to make it more comfortable to fly, adding the latest Sperry autopilot, a pressurized cabin, and hydraulic flight controls (replacing the cable, bell-crank, and pulley system of moving flight control surfaces, still the industry norm in the late 1930s). The AAF took delivery of its first C-46s in September 1941 with most of the original features except for the aircraft pressurization system; its chief advantage was seen in its increased cargo capacity—it could carry twice the cargo of the C-47 at a greater range, but not without a price.[70] The fact that the aircraft was only a few months' old when the United States entered the war meant that the C46's test and evaluation process was accelerated, and it was allowed to enter full operational status while still experiencing many problems. Arnold finalized his decision to send the C-46 to India in March 1943, and the planes began arriving two months later. Within its first five months of service it witnessed a 20 percent loss rate due to a variety of factors (to be covered in later chapters), all of which fell under the rubric of aircraft mechanical failures.[71]

The C-46's problems, identified early in its operational service, had as much to do with design flaws as with improper piloting technique. The hydraulic boost system (similar to power steering in an automobile) that Curtiss designers had hoped would make for an easier-flying airplane actually became a big problem in the field, first with the ATC's Alaskan Wing, then in the CBI. The C-46 was the first large aircraft in the AAF inventory to boast such a system (no bombers in 1943, including the B-17 and B-24, had such a system), and problems arose mainly due to the wide variation of temperatures experienced by the aircraft in flight and on the ground; the fluctuations between extremes of cold and heat caused seals to expand and contract, causing leaks and failures. Curtiss took quick action to repair this problem, adding a second, redundant hydraulic flight control system, but this just compounded the problem, with one report stating that this "in effect doubles the difficulty encountered in a single system," as it just led to twice the number of leaks in the system.[72] The problem got Arnold's attention, and he recommended that Curtiss make a major design modification and fit the airplane with the conventional flight control system that relied on balanced control surfaces, cables, and pulleys. Too far along to make such a major adjustment in the aircraft's design, Curtiss stayed with its original design, making modifications that eventually got rid the problems in this system, though most of these modifications—the AAF recommended sixty-eight such changes in the plane's early career—had to be made after the planes had arrived in India. This put a burden on the theater's already strained aircraft maintenance structure, with shortages of spare parts being a perennial problem.[73]

A May 1943 press release recorded the sentiments of a handful of C-46 radiomen who referred to the airplane as a "flying coffin," and while mechanical troubles undoubtedly led to a number of accidents, pilot error also played a part in a fair share of early problems with the C-46.[74] The plane was more challenging to handle, not being as "forgiving" as the C-47, and the systems were also more complicated than anything many of the new pilots would have flown. Added to this was a lack of procedural standardization to guide those novice flyers; strict "checklist" thinking was not a part of the prewar flying culture, reflected in a September 1943 report on the wave of C-46 problems. The report claimed that accidents were being caused by engines quitting over the Hump due to carburetor icing, which resulted from poor procedural guidance and knowledge on the part of the inexperienced aircrews.[75] Even in 1945, with two years of experience with the C-46 in the CBI, one Curtiss-Wright technical representative in India noted that most of the C-46 engine failures were "due to a lack of printed material or directives" for pilots to refer to in the proper application of carburetor heat, a device that kept ice from choking engines, which resulted in failure.[76] Some of the first C-46s sent to India did not have a proper carburetor heat system installed—something that may have been overlooked or due to India's tropical climate—but in a good number of cases investigators found that ice forming on the carburetor was the likely cause of power loss or engine failure.[77] Even so, a pilot's individual skill had much to do with how well Curtiss's new transport performed: an experienced civilian TWA pilot reported that he was able to take a C-46 to 25,000 feet when an AAF pilot was able to get the very same airplane to only 17,000 feet under the same conditions.[78]

By the end of 1943 most of the design flaws had been worked out of the airplane, such that it became the Hump's main airlifter. It was well suited for the theater, and it could carry a respectable load over the route's relatively short distance at altitudes that remained well clear of the terrain. It was only supplanted in its role as the Hump's mainstay after the summer of 1944, when conditions on the ground allowed a new airplane to see use in the theater.

The C-54, a militarized version of the Douglas DC-4, was a four-engine transport that made possible the Hump's vast tonnages in the operation's final year, thanks to a cargo compartment that approximated the size of a railroad boxcar. In rough terms, it was able to carry 20,000 pounds a distance of 1,500 miles cruising at 200 mph and became the transport of choice for carrying dignitaries on long-distance flights, including taking Churchill to Ottawa, Madame Chiang to the United States, and Roosevelt to the Cairo and Tehran conferences. Despite the C-54's size, speed, and range, its biggest weakness was its limited maximum flyable altitude, meaning it was not able to begin flying from India to China until the Japanese air threat in Burma was curtailed to the point where transports could fly a more southerly, direct route from Calcutta to Kunming over lower terrain. The C-54 was capable of cruising at 20,000 feet on four engines, but its three-engine performance reduced this to 15,000 feet, and crews usually had to plan flights with the possibility of an engine loss in mind.[79] Both C-47 and C-46 crews had to do the same thing in planning on the loss of an engine in flight, but it was easier to manually dump cargo from these smaller transports. This was not the case with the C-54, and three-engine performance had to be respected, making the northerly "high" Hump an impossibility if the larger transports were going to be able to maximize their possible cargo load, a load that usually averaged around seven tons per trip. Just as significant was the fact the plane's engines were susceptible to icing, thus stalling under moderate to severe conditions.[80] In addition, the C-54 was considered a very valuable transport, with every precaution taken to prevent the loss of each one of these aircraft.[81] All told, though, it was the C-54 that ushered in the Hump's so-called "era of big business," with the use of a transport that saw equal service as both a commercial airliner and a military transport.

A point of commonality among these three transports—the C-47, C-46, and C-54—is that none of them was designed primarily as a military airplane, pointing to a peculiar intersection between military air transport and commercial aviation production.[82] Under this arrangement there was an interesting commercial element at play: aircraft companies were usually eager to design and improve military transports because they could be easily converted to a commercial product that helped the companies turn a profit in the commercial sector. The AAF was cognizant of this fact and worked to steer military transport needs in a direction that was commercially attractive for companies like Douglas, Curtiss-Wright, and Boeing. A full year before the end of the war the AAF was already considering the possibility of converting its thousands of B-17 and B-24 bombers to commercial service, but judged them too small in volume to make suitable civilian airliners. Along these lines, C. R. Smith encouraged boosting C-54 production because the War Department could easily sell off extras after the war, given their attractive civilian role.[83] One negative aspect of this relationship came into play when civilian aircraft manufacturers were building airplanes that clearly had no commercial use, with companies finding it easier to work on projects that they knew would turn a postwar profit than those that would not. Gen. O. P. Echols, the head of the AAF's Material Command, after working on an arrangement that would have Lockheed build a transport for Pan Am, candidly remarked, "When you approach a manufacturer to undertake the development of a difficult military type, or when we endeavor to have him accelerate engineering work on military types or improvements thereof, he usually states that he is short of engineering help, but when the proposal for the development and design of a cargo airplane is made they seem to be able to find the necessary engineering assistance."[84] The success of the Hump airlift was a direct result of this curious symbiotic relationship between the troika of the aviation industry, commercial airlines, and military airlift. Such an effort would have not been possible without suitable planes, and such planes would not have been developed without the proper blend of cultural, geographic, and entrepreneurial factors that shaped U.S. commercial aviation.

Over time the Hump airlift would come to be defined by its geographic, physiographic, and meteorological context. The hazards of the route—summed up in jagged mountains and temperamental weather—would set the operation apart from its counterparts, like flights between Dakar and Marrakech, the Azores and St. Mawgan, or Anchorage and Adak. The aircrews that flew the missions started as a curious blend of commercial and military fliers, with the former being supplanted by the latter as the supply provided by the AAF's training establishment finally caught up with the demand created by the number of empty cockpits. Many of these new pilots, though, were thrust into an environment that demanded a high degree of flying skill, something pilots ephemerally refer to as "airmanship." The machines used to fly the Hump were solid, though not without their own problems. The C-47 would eventually prove to be too small to carry the loads dictated by the political dickering between Washington and Chongqing, the C-54 would be too heavy to fly the Hump until the Japanese air threat was pushed out of Burma, and the C-46—the transport with the ideal blend of size and range—would take almost six months of alterations in the field before it would be considered reliable. In the end, though, almost half of all the worldwide tonnage carried by the AAF's Transport Command would be carried over the Hump, an astounding fact considering the physical context.[85] What follows is an unfolding of that achievement.

"BARNSTORMING" OVER THE HUMP

MARCH TO DECEMBER 1942

By the beginning of April 1942 the situation in Asia and the Pacific was dire for the British and Americans. Japan had swallowed up a perimeter extending thousands of miles to both the east and south of the home islands and had begun to consolidate its gains by taking up a defensive posture that would secure territories extending in a wide arc from the western Aleutians, south through the Gilbert and Marshall Islands, west through the Solomons and bisecting New Guinea, encompassing the Dutch East Indies, and stopping in western Burma. Strategically the Allies had committed themselves to a "Europe-first" position as early as the Arcadia Conference, held just weeks after the attack on Pearl Harbor, focusing on challenging Hitler's advances on the Continent before bringing the weight of force against the Japanese. Logistically the Americans fixed overseas expenditures for the war in Europe over the war in Asia at a ratio of twelve to one, meaning operations like "Bolero," the preparatory supply of Great Britain in advance of a cross-channel invasion, was preferred over the competing demand to resupply the Chinese by air across north Burma from India. Making matters worse was the problem of transatlantic shipping due to the impact of an intensified German U-boat campaign that succeeded in sinking U.S. cargo at an annual rate of ten million dead-weight tons during the first ten weeks of 1942; the U.S. Navy was determined to counter this threat by convoying ships, but the short supply of convoy escorts made scheduling problematic.[1] Exacerbating the dilemma in the Eastern Hemisphere was the unhampered movement of the Imperial Japanese Navy astride both sides of India, in both the Bay of Bengal and the Arabian Sea, forcing the Americans to deliver supplies to Karachi in the west and haul them across the width of the subcontinent to Assam Province in the far northeast, a necessity forced by the fact that there was no Allied naval sea power present to protect the Port of Calcutta. It was under these conditions that the Army Air Forces would attempt to make good on Roosevelt's promise of February 9 to give the generalissimo "definite assurances that even though there should be a further setback [with the fall of Burma] . . . the supply route to China via India can be maintained by air."[2]

If movement abroad by sea was complicated by the threat of German submarines and Japanese surface ships, movement abroad by air in the spring of 1942 was relegated to a trickle, as the AAF did not take receipt of its first four-engine C-54 until that March and was forced to rely on the much smaller and shorter-range C-47 to do most of the work for the rest of 1942. The "Europe-first" priority was felt here as well with 43 percent of all transports sent to Europe; MacArthur's Far East Air Force theater was the second priority of transports, receiving 18 percent, and the CBI ranked third, garnering only 15 percent of the AAF's transport deployments for the year.[3] Transports allocated for Lend-Lease aid also went first to the European Theater, with Great Britain receiving 128 for the year versus the paltry 10 given to the Chinese.[4] Competing priorities were very much a reality of the war's first year in all theaters, but they took on a different face as far as China was concerned in 1942. While most Allied military efforts were geared toward operations like the possible invasion of western Europe in 1943, the looming Allied invasion of North Africa, or the "Cartwheel" operations in the southwest Pacific, the Japanese presence in China was viewed largely as an inert occupying force posing little threat to the Americans and British. In fact, the only "threat" stemming from China was the one posed by the generalissimo, with Chiang never missing an opportunity remind the Allies of how long he had been fighting the Japanese and how close he was to being forced to surrender if the requisite aid did not arrive. The Chinese would sustain only one major offensive during 1942, but the generalissimo never relented in the pressure he leveled against the Roosevelt administration, such that by the end of that year

the United States had committed the bulk of its newly formed air transport service—the AAF's Air Transport Command—to conduct its most robust effort of the
war to the resupply of China (see figure 6).

THE HUMP UNDER THE TENTH AIR FORCE

When Lewis Brereton's Tenth Air Force first arrived in India in March 1942, it
was charged with both flying and protecting the Hump airlift but had neither
the planes nor the personnel to do so. On March 29 the IJN attacked British
naval bases at Colombo and Trincomalee, sinking six vessels, including a cruiser,
an aircraft carrier, and thirteen merchant ships. This forced a diversion of the
Tenth's bomber force from planned operations against enemy positions in Burma
to counter this new Japanese threat off the coast of Ceylon, a naval threat that
did not disappear until the Japanese evacuated the Indian Ocean at the end of
April (they had been at sea since the previous November and needed rest and
refitting).[5] Col. Earl Naiden, Brereton's executive officer, was charged with directing the airlift that began the first week of April with a handful of airplanes and
aircrews based out of the RAF airfield at Dinjan (a British base in Assam with a
squadron of transports and Mohawk fighters); these crews were composed largely
of Pan Am pilots and copilots who were pulled from routes in Africa to augment
the remaining contingent of military, reserve, and civilian fliers who had left Morrison Field in West Palm Beach in mid-April. Ten of the Pan Am crews then inaugurated the command's first airlift, hauling 30,000 gallons of fuel and 300 gallons
of lubricants from Calcutta to the airstrip near Asansol (near Dinjan); from here
the cargo was carried to China two days later to be used to refuel Lt. Col. James
Doolittle's B-25s following their planned attack on Japan the next week.

This first airlift operation over the Hump was a point of friction for the
Americans and Chinese. Before Stilwell left the United States, Marshall briefed
him on Doolittle's attack—an unconventional air raid on the Japanese home
islands by carrier-based B-25 medium bombers that would recover to eastern
China. Stilwell informed Chiang of the details of the mission a month later, but
the generalissimo balked at the idea, fearing a Japanese reprisal on the provinces
where the bombers would be landing after the incident. A flurry of messages went
back and forth between Chongqing and Washington, with Marshall finally advis-
ing Chiang two days before the raid that it was impossible to recall the attack,

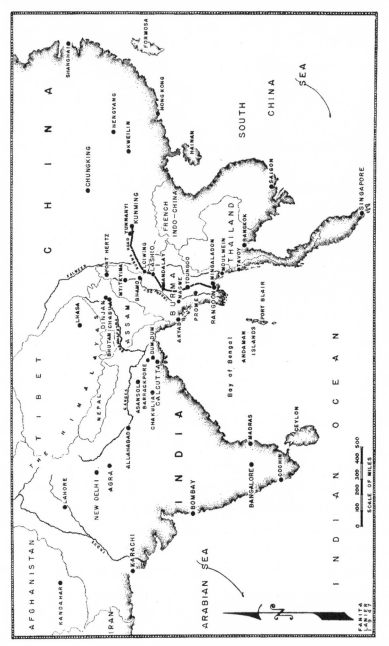

FIGURE 6. China-Burma-India Theater.

FIGURE 7. Hump Pilots in the "Barnstorming" Days. *Courtesy AFHRA.*

apologizing for the "misunderstanding," but adding that the Chinese could have the sixteen B-25s once they landed.[6] The Doolittle raid did succeed in striking Japan, but it also provoked–as Chiang had predicted–an eleven-week Japanese ground offensive in China's eastern Zhejiang Province beginning on May 11; the offensive was designed to destroy any airfields that the Americans might use in the future, while also punishing the local population for their work in helping rescue the U.S. airmen who flew in the raid.

German advances in Russia and the Middle East in April also tied in with the United States' airpower commitment to the Chinese, threatening to siphon off the understrength Tenth Air Force. On April 14 Eisenhower, acting as the army's assistant chief of staff, sent a message to London emphasizing the importance of holding the Middle East, fearing what the Soviet reaction might be if the British were pushed out of Egypt. To deal with this possibility, Marshall directed Hap Arnold to get the Tenth Air Force to full strength and then move it from

India to the Middle East, recognizing that "this diversion of the Tenth Air Force to another mission will adversely affect the Chinese situation" and that keeping Chennault's AVG force at full strength would serve as "assurances" to the generalissimo.[7] Altogether, the strategic situation did not bode well toward the end of April for the prospects of using airplanes to replace trucks over an "aerial Burma Road": the IJA would soon capture Lashio, the western terminus of the road; the IJN was threatening Allied shipping in the Arabian Sea; the German U-boat campaign was registering early victories in the Battle of the Atlantic; Rommel's desert campaign was gaining momentum in threatening a capture of the Suez Canal; the Soviets were still on their heels from German advances in the Caucuses; and U.S. air transport production was but a fraction of what it would be by the war's end.[8]

Upon arrival in India, Brereton established his headquarters in a posh hotel in New Delhi, with Col. Earl Naiden, his executive officer and airlift commander, running the airlift out of Dinjan over a thousand miles to the east. The forty-eight-year-old Naiden, an Iowan and West Point graduate, was no novice airman. Originally commissioned as a cavalry officer in 1915, he quickly transitioned to the aviation section of the Air Service two years later, earning his qualification as a junior military aviator in April 1917. By the end of that year he was the head of the American Aviation Mission to Italy and later participated in both the St. Mihiel and Meuse-Argonne offensives. Following the war he served as in instructor at the Air Service's tactical school (the forerunner to the Air Corps Tactical School) and was an exchange officer to the École Supérieure de Guerre in Paris. Known for his skill as a golfer—he was the Army Open champion in 1927—he was also among a cadre of notable military officers serving as one of the honorary pallbearers at former Air Service Chief Mason Patrick's funeral in 1942, along with other notables like John J. Pershing, George Marshall, Hap Arnold, Eddie Rickenbacker, and Carl Spaatz.[9] Naiden was a seasoned flyer with over 2,700 hours of flight time in pursuit, bomber, and transport aircraft, well qualified for the task of establishing the ferry line to China, which was still rife with obstacles.[10]

Arnold notified Naiden that seventy-five Douglas transports would begin leaving for India starting in mid-March, a contingent deemed sufficient to carry 7,500 tons per month.[11] Naiden then made a careful survey of the situation, planning to use the planes alongside CNAC transports, because Arnold had directed that CNAC be "used in an advisory capacity to the maximum extent," as they were the regional air transport experts. Naiden completed his survey two weeks later in the hope that the air route could go from Dinjan to Myitkyina—something made impossible by the Japanese Army in early May—though he stated that flights could bypass Burma and land in China, at Yunnanyi, once the monsoon was over in mid-October. The mission would be difficult at best: three airfields were needed for the seventy-five planes, yet only Dinjan was currently available. Two more fields could be enlarged to handle the transports, but no serious construction was possible during monsoonal rains, which were forecast to begin in mid-May, pushing the completion time back to November 1.[12] Because Dinjan was the only usable field until then, Naiden advised Arnold to limit the number of transports sent to India to only twenty-five, claiming that CNAC pilots informed him that regularly scheduled flights over the 10,000-foot ridges into Myitkyina were impossible due to the monsoon. In addition to the climatic threat were the Japanese, who had air assets within range of Upper Assam, prompting a request for a pursuit group to defend the transport bases. More significantly was Naiden and Brereton's fear that the Japanese would launch a ground offensive up the Ganges Valley, overrunning the airfields, although this was a move the enemy would not be able to sustain until 1944 due to the Japanese Army's commitment to keep forces in China and Manchuria in the event of a collapse of the Soviet Union.[13] And lastly, as if the weather and Japanese did not pose big enough problems, there was the matter of malaria, a disease that spiked during the wet monsoon that required a boost in medical personnel to handle the problem because the British in India where short of physicians.[14]

Forced to fly supplies across India from Karachi due to the Japanese naval threat near Ceylon, Naiden divided his command into two units, the Trans-India Ferry Command and the Assam-Burma Ferry Command. The division was a concession to the fact that supplies could be flown from Karachi to Dinjan easier than from Dinjan to Myitkyina, Yunnanyi, or Kunming. One negative byproduct of the division was the fact that sometimes Trans-India airplanes had to be offloaded at Dinjan, then reloaded onto an Assam-Burma transport parked next to it on the ramp, an unnecessary step that exacerbated manpower problems. Col. Caleb V. Haynes, originally sent to China to command a B-17 unit with plans to bomb Japan from eastern China, was charged with running the Assam-Burma-China portion of the route, relying on Pan Am commercial planes, pilots, and his own bomber crews to fly these early Hump missions.[15] Known as "Old Grizzly" by his men, Haynes was an accomplished pilot who won the 1939 Mackey Trophy for flying an XB-15 (a prototype of the B-17) to Santiago, Chile, to deliver earthquake relief; he was also one of the grandchildren of Chang and Eng Bunker, the original "Siamese twins" brought to the United States by P. T. Barnum in 1830.[16] Haynes's bomber crews added a needed boost to the airlift—some of the Pan Am crews sent by the company from Africa to India were refusing to fly the route in the face of the Japanese ground advance because, as civilians, they had no belligerent rights if they were shot down and captured by the Japanese.[17] When the Pan Am fliers left for the United States at the end of April, there were only five AAF transports in India, with twenty-eight set to arrive over the next few weeks. Myitkyina was bombed by the Japanese on April 28, further crimping the resupply route and forcing flights to now fly in a northerly arc from India to Kunming to avoid the advancing Japanese, who at the same time were overrunning Lashio, the western terminus of the Burma Road.[18] This prompted Roosevelt to issue another of his assurances to the Chinese, declaring, "The Japanese may cut the Burma Road; but I want to say to the gallant people of China that no matter what advances the Japanese make, ways will be found to deliver airplanes and munitions of war to the armies of Generalissimo Chiang Kai-shek. We remember that the Chinese people were the first to stand up and fight against the aggressors in this war; and in the future an unconquerable China will play its proper role in maintaining peace and prosperity not only in Eastern Asia but in the whole world."[19] At the end of April Naiden's meager force had delivered only a scant amount of supplies and would fare little better in May, delivering only 196 tons for both months combined.[20]

The early airlift was a haphazard operation at best. Haynes's Assam-Burma portion of the lift saw his crews frequently take off from Dinjan, with no weather reports or radio navigation help, into a solid wall of clouds that resulted from the Chota monsoon. The often-overloaded planes groaned to reach 10,000 feet, the pilots using only a compass and clock to determine their position, sometimes descending through a solid deck of clouds hoping that their navigation solutions were accurate. Haynes's executive officer was Col. Donald Old, a seasoned bomber pilot who came to the ferry group after serving as part of the U.S. mission to India. Old had a reputation among his crews as daily being "the first to take off and the last to land," and he became something of a legend when he supposedly warded off a Japanese fighter with a .45-caliber Thompson machine gun fired out of the back of his airborne transport.[21] Aircraft maintenance was handled by a small group of U.S. mechanics who arrived in India in February after a long voyage across the Pacific. The entire group was housed over ten miles from the airfield at one of Assam's many tea plantations, and ground transportation to and from the airdrome was scarce. Topping it all off was the daily fare at the mess hall, operated by Indians under British management, leading one contemporary to record acerbically, "The food was very different from American standards."[22] In the absence of an enemy warning system the crews launched in the darkness of the early morning to avoid enemy fighters, hoping to cram as many flights into a day as possible.

THE ALLIED RETREAT OUT OF BURMA

The Japanese push into northern Burma had achieved its intended purpose in closing the last of the four land routes into China, but overstretched supply lines forced the IJA to halt at the end of April. Struggling against poorly led and undersupplied British and Chinese forces, the ensuing Allied retreat meant that Naiden's transports were diverted from their Hump mission to delivering supplies to retreating Allied columns, dropping nearly four tons of rice to the Chinese Fifth Army in May and another eighty tons of supplies in June. One such regular recipient of airdropped supplies was General Stilwell during his storied two-week trek out of Burma on foot, refusing to fly out when Haynes landed to personally evacuate the CBI commander. The wounded from Toungoo and Mandalay were evacuated north to Myitkyina in the hopes of catching a flight back to India; one ferry pilot recalls the northern Burmese city as being "the Dunkirk of Burma" and remembers loading planeloads of wounded in the 120-degree heat with the "stench of gangrene everywhere."[23] The arrival of more airplanes—the transport complement was up to nineteen by May 24—allowed Naiden's ferry force to fly more missions, but his preoccupation with keeping the retreating troops supplied meant his command delivered only a meager twenty-five tons—less than seven full planeloads—to China during the month of June.

The Japanese Army's momentum into Burma provoked fears of a sweep into China. Myitkyina fell on May 8, and eastern columns of the IJA's Fifteenth

Army crossed the Salween River headed toward Kengtung, a city near Burma's border with China. Making matters worse was the fact that Stilwell was incommunicado, determined to make a statement of will and determination—something he claimed was absent in Chinese leadership. This prompted Magruder, the AMMISCA commander, to confer with the U.S. ambassador to China, Clarence Gauss, about the possibility of having the American Mission evacuate (in the worse case) into the Soviet Union, while recognizing "that nothing should be done which might in any manner arouse on the part of the Chinese the slightest suspicion that there is in American or other foreign circles any lack of confidence in the Chinese." Gauss went on to say that for himself, he was willing to risk being captured by the Japanese rather than giving the Chinese any impression that a U.S. retreat from Chongqing was imminent; he also suggested to Magruder that perhaps the mission "could decrease its numbers gradually" by incrementally having its members leave on outbound flights back to India. Gauss notified Secretary of State Cordell Hull of Magruder's concerns, who in turn asked Marshall to see that Magruder halted any intimations that his mission might be withdrawing from China, as such a move would be "highly prejudicial to the interests of this country in the Far East and the part which it has been and is hoped that China will play in the United Nations' effort."[24]

The need for air transports was becoming more pronounced with the enemy's success against Allied sea lanes, such that Roosevelt was forced to press portions of the commercial air fleet into military service. On May 6 he asked the airlines to abandon all nonessential domestic routes and directed Secretary of War Henry Stimson to commandeer and fit for military service those aircraft made available by this move.[25] Arnold also proposed to the president a week later that fifty B-24s could be diverted from prospective missions against Germany and refitted as C-87 cargo planes in the interest of bolstering the ferry route to China. The larger planes would have the range to fly to Kunming direct from Allahabad, India, over eight hundred miles west of Dinjan and well clear of the Japanese air threat in northern Burma. Arnold estimated that the fifty planes—half taken from British allocations and half from U.S. allocations—could deliver 1,200 tons per month to China, but that these converted bombers also represented over 400 tons of bombs per month dropped on Germany if sacrificed for the resupply of China. Eisenhower concurred with the air chief's suggestion, but on May 17 Roosevelt said that no action would be taken to divert the heavy bombers to the Hump, stating that mission would be carried out only by available DC-3 aircraft.[26] This provoked the generalissimo's ire, as he had somehow found out about the specifics of the bomber-conversion proposal.[27] Nevertheless, the decision meant the smaller transports would remain in range of Burma-based Japanese fighters, a threat that—unbeknownst to the Americans—was dwindling with the coming monsoonal rains.

At the end of March the Japanese Army's combat air contingent in Burma constituted five fighter *sentai* (a *sentai* was the equivalent of a U.S. squadron or German *Gruppe,* consisting of roughly twenty-five planes) and four medium bomber *sentai*. The fighter units were mostly equipped with the outdated Nakajima Ki 27 "Nate" aircraft and were so badly in need of being replaced with newer models that they all were pulled back to either the home islands, Formosa, or Manchuria by July, leaving only the 64th Sentai, a unit equipped with the newer Nakajima Ki 43 "Oscar" fighters in place for the remainder of the wet monsoon.[28] The four bomber *sentai* remained in Burma for the monsoon but did not begin attacking the Assam airfields until that October; the rainy season was devoted to the business of recovering from the drive through Southeast Asia and into Burma. The Americans took no chances with the possible air threat, though, launching their first B-17 attack from Dum Dum, India, against Myitkyina on May 12 and again on the 14th, 29th, and 30th; the last attack found no Japanese activity as the field had been rendered unusable by the raids.[29]

Japanese attacks did come, though not against India but rather against China's eastern Zhejiang Province on May 11. It was there that the IJA launched a reprisal offensive for the Doolittle raid, intended to destroy any airfields the United States might try to use in future missions against Japan while also punishing a huge swath of the province's population for its supposed collaboration with the attackers. Precise figures do not exist as to the damage wrought during the one-hundred-day campaign, but it is clear that at least twenty-eight principal cities were ravaged; in one of those cities, Zhuhsien, over 10,000 people were killed, 17,000 left destitute, 62,000 homes destroyed, 7,000 cattle stolen, and 70 percent of the local crops damaged. Looting was rampant and the destruction was gratuitous, with a dedicated incendiary brigade charged with the task of burning down those buildings left standing in areas marked for razing.[30] Following the attack the China Expeditionary Army withdrew to positions approximating preoffensive lines in order to conserve manpower, holding only the new areas that yielded deposits of strategic ores like tin, copper, and fluorite.[31] Despite the destruction—predicted by Chiang in his hesitancy in consenting to the Doolittle raid—the Americans benefited tremendously from the attack, able to sharpen their cryptographic skills against the flurry of Japanese messages that followed the raid, which translated into an intelligence advantage at the battles of the Coral Sea at the beginning of May and of Midway a month later. Ironically, it was this second battle—the most decisive naval victory of the war—that cemented the United States' Europe-first policy, solidifying Germany's position as the Allies' chief opponent, much to the chagrin of Chiang and the Chinese.[32]

A week after the Japanese launched their offensive against Zhejiang, Brig. Gen. Clayton Bissell, Stilwell's AAF liaison in Chongqing, recommended that the United States pressure the generalissimo into using ten of his eastern armies to defend the province's cities and airbases, employing U.S. aid as a reward for such a move and establishing the precedent that Lend-Lease aid would be tied to Chinese military performance. Marshall, specifically, and the War Department, generally, opposed Bissell's idea on the grounds that the United States had little leverage to apply to the Chinese when the airlift of promised supplies was going so poorly. Over 750 tons of aid was backed up in India awaiting transport over the Hump while Naiden's airlifters were preoccupied with dropping provisions to retreating Allied soldiers. The Japanese attack had all the marks of an all-out offensive, the likes of which had not been seen on the mainland since the Second Battle of Changsha in September and October of the previous year. The situation prompted Chiang to pass two messages to Marshall through Gen. Hsiung Shih-fei, the head of the Chinese Military Mission in Washington, stating, "China finds herself today in a more disadvantageous position than at any other time in this war, physically and psychologically. Physically because she is exhausted. Psychologically because she suffers from a certain amount of disillusionment due to the absence of expected Allied help." The message went on to recommend a U.S. ground offensive, the strengthening of the Chinese Air Force to 520 planes, and the monthly delivery of 5,000 tons over the Hump.[33]

AIRPOWER AND CHINESE MORALE

Arnold and the War Department continued to feel the pressure of making the Himalayan airlift a success, not only from the Chinese but also from the State Department and the White House. Stanley K. Hornbeck, a former Rhodes Scholar and the head of the State Department's Far Eastern division before the war, continually advocated U.S. support for the Chinese while serving as Cordell Hull's special assistant on Asian affairs during the war. In a memo penned concurrent with Marshall's response to Chiang's latest plea, Hornbeck wrote:

> *The number of planes needed for doing this job is ridiculously small in comparison with the relatively huge numbers we are sending to other fronts. Chinese morale has been preserved for many months past by the expectation of aid from the United States and Great Britain and assurances that she shall have aid by the United States. So long as the Chinese remain confident that such aid is going to reach them, there is fair chance of their morale holding up and resistance continuing. From now on there is only one way by which we can make sure of maintaining China's confidence: we must deliver goods. Deliveries can be made and an artery of communication between China and us can be maintained if we will but put into the job of creating and maintaining an air transport service such courage, such ingenuity and such effort as we have been and are putting into a variety of operations in other places and other contexts."*

He closed by stating, "What we most need to do at this moment is to get an air transport service into operation on a fair scale—and to do it now," something easier said than done.[34]

Hornbeck claimed that the number of planes needed to keep China supplied was "ridiculously small," and at the end of May that was a close approximation of the size of Naiden's 1st Ferry Group, which had received thirty C-47s by the end of the month but was suffering from a chronic shortage of spare parts and replacement engines. Arnold and the War Department were well aware of the problem but could do little to prevent it, and the situation would get worse before it got better. For example, in July twelve of thirty-two available aircraft were grounded for lack of parts, and again in September nineteen of fifty-four were grounded. Spare parts in general were in short supply, a perennial problem that persisted not just in India but throughout the entire AAF for much of 1943, the result of a procurement decision made by Arnold back in 1939. Normally in the 1930s when aircraft were purchased, a quarter of the purchase cost was devoted exclusively to spare parts for the order. Under pressure from the White House in 1939 to show strong numbers of whole aircraft produced, Arnold gambled and allocated his entire procurement budget to airplanes without the accompanying order of spare parts, planning on that money being available the next year to make up for this shortfall.[35] With the budget constraints just as tight in 1940, Arnold was forced to try to play catch-up by ordering spares for both that and the previous year's purchases, resulting in an overall shortfall of extra parts–20 percent of all new aircraft had been cannibalized for parts by the summer of 1941.[36] This caused a ripple effect of aircraft maintenance problems once the war began, and it persisted, most acutely in faraway theaters like the CBI, for the next two years. The problem forced innovative solutions like mixing and matching parts from different airplanes, seen in the creative example of using P-66 fighter engines to replace many of the flagging C-47 engines in Naiden's fleet. Vultee P-66 fighters were being diverted to China in the summer of 1942, and because they had the same engine as the C-47 (the Pratt & Whitney R-1830), Naiden wanted to see if the fighter's engines could serve as replacements for the transports.[37] The modification worked, and fourteen grounded transports were repaired for service in June.[38]

Indirectly, German air power and air transport also played a decisive role in impinging the Hump when it allowed Rommel's Afrika Korps to get under way after being pushed back to its April 1941 starting point at El Agheila in northern Libya. Hitler ordered Field Marshal Albert Kesselring's Luftflotte 2 (Second Air Force) from the Ukraine to the Mediterranean, a move that opened a flow of supplies and allowed Rommel to launch a fresh offensive on the night of May 26–27. Pushing east, the Afrika Korps marked its biggest success of the year in capturing the British stronghold at Tobruk, a victory that sent shockwaves throughout the Allied command structure. The garrison at Tobruk numbered 28,000 men, and the stores captured by the Germans were enough to sustain them in a drive designed to push the British out of Egypt. Hitler set aside plans to capture Malta– a move that would later come back to haunt him–and gave Rommel permission to continue on to the Suez Canal. Churchill, who was in Washington when the news of Tobruk's fall came, made immediate appeals for help from the Americans, help they gave with newly produced Sherman tanks as well as the repositioning of most of Brereton's India-based Tenth Air Force to Egypt, redesignating it the Ninth Air Force. The move brought needed relief to the Allied defensive in the Middle East, but in doing so it strained the limits of the Sino-U.S. military relationship.[39]

On June 23 the War Department ordered Brereton to stand up the Ninth Air Force in Cairo, prompting him to leave New Delhi two days later. He took with him his only heavy bomber unit, the 9th Bomb Squadron, the B-17 unit that Haynes had brought to India. He also took twelve C-47 transports, promising to return them once the emergency in North Africa was over (only eight were returned six weeks later; the rest were never returned).[40] Earl Naiden was left in charge of a skeletal Tenth Air Force and the ferry operation that now had fewer than thirty planes, over a third of them out of commission for maintenance reasons. This, along with a run of bad weather in June, led to the poorest month of tonnage delivered to China for the entire war, something that immediately became a weighty political issue in both Chongqing and Washington.[41]

On June 26 Stilwell had the unenviable job of notifying the generalissimo of the decision to send most of Brereton's air force to Egypt, provoking a thorny conversation with the Chiangs, who skillfully used the fact that the United States was reneging on promised aid to now press the Americans for more airplanes and tonnage. Stilwell began by saying he "deeply regretted" the loss, acknowledging that it would "reduce the tonnage of material sent from India." Chiang queried him on a number of details, many of which Stilwell did not know, but then began to press the U.S. commander, stating, "Since you are my chief of staff, my approval should be secured of the disposition of the Tenth U.S. Air Force"; he continued, "President Roosevelt in his telegram to me stated that he had ordered the transfer of the Tenth U.S. Air Force from India to China for use. His order cannot be lightly changed. If it were contended that the situation in Egypt is grave, I must point out that the Chinese situation in Chekiang and Kiangsi is no less critical." Madame Chiang Kaishek chimed in: "Every time when the British suffered a defeat, they took away our war equipment or that which had been promised to us. Such being the case there is no need for China to continue the

FIGURE 8. Chiang Kaishek, Madame Chiang, and General Stilwell, ca. 1943. *Courtesy U.S. Army Center of Military History.*

war"; she followed up with "What are we going to do about this? Can we stop the movement of heavy bombers to Egypt?" Stilwell replied that nothing could be done to stop the bombers, as Chiang and his wife most certainly knew; yet they continued to engage the situation from a position of regal naiveté in an effort to play out this elaborate bit of diplomatic theater. Chiang continued to express his displeasure, stating, "I am unhappy about this development. The China Theater of War is lightly regarded. Naturally I wish to know whether America and Britain consider it as one of the Allied Theaters." Madame then "helpfully" suggested to Stilwell, "You send some important member of your mission to Washington and place the matter before the high authorities there," with Chiang tossing the heaviest rhetorical salvo in applying simplified logic: "Since President Roosevelt in his telegram promised to supply China with planes and war materials she needs, what is being done amounts to disobedience of his orders. I do not suppose that [*sic*] President would approve of all this change. Less than ten per cent of what he had agreed to give to China has been supplied. I do not entertain any doubt that the President is sincere. What has been done is perhaps without his consent or knowledge. As chief of staff to me, you are responsible for seeing to it that the promised material is forthcoming."[42]

If he was anything, Chiang was a shrewd statesman who was operating in the best tradition of *yiwu*, working to squeeze from the United States whatever aid he could in an effort to solidify his own power base while also securing the Nationalist position against the Japanese and the Communists. And to remind Stilwell and the Americans what was supposedly at stake, Madame ended the conversation with this stinging rejoinder, "The Generalissimo must make a speech at the end of the fifth year [of the Chinese war] on 7 July. He must tell the Chinese people the truth at that time. The pro-Japanese element is very active. The Generalissimo wants a yes or no answer to whether the Allies consider this theater necessary and will support it."[43]

Roosevelt moved quickly to quell the furor, sending Chiang a telegram the next day that attempted to school the generalissimo on the global nature of the war, stating that if the Axis advance in the Middle East was not stopped, it "will result in the severance of the Air Routes to India and China, and seriously interfere with, if not interrupt, our sea lanes to India. It is imperative that the Middle East be held." Roosevelt followed up a week later in a message commemorating the fifth anniversary of the start of China's war with Japan—almost a verbatim response to Madame's challenge of a week and a half earlier. He stated, "You, the people of China, and we, the people of the United States and the United Nations, will fight on together to victory, to the establishment of peace and justice and freedom throughout the world."[44] The final result of the fiasco surrounding Brereton's departure to Egypt was a set of three demands by Chiang that continued to surface for the next year, though varying with respect to quantities. He wanted three U.S. Army divisions sent to China; he wanted five hundred combat airplanes "to be maintained continuously at the front"; and he wanted 5,000 tons of supplies a month delivered over the Hump, beginning that July.[45] These were all a reiteration of requests made through Hsian Shihfei the previous month and were levied with the unspoken threat of Nationalist capitulation to the Japanese.[46]

JAMES MCHUGH AND "IMPRESSION MANAGEMENT"

If the White House was tempted to buckle under Chiang's threats, a report sent by James McHugh, the U.S. naval attaché in Chongqing, surely served to quelled those fears by providing insight to the inner workings of Chinese politics as well as an assessment of China's danger vis-à-vis its war with Japan. In his October 5 report—one that captured Roosevelt's attention—McHugh dealt with such matters as Japan's military posture in China, the generalissimo's domestic power base, and Chinese morale with respect to the war. Regarding the Japanese military presence in China, McHugh wrote, "It has been self-evident since 1937 that the Japanese can go anywhere they want to go in China if they choose" and that "Chinese military leaders have been largely content to let them do so, adopting a strategy of 'magnetic resistance,'" one that will "give way under pressure and then flow back into the vacuum created by Japanese withdrawal." McHugh said that the Chinese leaders he dealt with, "speaking off the record," never professed to having ever driven out the Japanese in well-crafted counteroffensives, as the foreign press was wont to report, but were instead satisfied to engage the Japanese from a "defensive psychology." He stated the Chinese could continue to do this so long as the Japanese did not launch a "real invasion" of Yunnan or Chongqing. Based upon Japan's commitments elsewhere, McHugh concluded that the prospect of such an attack was unlikely.[47]

With respect to the generalissimo's authority in China, McHugh stated that Chiang was the supreme power in government—so much so that "no one even thinks of making a move without his prior approval" and "when he is absent the wheels of government practically stop." Out in the provinces he was an "idol—the personification of the glory of China and of resistance to the Japanese"; McHugh also stated, "Individuals may curse the Kuomintang and the Government (and they are practically synonymous), but they revere the Generalissimo."[48] McHugh's assessment was only barely inflated but not by much, considering Chiang's self-perception of being the embodiment of the Chinese state.[49] McHugh continued by stating that Chiang had "long since acquired the mental attitude toward foreign relations similar to that held in former days by the Emperor—namely that he is superior to ordinary processes and procedure and that his wishes must be met." McHugh observed that U.S. dealings with Chiang had largely fit into this paradigm, as the generalissimo had usually "named his own terms and got them"; when the Tenth Air Force was called to Egypt, Chiang called for Harry Hopkins, FDR's special assistant, and got "the next thing to his demand—a visit from Lauchlin Currie." A planned visit by Vice President Wendell Willkie the next spring was yet another instance of the United States' satiation of Chiang's imperial persona. McHugh finishes this point by stating, *"The important thing is that the Chinese people know this and credit the Generalissimo with much the same prestige over the foreigner as they formerly ascribed to the Emperor"* [underlined in original]."[50]

On the question of Chinese morale, McHugh recorded that, to his knowledge, Chiang had never "entertained the thought of any kind of compromise with the Japanese" and that even though the generalissimo had lost confidence in U.S. aid, "he would still remain anti-Japanese." McHugh wrote that many of the young officers in the Chinese army were staunchly anti-Japanese and would not follow Chiang if he did in fact agree to terms, and that many of the generalissimo's liberal opponents would use such an occasion to politically topple Chiang should he cave to Tokyo's demands.[51] McHugh also addressed the supposed "peace party" that held influence in China, one that was thought to include General He Yingqin and Kong Xiangxi (H. H. Kung), stating that they were actually loyal to Chiang but wary of taking a tough line in the war because of their respect for Japanese military strength (something the United States "lacked," according to McHugh) as well as their distrust of the United States' "good faith" toward its continual promises of military aid. McHugh closes this point by stating that he "had never been able to get any Chinese to discuss, even hypothetically, coming to terms with Japan" and that if any of them "think such thoughts they are apparently afraid to do so."

McHugh never thought that the Chinese would capitulate to the Japanese, but his larger fear was that the administration would botch the prospects of a solid postwar relationship with Chiang by failing to make good on wartime commitments, stating, *"The worst thing that could happen would be for us to decide that the Chinese can carry on for another year without any help and for this idea to penetrate the minds of the Chinese. If the Chinese ever get the idea that we have deserted them it will be an irretrievable catastrophe for our future relations with them* [underlined in original]." To sustain this appearance of U.S. support he went on to advocate Claire Chennault's plan to launch a China-based air offensive against Japan. In addition, McHugh acknowledged the important part the recapture of Burma would play, but "it is not absolutely essential to the support of a limited but very penitential air effort in China against the Japanese, provided the air transport service with India is expanded *and maintained.*" In McHugh's assessment, large quantities of supplies were not necessary to sustain Chinese morale—the important thing was the *appearance* of U.S. support. He went further, taking an indirect jab at Stilwell, who was a strong supporter of recapturing Burma as a means of reopening the Burma Road, and claimed that such a vision was misguided and that "an appreciable increase in the importation of war material into China would not produce a proportionate increase in Chinese military activity." Though the idea of using U.S. aid as an incentive for Chinese action was gaining traction in CBI headquarters, McHugh believed that such thinking revealed a "fundamental fallacy all too widely held and shared even by some foreign [i.e., U.S.] military officials in China." In McHugh's opinion, "The chief reason that Chinese military leaders desire Lend-Lease material is for the purpose of strengthening their own positions particularly for *post*-war purposes, not to extend a counter-attack against the Japs." He summarized Chiang's intentions: "China wants to go to the Peace table as strong as possible" and to "retain the physical means of maintaining themselves."[52]

McHugh's lengthy report was not confined to military matters; it also included his detailed observations about the Chinese economy, one that he believed to be decidedly agrarian, with rice being the most significant commodity. This macroeconomic characteristic meant that McHugh thought the Chinese could "carry on indefinitely" in the war because "she lives off her own fat," meaning that seasonal rainfalls for the planting and growing seasons were far more significant that foreign loans. McHugh insightfully carried this line of thinking a step farther, claiming that if there was a famine in Sichuan Province—the major food producer for Nationalist China—the impact would be catastrophic in amplifying any perception that the United States was ignoring the Chinese plight or abandoning them as allies, "for any deterioration in their economic situation from natural causes would be aggravated a hundred-fold by popular resentment against us for abandoning them." He sums up this point by stating, "The curious feature of such a situation would be, I believe, that the man in the street would blame us far more than he would the Japanese for his misfortunes."[53]

The impact of McHugh's report was both wide and deep. It was written confidentially and intended only for the Office of Naval Intelligence and Secretary of the Navy Frank Knox, but Knox shared it with Adm. Ernest King and Secretary of War Stimson, who shared it with both the president and General Marshall. It also made its way to the British chief of staff, Sir John Dill, who took efforts to discuss its contents with his U.S. counterpart. Roosevelt found the report interesting, as it undoubtedly resonated with his desire to tangibly display U.S. allegiance to China, but to do so without having such a display detract from the stated war priorities of the United States. Without knowing explicitly how McHugh's report shaped the president's thinking toward the Chinese, it is curious to note that U.S. military posture for the remainder of the war would largely fall in line with the analysis of this mid-grade naval officer who had felt he had to "shoot the works" because the "truth ought to be known in Washington."[54] In just seven months after McHugh's report reached Washington, Roosevelt would come to settle on an air strategy for the China Theater, one that depended on airpower for both air attack and air supply and one that also was more concerned with providing a visible show of U.S. loyalty toward China than with the actual military advantage gained by that support.

POOR TONNAGE FIGURES AND COMPETING PRIORITIES

Brereton's departure for Egypt at the end of June left very little U.S. airpower east of the Ganges, but Stilwell was glad to see him go, refusing to have him back once Montgomery's push toward Tunisia got underway. During his four months in India that spring, Brereton and his staff had garnered the reputation of being more concerned with enjoying the environs of air-conditioned New Delhi hotels and a "bevy of female stenographers" than in actually getting down to the business of organizing the airlift or providing Stilwell with air support or reconnaissance during the drubbing he took at the beginning of May.[55] From the start, Stilwell considered Brereton to be overly self-important, an impression only heightened by the fact that Stilwell was continually repulsed—to a fault—by even the scent of any such characteristic in fellow generals. Nor was Stilwell a fan of Naiden, remarking in his diary on June 25, 1942, "Brereton recommends Naiden for Major General!!—what slop"; he instead called for Brig. Gen. Clayton Bissell to take over the Tenth Air Force. Stillwell went on to claim that Brereton had caused a scandal in the command by getting too cozy with Mrs. Doris Jepson, the wife of India-based Firestone Tire executive Russell Jepson. She had moved from Bombay to New Delhi to serve as Brereton's personal secretary and, according to one source, was on the receiving end of a fair amount of "attractive underwear" bought by the Tenth Air Force commander with unit funds.[56] Naiden continued to run the airlift until August, when he was forced back to the United States with chronic stomach problems; before leaving he took steps to boost its meager production on July 15 by merging the Trans-India and Assam-Burma-China sectors into a single unit; even so, that month only saw seventy-seven tons carried over the Hump. By the midpoint of 1942 the prognosis for future deliveries to China was poor at best.

Hap Arnold never questioned airpower's ability to sustain the Hump, but he was nevertheless busy with building and shaping a strategic air weapon aimed at Germany and was ready to wash his hands of the airlift as a military operation. On July 19 Stilwell sent a message to Washington proposing that CNAC be placed under military control, but Arnold replied a week later proposing the exact opposite, that CNAC take over the operation in its entirety. Arnold had consistently recognized the latent expertise in commercial aviation, and he also knew that his air transport capability in mid-1942 was too small to handle the needs of competing theaters of war, so the AAF commander recommended to Stilwell at the end of July that CNAC take over the airlift completely.[57] Stilwell, ever suspicious of Chinese motives, was not enthusiastic about the idea, declaring it to be "unsound," as CNAC was owned in its majority by the Chinese government and was too mixed up in "internal Chinese politics." In Stilwell's opinion such an arrangement meant that CNAC would likely "show more interest in keeping up unessential commercial air routes within China than in transportation vital to the war"; he believed that such a move would be tantamount to admitting that "our Air Forces have failed" and that credit for the work already done in planning and organizing the route would "fall to CNAC, which has had little part in this." Stilwell went too far in stating that CNAC had little to do with the creation of the Hump, but as a theater commander his reaction to Arnold's suggestion was not surprising, given the fact that a CNAC-run Hump would leave Stilwell with no authority in airlift matters, something that he was not willing to relinquish. He declared, "My control of air transport in this theater is necessary both for political and military reasons."[58] It is difficult to predict the shape the airlift would have taken had it proceeded for the rest of the war under the direction of CNAC, but one thing is certain: had the airlift not continued as an explicitly U.S. military operation, the Roosevelt administration and the War Department would have been stripped of what soon became one of the United States' primary means of substantively displaying its allegiance to the Chinese, an allegiance portrayed in the regular stream of transports back and forth from southwest China.

Ever since Stilwell had been forced out of Burma the previous spring following a self-proclaimed "hell of a beating," he had been a continual advocate of reopening the Burma Road using Chinese soldiers trained and equipped by a U.S. detachment at Ramgarh, India. Marshall followed the direction of his theater commander and also argued for the recapture of northern Burma to reopen the overland supply route to China, but as preparations for such an offensive would take time, he strongly urged the buildup of the ferry route over the Hump in August 1942, claiming that its chief importance was to help the Soviets by mitigating the chances that the Japanese, if cleared of a strong occupying presence in China and Manchuria, would turn and declare war on the USSR. In an August 14 memo to the Combined Chiefs of Staff, Marshall stated that a quarter of Japan's land-based combat power was resident in China and if only ten of these divisions were released from service in China, they would, with their assigned air complement, "conceivably accelerate a Japanese attack against Siberia with its attendant repercussions on the Russian western front"; furthermore, steps needed to be taken to bolster the flagging morale of the Chinese army that was "dwindling to impotency."[59] The War Department had studied the possibility of keeping China supplied from Russia across the Silk Road but had concluded that such a move might serve as a casus belli and precipitate a Japanese attack on Siberia. U.S. officers who had spent time in the Soviet Union reported that Stalin had adopted a position of "armed neutrality" toward the Japanese and would risk no moves that might upset that delicate arrangement.[60] Given this, Marshall and his staff deemed that China needed to be given a continual "visible means of assistance" to prop them up and prevent a Japanese attack on the Soviets.

As the summer wore on, Chiang continued to apply pressure to the Americans, showing his dissatisfaction with the paucity of supplies coming over the Hump by recalling his ambassador from Washington, Wei Daoming. Stanley Hornbeck claimed that Chiang was justified in doing this, as the recall served as "an expression of exasperation" by the generalissimo, who had been "carrying a terrific political and military burden for more than 15 years." Hornbeck, ever the China advocate, praised Roosevelt for viewing the situation correctly but then

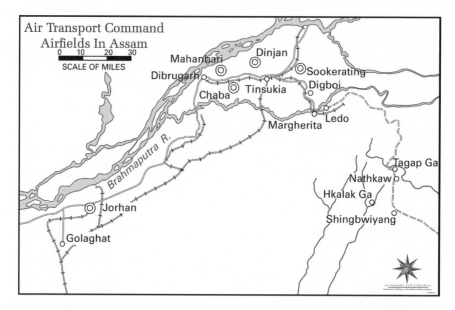

FIGURE 9. ATC Assam Airfields. *Courtesy U.S. Army Center of Military History.*

took to task the "various operating agencies of the Government" (a clear reference to the War Department and Army Air Forces) for finding "one reason after
another in impediment or prevention of the carrying out of declared policy."[61]
But Hornbeck's estimation that the Chinese air transport effort was being intentionally ignored was too simplistic, as transports were being used to support the
mass movement of men and supplies to Great Britain (for the planned cross-
channel invasion in 1943) and North Africa (for the launching of Montgomery's
offensive in October and the U.S. TORCH landings in November). In the second
half of 1942 alone, nearly 420 heavy and medium bombers were ferried to North
Africa for use against Rommel, gobbling up a sizable contingent of pilots and
cargo planes that were involved in actual fighting in that theater, naturally muting
the incentive to devote a considerable number of transports to China where little
fighting was taking place.[62]

The Hump effort also encountered a problem of a different nature in India
late in the summer when Mohandas Gandhi was arrested by British authorities in
the early morning of August 9 for his agitation in the "Quit India" campaign. The
arrest, meant to weaken the influence of the Congress Party, precipitated a back-
lash of riots that, though not directed at the Americans, still hurt the U.S. air con-

tingent in India, dependent as it was on local labor to build airfields and service aircraft. Exacerbating problems was the fact that the entire Bengal region was in the midst of a rice famine; it would claim some three and a half million lives, though famine-induced migration probably attracted labor to Assam where rice prices were reasonable.[63] Throughout the summer Dinjan had been the only serviceable airfield for Naiden's transports, but three other fields—Chabua, Sookerating, and Mohanbari—were supposed to be constructed with the use of local "coolie" labor as soon as the monsoonal rains abated (see figure 9).[64] Neither Brereton nor Naiden had the men or equipment to build the fields, despite the fact that Arnold had given them $10 million in currency to coordinate airdrome construction with the British.[65] Work at Chabua had begun the previous February when 2,600 native women were hired to break (by hand) the eleven million cubic feet of stone necessary to lay the runway.[66] Furthermore, local laborers refueled aircraft (something that had to be done manually, sometimes with five-gallon cans) and on-loaded and off-loaded cargo, jobs done by workers who often blurred the distinction between the friendly Americans and the British whom Gandhi was opposing, reducing the labor pool for these vital yet menial tasks.

Morale problems for airmen serving in India only compounded the challenges of the early Hump airlift. Promotions often lagged behind the rest of the air force for the simple reason that policy directives were easily lost in the shuffle of intercontinental message traffic. Furthermore, the 1st Ferry Group had to wrestle with the peculiar problem caused by the fact that its most experienced flyers were civilian airline pilots who were called to temporary military service, while those pilots who were "Regular Army" often had little flight experience. This breech promoted bickering between the two groups, seen in the remarks of one experienced civilian pilot: "It seems also that there is a lot of animosity toward the airline pilots by ranking army men over here caused by the fact that they realize we have considerable more experience in air transport problems than they possess and are afraid maybe we will replace them. The moral is 'The Airline Pilots cannot reconcile themselves to the incompetency of army management after seeing the efficiency of airline operations' and there will be friction and wasted effort as long as this condition exists."[67] The discussions about either merging CNAC into the ferry service or vice versa was undoubtedly colored by this unit dynamic, especially as CNAC pilots were paid a base salary of $800 per month for sixty hours of flying and $20 for each additional hour.[68] This salary was considerably more than that of a second lieutenant, who had a monthly salary of $367, with no incentive pay for extra hours flown.[69]

SLOW IMPROVEMENT AND JAPANESE COUNTERS

The airlift began to show signs of improvement by September with over four hundred tons of supplies delivered to China, a sixfold increase from just two months prior. Many airplanes were still grounded in need of replacement engines, but the fact that the remaining transports were being used only to fly the route between India and China and not for ancillary missions meant tonnages would begin to witness a slow rise. The monsoon was forecast to end in October, though Hump weather claimed its first victims on September 23 with a C-47 crash attributed to excessive icing; it killed the crew of two en route from Kunming to Chabua.[70] Just a week and a half prior to this crash the airlift witnessed another first of a different sort—the first night flight over the Hump. One of the ferry group's more experienced pilots, John D. Payne, took a handpicked crew through bad weather to Kunming, claiming he had only "hell and destiny" to guide him.[71] Proving the route could be flown at night was a significant accomplishment because darkness was an effective defense against the Japanese air threat, a threat that emerged the next month when the Burma-based IJA air arm began to resume its post-monsoon activities.

In a structure similar to that of the United States, Japan's army and navy both had separate air arms, though the service rivalry between the two often bordered on outright contempt, which forced both service air forces to evolve in strategically different directions. When the war first started in China in 1937, the IJN was tasked with supporting amphibious missions, and as the IJA had no suitable bomber with reasonable range, the navy was also tasked with strategic bombing missions launched deep into China's heartland, to include the well-known campaign against Chongqing. As plans for the looming Pacific War began to unfold in 1940, naval aviation was forced to shift its focus to the rehoning of fleet carrier duties, a skill that had lain dormant over the previous three years.[72] While the IJN's air force (IJNAF) was occupied with China in the late thirties, the IJA's air force (IJAAF) was busy with the Soviets, taking part in the unsuccessful venture at Nomonhan in 1939. And just as the Spanish Civil War shaped German airpower on the eve of World War II, so did the numerous Japanese skirmishes against the Soviets color its army's airpower plans. By 1940 the IJAAF was geared for a land war with the Soviets that would take place over Manchuria and Siberia, prompting the Koku Hombu (Air Headquarters) to call for the construction of short-range aircraft that performed well in cold climates, something that was completely out of step with the long-range flying conducted in tropical climates in the Pacific War.[73]

Japanese air operations against the Hump were staged out of bases in south and central Burma and came in the form of bomber attacks against transport bases as well as fighter attacks against airborne transports. Burma is shaped like the back of a human left hand, fingers together, and eight of the key Japanese air bases were located in a scattered arc stretching from just below the knuckle on the small finger to the joint of the thumb. If the fingers were spread apart the tip of the ring finger would approximate the location of Sookerating, the U.S. transport base closest to Burma, and the tip of the index finger would approximate the location of Kunming. (The farthest joint on the middle finger would represent Fort Hertz, and the next joint down would denote Myitkyina). This put the Japanese bases nearly five hundred miles from the Hump's flight path, and given the range limitations of the Ki-43 fighters, this meant that bomber escort fighters could remain over targets for only a short time and might even have to recover to a more northerly staging base like Myitkyina to refuel. The Ki-43 "Oscar" was a formidable aircraft, though, and at the time was considered the best fighter of the Japanese Army in terms of maneuverability and speed, but it lacked much of a punch, being only lightly armed.[74]

Attacks against U.S. bases were more prevalent than attacks against in-flight transports because it was much easier to strike an airfield than locate a single airplane using only the naked eye. It would not be until the following year, when the flow of U.S. transports picked up from a few flights to a few dozen flights a day, that the Japanese would even try to explicitly target the Hump route. It was difficult to pick out a single airplane without the help of radar, though early in the war Japanese pilots were found to have terrific eyesight, a discovery that ran counter to the prewar Allied conception that the Japanese would be racially inferior as aviators because of the shape of their eyes. As Alvin Coox points out, the Allies thought the Japanese were "myopic, night blind, poor at bombing and accident prone" because as babies "they were strapped to their mothers' backs, and thus they suffered from twisted vision and a wobbly sense of balance." Additionally the fact that rice was the main Japanese staple led some Allied pilots to assume such a diet was lacking in the proper vitamins and proteins necessary for good night vision. When Japanese pilots sank the *Repulse* and *Prince of Wales* in December 1941, some thought it must have been done by a special detachment of German pilots.[75] This was clearly not the case, and Japanese fighters constituted a legitimate threat to Hump flyers, but with range restrictions forcing the former to consider the latter as only a "target of opportunity" until later in 1943.

Opposing the Japanese in Burma were India-based British and U.S. fighter units, the latter falling under the purview of the Tenth Air Force. Chennault's China-based AVG "Flying Tigers" could also protect the transports, as his unit had been incorporated into the regular Army Air Forces in July, now called the 23rd Pursuit Group of the China Air Task Force; Chennault had also reentered the service and was promoted to the rank of brigadier general. Because the Japanese threat was closer to Allied units in India—whether attacking Indian transport bases or U.S. C-47s in the vicinity of Fort Hertz—the Tenth Air Force bore the brunt of Hump defense missions, forcing the relocation of the 51st Fighter Group from Karachi to Dinjan in October in response to an increase in Japanese reconnaissance missions over the Assam Valley (a Japanese Ki-46 "Dinah" reconnaissance plane was shot down over Dinjan on October 19). Then, on October 25, the Japanese launched their largest air attack in Burma in over six months, a well-orchestrated raid that saw Dinjan and nearby Chabua attacked simultaneously while a diversionary strafing attack was launched against Chittagong, a British-held city at the mouth of the Brahmaputra, over four hundred miles to the southwest. The Japanese also left one Hanoi-based *sentai* to patrol southern Burma while the bulk of its airpower was occupied with the targets in the north.[76]

Arriving early in the afternoon, the Japanese used twin-engine bombers Ki-21 "Sally" and Ki-48 "Lily" to attack parked aircraft, runways, and outbuildings, while using Ki-43 "Oscar" fighters to either strafe the airfields or fly top cover for the bombers. In all, the attacking force numbered fifty-four bombers and sixty-two fighters, with only three fighters shot down, six others damaged, and no bombers destroyed (according to Japanese records); over ten Allied P-40 fighters were destroyed on the ground and nine transports were destroyed or damaged beyond repair. The runway at Chabua was also cratered, and a nearby railway fuel dump was burned to the ground. The spartan conditions at both fields meant there was no firefighting equipment, so even the smallest amount of aircraft damage could turn into a blazing wreck in only a short time.[77] The Japanese followed up the next day with a raid on Sookerating, just twenty-five miles west of Dinjan and Chabua, this time using only Ki-43 fighters, which found a fair number of U.S. fighters airborne when they arrived just after noon. Some air-to-air combat ensued, but with little extra fuel to spend in long dogfights, the Japanese were forced to break off the attack with minimal damage done to the airfields. A third raid came the following day, again doing scant damage, but the string of attacks was halted on October 28 when an RAF unit attacked the Japanese base at Swebo, Burma (near Mandalay), forcing the Japanese to keep more of their fighters close to their bases as a protective measure.

The Allies considered the question of radar to provide early-warning for Japanese raids, but the rugged terrain facing the east—in the direction of the Japanese airfields—made it impossible to parse out an enemy formation from the usual ground clutter. Instead the Americans created a network of nine radio stations based between fifty and seventy-five miles east of the transport airfields to call in Japanese attacks so that fighters could be scrambled in time to meet the threat. The stations were positioned in the Naga Hills on the Indian-Burmese border; battery-powered radios were used to maintain strict silence so that approaching Japanese planes could be heard. Because the Japanese rarely attacked after dark, the evenings were spent using generators to recharge their batteries. The system was effective but was continually threatened after the Japanese learned of its presence and began launching limited ground offensives against the outposts in March 1943.[78]

The Japanese air raids both hindered and helped the Americans. The attacks had hurt the airlift effort for the simple reason that nine of the fewer than fifty C-47s that had been delivered up through September were rendered unusable. Added to this was the psychological impact of the attacks on the native laborers who were hired to work at the airfields, many quitting within days of the raids. In a bizarre twist, though, the attacks had the opposite effect on the transport aircrews, who were invigorated by the thought that their mission—one that could not be measured in bombs dropped or enemy planes shot down—had warranted the attention of the enemy. If the Japanese had thought that stopping the flow of supplies to China was worth an aerial offensive, then this gave a renewed sense of purpose to the Hump flyers.[79] The attacks also served to accelerate the placement of the radio warning network that served the transport bases well for the next two years until the Japanese 5th Air Division could be pushed back into southern Burma.

Despite the October air offensive, Hump tonnage continued to increase in November, growing tenfold over a four-month period. Still, that amount of tonnage was ridiculously small by the standards of military logistics, as the deliveries amounted mainly to fuel, ammunition, and stores for Chennault's P-40s and B-25s, which were doing their best to agitate Japanese positions in southern China. In China, the Japanese CEA had settled back into its mode as an occupation force following the Zhejiang offensive earlier that summer, with the Japanese High Command now fixated on the U.S. offensive at Guadalcanal. Additionally, there had been a tentative agreement among the Allies that an offensive would commence early in the spring of 1943 in an effort to reopen the Burma Road and increase the flow of supplies to China. Still, Chiang continued to make his pleas for more aid, though in a more conciliatory tone; he telegrammed FDR on November 24 asking for more planes to increase the "trickle of supplies needed for the functioning of the Chinese army and arsenals" to sustain that offensive.[80] But to simply add more transports to the ferry force was not sufficient to increase the airlift's production. What was needed at root was a complete organizational change, something that would take place on December 1 when ATC took over the operation.

AIR TRANSPORT COMMAND TAKES OVER

The AAF's Ferry Command had become Air Transport Command earlier that summer, merging the AAF's airlift and ferry responsibilities. From the start, the command was tasked with establishing a network of air routes that could connect all the world's inhabited continents; in doing so, it took on the shape of a growing commercial airline company rather than a combat aviation unit. Men like C. R. Smith fostered a command culture that thought in terms of mission efficiency—as in maximizing the payload for a given flight—and refused to be tempted by the "crisis management" mentality that dominated many of the headquarters of combat air force units. In an October 13 report submitted to Arnold, Smith argued that what the Hump airlift needed was not necessarily more planes but rather "singleness of purpose." Smith reminded Arnold that the original forecasts for the Hump predicted that 7,500 tons per month could be delivered once seventy-five transports were in place in India, based on the simple premise that a single plane could carry one hundred tons per month (even a moderately loaded C-47 carrying only three tons per trip would only have to make just over thirty round trips in a month to meet this quota, a reasonable goal). Smith sympathized with the maintenance problems encountered by the 1st Ferry Group but, even so, felt that the tonnage delivered to China should have been higher. To remedy the situation he proposed that ATC take over the airlift, either making it an extension of the existing trans-Africa-to-Middle East route or creating a new command altogether–to be run by ATC but dedicated solely to the flow of supplies over the Himalayas. Smith was convinced of the maxim that "the principal experience of the Air Transport Command is in air transportation, as contrasted with the experience of the Theater Commander being principally in combat and in preparing for combat." Bissell had never thought monthly tonnages could exceed 5,000 tons, but given the opportunity, Smith promised that he and ATC's commander, Hal George, could impose a fresh organizational perspective that would boost the airlift to new heights.[81]

Arnold's decision to turn the responsibility over to ATC was easy. It was also easy for George and Smith to decide to create a separate wing–the India-China Wing (ICW)–to bear this responsibility. Despite being the shortest of all ATC routes, the Hump was politically the most important, linking the Allies with China, both materially and morally, in what was to become an aerial "Burma Road." Three direct effects stemmed from ATC's assumption of the route. First, it ended the Hump's ad hoc "barnstorming" days. The Tenth Air Force was perennially undermanned and undersupplied, being in a low-priority combat theater, but now that the ICW-run airlift was to come under the umbrella of ATC–a command that would number over 200,000 personnel and 3,700 aircraft by the war's end–the airlift was wedded to a growing infrastructure of talent and equipment that held great promise.[82] Second, the airlift would get the "singleness of purpose" it needed because now it would be managed from Washington and not from either New Delhi (Tenth Air Force) or Chongqing (CBI headquarters). If Stilwell or Bissell wanted to use the transports for something other than the Hump, they would first need permission from Marshall or Arnold, a novel arrangement that was bound to be a sore spot as time wore on, but one that would allow Roosevelt political latitude in employing the airlift as a diplomatic marker to boost Chinese national will, serving as a stout display of U.S. commitment. Third, giving the Hump to ATC reduced the pressure for the recapture of northern Burma. Stilwell consistently claimed that tonnage delivered by airplanes could never match that delivered by trucks, so he insisted that Chinese national will depended on an opened Burma Road. Ironically, though, Chiang frankly cared little if the road was opened or closed, so long as supplies made it to China; having his troops trained and equipped by the Americans was a boon for him, and he had little desire in spending that martial "capital" on unnecessary forays into Burma. Those troops could be better used against his real nemesis, the Communists in Yan'an.

THE HUMP AND AN ASCENDANT
CBI AIR STRATEGY

JANUARY TO MAY 1943

O n December 1, 1942, the Tenth Air Force's 1st Ferry Group became the India-China Wing of Air Transport Command with Brig. Gen. Edward H. Alexander as its commander. The thirty-nine-year-old had served as the executive officer of Ferry Command from May to December 1941, working at the time alongside William Tunner, the man who would later direct the Berlin Airlift. Alexander's career had been fairly nondescript; he had earned his wings in 1929 and served in such positions as flight instructor, supply officer, and communications officer. Like many of his contemporaries, he had attended the Air Corps Tactical School, enrolling in 1937; afterward he was reassigned to the Air Corps' flying training arm for another two-year tour and was subsequently handpicked by Col. Robert Olds to serve as the executive officer at Ferry Command headquarters in the summer of 1941. After several months of busy staff work, Alexander volunteered in November to fly a B-24 ferry mission to Cairo to pick up Maj. Gen. George Brett, the deputy chief of the AAF. Alexander later admitted that he had been working seven days a week at headquarters and felt the two-week trip would provide a needed respite from the rigors of his desk job. He met Brett in Cairo just as the Japanese were attacking Pearl Harbor and so ended up as the general's personal pilot, flying him to meet with Chennault in Rangoon and Chiang in Chongqing. While in China, Alexander contracted Dengue fever and ended up staying in Chongqing at the generalissimo's home while he recovered over the next two weeks. Left behind by Brett, Alexander was ordered to remain in Chongqing to serve as air officer on Magruder's AMMISCA staff, a job that linked him to Stilwell when the latter arrived in China in February 1942. Thus, what started as a routine jaunt between Washington and Cairo grew into a nearly two-year odyssey that put Alexander and his India-China Wing in the center of Sino-U.S. political and military squabbles.[1]

When ATC assumed responsibility for the airlift at the start of December, Alexander was the ideal man to command the mission, having served as Stilwell's air advisor for the previous ten months and authoring the CBI headquarters' first air plan, "China Air War Plan," in September 1942. Described as "the conscientious, worrying type, who took a personal interest in the smallest details of his command," Alexander had the reputation for working "day and night, night and day, on the myriad complexities" of the airlift. Unlike the men who ran the airlift during the previous year, Alexander would be the first to try to make the Hump a success as a single, focused mission rather than an adjunct to the other air operations of the CBI, serving as the Hump's commander for the next ten months. According to Tunner, "He was up against a mountain of problems. He worked incessantly, but when he cleared up one matter, two others rose up to take its place." The problems took their toll, leaving him a "sick man" when he left the job in the fall of 1943.[2]

Alexander established his headquarters at Chabua, one of the newest airfields being built on one of Assam's many tea plantations; also open for limited service were the airfields at Mohanbari and Sookerating, all within thirty-five miles of the protection of the 51st Fighter Group at Dinjan. For aircraft he had approximately sixty C-47s, along with a dozen C-87s that were sporadically arriving from the United States.[3] His plan was to disperse the airplanes evenly among the three airfields so that a single Japanese attack would not be able to cripple the entire fleet, but the heavier C-87s needed a hardened runway, which meant they could be based only at Chabua, as Sookerating and Mohanbari were not yet paved. Not only did the airfields need paved runways but also paved "hardstands" where the planes could be parked for servicing, loading, and unloading without their wheels and landing gear sinking into the ground—which would

FIGURE 10. Brig. Gen. Edward Alexander (left). *Courtesy McGraw-Hill.*

become mud with monsoonal rains that May. Each field needed at least twenty-five hardstands, and Alexander was at the mercy of the British to coordinate all local construction, a situation that would give him fits throughout the spring and summer until Roosevelt and Churchill got involved.

Alexander was intent on beginning night flying to meet Stilwell's tonnage demands (the CBI commander wanted the ICW to deliver 3,683 tons of supplies to China for his "Yoke-force" project—the training and equipping of Chinese soldiers in Yunnan—over the next three months), but he had to wait for communication radios and navigation transmitters to be set up first to keep his crews clear of terrain, equipment that the 10th Army Airways Communications Service (AACS) Squadron would have in place by the end of spring. Morale was generally good among his crews, and Alexander was pleased at the surprisingly low rate of malaria and dysentery, the most common diseases among Americans in India. He also had only a handful of men with venereal disease and was more concerned with the cases of "neurosis" he saw cropping up among his pilots, something he deemed the result of a "lack of nerves." His pilots called it "hum-pitis" or being "hump happy," a moniker that would stick for the rest of the war. Alexander observed that men who served on the Hump for between six and eight months were prone to "ultimately crack up" if they were "kept on the job too long" and so recommended rotating these men to other wings within ATC. From the first days of his command he was committed to the welfare of his men, stating that his chief concern was "the saving of flight crews who have been plug-ging daily between India and China for many months," and—in a move that was probably ahead of its time—he requested vitamin pills to supplement the local food supply, in which such items as leafy vegetables were drained of normal nutritional value because most soil nutrients were washed away by heavy rains during the growing season.[4]

Despite Alexander's previous dealings with the CBI command structure—being a part of that command for most of 1942—considerable friction neverthe-less arose between his new wing and CBI leadership. The problem was rooted in the fact that Alexander was now leading an organization that was stationed within the CBI while being technically autonomous, taking orders from George and Arnold in Washington, not Bissell and Stilwell in India or China. Stilwell seemed to be largely content with this arrangement, as it relieved him of responsibility for the airlift; he had also gotten along well with Alexander and even told him in a memo, "I am glad that you were selected to command the India-China Wing," an uncharacteristic accolade for Stillwell to express in official correspondence.[5] The crux of the problem lay rather between Bissell (still the head of Tenth Air Force) and Alexander, the former determined to impose his authority on the airlift and the latter working to persistently divorce his command from the tentacles of local theater control.

Clayton Bissell had done a fair job as the Tenth Air Force's commander directing the Hump during the second half of 1942, but he had a difficult time relinquishing its control to Alexander. Even though Alexander was running the airlift out of his headquarters at Chabua, Bissell maintained that he controlled both the transport airfields as well as the prioritization of cargo, something that ran counter to War Department directives. Put simply, under the planned arrangement, Bissell (with the consent of Stilwell) was to assume the authority of determining what supplies were to be loaded on aircraft, while Alexander was to maintain control over where and when the planes flew. Bissell overstepped his bounds, though, by redesignating cargo destinations. On several occasions when supplies from the United States arrived at the port in Calcutta and were marked for delivery to ATC fields, Bissell would take it upon himself to redesignate their destinations according to the needs of the Tenth; this became problematic when items like spare aircraft parts were being sent to bomber or fighter units in India and not Alexander's transport bases.[6] This did not endear Bissell to Hal George at ATC headquarters in Washington, and the command relationship between the Tenth Air Force and the India-China Wing did not reach a decent level of co-operation until Bissell's reassignment to the United States in August 1943.[7]

Despite the harried relationship between Alexander and Bissell, the former was dependant on the latter for protection because the mission of the Tenth Air Force had shifted fully to the defense of the Hump route by the start of 1943. The radio warning network gave the fighter and transport bases no less than five minutes to scramble for inbound attacks that came sporadically during January and February. To counter the raids, U.S. bombers were sent against such Japanese positions as Mandalay, Bhamo, and Rangoon, hitting supply depots, fuel stores, and enemy aircraft.[8] By the end of February the 10th AACS Squadron had succeeded in linking the transport airfields with a growing radio network, February 28 saw operators in Kunming contact Brisbane, Australia, for the first time, marking the first time ever that a radio network circumnavigated the globe, an event of technological significance because from this point on communications could flow eastward to the United States from China rather than having to be passed on by the dozens of relay stations that lay in westward travel through the Middle East and Africa. The 10th also succeeded in setting up a low-power (one kilowatt) point-to-point homing beacon at Fort Hertz at the end of January, a navigation aid that served as a helpful reference marker at roughly the midpoint of the route. The beacon was crude, though, and provided aircrews with only a general compass heading for the station because its low power meant it had a range of only twenty miles. More important were the six directional finding (D/F) stations set up in India and China by the first week of April.[9] D/F stations broadcasted azimuth information as far as two hundred miles away so aircrews could triangulate their positions with a fair amount of accuracy, provided the mountainous terrain did not obstruct radio reception or other stratospheric phenomena (like solar flares or "night effect") did not skew a navigation solution.[10] D/F navigation was helpful to the Hump pilots, but its successful use was more art than science and was predicated mostly on user proficiency, which came only with hours of practice. The navigation aids also made the prospects for conducting twenty-four-hour flight operations more feasible, though adequate airfield lighting, both in terms of runway markers and ramp lighting for nighttime aircraft servicing, was still absent, making for only sporadic night flights over the Hump during the first half of 1943.

Back at ATC headquarters, now housed at an office building at Gravelly Point in Arlington, Virginia, the Plans Division put together a blueprint for Alexander that promised—under the most expansive conditions—to deliver 12,000 tons per month to China by that coming July and 50,000 tons per month by the end of the year.[11] The plan was a classic piece of wartime forecasting that reflected the chasm between the idealistic formulations of staff officers and the unfriendly realities faced by operators in the field. It was also consistent with the type of mechanistic thinking that shaped the most famous U.S. prewar air plan, AWPD-1, in which strategic bombing planners (led by Hal George, at the time the chief of the Air War Plans Division) simply calculated U.S. prewar bomber need based on the number and size of German war-matériel factories, the square footage of damage wrought by a single bomb, and the number of bombs a single plane was able to carry. In doing so, the necessary bomber fleet was determined by the amount of German acreage to be razed.[12] Like AWPD-1, this ATC plan simply looked at cargo-carrying capacity, distance between terminals, and aircraft speed and then deduced forecasts for Hump production. Admittedly the plan had a great many presuppositional flaws, but it is telling at one key point, that being the fact that ATC was already thinking of Hump tonnage possibilities in much larger figures than had ever before been considered. This may seem like a minor point at first glance, but for planners to seriously consider that such tonnage could be flown over the Himalayas bespeaks a command culture that thought in extravagant terms—though intangible or difficult to quantify, this mindset is perhaps one of the larger factors contributing to the airlift's future operational success. The thought that 50,000 monthly tons was even considered by ATC planners must have seemed like a typographical error to the likes of Stilwell, who never thought that anything more than 5,000 tons per month would ever be possible.[13]

THE CASABLANCA CONFERENCE

While Alexander was taking account of his air transport fleet in January, Roosevelt, Churchill (with de Gaulle and Giraud), and the Combined Chiefs of Staff were meeting near Casablanca, Morocco, from the 14th to the 23rd to hammer out Allied strategy for the coming year. Topics of discussion included the primacy of the U-boat campaign to counter German successes in the Atlantic, the invasion of Sicily once the gains in North Africa were consolidated, and the postponement of the cross-channel invasion until 1944. Airpower leaders also agreed to disagree on the dynamics of a profitable air campaign: the Americans insisted a successful one could be waged during the day, while the British were resolute that such an approach had been tried and found to be a failure, instead opting for nighttime bombing. At Casablanca they also discussed future plans for the CBI Theater with the proposal of a limited British invasion of Burma, code-named "Anakim," which was placed under consideration for the upcoming spring. Lastly, the conferees agreed to increase the flow of supplies to both the Soviets (reopening convoy routes to Murmansk) and the Chinese by increasing supplies delivered over the Hump.[14]

The idea of a British invasion of the Burmese coast had been considered during the previous month whereby a U.S.-supplied and supported force of Chinese soldiers would attack north Burma while the British launched an amphibious assault on the coast, but Chiang, ever suspicious of the British, pulled out of the planning just weeks before Casablanca. The generalissimo was continually wary of British intentions for several reasons, the most fundamental being that British imperial claims existed within the traditional orbit of Chinese geographical interests; Gandhi had warned Chiang that the British "will never voluntarily treat us Indians as equals" and that the Chinese could expect nothing better.[15] During the debacle of the Allied defense of Burma in 1942, Chiang felt the British had wanted to use Chinese troops only to cover their own retreat. It also did not help that the British were receiving the lion's share of Lend-Lease aircraft and supplies. Chinese mistrust of British sincerity about a coastal attack on Burma brought into focus a larger debate that was to dominate the theater for the next two years, namely the one between Stilwell, with his incessant arguing for a major Burmese ground offensive to reopen the Burma Road, and Chennault, with his extravagant claims that he could precipitate the downfall of Japan with a force of fewer than 105 fighters, 30 medium bombers, and a dozen heavy bombers.[16] Both had been making the case for their positions since the previous autumn, but it was at Casablanca that the debate was first tabled for discussion. During the conference's opening proceedings Arnold stated that Chennault's "exaggerated claims" still had merit as "there was no doubt that additional air forces in China would have a very great effect." Arnold hoped to eventually have 175 transports in India and was estimating a maximum delivery of 10,000 tons per month. In discussions two days later Roosevelt expressed that it would be politically expedient to send more planes to China because "periodic bombing raids over Japan . . . would have a tremendous morale effect on the Chinese people." Arnold did not disagree but tepidly stated that he "wished to see for himself whether or not an increased air force in China could be supplied."[17] To do so, he would go to China to investigate firsthand.

It was at Casablanca that Arnold's true sentiment about the Hump airlift began to show through, revealing him to be a lukewarm advocate of the operation; it is not that he felt the airlift was incapable of sizable deliveries, but rather that he saw little point in conducting an airlift simply to sustain Chinese national will. A couple of indicators give rise to this impression. First, at the end of 1942 Roosevelt promised Stalin one hundred U.S. bombers in the event of a Japanese declaration of war on the USSR; the promise was meant to placate the Soviet leader, who had just endured his toughest year of the war. On the heels of this offer Arnold chimed in that the Allies could send the Soviets three hundred transports at the rate of twenty per month, and this when U.S. production of all types of transports stood at an average of only 165 per month for the previous twelve months.[18] Rather than a surplus, there was actually a severe shortage of the aircraft on hand, as reflected in an order issued by Arnold just three weeks before his offer to the Russians in where he said, "No transport airplane of the DC-2, DC-3, or larger type will be used as a staff transport of any headquarters, command, or other activity of the Army Air Forces within the continental limits of the United States, except upon special assignment by this headquarters."[19] It was usual for headquarters' staffs to use cargo aircraft for official travel, but the scarcity of such airplanes in the inventory restricted this luxury. Given this fact, it is odd that Arnold would offer the Soviets three hundred transports less than three weeks later; clearly the air chief was more impressed with the need to sustain the Soviets through a regular diet of Lend-Lease airplanes than with rapidly bolstering the Hump airlift. Five months prior Stanley Hornbeck had complained that "various operating agencies" had not been giving sufficient attention to the resupply of China—it is not inconceivable that he was referring to Arnold's lack of conviction for such an operation.[20]

Second, Arnold never advocated the creation of a separate numbered air force in China. Numbered air forces—like the famed Eighth Air Force, responsible for the U.S. bombing campaign over Germany, or the Twentieth Air Force, which bombed Japan later in the war—represented that service's largest autonomous combat unit (the war ended with sixteen numbered air forces), normally commanded by a major general. Chiang tirelessly argued for the presence of a separate numbered air force in China under Chennault's command. Arnold respected Chennault as a tactician but felt he was logistically and administratively inept; because a separate numbered air force in China would be so small—as it could only be supplied over the Hump—he deemed it a senseless venture. Thus, Arnold was far more comfortable with the arrangement that Chennault command his own China-based task force under the purview of the Tenth Air Force in India rather than be given his own autonomy with a separate air force.[21] Arnold viewed the war in global cost-benefit terms, and giving Chennault his own air force in China provided only the benefit of making pinprick strikes against the Japanese army while costing a proportion of Arnold's air transport inventory.[22]

None of this is to suggest that Arnold was cool on the possibilities of air transport. Throughout the war he was a shrewd political-military thinker who perhaps did more to bring about the creation of the U.S. Air Force as a separate service than any other individual. He was an airpower advocate of the highest order and was as much a believer in strategic airlift as he was a believer in strategic bombing. But Arnold also had an air force to build and run, and while he supported the president's posture toward China as a subordinate, he did not share Roosevelt's grand vision for the place of China in the postwar world. Arnold traveled to China from Morocco after the conference and met with Chiang in Chongqing, summarizing his impression of the generalissimo by stating that the Chinese leader lacked "a global outlook" and persistently cried the familiar mantra "Aid to China! Aid to China!" Arnold said of Chiang, "Sometimes he gave evidence of quick thinking, but only at times. He had an orderly mind, capable of arranging details, and he asked very pertinent questions. However, the effort died out after the first few questions. There was no doubt that he had the power of life and death in his hands, as far as the Chinese nation was concerned, for as long as he wanted it, and he expected his subjects to remember that. Accordingly, he did not have to think his way through. It made no difference to him, so long as he had his way."[23]

Eleven months later at the Cairo Conference Arnold would remark, "Sometimes I wondered why we were saving China."[24] Arnold was not opposed to the Hump airlift. He simply thought that supplying China to sustain some ephemeral concept of national morale was unproductive and divert precious airpower resources from more pressing needs. As the war continued, Arnold eventually became a more outspoken advocate for the airlift, but only because it could be used to supply his India-based B-29s, which shuttled through Chengdu in Sichuan Province to strike targets on Formosa and the Japanese home islands. If Roosevelt represented the U.S. impulse to aid China over the Hump simply to preserve morale, Arnold would come to represent the desire to aid China over the Hump to the end of waging the nascent U.S. strategic bombing campaign against Japan.

ARNOLD'S TRIP TO CHINA

One other thing that Arnold took away from his trip to China was an appreciation for the challenges that confronted pilots who regularly flew the Hump. During the course of his trip to Asia Arnold spent time first in Karachi, then in Delhi. He then flew to Assam, and it was from here that his personal crew took off from Dinjan after dinner on February 4 for what should have been a two-and-a-half-hour flight. Instead the flight took over six hours. His crew got lost, mainly because they were flying at 19,000 feet without wearing their oxygen masks, and so—in what was surely a groggy state—made all manner of navigational errors that put them probably three hundred miles east of Kunming, potentially over Japanese-held territory. Thanks to some clearheaded intervention by Arnold, the crew was able to get back on course to Kunming, landing over four hours late to a reception of very worried senior officers who feared the worst for the United States' air chief.

Arnold's visit to China resulted in three broad actions. First, he would advocate bolstering the Chinese air force without the infusion of more Americans into the theater: "Due to the lack of shipping and the tremendous distance between the United States and China, everything possible should be done to keep down the number of Americans maintained in China"; so Arnold encouraged the merger of Chinese and U.S. fighter and bomber squadrons into a wing that would allow the Chinese to slowly grow in proficiency until the Americans could completely withdraw.[25] The result was the creation of the Chinese-American Composite Wing (CACW), composed of P-40s and B-25s. The unit endured to the end of the war and became the antecedent to Chiang's air force in Taiwan once his Nationalists had been forced to flee the mainland.

Second, Arnold's visit expedited the assignment of heavy bombers to China. Consolidated B-24 Liberators of the 308th Bomb Group would begin arriving in China that spring to begin bombing enemy shipping, ports, and bases, but the unit would also have to carry its own supplies into the theater to accomplish this mission due to the "lack of available cargo space on transports," which prevented ATC airlift support. The arrival of the 308th in China thus became the template for the "VLR" (Very Long Range), B-29 missions launched against Japan from China under the auspices of Operation Matterhorn the following year.[26]

Third, Arnold's visit to China prompted him to double the number of planes flying the Hump and establish a near-term target of 4,000 tons of supplies lifted over the Hump to support both the Chinese army and Chennault's air force. There is something different about Arnold's target tonnage, though. Unlike Chennault (who calculated his tonnage requirement based on the fuel needs of his P-40s and B-25s), Stilwell (who calculated his tonnage requirements based on the weight of ammunition and supply stores to train his Yoke-force), or the generalissimo (who arbitrarily called for increasing tonnages as a way to quantify his supposed level of desperation in the face of Japanese occupation), Arnold set 4,000 tons as a goal based on a realistic assessment of what he thought Alexander's wing should be able to lift. Doubling the number of transports in the ICW brought the wing's total to 125 aircraft. Arnold calculated that 90 of these—at least 70 percent of the fleet—should be available on any given day, a reasonable mark given the continual shortage of spare aircraft parts. He then figured that these 90 planes should be able to make at least twenty trips each per month, again a clear-eyed appraisal in view of the challenges of Himalayan weather. This totaled 1,800 round trips between India and China and, assuming that each plane would be at least half full, resulted in a monthly target of 4,000 tons.[27]

Arnold's tonnage target is noteworthy for one reason—it is strikingly low. One might expect him to be pressing George at Gravelly Point to speedily resolve the problems that prevented a heftier delivery of supplies, but, again, Arnold would only become keener on the Hump's output when it bore more closely on his desire to bomb Japan. The war in Europe was his first concern, and air transports for the invasion of Italy had to be set aside for Eisenhower's planners. Arnold likely appreciated both Stilwell and Chennault and their plans for bolstering China, but frankly the air chief was focused on winning the war through strategic bombing. From that perspective the recapture of Burma or the interdiction of Japanese coastal shipping held very little promise for eventual victory.

THE ICW AND "HUMPITIS"

Arnold's mandate to have the India-China Wing boosted to 124 aircraft was a step in the right direction toward increasing Hump tonnage, but Alexander was becoming more and more concerned about the fitness of his aircrews. Arnold had directed at least two crews per assigned aircraft, but Alexander felt this ratio was too low, as his men had been averaging over one hundred flying hours per month, a pace that was too high according to Col. Don Flickinger, Alexander's chief flight surgeon and a man who would later become something of a medical celebrity for parachuting into the Burmese jungle to help rescue downed CBS correspondent Eric Sevareid.[28] Flickinger conducted a careful study shortly after ATC took over the airlift and determined that seventy-five hours per month was the maximum any crewmember should fly because of the unusual rigors of the Hump. In mid-February Alexander had 112 crews and seventy aircraft at his disposal, or 1.6 crews per airplane, a figure that drove the tempo of operations too high as crews were forced to rest while airplanes sat idle. "Get me more aircraft crews if it is feasibly possible. I *hate* to see good, serviceable aircraft sitting on the ground with no one to fly them. An airplane doesn't need to *sleep*," wrote Alexander in a personal letter to Col. Robert Love, Hal George's deputy chief of staff.[29] Then, on January 20, Alexander reported that he witnessed the first case of a pilot "cracking," due to his "inability to take the mental pressure" of flying the route. To prevent this from spreading, Alexander requested a total of 308 crews to fly the complement of aircraft Arnold had ordered to India.[30] Additionally, Flickinger recommended limiting the wing's pilot's to seventy-five monthly flying hours, a novel move as the airlift was not considered a "combat mission," environmental conditions notwithstanding.

A comprehensive report, titled "Pilot Psychology, Fatigue, and Rehabilitation" and compiled by Flickinger protégé Capt. James Lowenthal in April 1945, asserted that "the hazards to which a pilot flying the 'Hump' was exposed were *real* hazards. The possibility of death, injury—of bailing out and walking back—none of these could be sugar coated. Icing, weather, Japs, night and instrument flight, motor failure at high altitudes—all were real potential dangers which no amount of minimizing could alter."[31] Of course, none of these dangers was unique to Hump pilots. Eighth Air Force bomber crews had to endure similar dangers, though in a milder climate and friendlier terrain, but conversely had to deal with German flak and fighters. Lowenthal's report recognized this disparity between combat and transport flying: "In combat the pilot was in close contact with his enemy. He must kill or be killed. During actual aerial combat, flying the airplane was secondary in importance to proper maneuvering in order to get the first shot. This was especially true of fighter pilots. Their primary mission was to seek out enemy planes and destroy them. This was not the case in the ICD, where the primary mission was to fly the plane."[32] (The India-China Wing was reclassified the India-China Division, or ICD, in July 1944.) Taking an interesting Freudian turn, the report claimed that this lack of a visible enemy actually served as a liability for the transport pilots: "ATC pilots, with rare exceptions, have not been out on missions where they have been shot down. They have not the desire to kill the enemy or the hate of the enemy which combat pilots have. But hate for a pilot is important, it helps protect the ego in that a person filled with hate is not nearly so likely to falter in the fulfillment of a dangerous mission because self preservation is partially disregarded. This ATC pilots lack."[33]

One can argue with the report's psychoanalytical conclusions with respect to the role of "hatred" in aerial warfare, but it becomes more straightforward as it continues:

> *Combat pilots during and after a mission knew they were an essential part of the war. They shot or dropped bombs. They realized a battle was going on. They saw the damage their bombs did or the enemy plane they shot down. Not so with an ICD pilot. He flew a load of cargo over the Hump. In the majority of cases he did not know of what use it would be and sometimes feared, with reason, that most of it would be wasted by the Chinese. To the ICD pilot, it was his flying which was the prime factor, not the fact that his cargo was essential to the war effort. He considered himself distant to battle campaigns.*[34]

Simply put, combat pilots witnessed the immediate results of their missions while Hump pilots–operating in the war's toughest climatic environment–were flying support missions that depended either on the exploits of Chennault's pilots or Chiang's soldiers for their ultimate value to be felt.

Exacerbating the "quasi-combat" nature of the airlift were the backgrounds of many of those Hump pilots who eventually developed cases of flying fatigue or anxiety, backgrounds that could be grouped into three categories: pilots who came to ATC directly from civilian life, those who came to ATC from tactical units, and those who joined ATC under duress. First, the report noted that many ATC flyers were civilian pilots experienced only in flying light aircraft. Lowenthal claimed these men flew only for the "gratification of a whim" and were "fair weather pilots with insufficient motivation to carry on with flying once they had their ego endangered." They were also "allergic to rumor," fearing for their lives before ever flying the Hump simply because they had believed exaggerated stories about the route's dangers. Lowenthal concluded of this group, "It was evident that flying for a 'whim' or hobby was insufficient to prevent them from quickly developing an anxiety neurosis."[35]

Lowenthal's second group were those who came to ATC because of "their ineptitude and inefficiency" in their prior assignments as fighter or bomber pilots. They were deemed unfit for duty with tactical units and so were transferred to ATC rather than being reclassified into other nonflying career fields. The report claimed that "these pilots should have never been graduated from any AAF [flight] school," much less pawned off on ATC because of the supposed simplicity of that command's mission. Pilots were needed everywhere in the AAF, and if a prospective fighter or bomber pilot failed his transition training to these combat aircraft, the personnel system deemed they should at least be qualified to fly transport–a point Lowenthal challenged.

The last group identified were those who came to ATC "under more or less duress," having been civilian instructors at the AAF's primary training schools when the Civilian Pilot Training Program ended, giving them the choice of either joining ATC or being drafted. Because these men were motivated to join ATC only so they could avoid possible service as infantrymen, Lowenthal claimed they were also prone to a certain degree of anxiety neurosis, being insufficiently motivated to sustain the rigors of Hump flying.[36]

Lowenthal found that older pilots were more apt than younger pilots to contract "humpitis." A survey of records showed that while only 11 percent of those who served in the ICW were thirty years old or older, that demographic represented almost a third of those pilots deemed psychologically unfit for duty; similarly, while pilots thirty-five years old or older represented only 4 percent of the wing's flyers, over 17 percent of this age group was deemed unfit for duty by the surgeon's office. Lowenthal's study attributed this to the fact that many older men had families (and thus were "risk averse"), lacked the required physical stamina to regularly endure the Hump's high-altitude, unpressurized environment, or simply did "not fare well on the diet which was served in Assam" and suffered from chronic indigestion or diarrhea. Regardless of age, those who reached "an anxiety state" displayed symptoms that started with a "lack of eagerness to fly," followed by an "out and out fear of flying, nervous tension; loss of appetite, restless sleep and increased fatigability, irritability and discontentment which were contagious and deleterious to the morale of other personnel, and loss of weight." If these symptoms were noticed early enough pilots could be rehabilitated by rotation to non-Hump missions, but if they were overlooked for too long, pilots would crumple and be useless for service for the remainder of the war in any theater of service.[37]

Alexander first began noticing this phenomenon among his flyers in January 1943, but solid figures for flight disorders were not recorded until the start of the following year. From January 1944 to October 1945 the ICW began tracking what it broadly called "flight disorders" in three categories. The first was aero-otitis, which referred to eardrum and sinus problems; frequent high-altitude flight also exacerbated flying fatigue cases and precipitated respiratory illnesses that weakened the immune system. The monthly average of crewmen who suffered from some form of aero-otitis was 16 percent. This preventable condition was treated with ephedrine, a remedy that was often in short supply in the theater.[38] The second disorder was flying fatigue, which usually resulted from flying between 100 to 150 hours per month; it affected a monthly average of 13 percent of the ICW crewmembers in 1944 and 1945. Significant is the fact that many of these cases were self-induced, especially during periods when, as will be covered later, men were rotated back to the United States based on a fixed number of flying hours rather than a number of months of required service. Crewmen often flew as much as possible as rapidly as possible so they could return home as soon as possible–often inducing their own "flying fatigue." The last category of disorder was "anxiety states," a label that referred to any of the neuropsychological problems that prevented men from flying for emotional reasons. The monthly rate here averaged just fewer than 3 percent; when translated into raw numbers, the monthly average was 141 crewmen.

As would be expected, there was a close correlation between fatigue and anxiety, both statistics climbing and falling together (see figure 11), Additionally, the peak period for both of these diagnoses was the second half of 1944, spiking in November when five out of ten ICW crewmembers were, at some time during the month, diagnosed with fatigue. The specific reasons for this will be covered later, but suffice it to say that the pressure for commanders to increase Hump deliveries while supporting the China-based B-29 attacks on Japan as well as Chennault's Fourteenth Air Force (one that was still reeling from the Japanese massive Ichi-go offensive in the spring of 1944), combined with the crewmen's

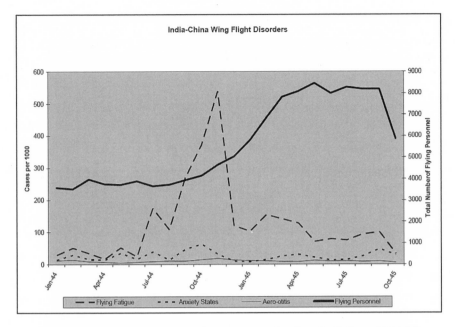

FIGURE 11. Flight Disorder Rates, January 1944–October 1945. *Source:* USAAF, ATC, ICD, Historical Section, *Medical History of the India-China Division of Air Transport Command.*

desire to accumulate flying time as fast as possible—all merged to make for a very weary group of Hump fliers in the fall of 1944.

Finally, how does "humpitis" as a condition confined to the ICW compare with the disorders affecting crews who flew combat missions in bombers? Both groups of fliers contained those who suffered from emotional disorders and had to be either temporarily removed from flying for rehabilitation or permanently grounded altogether. Bomber crews in the Eighth Air Force recorded emotional casualties numbering 42.7 per 1,000 men between 1943 and 1945, a number understandably higher than the overall U.S. Army rate of 36.7 per 1,000 men for the duration of the war.[39] In light of this rate, the ICW average of 25.5 per 1,000 men for the last two years of the war is noteworthy from two perspectives. First, one would expect the Eighth Air Force to have a larger number of emotional casualties: bomber formations would return to bases after missions, during the Eighth's darkest period, with nearly two out of ten airplanes missing. Examples like the two raids on Schweinfurt serve as reminders of the harrowing nature of World War II aerial warfare. But from a different vantage point the Hump's number of emotional casualties—though only 60 percent of that suffered by the Eighth Air Force—is remarkably high considering the fact that the weather and terrain were the airlift's most consistent dangers, not enemy flak or fighters. As Lowenthal remarked at the beginning of his report, the Hump's dangers were "real" dangers that surpassed the expectations of a group of men who carried to India an airline pilot mentality wrapped in a military uniform.

MORE AIRPLANES FOR THE INDIA-CHINA WING

At the beginning of March Arnold notified Alexander that brand new C-46s would be delivered to India rather than more worn out C-47s. Ten C-46s would be sent immediately, with thirty in place by mid-April; ten more C-46s would be delivered per month for the two following months so that fifty would be in place by the end of June.[40] Arnold's decision was an abrupt shift from the infusion of planes he promised Alexander when he was in China just four weeks earlier, and on its surface it seemed generous. But in reality it was done to shore up a logistical shortfall that resulted from the twin problems of a misinformed president and the AAF's worldwide shortage of C-47s.

When Roosevelt ordered the 308th Bomb Group to China that spring, he was told that the China-based heavy bombers would be able to strike enemy targets on the Continent (and eventually the home islands), all the while supporting themselves by flying their own supply missions back and forth over the Hump.[41] This was not possible, though, as the bombers would need regular airlift support to resupply the necessary bombs and fuel for their missions—just as Operation Matterhorn's B-29s would also need regular airlift support a year later. In his zeal to advocate his air strategy for China, it is likely that Chennault, known for being a poor logistician, wrongly gave the president the impression that the bombers could be self-sustaining and could support their own airlift needs.[42] However, when Roosevelt was notified that the 308th would be siphoning off regular supplies flown to China, he ordered an additional thirty aircraft to the Hump in a move probably intended to stymie any anticipated complaints by the generalissimo. But this, too, was a problem, as thirty extra C-47s were nowhere available for the tasking. Eisenhower, the designated Allied commander of Operation

Husky, the invasion of Sicily planned for that summer, had recently increased his desired transport complement, requesting five additional troop carrier groups (a total of 260 C-47s) for his paratroop divisions; without the additional planes his paratroopers would be forced to deploy to Africa at only two-thirds strength. Additionally, Gen. Douglas MacArthur was asking for fifty-two more transports to continue his operations in the southwest Pacific, while Gen. John DeWitt was asking for twenty-six planes to move troops to defend the Aleutians from a possible Japanese attack.[43] Because of these more pressing requirements, Marshall firmly advised the president to delay his order for the extra Hump transports but was rebuffed by FDR, who claimed he was confident that Marshall and Arnold could dig up the additional planes.

The extra transports were found, but not of the type expected. To deal with the rampant shortage of C-47s, Arnold called on Burdette Wright, a longtime friend and president of Curtiss-Wright, the company that built C-46s. Air Transport Command had been working with Curtiss to iron out production problems, but even as late as mid-February the command was complaining that predelivery inspections were overlooking numerous problems, which had to be repaired if ATC was ever going to take delivery of the transports. Then just three weeks later Arnold decided to send the fifty C-46s mentioned above to India, being assured by Wright that the planes could be made ready for overseas duty in a matter of weeks and thus solving Arnold's near-term shortage of transports. Unfortunately, though, the planes were not ready to be handed over to ATC at the end of March as Wright had promised, and problems with the prematurely delivered aircraft would persist throughout the rest of 1943, proving fatal when mixed with the dwindling experience level of the ICW aircrews.[44]

There is no reason to believe that Arnold was intentionally negligent in this matter. He routinely issued orders that were often sweeping in effect, leaving his staff to work out the details. And since there is no record of his discussions with Wright on the question of the C-46s, the two likely discussed the affair over the telephone, with Arnold being sufficiently convinced that his friend would hold up his end of the agreement. Problems aside, Arnold's commitment to send the new planes to Alexander was significant, as it represented over half the entire C-46 fleet at the time. But the air chief expected results from his decision, telling Alexander, "It's your baby now and it is up to you to see that it works."[45] Alexander

FIGURE 12. New C-46 Crossing the Hump. *Courtesy AMCHO.*

was encouraged by the news, replying, "The receipt of heavy transports here will do more to increase the tonnage to China and boost the morale of aircraft crews than you may possibly imagine." The C-46's cargo capacity—nearly double that of the C-47—would increase the tonnage per trip and the newer, more spacious aircraft was sure to be more enjoyable to fly once all the "bugs" were worked out. Moreover, he had notified Hal George two months earlier that the C-47s had trouble climbing above icing levels and were "entirely unsuitable for operations on this route."[46] Alexander was upbeat and hopeful for the prospects of higher tonnage forecasts and boldly exclaimed, "Weather and Japs only can stop this show now."[47] Little did he know the near-term problems the new airplanes would cause.

Arnold's decision to send most of the AAF's newest transports to India, which was intended to raise Hump tonnage, was also a result of Chennault getting his way with Roosevelt in arguing for a separate numbered air force in China. The Fourteenth Air Force was officially activated on March 10, but this was more of a formality than anything else, as Roosevelt was fairly convinced by the close of the Casablanca Conference that Chennault offered the greatest prospects for a China-based U.S. offensive against the Japanese. Stilwell disagreed, claiming that airfields were vulnerable and could be easily overrun by Japanese troops; Chennault would eventually prevail because he offered the greatest prospect of reward with only minimum investment. Additionally, Chennault continued to press his case by means of two separate paths into the White House that completely bypassed Stilwell and the War Department—to the frustration of both. First, Chennault's esteem with the Chiangs meant he could suggest something about U.S. strategy to the generalissimo that would invariably make its way to foreign minister T. V. Soong in Washington, who himself enjoyed a close personal relationship with Harry Hopkins, a man very close to the president. Second, Roosevelt, taken as he was by Chennault's panache, encouraged the airman to contact him directly should he have specific troubles in China, a move characteristic of the president, who frequently showed little regard for the formalities of the military chain of command. Chennault was known to have passed personal letters to Roosevelt by attaching them to correspondences that his executive officer, the well-known journalist Joe Alsop, was mailing to the president's secretary, Grace Tully (Chennault also famously passed a letter to Roosevelt through Vice President Wendell Willkie while the latter was touring China).[48] And while the creation of the Fourteenth Air Force was a gain for Chiang and Chennault, it was a loss for Stilwell, whose strategy for China—centered on the recapture of Burma—was muted by Chennault's air strategy for the remainder of the war.

PROBLEMS WITH AIRFIELD CONSTRUCTION

Alexander's springtime hopefulness had turned sour by April, with heavy rains all but stopping flights the last week of March. He told C. R. Smith, "The March tonnage figures to China are ridiculous"; only 2,035 tons had been delivered by the 24th, a figure far short of Arnold's goal.[49] Two weeks later Alexander sent a lengthy memo to Arnold warning that despite the infusion of new aircraft, tonnages would still remain low due to a listless British attitude toward completing the fields.[50] "There are today in all Assam available to this Wing, only 2 paved runways and 14 hardstandings from which to operate 43 B-24's and C-87s and 103 Douglas transports. All airdromes are unfinished, and the monsoon's rains have started," he wrote. Stilwell had gotten involved with General Wavell, the

British commander in India, but Alexander was still not encouraged, stating he expected no improvement "unless a powerful hypodermic is injected into British government construction agencies in India," especially as Alexander had been notified that Wavell took orders only from his own chain of command and that "it will require instructions from London to produce action here."[51]

Ten days later Arnold contacted Field Marshal Sir John Dill, the chief of the British Joint Staff Mission in Washington, reminding him that some time earlier Arnold had asked Dill to take action to speed up this construction. "This you kindly agreed to do" was Arnold's terse prompting, asking Dill to "expedite the construction of these new airdromes" or else witness stunted deliveries over the Hump.[52] Then, just days before the start of the Trident Conference in Washington, Arnold fell ill with a painful arrhythmia, causing his heart rate to reach 160 beats per minute. Marshall ordered him to stay in the hospital during the conference and appointed no replacement for Arnold. The matter of airfield construction rarely came up during the formal conference proceedings, a likely indication of Arnold's absence (Sir Charles Portal was the lone airman at the conference).[53] Instead, the British failure to stay on schedule with the airfields was handled outside of the conference: Stimson politely asked Churchill to tend to the matter because the airlift's growth depended on the "keenest concentrated effort in bringing in the fields"[54] The Americans were really at the mercy of the British to accelerate airfield construction; aviation battalions were dispatched from the United States to India in June, but transit time for these heavy units pushed back their usefulness to late autumn. Yet something happened at Trident that would go much further in helping the airlift than simply the construction of seven transport airfields, for it was at this conference that the Hump became a focal point of Allied strategy.

THE TRIDENT CONFERENCE

Roosevelt wanted to meet with Stilwell and Chennault before the conference, so both flew back together to Washington at the end of April to each argue for his own plan. They met in Marshall's office on the morning of the 30th. Chennault made his case first, proposing what was only a slight revision of the initial air plan he had presented to Roosevelt in a personal letter the previous October. Claiming that he needed 400 to 450 aircraft for his new Fourteenth Air Force and between

4,000 and 7,000 tons of Hump deliveries per month, he proposed to conduct a three-phased air campaign against the Japanese that would culminate with an attack on the home islands with heavy bombers. The first phase would focus on attaining control of the skies over China, something he felt could be done in sixty days in light of his past success as the AVG commander as well as the small size of the Japanese air force in China. The second phase called for the bombing of Japanese riverine transports, railroads, and coastal shipping to halt the flow of enemy supplies into China's interior. The third phase was to start in November and would culminate in the heavy bombardment of Japan itself, a campaign expected to be fruitful for the Americans, who had been recently studying the inflammability of Japanese target cities.[55]

Stilwell agreed that airpower could do great harm to the Japanese but again countered with his standard concerns, fearing that such an offensive by Chennault would provoke a Japanese ground assault that airpower would be unable to halt. Stilwell also wanted to see the United States train and equip 120 Chinese divisions to march east and push the Japanese off the coast, something that was unrealistic due to Chiang's dictatorial style and the makeup of the Chinese army, with its lack of 120 divisions that were even nominally loyal to the generalissimo. Regardless, Stilwell was dogged in his desire to motivate the Chinese to fight, even to the point of attempting to shroud the particulars of Hump deliveries; when Alexander briefed him on ATC's December 1942 plan to increase Hump deliveries to 50,000 monthly tons, Stilwell asked the airlift commander to keep the plan's details a secret, fearing that their disclosure "if fully known to the Chinese, would definitely commit them to a policy of inaction which would subvert the principal effort and objective of the United States in China." Stilwell also feared that knowledge of increased aid flown over the Hump would do nothing to slow down the flourishing black market in Yunnan Province, but would instead "increase the size of fortunes made from the sale of Lend-Lease materials," which would "increase the cupidity of certain influential Chinese and forever disappoint any hope of seeing Chinese armies with American arms take the field."[56]

The group broke for lunch, and Marshall, Stilwell, and Chennault met with Roosevelt that afternoon. There is no written record of the discussion, though it is likely that the president opened by sharing his views on the war in China, views that would already be skewed toward Chennault. According to Barbara Tuch-

FIGURE 13. Maj. Gen. Claire Chennault (left) and Gen. Albert Wedemeyer, 1944.
Courtesy U.S. Army Center of Military History.

man, Stilwell was largely despondent during the meeting; Marshall noted that the CBI commander sat with his head down and "muttered something about China not fighting," to which Roosevelt asked if he was sick and needed to be relieved. It is likely that Stilwell, a man of tremendous drive and passion, sensed that he was pleading a lost cause with the president.[57] In contrast, Chennault's biographer says of the meeting that the airman "could compensate with conviction what he lacked in depth or sophistication"; according to Chennault's memoirs, Roosevelt showed his enthusiasm for the air plan and asked if the Fourteenth Air Force could sink a million tons of shipping a year, to which Chennault replied: "If we received 10,000 tons of supplies monthly my planes would sink and severely damage more than a million tons of shipping." Roosevelt then supposedly "banged his fist on the desk and chortled, 'If you can sink a million tons, we'll break their back.'"[58]

As an aside, the Japanese high command did take notice of the growing

U.S. air presence in China, despite Chennault's wildly hopeful promises. On February 17, 1943, the Imperial General Headquarters ordered the China Expeditionary Army to "make every effort to strengthen its air operation" the following spring so as to "destroy the enemy's air strength and frustrate plans to raid the Homeland from bases in China." Air defense systems were to be bolstered, reconnaissance missions increased, fighter and bomber regiments reinforced, and the number of navigational aids boosted. Plans also included air attacks on Chennault's force in Yunnan Province. CEA commander General Hata had his staff put together "Operations Number Five," a five-month invasion of Sichuan Province by sixteen divisions designed to create a westward swath of destruction en route to capturing Chongqing, the capital, as well as Chengdu's airfields. Plans changed as the summer wore on, though, as the toll levied by the Guadalcanal campaign and the deteriorating situation in the Pacific forced the IGHQ to move five of its China-based divisions to the southwest Pacific and suspend the operation.[59]

The conference—dubbed "Trident" by Churchill—got under way on May 12 with heated discussions on the invasion of Italy dominating the agenda; deliberations on CBI strategy were also prominent, the focus of talks two days later. The Combined Chiefs met at the Federal Reserve Building the morning of the 14th to discuss the prospects of a Burma campaign, something that had been covered only slightly at Casablanca five months earlier, but one that the British were now decidedly against, chiefly because they saw it as a distraction from the more pressing war in Europe. Churchill's sentiment (recorded after the war) is indicative, as he recalls, "I disliked thoroughly the idea of re-conquering Burma by an advance along miserable communications in Assam. I hated jungles—which go to the winner anyway—and thought in terms of air-power, sea-power, amphibious operations, and key points. It was however an essential to all our great business that our friends should not feel we had been slack in trying to fulfill the Casablanca plans and be convinced that we were ready to make the utmost exertions to meet their wishes."[60] His feelings are unsurprising: the two British campaigns launched in Burma during the previous six months were dismal.

Sir Alan Brooke, the British chief of the Imperial General Staff, started things off by commenting on a plan written by Field Marshal Wavell, the senior British military commander in India. Wavell's plan was essentially written from the standpoint that any sort of conventional invasion of north Burma was bound to fail due to the numerous obstacles—to this end, it was a plan written to argue against such an operation. Brooke commented that even if such an invasion succeeded in opening the Burma Road during the fall and winter of 1943, it would still be many months before a substantial flow of supplies could be carried across that route. Adm. William Leahy, the U.S. chairman of the Joint Staff, then asked Wavell to personally comment on the problems he foresaw with such an operation, to which the latter droned on, enumerating so many reasons for not going forward with a Burmese campaign that he practically held the floor for the remainder of the meeting.

Wavell began with the problem of getting supplies to the invasion's launch point in Assam, going into detail on matters like the rise and fall of the Brahmaputra, the arcane system of ferrying railroad trains across that river (in lieu of railroad bridges), and the constraints on the cargo-limited meter-gauge trains that were designed to carry bales of tea and not heavy weapons, fuel, or munitions. He also detailed the region's rainfall record and the lack of qualified local personnel in operating road-building machinery. As far as aviation was concerned, Wavell claimed that over two hundred airfields had been constructed "at a very great effort" over the past year, which demanded "practically all of the resources which could be made available in India," but that these fields had been constructed in the interior and not in "forward areas" like Assam (due to shortages of native labor and equipment), making them ill suited for offensive operations. Topping off the logistical burdens of an Allied offensive into Burma was the matter of the Japanese, who had previously shown that they were "as good in defense as in attack"; Wavell did not wish to embark on an offensive unless his troops were prepared with "careful and lengthy training."[61]

Leahy interrupted Wavell's seemingly endless monologue to ask what then was "the best practicable action which could be taken to keep China in the war." Wavell shifted to what was to be the British default for the rest of the meeting, namely advocating the Hump airlift as a suitable replacement for the Burma Road. In the belief that the AAF was currently ferrying 6,000 tons per month with a goal of 10,000 monthly tons,[62] Wavell suggesting the airlift would be the easiest and most efficient way to continue to keep the Chinese and Chennault supplied. He also commented that if a large-scale invasion was not undertaken, that would leave all manner of men and resources to build more transport airfields, "which could achieve bigger results."[63]

Leahy then asked Stilwell to give his opinion on the matter. The CBI commander went on to argue for the absolute necessity of an Allied ground campaign supported by his U.S.-trained and equipped Chinese divisions, lest "the situation become dangerous" and the Chinese surrender to the Japanese—something he predicted would happen in the next year and a half. The meeting then devolved into disagreements over Wavell and Stilwell's arguments, the latter recording in his diary his disgust with his Allied counterparts: "British poor mouth. Can't–can't–can't."[64]

The Combined Chiefs met at the White House after lunch, this time with Roosevelt and Churchill. With the president presiding, the meeting again started with a reiteration of the importance of China to the Allied war effort. FDR stated, "It is no longer possible to simply tell China to take what she was given"; decisive action by the Allies was necessary. "An attitude of *It can't be done* could not be tolerated because it was certain something must be done," claimed Roosevelt. Churchill said he wholeheartedly agreed but—after a bit of diplomatic bantering between the two—could not see how operations in the swamps of Burma would boost Chinese morale. Instead he argued for something different, namely "a *passionate* development of air transport to China [all italics original]" as the suitable objective for the next six months. Wavell concurred, as did Air Chief Marshal Richard Peirse, the British air commander in India. Sensing the force of the British argument and Roosevelt's penchant for the expedient, Stilwell attempted to fire his last remaining salvos, but they fell largely on deaf ears. And rather than settling the debate between Chennault and Stilwell, Roosevelt suggested the Allies adopt both approaches by increasing aid *and* planning a ground offensive. This was not the first time the president tried to put an end to a disagreement by giving both parties what they wanted. He stated that he had never accepted the conventional tonnage limits on the Hump and that sufficient tonnage should be possible for *both* Stilwell and Chennault. Stilwell demurred, telling the president that he needed 2,000 tons a month for his Yoke-force (a figure whittled down from his earlier tonnage request that year); Chennault claimed he needed 4,700 monthly tons for the next four months. Roosevelt added the figures together, rounded them upward, and proposed that 7,000 tons a month be airlifted over the Hump, adding that this would surely please Chiang Kaishek as an initial tonnage goal to be met by July.[65]

The Combined Chiefs met again the following day and agreed to give first priority to building up the airlift to the rate of 7,000 tons per month by July 1 and 10,000 tons per month by September 1, along with seeing that air defense measures were in place to protect the effort. Roosevelt and Churchill spent the weekend at "Shangri-la," the president's name for Camp David in Frederick, Maryland; he would not broach the subject of the airlift again during the conference. On May 20 the Combined Chiefs again deliberated on the details of the effort to boost airlift tonnage. British Air Chief Marshal Charles "Peter" Portal wisely suggested that transport airfields be constructed to handle 20,000 tons per month, as it was easy to add more planes to the airlift but took longer to build airfield infrastructure. Admiral King, the U.S. naval chief, worried that expanding the airlift to this degree would likely increase the number of U.S. bomber attacks on Japan, something he was sure would provoke a heavy-handed Japanese attack on those airfields, a warning Stilwell regularly issued. King, a naval aviator and airpower advocate himself, usually sided with Stilwell, but he then endorsed bolstering the airlift—"though the opening of the Burma Road was a symbol to China, it might be possible to convince them that an air route would achieve the same result."[66]

By the close of the conference the Hump airlift had a tonnage goal dictated by the highest authority. For the rest of May and June the first 500 tons would go to Stilwell, with all remaining tonnage going to Chennault. Beginning July 1 the priority would switch, with the first 4,700 tons going to Chennault and the next 2,250 tons going to Stilwell (until Stillwell had received a total of 10,000 tons). Hump tonnage was to reach a rate of 10,000 tons by September 1, but the conference attendees did not discuss tonnage allocations beyond Stilwell's request of 10,000 total tons, a point of friction in the following spring. Stilwell had lost at Trident, but as CBI commander he still wielded the authority to allocate tonnages beyond what the Combined Chiefs had mandated, a feature of the lift that would cause problems once tonnages began to surpass initial expectations.

Chennault was clearly the biggest winner at the conference, securing the requisite tonnage for his isolated air force. Ironically, he had to do little talking, as Roosevelt and his administration seemed vexed by the prospects of a Chinese surrender and looked now to an aerial Burma Road as a symbol of U.S. commitment and allegiance to China. Whether the president wanted to use China to precipitate the collapse of the Japanese or simply to forge a lasting economic relationship with the largest nation in Asia, he made China a centerpiece of his wartime strategy. Churchill commented on this on the eve of Trident, stating, "The President and his circle still cherished extravagant ideas of the military power which China could exert if given sufficient arms and equipment."[67] Churchill also felt Roosevelt's fear of a possible Chinese collapse was overblown. True, conditions in China were bad, but they had been that way for some time now, and despite his constant rhetoric to the contrary, Chiang Kaishek was likely nowhere near the point of surrender. Nevertheless, it was at Trident that the Burma Road was replaced by the Hump airlift as the chief icon of Allied fidelity to China. There would be a ground offensive to reopen the road the following spring, but it would be ancillary to the larger Allied aims in the CBI as ever-increasing tonnage was airlifted across north Burma, with Roosevelt's mandated goals serving as a catalyst to the airlift's exponential growth.

Finally, the Trident Conference was the political catalyst that launched Hump tonnages to ever-increasing heights. ATC's assumption of the airlift the previous December put in place an operational infrastructure that, once developed, was capable of ferrying vast quantities, but such tonnages would go largely unrealized without the interventions of Roosevelt and Churchill, men who both favored the airlift but for different reasons. Roosevelt viewed the Hump as an operational shortcut to achieving a diplomatic end, one that would strengthen Chinese morale with only the minimum expenditure of military capital–the infusion of a handful of pilots and planes. Churchill viewed the airlift with a similar expediency, seeing it as a means of keeping Chiang's Nationalist soldiers out of British imperial holdings in Burma and India while requiring only the construction of a few airfields, not the blood of British soldiers spent in a lengthy jungle campaign. The conference also provided Alexander, the ICW commander, with all the backing he needed to overcome his unit's more pressing obstacles, but he now had fewer than six weeks to triple the tonnage his crews delivered to China. Roosevelt's mandate of 7,000 tons per month by July 1 gave the wing a fresh sense of purpose, though monsoonal rains, frequent aircraft malfunctions, and fresh Japanese "counter-Hump" operations would all conspire to frustrate the attainment of this goal.

"TEN THOUSAND TONS BY CHRISTMAS"

JUNE TO DECEMBER 1943

The Trident Conference gave the Hump airlift the political mandate it needed to become an important feature of Allied strategy. Roosevelt had been advocating the buildup of the "aerial Burma Road" since the fall of Rangoon the previous spring, but the operation was left to overcome its numerous complications with whatever resources were at the disposal of Air Transport Command. Now, however, Roosevelt would receive regular updates on the status of his order that 7,000 tons per month be airlifted by July and 10,000 tons per month by September—ambitious goals that in reality had little chance of being met on time. July and September would pass with neither mark being met; October saw tonnage peak at 7,240 tons but then depressingly slouch back to 6,491 tons the next month. Then in December—with the combination of sufficient operational infrastructure and demanding leadership—the India-China Wing easily surpassed the goal for that month, one that aimed to deliver "ten thousand tons by Christmas," and hauled 12,590 tons of supplies to China by the end of the month.[1] This near-doubling in tonnage from November to December marked the highest month-to-month percentage increase witnessed during any other period of the airlift.

No single factor was responsible for the increase. Intuitively one would assume that adding more planes and pilots to the Hump would result in more tonnage carried, but this gives short shrift to the operation's complexity. The

Hump's entire infrastructure required bolstering to include the need for more airfields (with suitable runways and hardstandings), better weather forecasting, a heftier radio network that would allow bases to coordinate arrivals and departures, more navigation aids to establish a formalized route structure, a stouter force of aircraft mechanics who were equipped with the tools and parts to effect repairs, a steady supply of P.O.L. (petroleum, oil, and lubricants) to keep the airplanes flying, reliable labor to load and unload airplanes, and a steady flow of supplies from Karachi or Calcutta to keep the planes full so they could make the most of each trip over the Hump. Even picayune factors could precipitate lengthy delays. Breakdowns on buses that carried crews the ten or twelve miles from their quarters to airfields, blown tires on landing airplanes that shut down runways and caused other arrivals to stack up into crowded holding patterns, batches of leaky carburetor floats for the C-46's radial engines, or even cooks with poor hygiene who set off outbreaks of diarrhea at bases—any one of these or similar factors had the potential to set back a day's flights. As Prussian philosopher of war Carl von Clausewitz aptly observed, "Everything in war is very simple, but the simplest thing is difficult," and he warned that an accumulation of these difficulties produced a "friction" not be easily overcome. Such was the plight of the ICW in the summer of 1943.

While politicians might bandy about Hump tonnage goals, Air Transport Command was immediately aware of the challenge posed by Roosevelt's order, requesting more airfields, more personnel, more aircraft, more in-bound tonnage, and better fighter protection. In addition to Chabua, Sookerating, Mohanbari, and Jorhat, the ICW also wanted Tezpur to be completed quickly, along with two other bases for a total of seven airfields, each with forty hardstandings. In general, the British government in India was not forthcoming in surrendering less flood-prone high-elevation swaths of land for airfields, as that land was occupied by lucrative tea plantations and would be turned over to ATC only with intervention from Churchill. In addition, over three thousand men were needed by September 1, a figure that more than doubled the size of the ICW; six hundred unskilled laborers were also needed for each base to load and unload cargo. Furthermore, ATC needed almost 120 C-46s (none were operating in India at the time of FDR's May 23 request) as well as increased tonnage along the so-called Assam line of communication, by which cargo arrived in Calcutta and made its way to Hump airfields via barge (a six-week trip), rail (a two-week trip due to the line's different gauges and the use of river ferries instead of bridges), or air.[2] Lastly, to defend the transport bases that would now occupy a 185-mile stretch of territory from Tezpur to Sookerating, the Air Staff requested an additional fighter group of three squadrons for protection, correctly anticipating the Japanese air attacks that would come that autumn.[3]

PROJECTS 7 AND 7-A

To meet Roosevelt's July goal the ICW had to increase its daily average to 233 tons. At the start of June it stood at only 78 tons. To strengthen the wing ATC launched its largest-ever mass movement of men and planes to India, aimed at building up the ICW to 535 aircrews (crews included a pilot, copilot, and radio operator) and 169 aircraft over a thirty-day period. Dubbed "Project 7,"[4] the plan was audacious, a fact that Arnold, George, Smith, and Alexander recognized; it was intended to double the ICW's manpower and airplane fleet, making it the size of the three largest U.S. airlines combined.[5] Arnold's order of March 4 to send C-46s to India was merged with Project 7 and was already running behind schedule when the first of the new transports, flown by civilian pilots, arrived in Karachi on April 21. It took over seventy-five hours of flight time for the airplanes to get from Miami to Karachi, and most were arriving in India overdue for the periodic inspections that were required every one hundred hours. Furthermore, because many of the pilots in India had no experience in the C-46, the ICW was forced to set up a transition school at Gaya to teach C-47 pilots how to fly the new airplane, a necessary nuisance that reduced the number of planes and pilots available to fly the Hump.

The size of Project 7 also required more planes and pilots than ATC had available to maintain its normal schedule of worldwide traffic. ATC was still responsible for ferrying combat aircraft to foreign theaters but could not concurrently sustain these missions, the Project 7 movement, and the additional crews that were being permanently assigned to the ICW. Requirements for combat aircraft for the invasion of Sicily were mounting in June and July—ATC ferried more airplanes abroad over this two-month period than any other similar period of 1943—so the command was forced to charter civilian airlines to do much of the work to get the Project 7 crews to India.[6] This translated into the cancellation of a number of regularly scheduled flights across the North and South Atlantic that resulted in a serious reduction in the import of certain materials like mica, a strategic mineral used as an insulator in high-voltage electrical equipment.[7]

Project 7 did succeed in boosting the number of planes and pilots needed to meet Roosevelt's goal, but it was a hollow success, as many of the planes needed substantial repairs. On June 11 Alexander reported that he had 156 transports assigned to his wing but that only 65 (or just over 40 percent) were available for Hump operations; a third of all of the fleet was unflyable and awaiting repairs, and the remaining planes were needed for the C-46 school, trans-India flights, and the in-theater movement of Project 7 personnel. He had 55 C-46s assigned to his wing, but a third of them were undergoing major repairs and modifications at long-term maintenance depots in India.[8] Many of the arriving pilots had little experience in heavy airplanes, some of them never having flown a twin-engine transport until they arrived in India. Paradoxically, the Air Staff claimed at the start of Project 7 that the Air Corps Training Command had promised Alexander's wing 220 two-engine pilots who supposedly had over a thousand hours of experience and were the "cream of their graduating classes" and "considered the most competent first pilots on two-engine aircraft available in the Air Forces."[9] This description bore little resemblance to those pilots who actually arrived in India. A third of them were only single-engine trained and required an additional thirty to fifty hours of flight training once they arrived in India. Flight qualifications aside, the rampant shortage of experience in the ICW was evident in the fact that three-quarters of all accidents by mid-July were attributed to novice flyers.[10] The problem would not go away soon: 55 of the 155 major accidents in the ICW from June to December 1943 were attributed to pilot error.[11]

Early in July Alexander realized that his wing was not going to meet the president's 7,000-ton goal and adjusted his forecast to 5,100 tons for the month. Then a week later he radioed ATC headquarters at Gravelly Point that further complications had forced him to reduce his estimate to 3,200 tons. The message was passed to Roosevelt, who, according to one witness, "made much ado about it" and asked for a detailed report that explained the problems.[12] The usual suspects of airplane malfunctions and aircrew inexperience were implicated, prompting Arnold to contact American Airlines and ask the company to divert ten of its C-87s as well as 159 flight and support personnel from the South Atlantic run to the Hump. Called "Project 7-A," the airline detachment was on its way to Tezpur ahead of schedule on July 24; arriving early and unexpected, they were forced to clear goats and cattle out of their unprepared quarters and set up their own messing facilities. The airline crews got little or no support from the army, as truck driving, furniture building, ditch digging, floor scrubbing, and latrine duties were second only to operational flight duties. Dysentery made conditions worse for the group, hitting most of the twenty-five flight crews and thirty mechanics. Nevertheless, the detachment flew its first flight over the Hump on August 2 with the help of ATC copilots, who introduced the route to the civilians.

Like their ATC counterparts, the Project 7-A crews flew only during the day, usually averaging one to two trips a day per available aircraft. The airline detachment suffered from the same shortage of spare parts as the rest of the theater, but the civilian mechanics were more seasoned than army maintenance troops in the ICW, so they were more skilled at reconditioning worn parts or improvising with other materials. The thirty American Airlines mechanics even had spare time to give additional training to army flight mechanics at Tezpur. The small detachment took a heavy blow on August 22, when they lost their first plane during a crash on takeoff that killed all five crewmembers. Two weeks later another plane was destroyed on the ground by a fire but was eventually replaced by another C-87. September saw many delays caused by required maintenance that kept at least three of the unit's nine planes grounded at any given time. With October came vast improvements as the unit's wealth of experience began paying dividends with each available airplane carrying an average of 103 tons per month. In terms of load efficiency, the airline crews consistently outhauled the ICW, averaging 91 tons per plane per month in August when their military counterparts were able to manage only about 52 tons per airplane per month. Airline experience easily translated into load efficiency: the detachment averaged 4.2 tons of cargo per trip for the length of its 120-day tour, an impressive statistic considering that a C-87 normally carried a maximum load of only 5 tons on Hump runs.[13]

Despite the influx of men and equipment with Projects 7 and 7-A, the obstacles to meeting the president's goals were still legion. The weather continued to cause problems, and monsoon rains were heavier than usual; C-46s sustained damage to their wing flaps during landings on Kunming's flooded runway in late September. The absence of pavement on taxiways made matters worse, with one

C-87 sinking up to its belly in mud at Kunming while taxiing after landing; rains at the Assam bases and the Kunming terminus were so bad that the entire route was closed down for a couple of days at the end of the month.[14] Heavy rains impaired both flight and ground operations, but when it was not raining, temperatures would soar to upwards of 130 degrees Fahrenheit, which made it impossible to work on airplanes without sustaining second-degree burns, forcing much maintenance work to be done at night. Dust reduced engine life, heat caused hydraulic fittings to fail due to the excessive expansion of fluids, and the continual lack of hardened parking spots meant that airplanes had to be shuffled around to high ground to keep their landing gear from sinking into the ground.[15]

Airfield construction was a constant bugaboo as well, even after Churchill got involved at the end of May, as the wheels of Imperial bureaucracy turned slowly. Renowned U.S. diplomat Henry Byroade, who served as an engineering officer in the CBI theater during the war and was responsible for coordinating much of the airdrome building in Assam, noted a greater sense of urgency among local authorities following the Washington Conference, though it was difficult to get much accomplished during the wet monsoon. Hasty work under such conditions also led to problems when one Assam runway completely washed out in a heavy storm due to careless construction.[16] An additional problem had to do with the rapid expansion of personnel in the ICW, which added over 2,000 men in less than sixty days and necessitated more buildings for lodging, messing, and mission planning. In early August Alexander was tempted to ask the British to relax airfield work to devote all their energies to building housing, but he was advised otherwise and told it would "not be fruitful or wise to ask the British to relax in any shape or form."[17]

The shortage of housing forced the ICW to use tents with brick floors, which Alexander considered "a menace to health" due to rampant malaria in heavy rains. In June he claimed that practically all of the men in the wing suffered from nonamoebic dysentery, which did not require hospitalization but hurt the wing in overall hours of work lost and took an expected toll on morale. Col. Don Flickinger, Alexander's chief flight surgeon, estimated that one out of five men might need to be hospitalized in August and September if adequate antimalarial measures did not reduce the mosquito population. The local food supply was poor as well, so Alexander planned to airlift food from Calcutta to feed his base personnel and their surrounding villages. This project had the added benefit of reducing the threat of food riots among the Indians.[18]

Aircraft maintenance posed one of the ICW's greatest challenges because of the continual shortage of spare parts, necessary C-46 modifications, and a lack of overall experience among the mechanics. The shortage of parts for the ICW posed the largest problem, and many planes were routinely grounded for lack of items like spark plugs, flight instruments, or generators. This was similar to what had occurred with the requisitioning of spare parts under Bissell a year earlier; shipments arriving in Calcutta or Karachi–labeled for delivery to ATC bases in Assam–were not forwarded to the ICW but rather pooled by Air Service Command (ASC), the AAF's theater supply arm. This forced mechanics at the transport bases to then requisition the parts–some of them being minor like those listed above–and wait for their arrival from the supply depots located either in Karachi or Agra, up to 1,500 miles away. Making matters worse was the fact that the transports were routinely treated with a lower priority than combat aircraft like fighters or bombers, putting the ICW at the mercy of the theater commander for badly needed parts.[19]

Another problem was the widespread "malassignment" of personnel in the ICW. According to usual army practice, soldiers were trained and coded for particular tasks needed by their units, but in the hastiness created by Roosevelt's tonnage goal, ATC headquarters was forced to send soldiers who were, say, trained as cooks but assigned as mechanics, or trained as logisticians but assigned to fill air traffic control billets. This was not a problem unique to the ICW, but it was worse there than anywhere else in the command, with 1,110 soldiers being misassigned, a number that represented a third of the ICW's enlisted force. Operations were slowed down as these unqualified soldiers needed training for their assigned tasks after arriving in India.[20]

CHANGES IN LEADERSHIP

The three months after the Washington Conference were not kind to the India-China Wing, which hauled only 2,383 tons in June, 3,451 tons in July, and 4,447 tons in August. Marshall and Arnold fed the president a constant stream of updates on the airlift's performance, but there were no easy fixes to the problems at hand. Roosevelt and Churchill met again for a week in late August in Quebec (the Quadrant Conference) to discuss primarily the war in Europe, though one of the matters addressed concerned the appointment of an overall Allied commander for Southeast Asia. Unhappy with the failed British foray into Burma earlier that spring, Churchill was eager to fix the disorderly command arrangement in the theater, and in doing so he and Roosevelt appointed Lord Louis Mountbatten as the head of South East Asia Command (SEAC for short, a moniker that Americans in the theater claimed really stood for "Save England's Asian Colonies"[21]). Prior to the Quadrant Conference, Chiang Kaishek had been toying with the idea of insisting on Stilwell's removal, as the two were consistently at odds and Chiang felt he had little utility for the U.S. general. The creation of SEAC changed this, though, as the command did not include China but did impose the specter of British Imperial rule over territories that were historic Chinese tributaries. As such, Chiang decided to keep Stilwell as a counterweight to the favored Mountbatten rather than push him aside and have to deal directly with the British.[22] Roosevelt was sensitive to Chiang's defensive reaction to the command's creation, so he asked Marshall and Arnold to assure the generalissimo that SEAC would help—not hinder—the war effort in China.[23] The creation of SEAC also altered the AAF's command structure in the theater; Gen. George Stratemeyer was appointed to serve as the commander of the India-Burma sector, a job that effectively gave him control of the U.S. Tenth Air Force in India but little more.

Stratemeyer got involved with trying to remove the obstacles to the Hump's success, as did Hal George, who went to India at the end of August, a trip prompted by the unlikely prospects for delivering 10,000 tons to China in September. George found nothing that surprised him while in India, though Alexander's leadership was increasingly being called into question with his failure to meet Roosevelt's goals. Stimson and Arnold sent Eddie Rickenbacker, the celebrated World War I ace, on a tour of Asia to encourage U.S. troops while also reporting on the problems with the Hump.[24] Rickenbacker's report listed eight reasons why the airlift was not meeting expectations, and chief among them was the "lack of capable and efficient management at the top."[25] Coincidently, Col. Joseph Mountain, the ATC chief of training, also went to India to seek solutions to the wing's problems, which he claimed were a result of poor supervision. His specific findings were damning. He witnessed one plane that tried to take off while its rudder lock was in place,[26] another that had to return to base an hour into its mission because the pilot discovered that it had never been refueled before takeoff, and a third with a crew who did not know how to turn on the plane's propeller deicers and were able to continue the flight only after Mountain showed the crew how so they could regain their airspeed.

Mountain's report went on to implicate Alexander and his staff for not correcting problems that he felt were "principally a result of the attitude which seemed to be prevalent in the Wing that once an order was given there was no necessity for follow up to see if it was carried out." True, the ICW was rife with maintenance problems beyond its control, but Mountain felt that Alexander was far too passive in confronting those problems. A "superstition" had sprung up among crews in July and August that something "mysterious and unknown" was causing C-46 crashes over the Hump—although the accident rate with the new planes was not too different from that of the C-87 (when compared using ton-miles flown). The influx of new fliers accompanied by the subsequent grounding of airplanes also gave rise to a spate of idle crews, which helped blow rumors out of proportion during casual conversation in the mess tent and around the poker table. One contributing factor here was the presence of dozens of navigators—there would be over 240 by October[27]—who were assigned to the wing but rarely used. Instead of sending these men back to the United States for duty elsewhere, Alexander felt it was unwise to relieve personnel while he was not meeting his tonnage quota, even if those men were trained for jobs of little use to the outfit.[28] Perhaps the largest blow to morale was the lack of a clear-cut policy stating just how long crews would have to stay in India; a rumor had sprung up that men would be allowed to rotate after a year, but during his visit Rickenbacker told the men that they should be prepared to stay in the theater for "a long, long time." Rickenbacker's talks were intended to boost morale. They did the exact opposite.[29]

Some of the problems Mountain identified were clearly out of Alexander's control, but his general observation of a lack of strong leadership in the ICW was on the mark. Even Col. Robert Love, ATC's deputy chief of staff and a close friend of Alexander, discretely told Hal George he thought it best if Alexander were replaced because the ICW commander was trying to run the entire operation from his headquarters rather than delegate responsibility to other agencies in the wing. "Alec is trying to keep too much in his own mind and not relying on the personnel he now has," wrote Love to George while the latter was inspecting the ICW in early September. Love's assessment was that "Alec has not realized the change that has come over the Staff with the growth of the Wing's activity" and that "the growth of this operation has been so immense and so rapid that Alec has not been able to keep up with proper administration, and in a desperate attempt to do this he has not delegated jobs to good men and forgotten about them until something went wrong."[30]

During George's September visit to India he brought Col. Thomas Hardin, the hard-charging prewar vice president of TWA and most recently the commander of the Central African Sector of ATC's Middle East Wing. Hardin went to India at the behest of C. R. Smith; the two had known each other since working together in Texas at Southern Air Transport in the mid-1920s, and it was Hardin who first taught Smith how to fly.[31] The two also worked together at American Airlines until Roosevelt appointed Hardin chairman of the Independent Air Safety Board (an antecedent of today's National Transportation Safety Board) in 1938. Two years later he took the job at TWA and stayed there until Smith cajoled him into joining ATC in May 1942. Unlike Smith, Hardin had military experience, serving first as a civilian transport specialist on the Mexican Punitive Expedition in 1916, then enlisting in the Signal Corps in 1918 and serving in France at the end of World War I. He earned his wings in the Air Reserve in 1922 and went on to organize Texas Air Transport in Fort Worth, the first contract air mail company in the Southwest.[32]

Hardin was known as a man able to handle tough jobs, though usually making few friends in the process. "C. R. feels that for an operating job under difficult conditions, Hardin may be our best man," wrote Love to George before moving Hardin to the Hump.[33] Smith was correct, as the demanding Hardin tolerated few excuses for poor performance. By late summer the ICW was divided into two sectors (similar to the arrangement a year earlier), with the west sector running trans-India loads and the east sector managing the Hump. Then on October 15 Brig. Gen. Earl S. Hoag replaced Alexander, but more significantly, Hardin was appointed the Eastern Sector commander. He talked the Tenth Air Force into giving him a stripped and worn-out B-25 that he used to fly to the Assam bases, regardless of the weather and sometimes with no copilot, where "he would arrive breathing fire because something had not been done or had been done wrong."[34]

FIGURE 14. Brig. Gen. Earl Hoag (left) with Gen. Brehon Somervell, July 1945. *Courtesy Harry S. Truman Library and Museum.*

Edwin Lee White, a veteran of this period of the Hump's history, records that despite Alexander's micromanagement, the Hump was still a "pilot-run airline," with pilots deciding how much cargo they were willing to carry and when they would depart and return. This abruptly changed in mid-September when Hardin was appointed the sector commander of the Hump run; he immediately set loading and load placement standards and disciplined pilots who failed to fly according to schedule. The most famous piece of Hump lore regarding Hardin is that, after assuming command of the sector, he supposedly flew a mission to China and back and declared upon landing at Chabua that "there was no weather on the Hump," nor would there ever be unless he said it was so. The story is likely to be apocryphal—Hardin was merely demanding, not maniacal—though it is true that once he took charge, pilots had to get supervisory permission to cancel a mission on account of weather and base commanders were held accountable for local performance. White records a firsthand anecdote that is telling:

I was with him on one trip from Calcutta to Chabua in his sinister B-25. We stopped at one field; it could have been Tezpur. The base commander, in accordance with the best military tradition, met the plane. Colonel Hardin said, "Pack your bags and come with me. I will be here about twenty minutes gassing up." "Yes sir," said the Commander, and hustled off. In about fifteen minutes he came with his B4 bag, climbed aboard and we took off. We landed at—let's say Jorhat, and again the Base Commander met us. Colonel Hardin stepped out, and greeted him by saying, "Colonel X, this is Colonel Z. He is relieving you at once. Pack your bags, take the next available transportation to New Delhi and wait there for further orders." There was nothing to say. He saluted and walked off. Colonel Z took his B4 bag and followed. We climbed back into the B-25 and left for Chabua. I asked the colonel, "What happened?" "Two weeks ago I pointed out a number of things wrong with maintenance there. Colonel X did not get them corrected. I think Colonel Z will." The subject was closed.[35]

Hardin came to be both feared and respected. He made his presence regularly felt at the six scattered bases under his jurisdiction, often confining his mornings to desk work at Chabua and his afternoons to flying to Mohanbari, Sookerating, Jorhat, Misamari, and Tezpur, which earned him the reputation as one who never asked his men to do something he himself was not willing to do.[36] He also was not one to let military regulations stand in the way of mission performance; while ASC routinely demanded strict adherence to all repair regulations, Hardin relied on his two decades of experience in running commercial companies, ignoring these standards when they became too cumbersome for field conditions. Smith spent a month in India inspecting the ICW at the end of 1943 and said of Hardin, "He has probably broken by now most of the Air Force rules about operations . . . if Tech Orders were now enforced here, I doubt that there would be an airplane in the air."[37]

September ended with the ICW still well short of Roosevelt's objective, hauling only 5,125 tons. The president was apologetic to Chiang in July after the failure to meet the 7,000-ton mark, stating, "I have been disappointed about the amount of material getting over the mountains."[38] T. V. Soong kept up the pressure on the administration nonetheless, reminding Roosevelt of the promise to

FIGURE 15. Brig. Gen. Thomas O. Hardin, 1944. *Courtesy AMCHO.*

supply Chennault's air offensive. Soong claimed that the attacks were "vital to the security of the great China base thus far preserved for the United Nations against heavy odds" and that should such an offensive fail to be executed or supplied, "the outcome will be very grave. What is needed is little and the stake is great."[39] The AAF hoped to start a B-29 bombing offensive at the end of 1943, but in October Arnold notified the president that the plane's production was running behind schedule due to labor problems, prompting a testy note from Roosevelt to Marshall: "I am still pretty thoroughly disgusted with the India-China matters. The last straw was the report from Arnold that he could not get the B-29s operating out of China until March or April 1944. Everything seems to go wrong. But the worst thing is that we are falling down on our promises every single time. We have not fulfilled one of them yet."[40] Despite the president's malaise, October's tonnage exceeded 7,000 tons and 10,000 tons looked within reach. But it was also in October that the Japanese Air Force in Burma began to take notice of the steady stream of U.S. transports and sought to halt it.

THE IJAAF RESPONDS

The Japanese recognized early on that U.S. airpower was playing a role in the theater and took both covert and overt strides to retard its growth. In June 1943, Japanese agents hired a twenty-one-year-old Chinese man in Anhui Province to provoke anti-U.S. sentiment among the Chinese locals through the distribution of leaflets demanding recourse for the supposed unequal treatment of Chinese by U.S. servicemen. The Japanese gave him a budget to execute the plot, but he was captured in Chongqing by Nationalist authorities at the end of August before it was launched. Had it been successful, he was promised $100,000 (in the Nanjing regime's puppet currency); instead he was shot by a Chinese firing squad.[41]

In another unconventional approach to interdicting the Hump, the Japanese reportedly set up false homing beacons that were designed to mimic the Americans' actual route of flight but whose placement would lead the transports off course, causing them to crash—though the spartan conditions under which IJA units in north Burma operated makes these reports questionable at best. A more conventional approach to cutting the Hump, though, was the IJAAF's assault on Hump transports that began in October 1943. According to Masa Tanaka, a 5th Air Division staff officer, the IJAAF in Burma was tasked with attacking the Hump that autumn as part of a larger move to wrest air superiority from the Americans in Southeast Asia.[42] The first transport shot down over the route was a C-87 piloted by Capt. John Perry en route from Yangkai (China) to Jorhat on August 9. No one witnessed the attack, but two radio operators in the area heard calls from the crew saying they were under attack and were looking for clouds to try to hide from the fighter, but the transport was never heard from again.[43]

Two months later the 50th Sentai launched Operation Tsuzigiri ("Street Murder"), which focused on the Hump airlift by sending eight Ki-43s to Myitkyina as a staging base for missions that hunted transports in the vicinity of Sumprabum, Burma, a town about fifty miles south of Fort Hertz. Japanese sources claim the 50th shot down a C-47, a C-46, and a C-87, all on October 13; U.S. sources confirm the C-47 and C-87.[44] The fighters refueled at Myitkyina, then quickly returned to their home base of Mingaladon, anticipating a counterattack. The 50th attacked again on October 20 using the same scheme, this time shooting down a Sookerating-based C-46 about forty-five miles south by southwest of Fort Hertz and destroying another C-46 three days later about thirty miles southwest of the earlier kill.[45]

The spate of Japanese attacks prompted a response by the Americans. Chennault contacted Col. William Fisher's 308th Bomb Squadron to launch a deception mission on the 27th in which a few B-24s would fly in a loose formation along a route that mimicked that flown by Hump transports. Because of the similarities between the B-24 and C-87—the two planes were practically identical—Chennault hoped the Japanese would attack the bombers, thinking they were unarmed transports. Japanese Ki-43s led by Captain Hashimoto again took off from Myitkyina and attacked and destroyed a C-46 en route from Yunnanyi to Chabua. While the transport was going down, the Japanese formation spotted the 308th's B-24s; thinking them harmless C-87s, the crews dropped their external fuel tanks and attacked the Americans head-on. One of the Japanese fighters failed to part with its drop tank and had to break off the attack, while another sustained a shot that caused an oil leak and forced the pilot to land on the west bank of the Irrawaddy, only to be captured by locals. A third Japanese fighter was also hit and forced to land, but the pilot made his way on foot to a Japanese-held outpost. U.S. sources claim eight Japanese fighters were shot down by the ruse, with a total of eighteen enemy fighters destroyed by the bombers over a three-day period. This is probably an exaggeration, but Japanese sources nonetheless concede that the ploy put an end to Tsuzigiri because the 50th Sentai could not spare missions that downed only a handful of U.S. transports.[46] The operation was ended, and IJAAF units shifted their strategy by attacking Hump airfields in India and China, something they did almost thirty times throughout 1943. In December alone the IJAAF attacked Hump airfields nine times in reprisal raids designed to pay back Chennault's deadly attack on the Japanese airbase of Shinchiku on Formosa on November 25.[47]

Three points of significance are shown by this effort to attack the Hump. First, the 50th Sentai must have been aware of the broader contours of the ICW's flight schedule and preferred routes of flight. There is no record of Japanese radar in the area, and it is likely that any such equipment would have been rendered useless by the terrain, so the Ki-43 pilots had to visually locate the transports, which usually flew alone, not in a formation that would have been easier to spot. The fighters were also forced to loiter and burn extra fuel while waiting for the unsuspecting transports, attested to by the 50th's use of drop tanks on the missions. It is possible that Japanese agents in either Yunnan or Assam were able to radio the takeoff times of the transports to give the fighters a close approximation of when to expect the transports, but the Tsuzigiri missions nevertheless burned much fuel and yielded little return, destroying one or two transports during a mission when there were dozens of Hump flights a day by that October. Japanese supplies in Burma entered via the port at Rangoon, and Allied air and submarine attacks were so effective that these supplies were reduced by two-thirds in 1943, shrinking fuel stores for the Fifth Air Army overall and the 50th Sentai specifically.[48] The fuel shortage only got worse with time as Japanese logisticians were forced to supplement their fuel supply with alcohol during the Ichi-go offensive in China in the spring of 1944. At the same time the Fifth Air Army was short of its semiannual fuel requirement by almost 30 percent, even after the preattack logistical buildup.[49] In the summer of 1943 the Anglo-U.S. Combined Intelligence Committee issued a report forecasting that the Japanese would likely "appreciate that the increasing use of the air ferry service to Kunming is indicative of the building up of a serious threat to her whole position in China" and thus attack the route to stop that buildup. But depleted fuel stores in Burma rendered this difficult for the Japanese.[50]

Second, the Ki-43 was a feeble example for a mid-war fighter. It was armed with two 12.7mm machine guns firing from the engine cowling, each synchronized to fire through the propeller arc; this gave the fighter a relatively slow rate of fire. Each gun also had only 250 rounds of ammunition, and the self-sealing protection on the fuel tanks was considered "rudimentary."[51] At this stage in the war the IJAAF pilots were probably as good as their German counterparts in Europe, but the firepower from the B-24's ten .50-caliber machine guns would have been a difficult for the Japanese pilots to handle.

Third, Tsuzigiri was significant because of the location of the attacks. The wreckages of the transports all fell within a box twenty miles deep and forty-five miles wide. This is noteworthy because it gives clues as to the transport's routes of flight, as each of them was shot down well south of Fort Hertz (see figure 16). This is important for two reasons. First, Hump crews in 1942 and 1943 reportedly flew well north of Fort Hertz to avoid the Japanese air threat. Standardized routes of flight did not come into being until the second half of 1944, when reliable navigation aids made such a structure possible, but even so, unit histories, personal memoirs, and even the history of the Chabua-based search-and-rescue detachment—men who were keenly concerned with knowing crews' planned routes of flight—recorded that the safest Hump route was thirty to forty miles *north* of Fort Hertz, a path that cut across north Burma via Kumjawng Pass and Bazik Pass. But the Tsuzigiri kills were between fifty and one hundred miles *south* of this path, putting the transports within easy reach of the Japanese Ki-43s that staged out of Myitkyina. Rather than flying a route that arced north, away from the Japanese threat, these transports flew the most direct route possible between the Hump bases in Assam and the Chinese termini of Yunnanyi or Kunming.

More interesting is the fact that these five transports were not alone in selecting a direct route from departure to destination. A representative plot of all transport crashes for 1943 (with known wreckage coordinates) shows amazing consistency, with fifteen out of seventeen crashing on what approximates a direct route of flight between Assam and the bases in Yunnan (see figure 17). The only exceptions were two flights at the start of November: a C-46 flying from Mohanbari to Yunnanyi that crashed at 14,000 feet in the mountains along the border of Tibet and China on the 1st and a C-47 flying from Yunnanyi to Misamari that crashed in high terrain on the 2nd.[52] Both of these crews were clearly flying routes

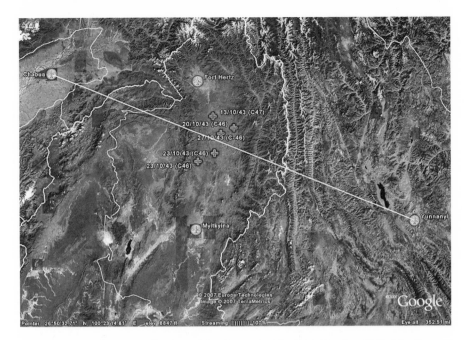

FIGURE 16. Transports Destroyed by Operation Tsuzigiri, October 1943. The five transports shot down by the IJAAF's 50th Sentai in the two-week period of October 13–27 are shown with date of crash (day/month/year) and type of aircraft. The Japanese fighters staged out of Myitkyina. The kills fall within twenty-five miles of the direct route between Chabua and Yunnanyi, approximated by the white line. All crash coordinates are based on Quinn's *Aluminum Trail* and the AAF's missing aircrew reports.

that kept them far north of the Japanese, a wise move since less than a week had passed since the last Tsuzigiri attacks on October 27. Nevertheless, crews would again resume the usual direct path once the Japanese threat subsided, flummoxing the new ICW commander, who wrote to a friend in December 1943, "The indifference of our flight personnel to the ever present threat of enemy fighters is one of the most amazing things in the world to me. The boys going over as 'sitting ducks' offer the most lucrative and perfect target in the world, which, fortunately, has been ignored as much as it has."[53] Ultimately, there are no positive figures as to the number of Hump transports shot down by Japanese fighters, but it was probably less than 5 percent of all those lost during the war, something attested to by Hoag's comment above as well as the crash plots. But what all of this does reveal is that pilots flew a route that arced in to northern Burma only when it

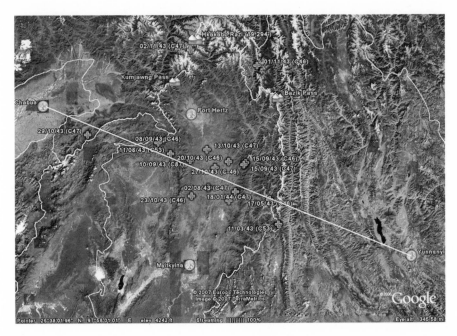

FIGURE 17. Transport Crashes, 1943. The seventeen transport crashes of 1943 with confirmed wreckage coordinates are shown with date of crash (day/month/year) and type of aircraft. The direct route between Chabua and Yunnanyi, represented by the white line, was preferred by most crews over the longer and safer route that arced north through Kumjang Pass and Bazik Pass. Note the location of Hkakabo Razi, the highest peak in Southeast Asia. All crash coordinates are based on Quinn's *Aluminum Trail* and the AAF's missing aircrew reports.

was absolutely necessary, despite the recommendation of printed flight charts. Clearly, Hump pilots were more than willing to take their chances against the Japanese fighter threat rather than against the high mountains of north Burma.

JAPAN'S "PEACE OFFENSIVE"

The Fifth Air Army's attack on the Hump was consistent with Japan's strategic aim to logistically isolate China. Reverses in the Pacific were forcing the Tojo cabinet to reconsider its China policy, and a significant shift was taking place during the Liaison Conference on September 21, 1943, with the execution of "peace operations" against Chiang Kaishek. Since the end of 1942 Tojo had sought active measures—both political and military—to bring an end to the China Incident. An end to hostilities would give the Japanese control of the length of the Chinese coastline and allow them free movement from Manchuria to Burma with the ability to shift troops between the Soviet and Indian frontiers. Additionally, ending the war in China would allow the Japanese to strengthen the Guandong Army and apply more pressure to the Soviets, who, until the Battle of Kursk in June 1943, were still on their heels against the Germans. Lastly, with Japan being a resource-poor belligerent, Tojo saw China as a possible replacement for resource-rich territories it tenuously held in the South Pacific; ending the war in China with favorable terms would solve this potential problem.[54] The terms issued at the September Liaison Conference stated that the Nationalists would not be required to declare war on the United States or Great Britain but would have to sever relations with them and demand the withdrawal of all of their troops in return for the removal of Japanese soldiers from Chinese soil except Manchukuo, a region of great industrial significance to the Japanese war-making complex. The gesture was intended to cause a rift between the Nationalists and the Allies by using the "peace enticement" (*youhe*) strategy and represented a change in Japan's political posture: the Japanese were now willing to negotiate with Chiang, having previously refused to even recognize the generalissimo's leadership in China. Prior to September 1943 the Japanese were content to settle for "surrender-inducement work" (*qufu gongzuo*), using military pressure to force Chiang's capitulation, but with the war going badly the Tojo government became more conciliatory. Sensing a shift in his favor, Chiang ignored the request for talks and instead used it to his advantage.[55]

Ever the shrewd politician, Chiang knew that the attention of foreign governments boosted his domestic and international stature. The Americans understood that timely messages from Roosevelt carried a certain persuasive power and influenced the internal workings of the Chongqing regime.[56] The Japanese could also strengthen Chiang's hand simply by seeking to parlay with him. George Atcheson, the U.S. chargé in Chongqing, reported: "According to our informant the Generalissimo, while having no thought of making any kind of peace with the Japanese, sometimes gives the appearance of not being unreceptive to such proposals because the fact that they are made to him gives him, against the backdrop of the generally deteriorating situation here, a sense of power. We are inclined to give credence to this explanation."[57]

FIGURE 18. Part of the "Aluminum Trail." *Courtesy AMCHO.*

To exert influence on Washington, Chiang used Japanese peace feelers to solicit U.S. aid. In late 1940 the Japanese offered to withdraw all their troops from China in exchange for Chiang's recognition of Manchukuo, a proposition he summarily refused while at the same time having Soong write to Roosevelt outlining "the gravity of the situation in China." The United States immediately loaned the Chinese $100 million (and the British loaned them £10 million) as another installment designed to bolster the supposedly precipitous government in Chongqing.[58]

Along with the peace maneuvers, the Japanese continued to keep military pressure on the Nationalists by launching their month-long Changde campaign in northern Hunan Province in November 1943. The campaign's explicit objective was to divert the attention of Guomindang forces in Yunnan training for possible action in Burma,[59] but it also served the general purpose of moving five Japanese divisions into crop-laden areas ripe for foraging and export. Since the start of the war in 1937, China had served as a source of food supply for export, and local Japanese commanders were rewarded for "capturing and handing to army logistics offices military materials and food belonging to the enemy."[60] Harvest-time offensives were not uncommon during a war in which Japanese units were usually required to provide for themselves, launching limited offensives designed to do little more than provide plunder and replenish supplies.[61] The late-autumn offensive culminated with heavy fighting at the Battle of Changde, which fell to the Japanese in early December, but they withdrew at the end of the month to preoffensive positions. Whatever the Japanese intentions, the offensive contin-ued to heighten U.S. fears of Chiang's possible concession to the Japanese, with Cordell Hull notifying the president that Japan "continues to make unsuccessful peace offers to Chungking" while Changde in Hunan Province was "reportedly in flames." Hull went on to report that Changsha (also in Hunan Province) would soon be attacked "with little possibility that the defense would be other than per-functory," bolstering the perception that the Nationalists were perpetually on the verge of collapsing.[62]

Hull's news reached Roosevelt during the Cairo Conference in Novem-ber, the only Allied meeting Chiang ever attended. The precarious relationship between the Soviets and Japanese prevented Stalin's attendance so Roosevelt and Churchill planned to meet first with the Chinese at Cairo the last week of Novem-ber, travel to Tehran to meet with the Soviet leader for a few days, then return to Cairo to tie up loose ends, this time without the Chinese delegation. The chief purpose of the conferences, also called Sextant and Eureka, respectively, was to hammer out the timeline of the Anglo-U.S. cross-channel invasion planned for May 1944, a date agreed upon at the Washington and Quebec conferences earlier that year but one that the British (again) wanted to postpone in favor of operations in the Mediterranean. This impacted strategy in Southeast Asia, as Mountbatten and Stilwell were planning on launching an amphibious operation in the Bay of Bengal (Operation Buccaneer) to entice Chiang to invade northern Burma to reopen the Burma Road, but the Allied invasion needed landing craft that were allocated for Europe. In all, the Cairo meetings were maddening for the Westerners, with Chiang reportedly "changing his mind about the proposed operations, confirming and withdrawing his approval in a bewildering succes-sion of orders."[63] Mountbatten later claimed that this first encounter with Chiang left Roosevelt and Churchill "absolutely mad," which might have accounted for the implied discrete order Roosevelt supposedly gave Stilwell to remove Chiang

FIGURE 19. The Cairo Conference, November 1943. *Courtesy Office of the Chief of Military History, U.S. Army.*

from power.[64] Sentiments aside, Chiang was agreeable to Buccaneer but continued to insist that the airlift to China must never be allowed to drop below 10,000 tons—a mark it had yet to reach.[65]

At Tehran a few days later, any disagreement over the date for Overlord was cleared up, thanks to Stalin's insistence that the Americans and British finally make a push in western Europe while the Soviets made a coordinated assault in the east. This, along with the U.S. insistence that the cross-channel invasion be followed by an invasion off the French Mediterranean coast, meant that all landing craft were tied up, pushing any prospect for an amphibious assault of the Burmese coast back to the end of 1944. Forced to go back on plans made just a week prior in Cairo, Roosevelt reluctantly telegrammed the generalissimo, asking if the Chinese would still be willing to invade Burma without the accompanying Allied coastal attack and assuring him that even if he was not, the United States would continue to concentrate "all air transports on carrying supplies over the hump to ground forces in China" for the possibility of Buccaneer in November 1944.[66]

Chiang was quick to take advantage of the Anglo-U.S. reversal. In a telegram sent just days after receiving news of Buccaneer's cancellation, Chiang began by commenting on Cairo's successfulness in silencing those Chinese who questioned the solidarity of the United States, Great Britain, and China. "In one stroke the Cairo communiqué decisively swept away this suspicion that we three had jointly and publicly pledged to launch a joint all-out offensive in the Pacific [of which Buccaneer was meant to be a part]." With the recent news of the offensive's postponement, though, Chiang warned that "if it should now be known to the Chinese army and people that a radical change of policy and strategy is being contemplated, the repercussions would be so disheartening that I fear of the consequences of China's ability to hold on much longer." Chiang went on to say that he was aware of the "advantage to be reaped by China as well as by the United Nations as a whole in speedily defeating Germany first"; but "the collapse of China would have equally grave consequences on the global war," and now Chiang's "task in rallying the nation to continue resistance is being made infinitely more difficult." Chiang went on to outline the only solution he saw to the dire situation:

> Because the danger to the China theater lies not only in the inferiority of our military strength, but also, and more especially, in our critical economic condition which may seriously affect the morale of the army and people, and cause at any moment a sudden collapse of the entire front. Judging from the present critical situation, military as well as economic, it would be impossible for us to hold on for six months, and a fortiori to wait till November 1944. In my last conversation with you I stated that China's economic situation was more critical than the military. The only seeming solution is to assure the Chinese people and army of your sincere concern in the China theater of war by assisting China to hold on with a billion gold dollar loan to strengthen her economic front and relieve her dire economic needs. Simultaneously, in order to prove our resolute determination to bring relentless pressure on Japan, the Chinese air force and the American air force stationed in China should be increased, as from next spring, by at least double the number of aircraft already agreed upon, and the total of air transportation should be increased, as from February of next year, to at least 20,000 tons a month to make effective the operation of the additional planes.[67]

MEETING THE GOAL

On November 30, the same day the conference in Tehran ended, the ICW closed out a most disappointing month. Delivering only 6,491 tons—11 percent less than the previous month—the wing also lost thirty aircraft to accidents. Making matters worse was the expectation that creative bookkeeping and around-the-clock operations were projected to set new records in November. Starting in October Hardin had his sector statisticians begin recording the fuel used to return from China to India—referred to as "reverse Hump tonnage"—as part of the total tonnage delivered to China. Hump flights had to fly to China with enough fuel for the return trip, whereas normal cargo missions anywhere else would be allowed to refuel at each destination. Because Hardin's transports were not afforded this luxury, he reasoned that he should be able to count the fuel they needed to return to India as part of their tonnage delivered to China, accounting for an extra 393 tons in October, or 5 percent of the month's loads. All in all, the practice was reasonable, especially considering that planes landing in China were regularly defueled if they had more fuel than they needed to get back to India—an often discomfiting practice for the aircrews.[68]

Around-the-clock operations were also expected to have remarkable effects on tonnage (Arnold even mentioned this to Roosevelt during Cairo's preconference meetings[69]), and all of the Eastern Sector bases began night flying on November 1 for their night-qualified crews. The absence of reliable runway lighting in China was what kept Hardin from issuing the order earlier (generator-powered lights were now replacing oil torches[70]), especially as he considered Yunnanyi's nearby mountains to be dangerous enough to allow night takeoffs only if airplanes had little or no loads on clear, moonlit nights and pilots had an unobstructed view of the terrain. Far from improving tonnage figures, night flying likely caused November's spike in accidents attributed to pilot error, owing to the rampant lack of flight experience in the wing and the general hazards associated with flying the route without adequate air-to-ground communications for nighttime operations (see figure 20).[71] Accident data does not delineate between day and night, but accidents caused by pilot error averaged five per month from June to October, then spiked to nineteen in November with the start of night flying—circumstantial yet damning evidence. On December 1 C. R. Smith wrote Hal George that "we are asking boys to do what would be most difficult for men

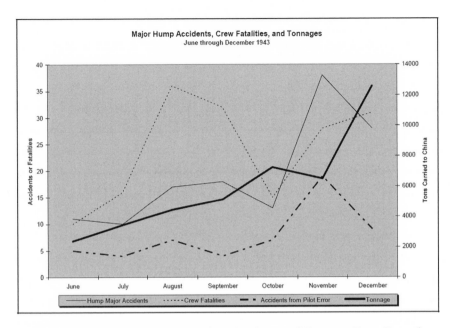

FIGURE 20. Major Hump Accidents, Crew Fatalities, and Tonnages, June–December 1943. Note particularly the jump in accidents from pilot error in November with the start of night flying. *Source:* USAAF, ATC, ICD, Historical Section, "A History of the India-China Wing, June through December 1943," pp. 451–52.

to accomplish; with the experience level here we are going to pay dearly for the tonnage moved across the hump."[72]

Pilot experience could only improve with flying time, but there were too many pilots for the number of flyable planes. A snapshot of one base, Mohanbari, on October 20 is indicative: there were 173 pilots (including both pilots and copilots) for twelve airplanes, five of which were ready to fly on a daily basis and seven that were continually undergoing repairs. The unit averaged eight trips a day (which would have used 16 pilots), which translated to an average of one flight every eleven days for each pilot, or three trips per month. As mentioned earlier, this took its toll on morale. As one inspector noted, the morale at Mohanbari was poor because "there are times when as much as two weeks elapse without a flight," and infrequent flying time did little to enhance pilot proficiency.[73]

Additionally, Hardin needed spare parts to get airplanes flying. In a paraphrase of one of his memorable quips on this matter, he likened the lack of critical parts in the wing "to a gentleman who has several sets of evening clothes, shoes and top hat but has no collar or tie. In such a case the outfit is useless."[74] To expedite the flow of spares, George inaugurated a weekly C-87 mission from the supply depot at Fairfield, Ohio, to India, likely the longest regularly scheduled route flown by anyone to date. Though only one of these flights made it to the wing toward the end of the year—most were forced by Air Service Command to stop and off-load their cargo at the depot at Agra—one of these so-called Fireball missions made it to the ICW in November, followed by several more in December, a factor that slowly helped improve the wing's number of in-commission aircraft.

Something else that helped was the addition of fifty-six airplanes to the ICW under the auspices of Project 8, ATC's plan to deliver lengths of six-inch-diameter pipe to Burma and China to build a fuel pipeline that eventually stretched from Calcutta to Kunming. The pipeline was approved by the Combined Chiefs at Quebec and was designed to serve both air and ground assets; it would follow the same route as the Ledo Road, an innovation of Stilwell's designed to eventually extend the Burma Road west another five hundred miles to Ledo in India. The road, built largely by African Americans serving in U.S. Army engineering battalions, was started in March 1942 at the railhead at Ledo, about forty miles east of Chabua. It snaked six hundred miles to Bhamo in Burma, where it would intersect with the older Burma Road and be renamed the Stilwell Road by Chiang in January 1945. By September 1943 Fort Hertz was deemed safe enough from Japanese encroachment to use it as an off-load point for piping needed by the road's engineers, so sixteen C-47s were given to Hardin specifically for the job, along with another forty C-46s intended to carry pipe to China to begin the line westward from Kunming to carry the 15,000 tons of materials needing airlift.[75] Project 8 was supposed to remain distinct from the rest of the Hump operation, but it did not take long for its tonnage figures to bleed into the regular accounting of daily Hump tonnage. As such, Hardin began using the extra C-47s for regular Hump flights the day after they arrived, as pipeline deliveries were delayed. He did the same with the extra C-46s that arrived in early December as well.[76]

The combination of more flyable airplanes (thanks to the influx of spare parts and Project 8's extra planes) and Hardin's demanding leadership led to more trips and tonnage over the Hump, finally surpassing the president's

10,000-ton mark. The ICW's entire fleet now numbered 230 aircraft, 23 more than in November with all of those added planes being either C-46s or C-87s. The Eastern Sector flew 3,155 trips in December, averaging 100 per day, nearly doubling the number flown in November; both months enjoyed good weather. To help December's "push," the Air Staff had two dozen B-24s of the Tenth Air Force remain in India to augment the airlift before their rotation back to the United States. The planes needed slight modifications to make them "Humpable" and were used mainly to ferry fuel and bombs to China, helping also to boost the airlift.[77] Morale, which had been in the doldrums with the posting of November's tonnage figures, began to lift as December's daily numbers were released, and by mid-month the slogan of "ten thousand tons by Christmas" became ubiquitous in the wing.[78] According to one witness, "Hardin was everywhere, inspecting, suggesting, encouraging and expediting the work"; he was "feared and hated by the incompetent and slack" but also "loved and respected by the competent and aggressive."[79] The tonnage mark was actually surpassed on Christmas Day, and thanks to the time difference, FDR got the news on Christmas morning. So elated was Roosevelt that he awarded the Presidential Unit Citation to the entire ICW, an award normally restricted to only combat units.

The achievement of Roosevelt's 10,000-ton mark is best viewed against the backdrop of all of 1943. The ICW had overcome innumerable obstacles, both materially and morally, in breaking through what had become a sort of "glass ceiling" in Hump tonnage; there was nothing magical about 10,000 tons save the fact that Roosevelt could now claim he had made good on his promise to Chiang in an effort to "keep China in the war." All of 1943 had been difficult because the size of the ICW was increased too fast. Curtiss-Wright C-46s that began to arrive in May and June proved to be more a hindrance than an immediate help, needing an array of modifications that should have been done before delivery from the factory. The summer's monsoon also gummed up the works, and the influx of inexperienced pilots put a further strain on the wing, with August and September being the unit's most inefficient months.

As Churchill once quipped, there are "lies, damned lies, and statistics," but the best way to summarize the variables impacting the wing's performance and compare the monthly periods from December 1942 to December 1943 is in terms of efficiency, defined as Hump trips per assigned aircraft, not tonnage (see figure

21). What becomes clear is that the Hump saw its peak efficiency in December 1942 while it was still a small operation flown by fairly experienced crews in reliable C-47s that were able to carry only a paltry 1,227 tons. This efficiency dropped in January with the addition of more C-47s (and fewer pilots to fly them—recall Alexander's call for more pilots because "an airplane doesn't need to sleep"), but then recovered the following month. More airplanes were added in March and April, but still short of pilots, many planes sat idle. May witnessed the late arrival of a few of Arnold's promised C-46s, but the monsoon got started at the same time and slow airfield construction also made operations difficult. June 1943 saw the nadir of efficiency: the wing flew fewer than four trips over the Hump per the number of aircraft assigned, a testament to the influx of unmodified C-46s and unqualified pilots. The situation remained unchanged throughout July, August, and September while pilots received extra flight training at Gaya and spare parts slowly trickled into the theater. From a low point in September, efficiency began to rise with the correction of past problems and Hardin's demanding influence on his sector's flying culture through his unique blend of airline expertise and martial coercion. October saw a jump in efficiency, which leveled in November but then spiked in December. The wing approached its efficiency marks of the previous year, but this time carrying ten times the cargo. Hardin's work earned him a month-long leave back to the United States, and Hal George and C. R. Smith both commended his efforts to Arnold, stating, "If it is possible to give credit to one man for his excellent results that are now being accomplished in the Hump operations, that one man is Colonel Tom Hardin."[80]

The increase in efficiency also came with a price in the form of 155 major accidents and 168 crew fatalities between May and December 1943. The costly trend would not change soon, either, as tonnage delivered was considered more valuable than normative safety precautions. No sooner was the 10,000-ton goal met than AAF leaders in India began warning of the dangers of striving for higher tonnage goals. George Stratemeyer in New Delhi strongly recommended against planning for more than 10,000 tons, claiming, "Any tonnage over that amount should be considered velvet."[81] But tonnage requirements would double over the next eight months, double again in five more months, and nearly double for a third time six months after that (though for slightly different reasons). Chiang had pushed too hard at Cairo, and Roosevelt was now less inclined to send supplies

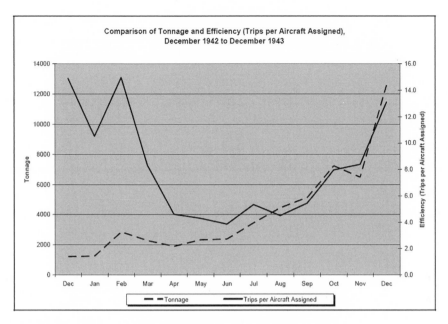

FIGURE 21. Monthly Tonnage and Efficiency. The solid line marks the number of trips flown over the Hump per the number of aircraft assigned to the ICW. *Source*: USAAF, ATC, ICD, Historical Section, "A History of the India-China Wing, June through December 1943," pp. 446–47.

simply to bolster some hazy concept of Chinese national will. Although the president was still dogged in his determination that China would play an important part in the postwar world, in 1944 China would come to be regarded as vital in terms of military strategy as a launch pad for B-29 bombers or a departure point for an invasion of Japan and, in doing so, would witness a remarkable increase in Hump tonnage.

THE HUMP GOES TO WAR

JANUARY TO SEPTEMBER 1944

The close of 1943 marked a turning point for the Hump. Roosevelt's goal of 10,000 tons per month was finally met, a point of significance if for no other reason than it represented the U.S. commitment to support China in its war with Japan. Since before Pearl Harbor, Chiang Kaishek's government had been pleading for military aid, which came in three forms: direct supply of Lend-Lease equipment to the Nationalists under the coordination of the China Defense Supply Company (CDS), the training and equipping of Stilwell's Yoke-force of Chinese soldiers preparing for the invasion of Burma, and Chennault's Fourteenth Air Force, focused on crippling Japan through China-based airpower. Stilwell and Chennault had been at odds through much of 1943, with the latter getting the upper hand in securing the president's favor—after all, an air campaign held out the promise of being a much tidier prospect than a grueling Burmese ground offensive. This "air strategy" for China was now made complete with the Hump's growing success as it served as an "aerial Burma Road." Long the icon of China's succor, this new Burma Road—now traversed in the skies at 17,000 feet—had by late 1943 become more important in *symbolic* terms than purely *material* terms. The India-China Wing's delivery of 12,590 tons in December gave Roosevelt substantial evidence to prove to Chiang that the United States stood behind its Chinese ally, evidence intended to sustain Chinese national will, which seemed perpetually on the verge of yielding to Japanese terms. Ironically, though, the attainment of the tonnage goal coincided with a shift in U.S. policy that no longer valued China for China's sake but instead for its geographic proximity to Japan. The Hump was squarely in the middle of this shift, as the airlift's mission transformed from one designed to sustain China to one bent on the destruction of Japan by securing the western flank in the larger war in the Pacific.

To meet the new objective, the airlift would grow over the next nine months—from January through September 1944—in terms of both size and institutional maturity. Operating procedures would be standardized, routes of flight between India and China would be formalized (thanks to the installation of ground-based navigation aids), and the wing would be reorganized to mimic the layout of a civilian airline company. The airlift would double in size, and the stream of supplies flowing in on the Assam line of communication (LOC) would correspondingly increase, though in fits and starts. The first nine months of 1944 also saw the Hump in the middle of a land war in Asia as the target of Japanese ground offensives in India and China that nearly blocked the airlift altogether. Lastly, the most significant tonnage-boosting factor in the Hump's forty-four-month history would also take place during this period when Stilwell's offensive pushed Japanese forces out of central Burma, allowing flights to fly direct from Calcutta to Kunming and ushering in 1945's "era of big business."

THE QUESTION OF EXPANSION

Meeting the 10,000-ton objective provoked words of caution from those within the airlift community. Earl Hoag felt that the Hump's saturation point lay somewhere between 12,000 and 15,000 tons and warned against any attempt to strive for 20,000 tons per month. C. R. Smith, back at Gravely Point after his seven-week visit to the ICW, was equally cautionary in his trip report: "The target of 10,000 tons having for several months been met, there is the danger that many in AAF will believe that the job is 'in the bag.' Nothing could be farther from the truth; there remains much to be done to get this operation out of the 'emergency' category, and diminish the cost of the operation in lives and airplanes. For a long time to come this operation will require the interested attention of AAF and action must be taken to cure some of the existing deficiencies in the India-China transport operation."[1]

The Hump was in the "emergency category" at the start of the year, but this would not diminish the airlift's expectations as Stilwell ordered Stratemeyer to renew his survey of the airlift's maximum tonnage.[2] The Air Staff had in fact been considering a 20,000-ton objective as early as December 13, 1943, most likely as a result of the influence of Soong and Chennault. Regardless of the determining factors, the remainder of the airlift's history would be characterized by an operational inertia that viewed tonnage as an end in itself rather than as a means to an end.

Many of the problems present the previous summer still persisted into the new year. The Assam LOC was still weak; several bases halted flying in the first quarter of 1944 for days at a time due to fuel shortages. Fuel was the most frequent cargo on Hump flights, and its shortage kept flights on the ground either because the planes could not fly or because they had no cargo to carry. This did little to assuage the push for monthly tonnage, though, as Hardin remarked, ". . . words fail me. When you run out of cargo haul that goddam rock off. That would be helpful."[3] The Assam LOC had been a perennial problem largely because the Americans were at the mercy of Imperial administrators who probably echoed the prevailing British disenchantment with the United States' strategic view of China's place in the war. Stratemeyer had complained of fuel shortage forecasts as early as the previous fall, involving the U.S. Army's chief logistician, Lt. Gen. Brehon Somervell, who coordinated the militarization of both the Assam railroad and the Port of Calcutta, freeing the line from the influence of local politics.[4]

The militarization of the LOC meant an increased flow of supplies to the Assam airfields and forced the use of more unskilled local laborers. Each of the bases employed roughly 425 Indians, half the size of a state labor battalion, with one out of five workers absent on any given day. This left about 340 to work the wing's round-the-clock cargo loading and refueling duties, or just over a hundred to cover each of the day's three shifts. Since it took upwards of twenty laborers to handle each arriving or departing aircraft, this meant that a maximum of four airplanes could be serviced at any given time. To increase the throughput of airplanes, Hoag wanted to double his force of laborers, either locally (thus needing British involvement) or with the import of Chinese workers that he deemed as being "physically stronger and perhaps a little more efficient in this work than the Indians in Assam." Earlier Hoag had notified Washington that African American troops would also suffice to fill the billets but stated that he was not optimistic this request would be met as the War Department was restricting the flow of all service troops to the CBI until the war in Europe was in hand.[5] The need for more ground-handlers did not soon evaporate, and Hardin again requested 2,500 African American soldiers for the Assam fields in April, asking that the first 1,000 of this group be sent immediately so as to free up the hundreds of mechanics and other technicians who were being pulled away from their regular jobs to work on loading and refueling duties.[6]

AIR TRAFFIC CONTROL

On the flying end of the airlift, a more robust air traffic control system was badly needed not only to prevent crews from getting lost but also to manage the larger fleet of planes crossing the Hump. Hardin recognized this weakness soon after taking command of the Eastern Sector, telling Hoag he thought the lack of navigation aids (or "navaids") was the weakest part of the entire operation and was to blame for the run of airplane crashes in November 1943.[7] At the start of 1944 aircrews were still flying their favorite routes to and from China, a problem for two reasons. First, this meant it was impossible to smooth the sequence of arrivals, so many planes had to hold over Kunming for hours as a result of airfield congestion, burning precious fuel and flight time that could be used for additional flights on a given day. In one extreme example a crew was forced to hold for four and a half hours while arrivals and departures were sorted and given clearance to land or depart.[8] The lack of a reliable route structure also meant that many crews got lost and either had to bail out after burning all their fuel or crashed in high terrain. As previously mentioned, low-power beacons served as rudimentary position markers, not a true navigational aid, and only validated a crew's position along the way; radio ranges instead operated as the backbone of the airway structure.

Unlike the portable ground-based navaids used today, radio ranges were made up of four 125-foot antenna towers arranged in a square, with a fifth tower placed in the center. The four outer antennas would broadcast signals: either a Morse code A (a dot-dash sound) or N (a dash-dot sound), depending on their location (see figure 22), with the transmission directed outward for a maximum distance of two hundred miles. Crews would navigate by tuning to its broadcast frequency, determining their position based on the tone they received, either A or N,

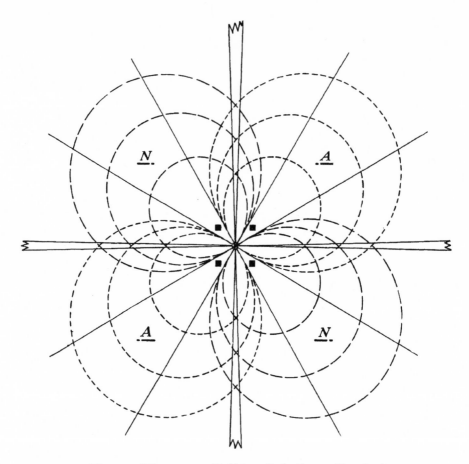

FIGURE 22. Theoretical Transmission Field for a Radio Range. Note the four antennas arranged in a square; a fifth antenna in the center transmitted voice signals. The four areas where the *A* and *N* overlap produced the overlapping dot-dash and dash-dot tones, which sound like a steady tone and told pilots they were "on the beam."
Courtesy McGraw-Hill.

and distinguishing between the relative strength of each tone. So, for example, if a crew was in the upper-left *N* quadrant of the diagram, all they would hear would be a pure dash-dot tone, but as they flew east they would begin to hear the dot-dash tone. The *A* signal would strengthen as they approached due north of the radio range, with the *N* signal getting fainter as they flew into the northeast quadrant of the diagram. Normally crews navigated by attempting to fly in the area where the *A* and *N* intersected; it was here that the dash-dot and dot-dash signals perfectly overlapped, producing a steady tone that meant the airplane was "on the beam." Radio ranges were the foundation of civil airways in the United States at the start of the war, but their proliferation did not relax the challenge they posed to their users, who had to determine their position relative to the antennas based on Morse code signals they heard in their headsets.[9]

This form of navigation was challenging along airways at altitude and was even more so while flying instrument approaches close to the ground. Low-pressure systems usually meant low ceilings, and a pilot would not break out of the weather and see the runway until he had descended on instruments (like a radio range) to only a few hundred feet above the ground. Chabua had just such an approach where the pilot flew directly over the range at 3,000 feet and descended to 2,000 feet, flying a course directly away from the runway for three minutes (see figure 23). After the time was up, he executed a "procedure turn" (making a 30-degree left turn, flying for one minute, then making a 180-degree right turn to intercept his inbound course) while descending to 1,500 feet. Using the Morse code signals, he then turned to intercept the inbound course to the runway; once he got over the range, he began his final approach, descending to 670 feet—or 350 feet above the ground. Hopefully he would break out of the weather on final approach in time to land; if not, he executed a "missed approach," climbing back to altitude and contacting air traffic control for further instructions, all the while navigating his aircraft based on the radio range's aural signals.[10] The entire procedure was straightforward enough in the flat terrain of the Brahmaputra Valley, but in the hills of Burma or China low-altitude instrument flying required extra finesse.

The Army Airways Communication Service (AACS) was put in charge of building and operating the ranges while also increasing the number of air traffic control frequencies to help manage the flow of arriving and departing aircraft. By November 1944, monthly arrivals at a terminal like Kunming averaged one every five minutes, day or night, so it was imperative that this traffic was controlled to prevent mid-air collisions, provide arrival information for ground crews, and help plot and track lost aircrews who needed assistance. AACS's work was slow and cumbersome, but once completed it enabled a flow of traffic that rivaled that seen in today's major airline markets like Washington, Atlanta, Boston, or Chicago.

Bolstering the air traffic control system was also important because it was an

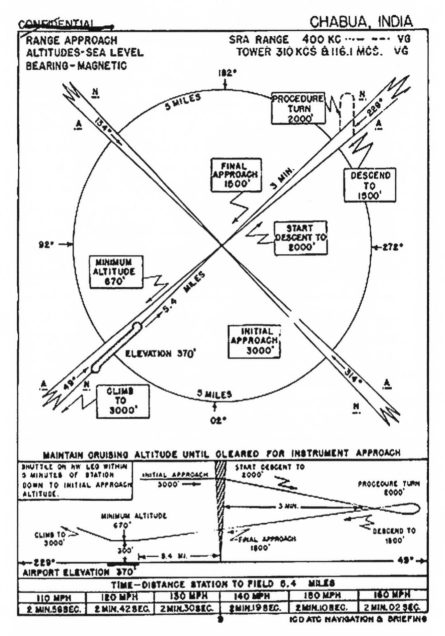

FIGURE 23. Chabua Range Approach. The Chabua radio range (depicted by the four transmission signals coming from the center of the plan view) was the navigation aid for this approach, allowing a plane to descend to 350 feet above the ground in poor weather conditions. *Source:* "Chabua Range Approach," author's files.

integral part of the way U.S. pilots were trained. Unlike the British, the Americans were trained to lean heavily on direction given by controllers, a difference that was highlighted later in 1944 when the ICW tried to standardize air traffic regulations with British units operating in the Western Sector between Assam and Karachi. British flying units were supplying controllers to work at U.S. airfields but the differences between the two flying cultures was enough to threaten the workability of the arrangement. As the unit historian at the U.S. airfield at Jiwani records:

> *The differences which are basic, might be expressed thus: with the British, it is up to the pilot to find his way to the next station and get ready to let-down [fly an instrument approach for landing], with a bare minimum of guidance. We, on the other hand, have made every airway, from takeoff to landing 2,000 miles away, as safe as a city street. The British pilot is the captain of a ship, navigating her between uncharted reefs and shoals and through vast unknown stretches. The American pilot is a taxi driver stopping at red lights, listening for whistles, given the proper signals for left and right-hand turns. . . . If we used the casual British procedures, our pilots— who had never had to be as good navigators as the British—would be plopping into the drink all over the Arabian Sea.*[11]

These cultural differences also extended to the ground. In 1943 the Americans requested that the British build a "greenhouse" type of control tower atop the operations building at Jiwani that would allow an omnidirectional view of the airdrome. Instead all the Americans got was a "thick roofed room with windows which permit vision only to 45 degrees above the horizon—thus offering endless opportunities to lose track of aircraft."[12]

CREW ROTATIONS

The wing's successful closeout to 1943 boosted its corporate morale, but individual morale was shaped more by the unit's rotation policy than anything else. When ATC took over the airlift in December 1942, there was no set rotation policy. Rumors abounded, and many thought the AAF would rotate individuals back home after a year of service, but a stated policy was not established until Hoag and Hardin replaced Alexander in the fall of 1943. At the end of October

1943, Hoag began asking ATC to set the policy at 1,000 hours of service in the theater, a demanding request that originated from Hardin. Hal George felt this was too high, seeing Hardin as a "particularly tough individual" who had all the "fire and enthusiasm of a crusader" but thinking that crews would wear out before reaching the mark.[13] Instead George set the policy at either nine months of Hump duty or 675 flying hours, whichever came first. After crews met this mark, they would then be rotated to the trans-India Western Sector, where they would have to serve for another nine months or fly an aggregate of 1,000 hours (whichever came first) before they were allowed to return to the United States.[14]

This policy seemed reasonable at first but came into question by the inspector general in February when he noted that operational fatigue was on the rise in the wing; he invited the surgeon general to introduce a revised policy with Flickinger, the ICW's chief doctor, who recommended no more than 450 Hump hours or 1,000 trans-India hours.[15] Hardin met with Flickinger, and the two reached a compromise: Eastern Sector Hump pilots would fly a total of 650 hours and Western Sector pilots 900 hours before being eligible to return home. Hardin defended his policy primarily on the grounds that it raised morale and instilled in his pilots "a diligence and sincere desire to accomplish the mission." He was afraid that if pilots were allowed to rotate after a set period of time, there would be a "tendency to wait out the accomplishment of such a minimum period rather than to extend every effort toward accomplishing the mission of the Wing."[16] Hardin's assessment was correct, as his crews worked hard to accumulate hours, but there was a growing fear throughout 1944 that the rush for hours led many to wear out prematurely. As seen earlier, pilot fatigue abruptly rose in June and did not return to a normative rate until the end of the year, bringing the time-based system again into question. There was no easy solution, though, as a date-based system undoubtedly bred slackness while the time-based system facilitated an overzealousness that could at the same time drive tonnage figures up while driving pilots into the ground.

Tonnage figures for January and February hovered around 13,000 tons as the wing slowly tried to establish an operational rhythm. In March Hardin would replace Hoag as the overall commander of the ICW. Complaining that he was unable to visit his transport bases due to the lack of a good executive officer, Hoag rarely strayed away from the confines of his headquarters in New Delhi, leaving Hardin to do much of the field work. Hoag had served well nonetheless, with George sending him to command the European Wing in preparation for the Normandy invasion. Japanese attacks against Hump airfields had also fallen off in January and February, as the Tenth Air Force had launched a series of bombing raids against Rangoon and Mandalay to keep IJAAF fighters busy with the defense of Japanese positions and distracted from attacking the Hump.[17] Despite these efforts, the airlift would come closest to being cut off that spring as the result of a Japanese ground offensive into India that came within miles of cutting the Assam LOC and threatened to overrun several of the transport airfields.

U-GO, HA-GO, AND PREPARING FOR ICHI-GO

In early 1944 the Americans captured the Marshall, Caroline, and Mariana Islands in the Pacific with the Japanese clearly back on their heels; to confront these reverses the Imperial General Headquarters planned to launch near-simultaneous offensives in India and China. The first, Operation U-go, had a threefold purpose: block the Hump's supplies to China by cutting the Assam LOC to the ICW airfields in Assam, preempting a possible Allied invasion of Burma, and inciting an Indian nationalist uprising that would hopefully spread across the subcontinent. The second offensive, Ichi-go, was more involved and was the largest Japanese land offensive of the war; it was designed to consolidate gains from Manchukuo to Indochina and give the Japanese control of continental lines of communication in the face of the advancing U.S. juggernaut in the Pacific. Ichi-go also sought to overrun the growing number of U.S. airbases in China used to launch attacks against shipping in the East China Sea and against the home islands.

The Japanese had long disdained the "material and spiritual" help that the Hump airlift gave the Chinese, seeing it as "performing the part of a camphor injection" in sustaining Chinese morale. As early as August 1942 the IGHQ had ordered the Fifteenth Army to draw up plans to "facilitate air operations by capturing and securing the strategic area in the north-eastern part of Assam Province and the vicinity of Chittagong and also to cut off the aid-Chiang [Hump] route."[18] This plan, called "21-go," was targeted for launch in October 1943, but Generals Iida (commander of the Fifteenth Army) and Mutaguchi (charged with the defense of north-central Burma) called for more time to prepare; the swiftness of the Japanese advance in the first half of 1942 produced a "victory disease" that was overly ambitious and quickly tempered by the reality of overstretched supply lines.

Delaying the launch of 21-go until 1943 assured its ultimate cancellation. U.S. successes at Guadalcanal drew off Japanese reserves in Southeast Asia, and the victory at Midway meant the IJN would not be able to sustain operations in either the Bay of Bengal or the Arabian Sea. Subhas Chandra Bose visited Tokyo in June 1943, urging the Japanese to invade northwest India, and sufficiently impressed the Tojo government that his collaborationist Indian Nationalist Army would be allowed to accompany a Japanese attack in the hopes of sparking a general anti-British revolt. General Mutaguchi, now the Fifteenth Army commander, had also undergone a drastic transformation once 21-go was cancelled. When the IGHQ had ordered plans for 21-go, he had balked, pointing to the impossible terrain in northern Burma. But just a few months later he had to deal with Orde Wingate's *chindits,* a special forces battalion inserted into Burma and supplied by airdrop. Mutaguchi had defeated the British at Singapore and reasoned that if the British could operate in north Burma, then naturally the Japanese could do the same. He also began to develop a messianic air about his place in the war, having been the regimental commander of the Beijing Garrison in July 1937, recording in his diary, "I started off the Marco Polo Incident, which broadened out into the China Incident, and then expanded until it turned into the Great East Asia War. If they [the Fifteenth Army] push into India now, by my own efforts, and can exercise a decisive influence on the Great East Asia War, I, who was the remote cause of the outbreak of this great war, will have justified myself in the eyes of our nation."[19] Mutaguchi reasoned that a thrust into India could both serve as a launch pad for Bose's army, thereby fomenting Indian independence, precipitating Britain's withdrawal from the war, and allowing the Japanese to link up with the Germans across Persia, as well as cut off Chiang's supply route and solve the China Incident by causing Chongqing to fold. His lofty ambitions were matched only by the size of his coming losses during the invasion.

The cancelled 21-go was replaced with U-go, an attack aimed at Kohima and Imphal. In February, three weeks before U-go kicked off, the IJA attacked the British on the Burmese coast at Arakan (see figure 24) in an offensive intended to divert Allied attention and dim the prospect for resupplying the British from the

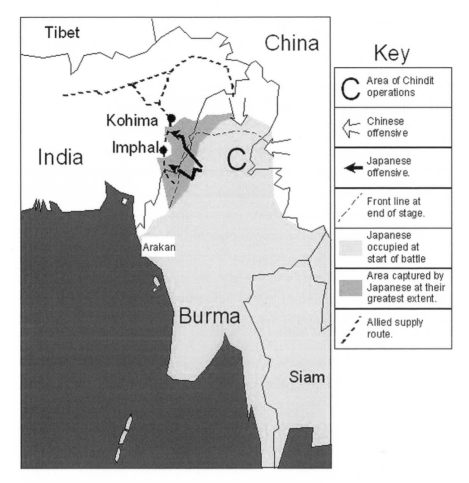

FIGURE 24. Arakan, Imphal, and Kohima, February–May 1944.

coast. As an aside, the selection of Mountbatten, an admiral in the Royal Navy, as SEAC the previous summer had left the IGHQ with the impression that British designs against Burma would come from the sea, prompting them to first secure the coast with Operation Ha-go. The attack held implications for the ICW, as it was the first to provoke a string of "diversions" from the wing's primary mission of supplying China; the ICW was responsible for dropping supplies to the radio warning network outposts established the previous summer, but the priority of Roosevelt's tonnage goal meant this mission now fell to Troop Carrier Command (TCC) units in India. TCC was specifically trained to airlift and airdrop the necessary troops and supplies in combat zones, operating often out of austere locations that were dangerously close to the enemy; these units had an important role in the story of the Allied recapture of Burma, but their fleet was too small to meet the Japanese offensives that began in February 1944, and they were forced to call on supplemental help from ATC units in India.

On the night of February 24, the ICW's Eastern Sector Headquarters at Chabua received a wire requesting twenty-five aircraft to help TCC for a special resupply mission within the next thirty-six hours. The duty officer at the time—not used to receiving such urgent messages—thought little of the request and did not notify Hardin's staff until eight o'clock the next morning. Even with the loss of precious time, the Eastern Sector still managed to get all of the planes to their proper staging bases by the next morning, timeliness that surprised the TCC units; relations were good between the ATC and TCC crews, though the latter regarded the former to be cut more from the cloth of airline pilots than combat aviators.[20] The assessment was accurate, but the ICW consistently showed its mettle as crews air-dropped supplies to the encircled 17th Division near Arakan. Cargo doors were removed from the C-46s, which needed four to five British "kickers" to push out supplies when over the drop zones. Normally the planes logged nine hours of flight time daily on Hump runs, but the Arakan missions reduced this to less than two hours a day. Still, the flying was much more hazardous, as the ATC pilots had to evade dangerous ground fire near drop zones.

Less than a month later Mutaguchi began his attack on Imphal, prompting another call for ATC to supplement TCC, now with twenty airplanes. This time the situation was graver, as the Japanese had managed to capture Kohima, a key village along the Manipur Road to Imphal and only thirty miles from Dimapur, a town along the railroad that supplied the Brahmaputra valley airfields. British general Claude Auchinleck was characteristically dry about the potential danger, even though ATC at Gravelly Point drew up plans to keep the Hump going should Assam and Bengal fall to the Japanese.[21]

Similar to the resupply of the 17th Division at Arakan, the ICW crews again flew well, though under conditions very different from those of their normal Hump runs. Crews were forced to serve as their own air traffic control, making "blind" calls over the radio: "Flying 90 degrees out of Silchar. Altitude 9,000. Altimeter setting 2992. Look out."[22] One crew arriving at Tulinal tried to land to the southwest into the wind, but the runway controllers used flares to wave it off twice, signaling for it to land in the opposite direction (with the wind). The C-46 was much heavier than TCC's C-47s that frequented the field and needed more runway for landing. The plane's brakes failed while trying to stop at the higher landing speed (a result of the tailwind), ended up in a ditch off the end of the runway, caught fire, and was destroyed. Birds also posed another problem to Hump pilots, who had little experience with low-level flight; vultures riddled the countryside thanks to the numerous dead, and a well-placed bird strike could take down an aircraft as easily as a round of flak. More daunting was the Japanese Air Force, which began attacking the transport fields on April 20, shooting down two ATC C-46s on the 24th and 25th. Japanese fighters attacked Tulinal on the 26th, destroying no planes but killing one pilot and critically wounding another. British fighter cover brought an end to the air attacks, and Mutaguchi's invading division was forced to withdraw in May, but only after fierce ground combat that came within twenty-five miles of the Hump's rail line at Dimapur.[23] So certain was Mutaguchi of victory before the attack that he gave an order to prepare to move his Fifteenth Army's "comfort women" to Imphal ten days after the attack started in March. Now he was forced to retreat after losing 60,000 troops, a striking blow when compared with the loss of only 17,000 Indian and British troops.[24] Altogether the ICW crews hauled nearly 7,000 men and delivered 1,600 tons of supplies while evacuating over 5,000 wounded during their three-month hiatus from regular Hump duties.[25]

Hardin's final report on the ICW's Arakan and Imphal missions called them "diversions" because they distracted the wing from its primary task. It is impossible to determine precisely how much monthly Hump tonnage figures were reduced by supporting the war in Burma, but a glance at the overall tonnage statistics makes its impact obvious, with no appreciable rise until June. Leadership within the ICW groused about this, and Hardin radioed George that "these troop movements are battle emergency operations, are justified, and nothing can be done about it until Troop Carrier is able to handle such requirements, but it's hell on the Hump."[26] Hardin was not the only one who disliked the digression. The Joint Chiefs of Staff (JCS) also disliked Mountbatten's making decisions about the Hump without first consulting the Allied Combined Chiefs. At Cairo the previous December Mountbatten claimed he needed 535 additional transports for his planned invasion of Burma the following spring, dubbed "Tarzan." The JCS were not happy with the request but made arrangements to meet it, working out a schedule that would impact only the China airlift in March and April. Then, when Stalin demanded Overlord be launched the coming summer (leaving no landing craft for the invasion of Burma), Tarzan was cancelled, and the need for air transport became moot. But now with Mutaguchi's offensive, the need again arose, and Mountbatten again had to go cap in hand to the CCS. Thus, the twenty-five ICW planes that supported Allied troops at Arakan and the twenty that supported those at Imphal and Kohima had to be approved by the CCS, as those airplanes remained under CCS control. Little did those crews know that their missions required the close scrutiny of the highest Allied operational command of the war because of the political implications of their "diversions."[27]

This was not a case of micromanagement on the part of the CCS or JCS for the simple reason that the Hump airlift carried much political weight. Mountbatten's complaints that he should be allowed to run the Hump fell on deaf ears, as tonnage allocation increasingly became a feature of global strategy rather than the province of theater commanders. Prior to Cairo, it looked as though Chiang might commit his Yoke-force troops to the recapture of Burma, but the cancellation of Buccaneer (and Tarzan) made these prospects dim. Brig. Gen. Frank Roberts, the head of the Strategy and Policy Group of the Operations Division (OPD) felt that the most China could offer would be to serve as a base for U.S. air attacks against Japan and any hopes that the Chinese could secure an overland route to the China coast in either the East or South China Seas was a mirage. In January his office recommended that the United States rely exclusively on the airlift to build up the airbases in China while also capturing Myitkyina to shorten the Hump route of flight (noting that any moves to continue the Ledo Road project were a waste of time) and defer any sizable equipping of the Chinese army until Nimitz's Pacific Fleet reached the China coast, presumably in late 1945.[28]

Roberts's position was considered too politically insensitive to U.S. relationship with Chiang, but by early March it had influenced JCS planners, who stated: "It now appears that the Pacific advance to the Formosa-Luzon-China Coast area cannot, except for air support, be materially aided by the SEAC and CBI theaters. . . . It would seem logical then, that all efforts in that area should be directed toward nourishing the air forces in China so that they, by an all-out effort, can support our assault from the Pacific."[29] India still held a prominent place in Allied

FIGURE 25. Internal and External Birdstrike Damage. Note the bird's head near the rudder pedals in the top photo. *Courtesy AMCHO.*

planning up through the first quarter of 1944, but this began to wane in April, with OPD stating: "During the past month, the strategic plan for the defeat of Japan has progressed to a point where it now appears probable that there will be no major land campaign in China supported from India and it is very doubtful that it will be possible or necessary to launch a major amphibious operation from India in support of the advance along the Philippine-Formosa-China Coast line."[30]

The Japanese offensive into India coupled with the Americans' success in the Pacific muted the prospects of using India as a launch pad for an assault on China, but Chiang's refusal to release his Yoke-force to Stilwell for action in Burma also dimmed the prospects of opening an overland route from Calcutta to the southeastern coast of China. PAC-AID was the name of the massive logistical operation that made coastal China a supply depot for the approaching Pacific Fleet. Ideally, PAC-AID stores would be best stocked with fuel and ammunition delivered overland from Calcutta, across the Ledo Road and Burma Roads into China, and then to the coast somewhere across from Formosa, but this plan was slowly being supplanted by the notion that PAC-AID stores could just as easily be filled by the Hump airlift, especially if the more capable C-54 could haul loads on direct flights from Calcutta to Kunming.

Allied strategy was muddled in April, proceeding along three lines. OPD and the War Department were gravitating toward reliance on the Hump to meet PAC-AID's logistical requirements while Stilwell was running cross-purpose in his determination to open the Ledo Road. As for the British, after Cairo and Tehran they had planned on expending a minimum of effort in Burma—only enough to capture key airfields—with Mountbatten claiming that Stilwell's direction was "out of step with global strategy" and that instead it would be more fruitful to follow an amphibious line of attack across Sumatra and Malaya,[31] a direction likely more attuned to British Imperial claims in Southeast Asia. Timing was the key factor with all three approaches, as the root question revolved around which plan was able to reach the China coast in time to support the Pacific Fleet, projected to arrive in late-1945. Landing craft were needed for the war in Europe and could not be released until after the invasion of France, pushing back the timetable of Mountbatten's "end-around" strategy. The Ledo Road could be pushed through to Kunming (once it joined the Burma Road), but to what avail? Supplies would still have to travel well over a thousand miles by truck to reach the coast on dilapi-dated Chinese roads and would not arrive until late 1945. Clearly the plan to stock PAC-AID could best be accomplished by air, thus becoming the Hump's strategic focus in the spring of 1944 and remaining so until the end of the war.

This did not mean that Stilwell was left out to dry in the spring of 1944, but the War Department shared his passion to reopen the road through Burma only up to the point where Myitkyina was recaptured. "Mitch" fulfilled two roles in American planning: as a convenient refueling stop for cargo-laden airplanes (an airplane that carries less fuel can carry more cargo) as well as a staging base for Allied fighters protecting the transports. Despite this difference of vision between Stilwell and the War Department, Roosevelt was becoming increasingly weary of Chiang's recalcitrance and reports of an imperiled China. The generalissimo would not commit his Yoke-force troops to Burma, claiming on March 27:

Seven years of war have taxed China's material and military strength to such an extent that to insist upon her doing something beyond her power would be to court disaster, the consequences of which would seriously affect not only Yunnan and Szechwan, but also the whole situation in this theater of war. Should this happen, the Japanese would invade Yunnan and Szech-wan, the revolt in Sinkiang [Xinjiang] and the communists activities in Shensi [Shanxi] would assume a new aspect in furtherance of their plan of bolschevizing [sic] this country so that our Government would not be in a position to do its part in this global war, and the Allies in East Asia would be deprived of a base of operations against Japan.[32]

Roosevelt would not hear of it. A week later he sent a strongly worded message to Chiang with a veiled threat to revoke military aid if the Yoke-force failed to cross the Salween and invade northeast Burma, which would have the effect of divert-ing the Yoke force's April allocation of 734 tons to Chennault and rescinding the contracts with CNAC, in turn requiring the airline to return all the U.S.-loaned aircraft. Backed into a corner, Chiang relented and had his minister of war, He Yingqin, explain to Marshall that "China has always realized her position with regard to offensives by United Nations, and it has only been because of time and lack of essential equipment that such action has not taken place before this time."

General He went on to say, "You can rely on China doing her share, but it is hoped that you understand her difficulties"; he ended unconvincingly with "Decision to move part of the YOKE Force across Salween was made on initiative of Chinese without influence of outside pressure, and was based on realization that China must contribute its share to the common war effort."[33]

It is important to note that Yoke-force troops were not the only Chinese soldiers participating in Stilwell's project to open the Burma Road. At the end of March—before Roosevelt's ultimatum—China agreed to send 17,000 troops from Yunnan to Assam to supplement the northeastern invasion of Burma. To move the troops, Stilwell arranged to have them airlifted from Yunnanyi to Sookerating in a move designed to have only a slight impact on the Hump. Starting April 3, crews that had just off-loaded their cargo at Kunming would take off and contact the control tower at Yunnanyi to see if there were any Chinese troops ready to be picked up. If there were, the plane would land, load as many as 46 soldiers, and head to Sookerating; in eight days 17,518 soldiers were moved in an operation that only impacted Hump tonnage by slowing down the flow of traffic with additional stops.[34] The soldiers then left Sookerating and joined up with Stilwell's X-Force, which crossed the Chidwin in April into northeast Burma. The contentious matter of the Yoke-force troops, though well equipped and trained, was as much an issue of politics as that of military necessity.

Chiang Kaishek had valid reasons for not wanting to commit the Y-force to Burma at the end of March. Troops from Outer Mongolia had invaded Xinjiang Province, reportedly accompanied by Soviet military aircraft. His intelligence network was also picking up signs of a Japanese buildup north of the Yellow River in Henan Province, a harbinger of another Japanese offensive. Perhaps most importantly, though, Chiang had seen how his best troops in 1942, his German-trained Fifth and Sixth Armies, had been squandered by Stilwell in Burma, and he was hesitant to revisit that catastrophe. The British scurried out of Burma in 1942, showing little regard for Chiang's forces, which prompted him to request Buccaneer, the amphibious invasion of the Burmese coast by the Royal Navy, as a security deposit of sincere motives. When Buccaneer was cancelled, Chiang's suspicions of the shallowness of Anglo-U.S. intentions were confirmed, evoking understandable caution toward letting Stilwell again use them. Additionally, standing troop strength was more essential to the maintenance of Chiang's regime than actual military victories, further justifying his reluctance to send his troops across the Salween. It was only under strong U.S. coercion that he finally gave his consent.

ICHI-GO

Within days of the Chinese commitment to deploy the Yoke-force to Burma, the Japanese crossed the Yellow River in what was to be their largest land-based operation of the war. Planning for operation Ichi-go had been under way since autumn 1943 and was primarily motivated by the fear that Japan might soon lose access to its sea lanes from the Dutch East Indies, Southeast Asia, and the Philippines. Prewar projections forecast that 1.8 million tons of Japanese shipping would be sunk by the Allies in the first two years of the Pacific War, but in fact 3.8 million tons were lost in the first twenty-one months, 55 percent at the hands of U.S. submarines and another 24 percent by Allied airpower. When the Pacific War began, Japan's seaborne transport capability stood at 5.5 million tons, but it would be reduced to 77 percent of this figure in just two years. Along with the loss of shipping was the loss of petroleum, steel, and rice, all in short supply due to the U.S. threat to Japan's Asian sea lanes.

In November 1943 the IGHQ called for a plan to circumvent this problem by establishing internal lines of communication on the continent, divorcing the Japanese from dependence on widespread sea control. To do so, the IJA would launch an offensive aimed at capturing the key points along the Beijing-Hankou and Hankou-Guangzhou (Canton) railroads, pulling up tracks from the Liuzhou-Dushan section and relaying these rails from Liuzhou to Liangshan (on the border with Indochina). The Japanese also planned on adding 200 locomotives and 2,500 freight cars to increase the line's throughput. The end result would be a 2,000-mile railroad from Peking to Hanoi that could serve—at least in theory—the supply needs of both the CEA and troops stationed in Southeast Asia as well as provide a route from the East Indies to the home islands with little reliance on shipping.[35] In achieving this goal, the Japanese high command also hoped to destroy U.S. airbases that were interdicting the flow of supplies within China as well as those destined for Japan. The Japanese were also concerned about the prospect of U.S. air attacks against the home islands, foreshadowed by Doolittle's famous 1942 raid, though it would be many months before the United

States would have airplanes available to strike Japan from the continent. U.S. airpower was a target of the ground offensive, but only insofar as it facilitated the flow of supplies by the eradication of the air threat. It is tempting to read events backwards and contend, as several have, that Ichi-go was a preemptive attack to check Operation Matterhorn, the United States' B-29 offensive against the home islands, but this would be guilty of anachronism because the Japanese offensive began before the first B-29 arrived in Asia.[36] At bottom, the primary objective of Ichi-go was the establishment of internal lines of supply to make up for the fact that prewar Japanese planners had grossly underestimated the capability of the United States to recover from Pearl Harbor.[37]

Ichi-go was planned in two stages. The first, the Henan (Honan) phase, would cut south toward Zhengzhou (Chengchow) and on to Wuhan (Hankou), following the rail line and connecting north and central China. The second phase would drive south from Wuhan to Hengyang, then southwest through Nanning to Liangshan and the border of Indochina (see figure 26). The operation would be the largest of its kind launched by the Japanese during the war, using 400,000 troops supported by 70,000 horses and 12,000 vehicles; the heavy reliance on horses was a testament to the chronic shortage of fuel; ethanol was already supplementing a significant portion of petroleum stores.[38] The operation began on April 18 with 140,000 men crossing the Yellow River in central Henan Province in a weakly defended area. Chinese troops reeled under the weight of the attack, which was able to move quickly across the flat Henan plain; those that did fight were easily decimated while most others simply melted away. The capture of Luoyang (Loyang) on May 26 saw 21,643 Chinese soldiers killed at the price of 1,061 Japanese; between May 9 and 20 over 32,000 Chinese were killed compared with the loss of only 760 Japanese.[39] The performance of Chinese troops was uneven. Some fought well while others dissolved when engaged by the Japanese. As Ch'i Hsi-Cheng points out, the speed of the Japanese attack caused many Chinese soldiers to cut and run, abandoning vehicles and weapons; after the Japanese had forced remnants of Tang Enbo's thirty divisions to flee to the mountains in western Henan, he was ordered to have his troops "take up 'garrison duties,' to 'conduct guerilla warfare,' and to engage in 'regroupment and training,'" terminology that was intended to shroud the fact that his force had completely lost its combat effectiveness.[40]

Ichi-go's second phase began on the heels of the first but moved more slowly on account of the terrain, the lack of air superiority, and lengthening supply lines. Many lakes and rivers had to be crossed south of Wuhan, and the course from Changsha to the Indochinese border was riddled with mountains, at times slowing some heavy units to only one kilometer a day.[41] Chennault's Fourteenth Air Force still dominated the skies over south-central China, forcing the CEA to restrict its movement to nighttime, disperse its supply depots, reinforce its antiaircraft artillery units, and requisition squadrons from the Fifth Air Army in Burma.[42] Chiang ordered his local commanders to fight to the death, executing the commander of the Fourth Army at Changsha for losing the city. The Japanese met some of their stiffest resistance at Hengyang when Fang Xianjue held out with 16,000 men for forty-six days before being overwhelmed on August 8. Hengyang housed the largest airbase in Hunan and was also the key city on the Wuhan-Guangzhou railroad, and the Japanese paid dearly for it with the loss of more than 20,000 men.[43] Two months later the Japanese 4th Field Railway Command was still trying to repair the destroyed spans along the route from Hunan to Guangxi but was having a difficult time because of the scarcity of building materials, thanks to the work of loyal Chinese units in the area who remained active by denying rails, ties, and bridge beams to Japanese engineers.[44] Meanwhile, the U.S. airfields at Lingling, Guilin (Kweilin), and Liuzhou were wide open for attack.

The impact of Ichi-go on day-to-day Hump operations was minimal throughout the spring and summer. The wing would be called upon to evacuate personnel once the offensive turned west toward Kunming in late summer, but until then business continued as normal between Assam and Yunnan Province. The headquarters relocated in mid-April to the tea plantation at Hastings Mill, a move that thrilled no one on the staff because they would exchange the comfortable surroundings of New Delhi for the squalor of Calcutta. Stratemeyer wanted all air assets in India to have their headquarters collocated, a reasonable wish designed to maintain some semblance of unity of command. The wing also scored its best safety record in April, losing only one aircraft over the Hump (there were thirteen total accidents in April, five of them "washouts," or complete losses, but only one loss over the mountains). Hardin attributed the low rate to the wing's "intensive training program" that covered all phases of flight, from takeoff to landing, including night operations, navigation procedures, and the use of com-

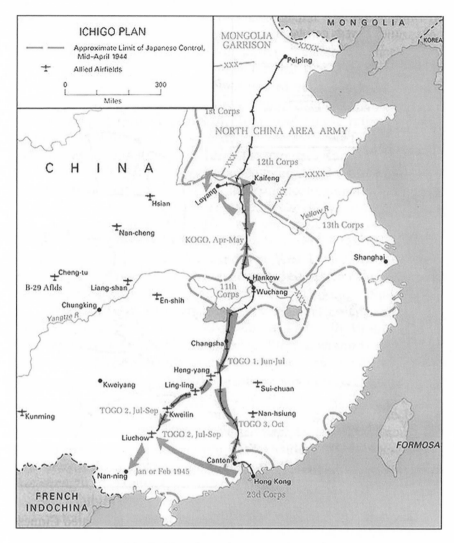

FIGURE 26. Ichi-Go Plan. *Courtesy U.S. Army Center of Military History.*

munication and navigation radios, though he was cautiously optimistic that such a record could be sustained, especially with the monsoon starting in May. Spare part shortages continued to plague the wing to a "dangerous degree" and would continue to do so unless the timely influx of emergency shipments made up for shortfalls.[45] By far the biggest factor affecting ICW that spring revolved around Operation Matterhorn, as strategic bombing planners in Washington were convinced that the mission could be accomplished without any help from ATC. They quickly discovered this was impossible.

OPERATION MATTERHORN

In April 1944 the Twentieth Air Force, the AAF's most unique numbered air force, was activated. Many characteristics set it apart. First, it flew the most advanced U.S. aircraft of the war, the Boeing B-29 Superfortress, a bomber originally conceived out of the fear that Great Britain would fall to the Germans and make necessary a long-range bomber capable of striking continental Europe from Iceland. It had a combat radius of 1,500 miles, was able to carry ten tons of bombs, and had a crew of ten that flew in the comfort of a pressurized cabin. Lead-computing machine guns were optically aimed but remotely controlled, like the B-17G's chin turret (the only two successfully fielded remote-controlled defensive armament systems of the war—by any belligerent), and bombardiers could score closer hits in bad weather thanks to the plane's radar. Technologically speaking, the B-29 was a quantum leap in bombing capability, and its long-range "global" capability meant it would remain under Arnold's command for the remainder of the war. Even the unit's name was unique, always referenced in roman numerals, "XX," and breaking from the conventional approach in sequentially numbering air forces (with arabic numbering). Normally the next numbered air force would have been the sixteenth, but Arnold thought that the twentieth was unique and named it after the twentieth century. But it was this uniqueness that led to problems once the Twentieth went to war.

Normally a numbered air force fell under the direction of the theater commander, but as a global command, the Twentieth fell under Arnold instead of Stilwell.[46] None of this was by accident, as Arnold and his deputy, Lt. Gen. Lawrence Kuter, were both long-time advocates of the merits of strategic bombing and felt they could best execute a European-style bomber offensive against Japan as long as they had exclusive control. But the stand-alone nature of the Twentieth worked against the unit: its "first among equals" status created the mistaken impression that it could deploy anywhere and fight autonomously. Thus, the initial plans for the Twentieth to bomb Japan from India included no outside support. Brig. Gen. Kenneth Wolfe, the commander of the 20th Bomber Command,[47] planned on using his own bombers and a complement of transports to first ferry the command to Calcutta, then use those same planes to begin flying over the Hump to stockpile bombs and fuel at Chengdu in Sichuan Province. Once the stockpile reached an adequate level, the bombing missions could begin with the planes taking off from India and stopping at Chengdu for fuel and bombs en route to bombing Japan. The bombers would recover to Chengdu after their missions, which took ten to twelve hours, and finally return to the security of one of the five B-29 bases in Calcutta.

The complicated logistical arrangement did not work, mainly because Wolfe's own planes spent more time prepositioning their own supplies than actually flying bombing sorties; one member blithely referred to the unit as "a goddam trucking outfit."[48] The first B-29s arrived in India in April, with the first attack scheduled for June; by the end of May the Twentieth had logged a total of 2,867 B-29 flying hours, with 2,378 accounting for transport missions and 439 for theater training, an average of less than two hours of training for the command's 240 crews (so tight were its logistical needs that bomber crews practiced formation flying on transport missions over the Hump). Despite this and the efforts of the 20th Bomber Command's own fleet of C-87s and C-46s, supplies could not be ferried fast enough and help from ATC was necessary. Smith anticipated this in May and wrote Hardin—who was busy being tasked to simultaneously support Mountbatten, Stilwell, Chennault, and now Wolfe—that he should do his best to keep a flexible attitude. "Not being the responsibility of a theater commander, 20th Bomber has been a bit shy about channeling their air transportation requirements in the usual manner, feeling *they* must take the responsibility for seeing that their goods move by air," wrote Smith. He explained to Hardin that ATC was trying to convince Wolfe that ATC could meet his command's transport needs more efficiently than using B-29s as airlifters and wryly closed his letter by claiming, "Only by doing people's work for them well will keep them from the idea that they should do it themselves."[49]

Smith's desire to help Matterhorn was not necessarily an attempt at intra-service camaraderie. Since April, the ICW had been called upon to support the Twentieth with airlift, though in an ad hoc manner. The ICW was also forced to support the Twentieth with maintenance, fueling, and loading help, all of which could be done more efficiently if the ICW were allowed to formally manage the bomber command's transport needs. Additionally, by the end of April, support for Operation Matterhorn had risen to the top of the theater's list of priorities, supplanting the PAC-AID buildup of stores, Stilwell's Y-force, and the Fourteenth Air Force's Hump requests. This being the case, it was in ATC's best interest to subsume as much of the airlift work as possible because "ATC is the basic agency for hauling stuff by air for the Army," remarked the former airline executive.[50]

To make Matterhorn work, lots of "stuff" had to be hauled over the Himalayas. In July, August, and September nearly 12,000 tons of fuel and bombs were carried from Calcutta and the Assam Valley to Chengdu in support of the seven bombing missions that dropped 813 tons of bombs. Put another way, every 500-pound general-purpose bomb dropped on Japan during that period required the equivalent of one fully loaded C-46 delivery over the Hump to China. The fact that the operation dropped over 4,730 tons of bombs during its brief history meant that some 69,000 tons overall had to be airlifted to China by 20th Bomber Command and ATC transports, the same amount of tonnage carried in the first *twenty months* of the entire Hump airlift.[51]

It is not difficult to carp on Matterhorn's unwieldy logistical needs, all of which were clear to the operation's planners from the beginning—which is why it was always the intention to move the bombers to the Pacific once the Marianas were secured. In fact, it was not accidental that Matterhorn's first attack on Japan—the first strike against the home islands since Doolittle's April 1942 raid—took place on June 15, the same day as the U.S. invasion of Saipan. Wolfe had to bend over backward to make this attack on the coke ovens at Yawata a reality, but he did, giving his crews valuable experience during the long-range mission. The experience gained during this raid and the ones that followed proved to be where Matterhorn's real value was felt. The planes had been rushed through production, with the AAF uncharacteristically purchasing the bomber before it was ever built; as such, it was rife with problems when it first came off the assembly line at Wichita. As Curtis LeMay, the man who replaced Wolfe as the head of the Twentieth, quipped: "The B-29s had as many bugs as the entomological department of the Smithsonian Institution. Fast as they got bugs licked, new ones crawled out from under the cowling"[52] But at the end of the day, it was during Matterhorn that many of the mechanical bugs and operational nuances of employing the big bomber in combat were worked out, helping smooth the command's operations once the planes relocated to the Pacific. It was also during Matterhorn that the Japanese began to recognize the flaws in the air defense system of their home islands.

The development of the B-29 was no secret in the United States, and the IGHQ was anticipating its arrival in the theater. The Japanese espionage network noticed the buildup at Chengdu, a location that the IGHQ felt was too far to hit anything other than western Japan. At Cairo, Chiang had agreed to commission local labor to build four airfields in the Sichuanese city, 170 miles northwest of Chongqing. Nearly 300,000 laborers—most of them farmers—worked for weeks, laying hand-chiseled rock that was then crushed beneath the weight of hand-drawn, ten-ton stone rollers.[53] IJA Type 100 reconnaissance aircraft had inadequate range to reach Chengdu to survey the progress of the growing operation, but preparations were made to strengthen observation posts and radar sites along the Beijing-Hankow and Tienjin-Pukou railroads that were designed to plot the track of the bombers and anticipate their targets. Fighters were withdrawn from the front in Hunan, but the lack of any airborne radar meant a reliance on inadequate coverage from the ground-based radar, so the B-29s were seldom intercepted. The best option for the Japanese was to attack the airbases at Chengdu, something that was done with outdated Type 99 light bombers equipped with internal auxiliary fuel tanks for the long flight. Japanese sources record one successful night raid on September 8 that claimed seven B-29s burned and eleven others destroyed on the ground, though the AAF's official history makes no mention of the attack.[54] By December, Matterhorn as a China-based operation had outlived its usefulness, and the 20th Bomber Command would relocate to airbases in the Marianas for the remainder of the war.

SUMMERTIME JUMP

To meet the theater's increasing logistical demands, in mid-July Hap Arnold set a Hump tonnage goal of 31,000 monthly tons by December. The JCS also realigned tonnage priorities, now placing the Fourteenth Air Force at the top of the list, followed next by PAC-AID, Matterhorn, and the supply of Chinese troops outside the orbit of Stilwell's Y-force. The India-China Wing had also grown to such massive proportions that it underwent a name change in June, now called the India-China Division (ICD), nomenclature consistent with normal army usage.

Under the ICD were four wings, India, Assam, China, and Bengal, the last of which became active at the beginning of 1945 with the first direct flights from Calcutta to Kunming. Hardin, ever the consummate operator, had worked hard to eliminate the staff positions of those doing redundant work in the old Eastern and Western Sectors of the ICW (and in doing so managed to cause some rancor among those who preferred the comfortable confines of an office to the rigors of daily Hump sorties), but the organization was becoming too unwieldy and needed the organizational adjustment to allow for further growth. Plans were set to increase the division's fleet to 440 transports operating from eleven different airfields by the beginning of 1945, a far cry from just two years prior when one-tenth that number were used.[55]

The summertime expansion of the Hump was by no means a forgone conclusion in 1944. Matterhorn was forced to rely on the ICD for a time, but once LeMay got his command into an operational rhythm—as syncopated as that rhythm was—ATC-support became unnecessary. Stilwell's offensive seemed well in hand with the recapture of Myitkyina in May, and the CBI commander was long since fed up with the hopes of reforming the Chinese Army by supplying Chiang's troops en masse. He was pleased with the performance of Chinese troops when they were trained, supplied, and led by Americans, but he knew little good came of supplying Nationalist troops beyond his purview, especially when Chiang was keeping arms from Chinese units in direct contact with the Japanese, but under the command of generals the generalissimo did not trust.[56] This left PAC-AID (also called "Enterprise") as the ICD's preeminent mission, with the charge to deliver 51,586 tons to the China coast by January 1945.[57] This was complicated by Ichi-go but was still considered vital to the support of a potential U.S. invasion of Formosa. U.S. strategy was still not settled on whether to approach Japan from Formosa or the Philippines; PAC-AID, by virtue of its geographic proximity (the distance between Formosa and the mainland being only one hundred miles) was of greater utility to the former. Douglas MacArthur, the promised liberator of the Philippines, was an advocate of the latter; Chief of Naval Operations Ernest King pushed for the capture of Formosa. The requirements for Hump tonnage thus awaited closure on this decision.

The division's expansion is most clearly seen in its productivity from May to August, months in which the wet monsoon usually curtailed tonnage. Instead, this four-month period witnessed dramatic growth: 11,383 tons in May, 15,845 in June, 18,975 in July, and 23,676 in August. Roosevelt hailed the breaking of the 20,000-ton mark at a press conference, calling it an "amazing performance" and "an epoch of the war." Churchill likewise commemorated the event in an address before the House of Commons, albeit in more flowery prose:

> *It is well known that the USA has been increasingly engaged in establishing an air route to China capable of carrying immense supplies and by astounding efforts and at a vast cost they are now sending over the terrible Himalayas, or "Hump" as it is called in the armies, I will not say how much as the Burma Road has ever carried in its palmist days or ever will carry in days to come. . . . This incredible feat of transport at 20,000 or 22,000 feet in the air, over ground where engine failure means certain death to a pilot, has been performed by a grand effort which the USA has made in their passionate desire to aid in the resistance of China. Certainly no more prodigious example of strength, science, and organization in this class of work has ever been seen or dreamed of.*[58]

Despite the accolades, U.S. policymakers found themselves questioning the wisdom of exclusively supporting Chiang. The Office of Strategic Services (OSS) sent a mission to Yan'an to meet with Mao Zedong to discuss how the Communists might best fit into Allied strategy against the Japanese, while Stilwell's relationship with Chiang had devolved to a point of uselessness, with the American's scorn reaching fever pitch. On September 9, with nothing to stop Ichi-go in Guangxi, he recorded in his diary: "Disaster approaching Kweilin. Nothing to stop Japs. About 50,000 demoralized Chinese in the area against 9 jap divs. Chinese have no replacements. Jap units are filled up. It's a mess, & of course all they think of is what we can give them. [Gen.] Sun Fo wants us to fly in American troops!!! [Gen.] Yü Ta Wei wants weapons. So does [Gen.] Pai [Chongxi]. What they ought to do is shoot G-mo [Generalissimo] and [Minister of War] Ho [Yingqin]."[59]

Lastly, OPD correspondence openly acknowledged that a measure of supplies still had to be shipped directly to the Chinese, if for no other reason than to serve as payola to bolster Chiang's domestic esteem. "In addition to the purely military tonnage that must go over the Hump for ground forces, there is a certain minimum allocated to key Chinese ministries upon the heads of which the Generalissimo must depend if he is to maintain himself in power."[60] In 1942 the War Department regarded Chiang with a degree of skepticism that had soured into a palpable cynicism over the next two years. And despite the fact that in Ichi-go the Chinese had suffered their greatest military defeat since the war began, U.S. aid to the Guomindang would shrink, despite soaring tonnages over the Hump. Between August 1944 and October 1945—surely a period of great domestic distress for Chiang—Hump deliveries to the Nationalists totaled 19,542 tons while total Hump deliveries totaled 587,688 tons. Put another way, Chiang's government got three pounds of supplies for every one hundred pounds that crossed the Hump.

The summer's events served to crystallize the way the Americans and Chinese would proceed for the duration of the war. First, the Americans put aside plans to take Formosa in September when Adm. William "Bull" Halsey's fleet made incursions into Luzon, finding the northern Philippine island lightly defended. The logic for taking Formosa was in line with the general Pacific strategy of bypassing strongholds to take positions more lightly defended by the Japanese; it was assumed that the Philippines would be such a place worth bypassing, but Halsey proved this otherwise. As a result, MacArthur would have his way and the U.S. advance toward Japan would be settled the following month. Added to this was the complication Ichi-go posed on the use of China's southeastern coast as a supply depot with no clear land route from Kunming to the coast. Furthermore, Chiang's armies that tried to block Ichi-go were decimated, but the generalissimo was still gaining the upper hand with the Japanese. The seizure of the Marianas precipitated the fall of Prime Minister Hideki Tojo, and his replacement, Koiso Kuniaki, was proposing a settlement with Chiang based on "full equality." Peace terms from the previous autumn called for the Nationalists to denounce their alliance with the Americans and British, but Koiso's terms were softer. Chiang would not be required to break off relations with the westerners or declare China's neutrality. Japan would withdraw its troops once the Allies did likewise, and a treaty of friendship would be worked out between the two Asian nations. China would be allowed to determine the status of Inner Mongolia and would also regain sovereignty over Hong Kong. But as with the autumn 1943 terms, the Japanese still required the status quo with Manchukuo—which Chiang rejected out of hand. In September Koiso called on retired general Ugaki Kazu-shige to lead a peace mission to Chongqing,[61] but Chiang refused to meet with the delegation, sensing he only had to hold out for a better prize.

September also marked a shift for the ICD. Tom Hardin had spent a year running the airlift, playing an instrumental role in seeing it pass the 10,000-, then 20,000-ton mark, and it was time for him to rotate back to the United States. His replacement was Brig. Gen. William Tunner, a man who would build on the foundation laid by Hardin to see the Hump realistically target the 100,000-ton monthly mark. Tunner brought with him a cadre of seasoned airlifters to run his headquarters, ushering in what affectionately became known as the "era of big business." To make this a reality, the division would begin adding the C-54 to its inventory at the beginning of October, with the massive transports doubling the loads carried by C-46s. The new Douglas transport, the first truly intercontinental airlifter to ever be built, was designed to carry a five-ton load from San Francisco to Honolulu. With the Japanese cleared out of northern Burma, the more southerly (and less mountainous) low Hump opened, and the ICD's leadership could begin imagining a route directly from the port city of Calcutta to Kunming, removing the perennial obstacles of the Assam LOC. The wing had performed well during the first nine months of 1944, despite the "diversions" of India, Burma, or Matterhorn, missions that irritated Hardin but were nonetheless vital to the Allies' progress. By 1944 the ICW's leadership thought of victory in terms of a monthly tonnage—naturally disparaging those things that chipped away at this figure—though success or failure could not be reduced simply to a tonnage figure. The airlift still represented the only line of connection between the western theaters of India, the Middle East, and Africa and the eastern theaters of the Pacific, Southwest Pacific, and East Asia. And its very existence represented a victory of sorts, especially in the face of Japanese offensives into India and south China earlier that spring.

THE HUMP BECOMES AN AIRLINE

OCTOBER 1944 TO AUGUST 1945

China's role in Allied planning waned from autumn 1944 until the end of the war. The decision to merge MacArthur's and Nimitz's twin drives at Luzon rather than Formosa meant that China would slowly recede in strategic importance and remain a factor in Allied planning only for three reasons. First, as with the PAC-AID deliveries scheduled throughout the end of 1944, China was seen as a lodgment for stores and equipment for future operations against the Japanese home islands, as Kyushu, the southernmost island, was only five hundred miles from Shanghai. Second, should the Soviets enter the war against Japan (something agreed upon in principle at the Tehran Conference in November 1943 and in specifics in Moscow a year later), U.S. planners deemed it important to consider a coastal invasion of China to meet up with Russian troops who would be driving south through Manchukuo. Third, China also had to remain part of U.S. planning if for no other reason than the unthinkable prospect of having to defeat the Japanese everywhere in the Empire rather than securing a recognized general surrender from Tokyo.[1]

Ironically, the diminution of China's strategic value did not correspond to a reduction in Hump tonnage requests; rather, ICD deliveries soared to unbelievable proportions, with 75 percent of the Hump's wartime total of over three-quarters of a million tons being delivered in the war's final year. The reasons for this were twofold. First, despite the War Department's tepid backing for the reopening of a land route from India, it still placed value on China's location in view of the growing prospect of an invasion of Japan. The United States had invested millions of dollars of aid in Chiang's government and was still holding out for a hopeful return on that investment, however meager the likelihood. Second, Hump tonnage would jump in the war's last year as a result of an operational inertia made possible by the coupling of a mature air transport infrastructure with leadership bent on maximizing airlift efficiency. Brig. Gen. William Tunner replaced Hardin in September, inaugurating what the AAF's official history calls "the era of big business" by building on the efforts of his predecessors.[2] This was timely because the robust airlift would become more capable and flexible than all other means of supply. To get the newly renamed Stilwell Road (the merger of the Ledo and Burma Roads) to a place where it could deliver 60,000 monthly tons meant delivering 5,759 trucks and 56,500 support troops to the theater, when air transport promised the same tonnage with only the addition of 150 aircraft and 5,000 troops. These figures neatly reversed the orthodox belief that land transport using trucks was inherently more efficient than air transport. Plainly, given the rugged terrain and distances involved, air transport was significantly *more* efficient in this case.[3]

The investment of the previous two years would begin to pay off as an abundance of airfields, a steady supply of pilots, a revitalized maintenance system, and a mature airways structure put the ICD on par with any commercial air carrier of the 1940s. In short, the Hump airlift would become an airline capable of rivaling any contemporary competition in efficiency and capability.

CBI STRATEGY IN AUTUMN 1944

In autumn 1944 four factors dominated the CBI's landscape and served to shape the larger context of global strategy. These included the replacement of Joseph Stilwell with Lt. Gen. Albert Wedemeyer, Japanese success in the last months of the Ichi-go offensive, the disappointing impact of the Matterhorn B-29 attacks, and the introduction of a new airplane to the airlift.

Stilwell's recall from China in October marked the culmination of tensions between Washington and Chongqing. Chiang had suffered humiliation the previous April when the War Department threatened to withdraw aid unless the generalissimo consented to order the Yoke-force across the Salween to attack the Japanese in northeast Burma. To his mind, Guomindang troops were squandered by Stilwell in the summer of 1942 during a period when southwest China was vulnerable to what appeared to be a Japanese juggernaut; with intelligence reports indicating yet another Japanese buildup in April 1944, the generalissimo was in no mood to again deploy his best-trained and -equipped force back into Burma, especially when the Hump airlift was humming along. The Japanese had extended their reach deep into south-central China by late September, and Stilwell was furious that Chiang's decision making was shaped more by political than military considerations. The generalissimo had withheld aid from generals with suspect allegiances and had refused to move his armies dedicated to keeping the Communists fixed in the northwest. To deal with this, Stilwell succeeded in persuading the president to ask Chiang that the U.S. general be placed in command of all Chinese forces—Guomindang and Communist alike. The request infuriated the generalissimo, who, in a meeting with the GMD Central Executive Committee, called it a bald-faced attempt at "imperialism."[4] Acceding to such a request was impossible for Chiang to accept without shattering his already tenuous support base. Chiang was able to endure Stilwell's New England brusqueness and acerbic character insofar as it meant the infusion of U.S. aid on Chinese terms, but to relinquish control of his armies to the American meant political suicide. As for the Americans, by late summer Roosevelt came to regard Stilwell's recall as politically expedient, as a means by which to separate himself from a possible collapse of China, telling Chiang that "a full and open explanation of reasons for General Stilwell's recall will have to be made" and warning that "the American people will be shocked and confused by this action and I regret the harm that it will inevitably do to the sympathetic attitude of the American people toward China."[5] If Chiang no longer wanted Stilwell because he threatened Chinese domestic politics, then FDR could use the recall as a means of displaying the generalissimo's recalcitrance, a useful move that would distance the White House from any possible culpability should China collapse.

Albert Wedemeyer was no novice to the theater. He had served in the Philippines before the war and had also worked as Mountbatten's chief of staff at SEAC headquarters. His diplomatic demeanor meshed well with Chiang's ego, though Wedemeyer's mission in China during the war's last year carried less importance with Washington than Stilwell's did two years earlier when China's role in Japan's conquest was still prominent. But where Stilwell's self-perception of his own mission was more messianic—seeking to reform Chiang's government by reforming his army first—Wedemeyer's vision was more focused. Like Stilwell, he too embarked on a plan to build a U.S.-trained and equipped force, this time aimed at a drive to the coast designed to open a port for the direct infusion of Allied supplies. This plan called for the buildup of thirty-six Chinese divisions with U.S. advisors attached to command elements at all echelons; all orders had to be vetted through both the Chinese commander and his corresponding U.S. advisor before action was taken, a setup designed to prevent Chiang from privately issuing personal orders.[6] Wedemeyer easily secured approval from Chiang to carry out the plan, as the generalissimo was undoubtedly lured by the prospects of a seemingly endless supply of U.S. aid. Should the Americans again push the limits of controlling his armies, Chiang felt he could more easily sway the conciliatory Wedemeyer.

The Japanese offensive had to be stopped before the Allies could contemplate any notions of a drive to the coast. The fall of Hengyang in early August 1944 opened the road to Guilin and Liuzhou, two of the larger Fourteenth Air Force bases, and with little Chinese opposition to stop the drive, the Americans began to scuttle the fields. Japanese troops entered Guangxi Province, taking Guilin and Liuzhou in November and forcing Chennault to withdraw his air units to the west and vainly demand the release of B-29s to counter the attack. From the start of the offensive Japanese commanders had been ordered to attack Chinese strongholds, wary of Chongqing's propensity for avoiding battle until they had forced the Japanese to overstretch their supply lines, only to launch a counterattack with better equipped forces. Japanese directives repeatedly told commanders to single out elite Chinese units, explaining that once they had been defeated, the regional forces would dissolve. As a result, casualties quickly mounted, with 108,000 Chinese killed or wounded (according to Chinese sources) out of 286,000 troops in the offensive's Hunan phase alone. By the time the Japanese entered Guangxi, the Nationalists were able to scrounge together only between 60,000 and 70,000 battle-weary men to meet the Japanese advance. Strategically speaking, the Chinese would bend but never break, but with the pending fall of the Philippines and

the invasion of Okinawa on the horizon, the reasons for a renewed U.S. investment on the continent seemed hollow at best.[7]

Except for the incendiary attack on the Japanese supply depot at Hankow
later in December, Arnold refused to allow the B-29s to be diverted from their
strategic bombing mission of the home islands to the ground war in China, especially as any threat posed by Japanese ground forces against the bombers' staging
bases in Chengdu seemed remote. Chengdu was over five hundred miles to the
northwest of the most advanced Japanese columns at Guilin, and there was little
fear that these armies, overextended as they already were in September, would
be able to make the trek over the difficult terrain of Guizhou and Sichuan to pose
a problem to the big bombers. Besides, Matterhorn was having its own problems,
even under the command of Curtis LeMay. Twelve missions had been launched
by the end of October (not counting the initial training raid against Bangkok),
with an average of one out of every four airplanes failing to make it to the target,
usually for mechanical reasons. The attacks were impressive for the distances covered by the bombers, but the long flights meant fuel had to be traded for bombs;
as a result, each attack averaged only 170 tons of bombs dropped by fifty-four
B-29s, or 3 tons per plane, a paltry amount for an aircraft with a 10-ton payload
(by way of comparison, the attack on Schweinfurt and Regensburg in August
1943 dropped 724 tons of bombs[8]). LeMay was able to experiment with incendiary bombs, using them exclusively against Nagasaki on August 10 and Hankow
on December 18 and later keeping the load ratio at roughly one ton of napalm
bombs for every two tons of high-explosives (see figure 27).[9] Thus he was able to
test the assumptions made by planners two years earlier who claimed that Japanese industry was uniquely susceptible to firebombing due to the inflammable
composition of urban areas.[10] Nevertheless, the days of the 20th Bomber Command in China were numbered. China had been planned as a temporary excursion for the unit only because the airplane was (hypothetically) ready for combat
before the Marianas were captured; with the islands now under U.S. control, the
bombers could be reassigned to the Pacific.

The final factor that shaped the theater's strategy in autumn 1944 was the
arrival of the Douglas C-54. The "Skymaster" was capable of hauling ten tons
1,500 miles, but it had heretofore been unusable for Hump operations because it

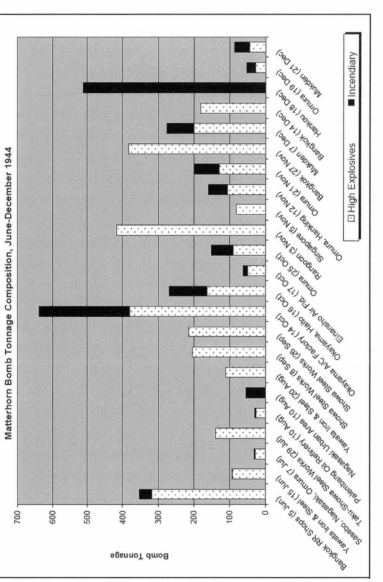

FIGURE 27. Matterhorn Bomb Tonnage Composition, June–December 1944. *Source.* "20th Bomber Command Digest of Operations," December 31, 1944, NARA II, RG 18, Entry 10, Box 27. The chart shows the comparative tonnage composition of high-explosive and incendiary bombs used during the Matterhorn B-29 attacks. Note the exclusive use of incendiaries during the August 10 attack on Nagasaki and the much larger payload of fire bombs used against Hankou (Wuhan) on December 18.

was unable to maintain adequate altitude when threatened by icing conditions. The first C-54 was sent to the Hump in the middle of 1943 to test its performance over the Himalayas over a two-month period, and the findings were not good. On paper it seemed like the aircraft was ideally suited for Hump operations—an enormous cargo compartment and four engines capable of lugging the load—but toward the end of its test period it began to encounter icing that choked its engines and caused them to fail in flight. The reason for this was not the airplane's lack of power to climb over the mountains but just the opposite. To cruise at 18,000 feet the airplane had to fly at a lower RPM than normal (or else burn excessive fuel), making it highly susceptible to failure in areas of moderate and severe icing. This was not a problem for the two-engine transports because they had to operate at a higher RPM to maintain altitude. As for the four-engine C-87, it was designed as a high-altitude bomber and thus had turbosupercharged engines, which allowed it to operate at any altitude up to 30,000 feet and so avoid icing.[11] The C-54's engines were not turbosupercharged and so could not outclimb the icing—but also could not fly at a lower altitude without the threat of engine failure.[12] Thus, partly because of what was really an engineering characteristic, the Skymaster was kept off the Hump until after the Japanese forces in Burma were pushed far enough south to allow the planes to fly the low Hump by way of Myitkyina, as opposed to "Route Able," the route that covered higher terrain over Fort Hertz.[13]

Furthermore, less than a tenth of the aircraft's total wartime production was available by the end of 1943 (at this point 98 C-54s had been delivered to the AAF; the service would receive 1,089 by the war's end). Additionally, production was slowed by labor problems with the Douglas plant in Chicago because of its proximity to Detroit. The auto industry was paying better wages than the aircraft industry, drawing off skilled workers and shift supervisors and forcing Douglas to transfer key personnel from factories in Tulsa to increase the output of Chicago's plant.[14] And the final factor that colored all U.S. aircraft production was the emphasis to churn out combat planes like fighters and bombers over transports. The ICD would eventually receive only a tenth of the United States' total production of the C-54s (the division had thirty-eight in January 1945, increasing to a peak of ninety-eight in August), but the massive payload of these airplanes nonetheless made possible the record tonnages of the war's last year.

INSTITUTIONALIZING THE HUMP

The sharp increase in Hump tonnage during the summer of 1944 did not come without a price. The accident rate was again climbing, and reports had made their way back to Gravely Point that ICD morale was in the doldrums. Hardin had officially been in charge of the airlift only since March, but it was his energy and drive that had fueled the operation past the 10,000- and 20,000-ton marks. C. R. Smith was concerned that his long service overseas (he had been assigned to overseas wings for the past two years) was wearing on his judgment and so suggested to Hal George that he be replaced by William Tunner, an ATC staff officer who managed personnel for the Ferrying Division. Tunner, a West Point graduate (class of 1924), had the reputation of being a personable and conscientious officer, though he had little command experience. Smith thought him to be well suited for the job, and George offered him the position, though Tunner was initially cool to the proposition. In a 1976 interview Tunner claimed that he "didn't particularly like the idea because anybody who goofed in the Ferrying Division was on the roster to go to India. It was the end of the line . . . and I felt like I was joining all the bad boys."[15] By 1944 the Hump's reputation was dismal, with returning officers going "out of their way to tell you how much they hated it"; it had come to be regarded as "the place to which you exiled officers you wanted to get rid of." In his memoir Tunner later confessed that ATC would levy pilots from his Ferrying Division (while he still worked at Gravely Point) and that he and his personnel officer did not hesitate to send to the ICD "those men my base commanders [of the other ferrying airfields] felt they could best do without," as the "misfits were not wanted in any outfit."[16] Now, in a neat turn of irony, Tunner would be the commander of those self-same "misfits."

Tunner's marching orders were threefold: boost morale and lower the accident rate while increasing tonnage. Medically, the division was experiencing a summertime spike in malaria, diarrhea, dysentery, and upper respiratory infections. Flying personnel removed from duty in September were averaging over a week per month convalescing, almost doubling the same statistic earlier in February. To combat what was really a theaterwide problem, antimalarial schemes were devised to cut down on disease transmission by fitting DDT-laden B-25s with spraying equipment to douse mosquito-breeding areas near bases and camps. All told, these "Skeeter Beaters" dumped 12,000 gallons of pesticide, but

FIGURE 28. Brig. Gen. William Tunner. *Courtesy AMCHO.*

it was difficult to control the insect population during summertime monsoonal rains. Additionally, venereal disease was a perennial CBI problem, though the ICD managed to keep its infection rate lower than that of the rest of the theater. Characteristically, the Americans sought to combat the problem through fear-based troop education, though nearby brothels made temptation irrepressible. Prophylaxis stations were eventually made compulsory, and the high disease rate among local prostitutes was advertised by commanders. But the most effective VD deterrent came in September when a U.S. soldier was stabbed to death by some Indians after being caught with a prostitute in the open air near New Delhi's Lodi Tombs. News of the murder spread quickly and had a marked impact: prior to the death the daily administration of prophylactic treatments hovered around fifteen, jumping to ten times this number immediately after payday; but within thirty-six hours of the murder the daily administration of prophylactics halted altogether, and for four days none were administered throughout all of Delhi, an unprecedented statistic, with a total of nine administered two weeks after the incident.[17]

Adding to morale problems was the general culture shock experienced by most Americans serving in India, who had never spent any prior time in Asia. The servicemen found certain customs raw and crude, as in the daily collection of "night soil." One unit historian in New Delhi dryly commented that indoor plumbing was a rare luxury, so "the people go out in the morning and at appropriate times during the day to the street gutter, where they squat flatfooted in the national posture, and relieve themselves. It is customary to face the wall while defecating in public, as these people are extremely modest, and their delicacy in such matters is great." Youths or teenagers would then scoop up the open sewage and load it onto cattle-driven carts to be loaded onto railway cars for transport to a refuse site ten miles north of the city limits. For those wealthy enough to have indoor plumbing, a brass bowl and faucet replaced toilet paper.[18] Hindu religious practice was also viewed with a sense of bewilderment by Americans who were hassled by members of the Hindu Jain sect, who took issue with any killing, including that of the robust mosquito population; the Jains went so far as to cover their mouths and noses with a cloth to keep from accidentally inhaling a small bug or parasite and inadvertently killing it.[19]

If cross-cultural matters were a source of consternation, so were internal ICD relations between white and African American servicemen. Most of the ICD's African Americans were in unskilled jobs, but one standout was Pfc. Curtis Green, a clerk-typist who sent a letter of complaint directly to Tunner on behalf of the other African Americans in the division. His grievances fell into four categories: slow promotions, frequent racial slurs by whites, the singling out of black soldiers for discipline (when whites were intentionally overlooked), and the segregation of rest camps, with only one camp in the theater opened to African Americans. According to Green, promotions were slow because black soldiers were denied skilled positions based on the assumption that low IQs necessitated such a policy, an assumption Green claimed was patently wrong. Racial slurs were frequent, and most African American soldiers silently bore up under the harassment; but when they did not, they were sometimes court-martialed—depending on the severity of their reply. Tensions also rose when 2,000 African American troops were denied the privilege of taking weekend leave into Dibrigarh, the reason being; they were told, that "Negro troops were not capable of behaving themselves in this city" whereas the real reason was, as Green points out, because a

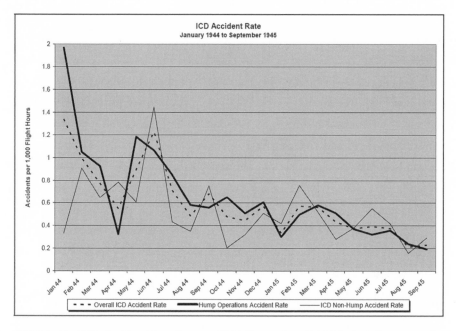

FIGURE 29. ICD Accident Rate, January 1944–September 1945. The bold line notes the accident rate per 1,000 flight hours of Hump operations, whereas the dashed line denotes the overall ICD accident rate and the thin line the non-Hump ICD rate. Notice the steady decline from January to August 1944 (after which Tunner replaced Hardin) and the sudden jump from January to March 1945, which later prompted Smith's ire toward Tunner. The low rate in April 1944 was the result of excellent flying weather between winter and the monsoon, *Source:* USAAF, ATC, ICD, Historical Section, "History of the India-China Division, Air Transport Command, 1945," p. 539.

new Enlisted Club was opening in town and "the company of the Negro soldiers were not desired." Tunner replied to Green a week later with the obligatory statement: "Every effort is being exerted to assure that racial discrimination is not allowed to exist in this command"; Green's complaint was an example of the general racial hue that shaded U.S. wartime race relations.[20]

Adding fuel to morale problems was the accident rate, which averaged nineteen per month during the first half of 1944, or about two every three days. Despite these numbers the overall trend was downward (see figure 29), with April witnessing only four total accidents due to a weather lull between winter and the wet monsoon. Arnold was concerned about the raw number of accidents and called for George's explanation, to which the ATC commander sardonically replied that there were only two ways to make the operations "safe"—to fly only when the weather was "indisputably good" or to "stop flying altogether." George continued, "Based on the strategic military importance of this operation, we are, I believe, safe in asserting the operation has, without a doubt, been required . . . [and] that the 'price' we have paid [in accidents] is entirely justifiable."[21] Hardin was not as methodical as Tunner in reducing the accident rate, but his local training programs and the increasing experience with the C-46 had gone far in arresting the problem. Nevertheless, the scrutiny facilitated Tunner's takeover of the division, with Gravely Point hoping a more safety-conscious commander could reduce the airlift's fatalities.

Pilot proficiency was still a problem in 1944 and would remain so for the rest of the war. C-46 pilots frequently misapplied carburetor heat in icing conditions, resulting in a number of engine failures that led to accidents. Takeoff accidents were also on the rise in the spring of 1945, caused by such factors as a premature reduction in power too soon after liftoff, a failure to reference instruments during night takeoffs, or by accidental application of slight brake pressure throughout the takeoff roll, which kept aircraft from getting airborne before reaching the end of the runway.[22] Exacerbating all of this was the rising rate of flying fatigue—too many pilots were flying too much. On the extreme side there were reports of pilots flying 165 hours per month—or about one Hump run per day—in an effort to earn the hours required to rotate back to the United States (see chapter 4). In September 44 percent of the division's pilots were flying over one hundred hours per month, and the following month this was up to 53 percent. To put a stop to this, Tunner established a new rule whereby a pilot could fly a maximum of only sixty hours every fifty days, and twelve hours of rest was required between flights. Tunner also planned on building jungle indoctrination camps designed to acclimate crews to the local environment so they could do recreational hunting, fishing, and camping—an idyllic prospect with most pilots in late-1944 concerned only with getting 650 flight hours as rapidly as possible, with little time or interest in exploring the Indian countryside.[23]

Before assuming command, Tunner made a survey trip to the ICD in June 1944 to take stock of the situation and was struck by the bedraggled personnel and their lack of military bearing. Replete with beards, handlebar moustaches, and sloppy uniforms, Tunner was taken aback by the absence of "common courtesy," recalling that he "began stopping to talk briefly with each group, asking such questions as how long they had been in the theater, what their duties were. Most stayed where they were, answering me in monosyllables, with bored expressions on their faces. One or two would stagger to their feet and give me a sickly smile."[24] Armed with this impression, Tunner made it his chief initiative upon arrival in September to infuse military discipline, instituting daily 8 A.M. staff meetings, requiring his base commanders to sharpen the appearance of their airfields, and organizing parades and inspections. As expected, there was initial resistance, but eventually Tunner's goading on the importance of aesthetics began to pay off and his crews began to behave with a sharpness in line with their appearance. Before he left Washington, Tunner was also able to handpick his staff and took with him to India a bloc of senior officers who all fell in line with his vision for the division. Two positions he gave particular attention to were public relations (filled by Gordon M. Rust), and statistician (filled by Kenneth Stiles). Rust had a cadre of artists and writers at his disposal with which to create all manner of posters, circulars, and even an ICD-wide weekly newspaper. The *Hump Express,* with a circulation of 35,000, was complete with Associated Press headlines, comic strips, and sports scores.[25] In the area of statistics, Stiles—in vogue with the "organization man" methodological culture prevalent among post-Depression U.S. businessmen—worked tirelessly to divine patterns and trends in any number of the dizzying categories of statistics that could be accumulated by an airlift unit, all with an eye toward isolating potential problems and forecasting future tonnages with a fair degree of accuracy.[26] The ICD was steadily growing in terms of the number of men, airplanes, and operating bases, with Tunner assuming the role of the CEO of a large commercial airline as much as he was a military commander.

The end of 1944 saw the emergence of a symbiotic relationship between the ICD's expansion and its effectiveness. Strategy makers began to view the unit as the best option for supplying China because it required little additional infrastructure (most airfields were complete by mid-1944) and could be just as easily expanded as it could be contracted, displaying something of the inherent flexibility of airpower. The airlift's record from December 1943 to September 1944 had given it the reputation of being capable of lifting as much as was required as long as the planes and pilots were available, so forecasts of 100,000 monthly tons by January 1946 were deemed not only possible but probable. Tonnage figures for

FIGURE 30. The ICD's Statistical Control Division. *Courtesy AMCHO.*

the last three months of the year were impressive: nearly 35,000 tons were delivered in November. Ichi-go's 1944 onslaught made Chennault the first priority for deliveries, but the perennial lack of adequate ground transportation in Yunnan made it impossible to carry supplies much beyond the Kunming terminus. In May 1944 a plan was hatched to fly seven hundred trucks and 2,000 tons of spare parts into China, but the fall of Guilin and Liuzhou in September and October cancelled this.[27]

Transportation limitations were also being felt by Japanese troops who had pressed into Guizhou Province in early autumn. Japanese records state that 3,500 tons of supplies left the Wuhan depot each month but that this had been trimmed to 2,500 tons by the time they reached Hengyang, 270 miles to the southwest; by the time they got to the border of Guizhou, this was further reduced to 600 tons, with only 300 tons reaching Hengyang each month—enough to keep a single U.S. division supplied for a day and a half.[28] Support was given as units from northern

Indochina crossed into China and connected the line of occupation from Hunan to Hanoi, completing what was to be the eastern extent of Japan's inner defense region. Wedemeyer took over from Stilwell in the midst of this and feared a Japanese drive to capture Kunming, though logistical realities made this unlikely with advanced Japanese units relying largely on captured stores.[29] The IGHQ ordered the new CEA commander, Gen. Okamura Yasuji, to halt with the capture of the Guizhou airfields, but the Americans were led to think Kunming was a target of a ground offensive when the Japanese Eleventh Army—acting on its own accord—began a westward drive into Guizhou Province. Motivated by Japanese setbacks in the Pacific, the Eleventh's commander, Kozuki Yoshi, was determined to operate in the spirit of the "Sho" ("to conquer") directive, issued by Tokyo that autumn and designed to inflict as much damage as possible on the enemy.[30] The Eleventh's solitary drive would eventually end at Dushan, three hundred miles east of Kunming, but not until Wedemeyer made hasty arrangements to airlift Chinese troops in Xian (Hsian) and Burma to stiffen Kunming's defenses.[31]

ALPHA, COTTON TAIL, AND GRUBWORM

Wedemeyer's proposal to airlift troops to defend Kunming was met with mixed feelings from the War Department, SEAC headquarters, and Chongqing. Hump tonnage would not be reduced, but the move would require 6,620 tons that could be used by Chennault. The 20th Bomber Command would also have to curtail its December plans from 349 to 276 sorties. Mountbatten no longer had need of the Chinese Fifty-third and Fifth Armies on the Salween front, but he was reluctant to give up any transports to move them back to China.[32] It was only after he was chided by Marshall and the CCS—who reminded the SEAC commander that transports were diverted to him to help him fend off the A-Go and U-Go offensives earlier that year—that he consented to give up use of Troop Carrier Command and Combat Cargo (ComCar) units assigned to his theater.[33] As for Chiang, he was pleased to be getting his Burma Expeditionary Army back on Chinese soil but was more muddled with the prospect of moving the Fifty-seventh Army from Xian, as it was positioned there chiefly to serve as a blocking force against Communist troops to the northeast.[34] Wedemeyer wanted to move 60,000 troops from Xian to Guiyan (in Guizhou Province, between the Japanese Eleventh Army and Kunming), but Chiang recommended moving 100,000 troops instead, but

FIGURE 31. Operation Grubworm's Loading Difficulties. *Source*: Operation Grubworm Historical Data, January 29, 1945, 830.04-2, AFHRA.

only after waiting thirty days. The motive behind the delay is unknown, but the offer to shift troops—even those counted among the Communist blocking force—was, as we shall later see, politically helpful to Chiang, who needed to bolster his power base in the south.[35]

The airlift of the Chinese troops from both the east and west was the dominant topic in the theater during the last six weeks of 1944, carried out by ATC, TCC, and ComCar units. The entire effort to defend Kunming was referred to as the "Alpha Plan," with ATC aircraft beginning the movement of over 18,000 troops from Xian to Chanyi on December 4.[36] Wedemeyer was leery of the value of these troops and so took more comfort in the Sixth Army's move from the Salween that started the next day. The ICD portion of the operation was called "Cotton Tail," but the Hump pilots fell under the operational control of the Tenth Air Force, which dubbed the operation "Grubworm." The Cotton Tail portion of the lift began on December 13 and moved over nearly 12,000 troops from Myitkyina to Chanyi. TCC and ComCar units carried another 14,000 troops into China,

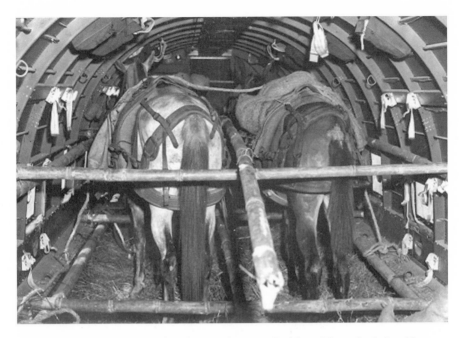

FIGURE 32. Solution to a Grubworm Transport Problem. The makeshift stables in the back of C-47s proved a success, as only one out of 1,500 animals ever broke free during flight. *Source:* Operation Grubworm Historical Data, January 29, 1945, 830.04-2, AFHRA.

along with almost 1,600 horses, probably the most unique cargo ever hauled over the Hump.

The lack of motor vehicles made the horses invaluable to the soldiers, though their movement took some extra planning. Animals had been carried over the Hump before, but not in these numbers, and potential problems cropped up at every turn. First, getting the animals into the planes was a chore, as most were opposed to climbing the steep ramp into the C-47's cargo compartment (see figures 31 and 32). To get around this, the animals were coaxed up a shallow ramp onto the back of a flatbed truck, which was then backed up to the cargo doors. Next there was the problem of securing the horses for what would most likely be a turbulent flight. Bamboo poles were cut to divide the cargo compartment into "stalls," two hundred pounds of hay were set down to soak up manure and urine, and the horses' halters were secured to the partitions. After a few tries it was found that four or five of the small Indian Tonga ponies (averaging only fourteen hands high and weighing between six hundred and seven hundred pounds) were the ideal maximum load; each trip carried a U.S. soldier who was experienced with horses. The horses were not sedated for two reasons: the crews feared the animals might act up if the doping wore off during the two-hour flight, and the high altitude served as its own sedative, keeping most of the animals docile. Impressively, of all the horses carried, only one got loose during its flight, going wild and nearly kicking a hole in the side of the fuselage until the crew chief—an experienced hostler—was able to subdue the animal. Other that this, Grubworm went off without a hitch, and the ComCar pilots later admitted they enjoyed carrying the animals more than Chinese soldiers, as the stench of manure was preferred to that of vomit.[37]

In the end the troop movement was unnecessary because Wedemeyer overestimated the IJA's intentions. The Japanese were able to destroy the Guangxi airfields, but the bases in Sichuan were well beyond Okamura's logistical reach.[38] U.S. success in the Pacific had drawn off troops for the defense of Okinawa, and the possibility of a Soviet invasion of Manchukuo meant the Japanese needed to keep ten to twenty divisions ready to reinforce the Guangdong Army.[39] The moves did help Chiang, though, who was working to consolidate his military base after the carnage of Ichi-go, and the repositioning of nearly 50,000 loyal troops in Yunnan and Guizhou served to bolster his stature in a part of the country with tepid loyalty to Chongqing. Far from reeling under Ichi-go's weight, Chiang sought to use the Japanese to eliminate dissident factions. He denied arms to Xue Yue—who was well positioned to defend Hengyang—because of the general's questionable loyalty. He had also hoped that local commanders like Yu Han-mou, Chang Fa-kwei (Zhang Fakui), and Tsai Ting-kai (Cai Tingkai) would be eliminated by the Japanese. In addition, Chiang was wary of the loyalties of Li Chi-shen, a prominent politician in Guangxi, as Li had approached the U.S. Consul in Guilin during the summer of 1944 to solicit U.S. help in establishing an anti-Chiang government in the southeast. Furthermore, John Paton Davies in Chongqing reported that a U.S. landing on China's southeast coast had the potential of precipitating an open announcement of independence by these anti-Chiang elements that were looking to coalesce around U.S. military power in overthrowing the generalissimo. Davies reported that the poor performance of

FIGURE 33. Off-Loading Chinese Nationalist Troops. *Courtesy AMCHO.*

Chinese troops in Guangxi during the defense of Guilin and Liuzhou was due to their understanding that Chiang "desired their liquidation," such that "they avoided contact with the enemy and sought to retain their forces intact."[40] This was seen in the extreme when 1,500 troops deserted at Yunnanyi in the midst of an airlift effort to carry them from Chongqing to Baoshan, costing the ICD 250 plane-hours of flight and wasting 22,000 gallons of gas.[41] To counter this timorousness, Chiang was glad to play off of Wedemeyer's fears of the Japanese Eleventh Army's thrust toward Kunming as an excuse to consolidate more loyal troops in southern China. This would not be the last time that Chiang would make use of U.S. air transport to reposition his troops to maintain a political advantage.

Lastly, the troop movements did little to warm relations between the Air Transport Command pilots of the ICD and the transport pilots who flew for TCC or ComCar. ATC fliers already had the reputation of being overpaid prima donnas because many of them flew for both the reserves and airlines (making a considerable income). Many of the reservist/airline pilots flew for the Ferry Command and so seldom saw regular service in the CBI (as in the example of American Airlines and Project 7A discussed in chapter 5), but the stigma still managed to attach itself to the broader population of ATC pilots. With airline pilots earning three to four times the salary of a regular army pilot—the reservists being paid as contractors for the War Department—it was not difficult for the regular officers to feel the twinge of inequity, especially when they could point to the influential positions of airline notables within ATC, like C. R. Smith, Lt. Col. John Steele (Pan Am's operations manager), and Col. Larry G. Fritz (a prewar executive with TWA).[42] Making matters worse was the fact that the media often confused any transport operation in Asia as that of the ICD, as in the case of a January 21, 1945, news report on the abovementioned troop movements. It gave sole credit to the "seasoned pilots of the Air Transport Command, who ferried troops and their equipment to Yunnan Province, and said the job was tougher than flying the 'hump' from India."[43] The TCC and ComCar units that did most of the work were summarily ignored, doing little to endear them to the ATC fliers.

MISSION DISSATISFACTION IN THE ICD

Overall, the Cotton Tail and Grubworm movements were uneventful. The only incident involving the troops occurred on the operation's last day, January 5, when a Chinese soldier waiting for a plane accidentally brushed a hand grenade off his belt that exploded, injuring eleven soldiers (but not the one who had been wearing it).[44] Had the operation taken a few more days, though, it could have meant disaster for the crews and passengers, as the Hump experienced its worst weather on record on the night of January 6–7. Referred to as "Black Week," the weather was the worst ever recorded by the Tenth Weather Squadron, with updrafts of 5,000 feet per minute, altitude crosswinds of ninety to one hundred miles per hour, severe icing, sleet, and hail from 15,000 feet all the way up to 38,000 feet. The few existing radio frequencies carried continual calls of "May Day" by airborne crews. A pilot report by Lt. Thomas M. Sykes was typical: "With our airspeed going from 300 to 40 mph, the rate of climb went up 4,000 feet a minute and suddenly we were on our back. While hanging in my safety belt and with dirt from the floor falling all around, I realized that it would be impossible to bail out. The co-pilot and I fought with the controls until we finally righted the ship at 21,000 feet. We made a complete 180-degree turn and were headed in the direction from which we had come." All told, nine ICD aircraft were lost in the storm, including eighteen crewmembers and nine passengers; CNAC lost three aircraft, and three more airplanes were lost between the Tenth and Fourteenth Air Forces.[45]

Tunner could do nothing to control the weather, but he took an active role in guarding against slumping division morale. He established "morale boards" at each base where soldiers could go to air grievances and make recommendations for improvement. There is little evidence that this approach served as anything other than an institutionalized "suggestion box," though he did continue to emphasize amenities and aesthetics, publishing a "Dream Base" book chockfull of photos of the best dining halls, operations rooms, theaters, and the like among his bases in order to foster unit pride. He also took measures to censor the spread of news he felt would be detrimental to morale. In mid-December a story broke in the *New York Times* and *Chicago Tribune* about a massive smuggling operation, run by Americans between India and China, under the headlines "Smugglers Infest Air Run to China" and "Convict Yanks as India-China Air Smugglers."[46] The stories actually did not originate from U.S. reporters but were first reported by war correspondents in the *CBI Roundup,* an in-theater publication. Maj. Gen. Daniel Sultan, now the commander of the India-Burma theater, allowed its release because he feared that it would otherwise be spread by rumor. The *Hindustan Standard,* a paper that cared little for the Anglo-U.S. presence in India, reprinted the story, which was then carried a few days later by U.S. newspapers. Tunner pleaded with the theater commander to block the story's release, but Sultan was unmoved. To counter the report's allegations that over $4 million had been netted by smugglers flying between India and China over the past two years, Tunner released his own report claiming that only seven out of the three hundred cases in the report involved the ICD, all of them minor and involving small amounts of cigarettes, liquor, or sulfa drugs.[47] A year prior, Alexander had noted a small degree of smuggling when he first took command of the wing in January 1943, and this likely persisted; later that year two ATC pilots were caught selling pens, watches, and other valuables in Karachi and were court-martialed for the offense.[48] The temptation to turn a profit on price differences between India and China was ubiquitous, and it was equally difficult for Tunner to keep his men upbeat about the importance of the unit's mission when they witnessed a general malaise and weariness for the war on the part of the Chinese. It was not uncommon for houseboys to serve as intermediaries between U.S. fliers and "fences" in town, with hundreds of dollars routinely changing hands—making the war, in the words of one unit historian, "a profitable venture."[49]

The battle cry among ICD flyers to "keep China in the war" had lost its vigor by late 1944 as the Americans saw firsthand the futility of their efforts, expressed in the sentiments of a thirty-two-month veteran of the theater who stated, "Somehow I felt that my three years here have been wasted."[50] Petty thievery of ICD stocks by locals was rampant because it was impossible to cordon an entire airfield. Vehicle theft got so bad that soldiers routinely removed the distributor cap and wires after parking a car to ensure it would still be there when they returned. Crews were also disheartened when they witnessed Chinese in civilian clothes taking receipt of cargo recently delivered, only to be loaded into trucks that were likely bound for the black market. Fuel, a commodity literally worth its weight in gold, was regularly stolen in drum lots and siphoned off into smaller containers, a smuggling system that reminded some of the older pilots of the United States' experiment with Prohibition (see figure 34).[51]

There were also frequent reports of Chinese working for the Japanese by sabotaging transports; in one case a plane had engine trouble before takeoff and

FIGURE 34. Innovative Fuel Smuggling. Captain Ogle, a P&T officer in Kunming, models a harness discovered on a Chinese civilian in 1944. *Source:* USAAF, ATC, ICD, Historical Section, "History of the India-China Division, Air Transport Command, 1944," 3:926.

taxied back to parking, where socks were found stuffed in the exhaust. Another pilot had trouble with an aileron while he was performing preflight checks preparing for a nighttime takeoff. He shined his flashlight out the window at the wing only to see a Chinese guard shredding the left aileron fabric with his bayonet; the saboteur was never captured.[52] This permeability between the Japanese and Chinese was not confined to the local level, either. The Alpha troop movement was kept a strict secret, with only the highest authorities in the U.S. and Chinese governments aware of the mission. But three days after the plan was first passed to the generalissimo, Tokyo Rose, the well-known radio propagandist, broadcast the entire plan, including such details as pickup and arrival bases, the number of troops to be moved, the number of planes, and the mission's objective. It was within this context that one witnessed a corresponding rise in the cynicism of Americans and their involvement in local smuggling.

To counteract the withdrawal of air units from China, the Japanese made the most of espionage. Rarely did a nighttime bombing raid on Kunming occur without small signal fires suddenly appearing in nearby hills only minutes before the bombers would arrive overhead, helping the Japanese pilots triangulate their positions to locate the airfield. At a B-29 base in Chengdu, signal flares were mysteriously fired from each end of the runway just as the attacking bombers appeared over the field. Four Americans fleeing for cover during another attack came across Chinese who had just set off flares on the approach end of the runway only moments before the Japanese bombers arrived. Poverty-stricken locals were susceptible to bounties offered by the Japanese, who promised CN $10 million for destroying a bomber, CN $5 million for a destroying a fighter, CN $5 million for killing flight personnel, and CN $5 million for inflicting crippling damage to a U.S. air base.[53] Chinese officers were even suspect, exemplified by a captain who was discovered taking "voluminous notes" at Kunming in October 1944. He was brought into custody and questioned in the presence of ranking Chinese officials, claiming he "was doing it for practice" and was summarily set free. One American present at the interrogation sarcastically commented that he doubted that the information the captain was gathering was "solely for local consumption."[54]

PILOT ROTATION AND PRODUCTION-LINE MAINTENANCE

There was little Tunner could do to alter the difficult operating environment, but his penchant for a neat and orderly division was beginning to bear fruit as mission efficiency slowly began to increase. One of his chief means of doing this was by revamping the entire maintenance system by replacing the old crew chief-centered system with an assembly-line approach called Production-Line Maintenance (PLM). PLM was being used in the United States at training bases and was designed to better handle a high volume of traffic by using various teams to inspect or repair certain systems on airplanes. Under the old system the plane's dedicated crew chief (a flight mechanic) was responsible for all work on that particular airplane, "from changing a tail wheel to adjusting a propeller power unit."[55] Under the new system the plane would be serviced by up to seven different stations, each one checking a specific part of the airplane like the engines, radios, oxygen system, instruments, and so forth. Theoretically this would reduce the number of overall mechanics while also allowing them to be experts on only one system rather than the entire aircraft. This was attractive to Tunner, who was beginning to receive daily arrivals of new C-54s; yet he had few mechanics qualified to service the airplanes. At Kurmitola in January only 15 percent of his crew chiefs had more than a few weeks of experience on the aircraft, and at Shamshernagagar only 4 percent of the mechanics had any experience on four-engine aircraft. Tunner's fleet was forecast to grow to 602 aircraft, for which he would need over 10,000 mechanics when he had only 7,000. PLM would solve this problem by allowing him to hire unskilled locals to do jobs like replacing spark plugs and washing airplanes while also making the most of skilled non-U.S. help in the form of a hundred German-trained Chinese crew chiefs who each had upward of a decade of experience.[56]

Tunner had no experience with PLM but was given the idea by Col. Robert Bruce White, who was intimately familiar with it. Tunner made White the ICD's maintenance chief and put him in charge of the rocky transition that was met with resistance from all quarters during an initial tryout at Jorhat in February 1945. Experienced mechanics did not like the arrangement because it required them to repair systems in a prescribed manner in a day when most repairs relied on a mechanic's favorite technique, not a shop manual. Nor did pilots like it, fearing that because no single man fixed the plane, the repairs were likely to be shoddy or incomplete because of the "impersonal" nature of the system. The low motivation to make PLM work caused problems, and repairs actually took longer under the new system. Pilots' fears were given some validation when a series of crashes took place a couple of weeks after the trial's beginning, leading to the assumption that incomplete repairs were to blame. White was determined to make the system work, though, and threatened to "kick" some local commanders "into the Brahmaputra" if they did not "get with the program"; by the end of March PLM was gaining some steady acceptance as the maintenance utilization rate was showing a steady increase.[57]

PLM was a good solution to a shortage of qualified mechanics in the midst of a growing fleet, but solving a looming shortage of pilots was not as easy to handle. When Tunner first took over the division, he decided to maintain the status quo in rotation policy for his aircrews, fearing that tampering with the requirement for 650 hours would only contribute to an atmosphere of "unrest, uncertainty, and dissatisfaction" and that the policy had to remain in place to "bring a feeling of stability to our crews."[58] With the wing growing, though, he would be forced to increase this requirement by March 1945. Hardin had been the first to institute a strict hour-based system of rotation, rightly sensing that it motivated his crews to fly. But by spring 1945 pilots were gaining flight time too rapidly, allowing them to rotate back to the United States and creating a perennial vacuum of Hump-experienced aircrews, a factor that kept the accident rate higher than desired. To combat this, Tunner proposed upping the hour requirement to 750 hours and forcing all aircrew to remain in the theater for at least one year. The announce-ment was bound to be met with resistance, so Tunner planned to compensate the pilots by being "generous" with "rehabilitation camp periods and with leaves," while again proposing to develop "hunting and recreational facilities at our jungle camps" and to "generally go overboard looking after the welfare of the individual pilot."[59] Half of the division's accidents were being caused by the bottom one-quarter of its experience pool, so Tunner thought that extending the duty require-ment was the best way to solve the problem, even though the policy caused an uproar in the division to such a degree that two months after it was implemented he was begging George for more pilots: "Due to their strong reaction to the pres-ent plan [one year and 750 hours] I am inclined to agree that that we should make a concession," proposing to keep the flying requirement at 750 hours but with a reduction of the in-theater time to ten months.[60] Apparently the pilots did not consider the "generous" leaves and opportunities for a jungle retreat as adequate payback for increasing the time requirement.

Tunner did help to improve morale among ground personnel, though, by requiring soldiers to stay in the unit for only two years. Yet by the following sum-mer he was anticipating a shortage and had his personnel officer devise a clever incentive plan that allowed men forty-five days of leave in the United States if, at the eighteen-month point in their tour, they agreed to come back to India for twelve more months. There is no data that records how many took this option, but there were reports that members of Tunner's headquarters were pressur-ing men to stay in the theater longer, drawing the ire of Smith, who threatened Tunner: "Unless you take immediate and positive action to limit pressure being placed on your people to volunteer for a second tour of duty, we will have to take such action to control it from this end."[61]

JAPAN'S LAST GASP: THE SPRING '45 OFFENSIVE

Hump tonnage continued to rise at the start of 1945, and the 44,099 tons delivered in January represented a 38 percent jump from the previous month. The following month Wedemeyer submitted his newly drafted Beta Plan to the generalissimo, one that sought to use the U.S.-trained Chinese divisions and a heavy complement of Tenth and Fourteenth Air Force aircraft to thrust eastward and open a path to Fort Bayard, a coastal town on the Liuzhou Peninsula. If successful, the Americans would have access to China directly from the South China Sea. The generalissimo approved the plan, and Wedemeyer went to Washington to gain approval from the War Department as planners in India and China made arrangements for the increasing tonnage—via the Hump, the Stilwell Road, and the pipeline—needed to execute the plan. April through May and June through August required 77,000 tons and 87,000 tons, respectively, to support the thirty-six divisions and their air contingent. Forecasts for such deliveries were below this mark by 12,000 to 25,000 tons, and when the army's Service of Supply offered to again bolster the Stilwell Road to increase tonnage, planners decided against it because the investment of added trucks and support personnel was too high. Conveniently, the B-29 bases in Calcutta had recently been vacated by 20th Bomber Command, so those fields became an ideal spot to reopen as C-54 airfields to increase the number of direct flights to Kunming. The new airplane's impact was significant, seen most vividly in July 1945 when air, road, and pipeline combined to deliver 119,800 tons to China, just shy of the goal of 129,000 tons; the airlift carried the largest share, 71,000 tons, when it was originally forecast to carry only 20,000 tons.[62] In addition, tonnage delivered over the Stilwell Road included the weight of the vehicles used; many of those trucks were permanently left in China.[63] The impact of the C-54 was being felt, all the more significant because it was not arriving in India in the numbers hoped for; original plans were to redeploy C-54s from Europe to Asia once the war with Germany was over, but changes committing many of these transports to the redeployment of U.S. servicemen back to the United States meant there were only twenty-two more C-54s working the Hump on V-J Day than there were on V-E Day (see figure 35).[64]

Hump deliveries continued to be an expression of U.S. policy in February with a delivery of U.S. medical supplies to Communist troops in Yan'an. At the

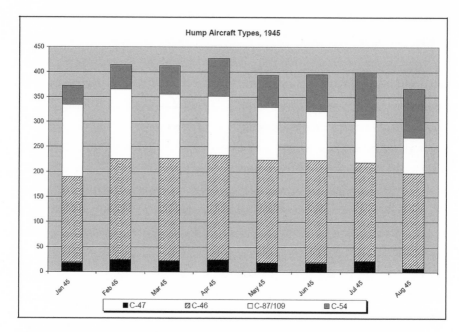

FIGURE 35. Hump Aircraft Types, 1945. Fleet composition for the Hump portion of ICD's mission was relatively static throughout 1945, which shows that the division relied on better maintenance procedures and more efficient operations rather than sheer number of planes to account for the impressive tonnage figures delivered to China. *Source*: USAAF, ATC, ICD, Historical Section, "History of the India-China Division, Air Transport Command, 1945," p. 85.

beginning of 1945 U.S. policy toward China in the near term was the unification of Chinese war resources against Japan; the long-term objective was to develop "a united, democratically progressive, and cooperative China."[65] This did not mean that China was expected to be united under Chiang, but it also did not mean that the United States would begin arming the Communists. As an intermediary position the ICD could deliver Red Cross medical supplies to Yan'an. A single crew delivered medicines, sulfa, microscopes, X-ray equipment, and surgical supplies to the Bethune Memorial Peace Hospital run by Dr. George Hatem (Ma Haide), a Lebanese American physician trained at American University in Beirut and Geneva and working for the Communists. Dr. Hatem said of the plane's cargo that it was "more medicines than I've seen in the last eight years put together."[66] The delivery was more symbolic than anything else, serving as a tangible expression of the United States' readiness to help any group in China willing to fight the Japanese. The U.S. observer mission—the so-called Dixie Mission—had been working with the Communists since the beginning of the winter of 1944 as U.S. policy slowly began to divorce itself from Chiang's government.[67]

At the same time that the United States was exercising other options in China by working with the Communists, the Japanese were again softening their position toward the Nationalists. Tokyo had ordered Okamura to attempt to open talks with Chiang in December 1944, which he conducted via radio with Yuan Liang, Chiang's representative in Shanghai. Okamura again offered to end the war with a Japanese withdrawal to Manchukuo, but Chiang insisted that the Japanese withdraw to Korea. In February Okamura met with Yuan and called for the two sides to show restraint toward each other but was not authorized to relax the Japanese terms. In mid-March, with the fall of Okinawa on the near horizon, Koiso desperately summoned Miao Bin, the vice president of the Examination Yuan in Nanjing's puppet government who claimed he was authorized to negotiate terms on behalf of Chongqing, offering supposed "Sino-Japanese comprehensive peace proposals." Terms included the dissolution of the puppet government with Chongqing simultaneously recognizing a National Government Nanjing Rear Area Office (*lishoufu*) made up of prominent citizens. Following this, Chinese and Japanese representatives would meet in Macau, and once terms were signed, Chiang's government would return to Nanjing. Koiso presented Miao's proposal to the Supreme War Council, but it was refused by war minister Sugiyama and foreign minister Shigemitsu, who questioned the authenticity of the offer. The emperor also rejected the move. So Koiso resigned in the midst of a loss of confidence and was succeeded by Suzuki Kantaro, who, by the summer of 1945, had absolutely no leverage with Chongqing.[68]

Militarily the IGHQ ordered Okamura to begin assuming a defensive posture in China in the event of a U.S. invasion of China by fortifying the coast with three divisions and consolidating its position between Shanghai and Hankow. In the absence of a solid air force he launched a spearhead to take the U.S. air base at Laohekou, about 350 miles northeast of Chongqing, and Angang, 100 miles west of Laohekou. Fearing that the Japanese might press all the way to Zhijiang (or Chihchiang, in Hunan Province), 270 miles southeast of Chongqing, Wedemeyer again took action to coordinate a blocking force, again calling for the airlift of Chinese troops. He notified the ICD of the requirement to move the Chinese New Sixth Army's 22nd Division from Kunming to Zhijiang to block the capture of the U.S. airbase there. Code-named Operation Rooster, ATC began the airlift of 11,000 troops and 1,300 animals on April 21 using C-46s and C-47s. Thirty C-46s were pulled from Hump duty to supplement the operation, such that an even 100 transports were available for the haul. Whether the operation's details were compromised is uncertain, but within hours of the arrival of Rooster's head-quarters detachment at Zhijiang, the field came under attack by a handful of Japa-nese saboteurs, eliciting haphazard gunfire from nervous Chinese troops; enemy snipers were also located around the field and a U.S. fighter pilot on the ground was shot in front of the alert shack. The airlift was completed in nine days without a single incident or accident, prompting a second phase that began on April 30; more than 14,000 troops and 800 animals were carried with only one accident. The Japanese never succeeded in capturing Zhijiang, as their own supply lines were stretched to the limit, but the rapid infusion to the area of over 25,000 troops in less than two weeks undoubtedly played a part in halting Okamura's offen-sive.[69]

Troop movements on a whole were usually uneventful. They became a regular feature of the ICD's mission in 1945; the division moved more than 75,000 Chinese soldiers in its four largest moves between January and July, and a problem arose on only a few occasions. One incident occurred in July 1945 with a load of eighteen Chinese soldiers, who were being carried from Chanyi to Nan-ning when bad weather forced the plane to land at Poseh. The crew decided to eat dinner while waiting for the weather to pass, and when they returned to the airplane they found that the soldiers had refused to deplane. The pilot wanted to wait until the next day to continue the trip, but the soldiers' belligerence prompted him to make the best of the situation and make the flight to Nanning. The crew was able to avoid thunderstorms but encountered some severe turbu-lence that caused one soldier to cut his head, which the radio operator bandaged. Upon landing at Nanning the crew deplaned, waiting for the soldiers to be picked up, but were suddenly lined up against the side of the airplane with a Chinese ser-geant shouting orders to his comrades to fix bayonets and charge their weapons in what looked to be a plan to execute the aircrew. A U.S. infantry officer at the field stepped into the fray and ordered the sergeant to have his men put down their weapons, though it was only due to the timely arrival of a high-ranking Chinese officer that the soldiers relented. The roughed-up crew quickly boarded their airplane and took off, with no clue as to why the soldiers threatened to kill them. From this time forward all Chinese soldiers were required to stow their weapons in the radio compartment, and all crew members were equipped with side arms on troop-carrying trips.[70]

A second incident was not isolated but instead was reported by a number of aircrews throughout the summer. Planes were landing with fewer troops than they loaded, leading to the puzzling question of what happened to the missing soldiers. Some pilots thought that soldiers used the flights to get rid of unwanted comrades, as one pilot reported seeing an NCO kick a conscript out of the plane's open door—at altitude—during one flight. In an extreme example one C-46 on April 16 landed with only forty-three troops when sixty-five had been on board before takeoff. The remaining soldiers claimed the missing twenty-two had jumped out of the plane after takeoff, some while the plane was still close to the ground, others at altitude, grabbing one of the plane's few parachutes. Soon after replacing Stilwell, Wedemeyer remarked of the Chinese conscript, "Conscription comes to the Chinese peasant like famine or flood, only more regularly—every year twice—and claims more victims. Famine, flood, and drought compare with conscription like chicken pox with plague." It is likely that conscripts (and even regulars) saw the flights as a possible means of escape and were willing to risk the jump, thinking their odds were better at surviving the fall than surviving another day in the army.[71]

TUNNER'S AIRLINE

From April through July 1945 the ICD was showing the marks of an efficient and effective air transport machine. Hump tonnage increased 60 percent during this period alone, though with no appreciable increase in the size of the fleet. In addition to special troop movements, the division had expanded to over forty bases and was flying a complex route structure that looked similar to the trunk-line and feeder-route structure of contemporary airlines. The main routes were between Karachi, Calcutta, Assam, and Kunming, with feeder routes to the dozens of other terminals operated by ATC. The air traffic control system was mature enough to manage the dozens of aircraft airborne at any given time, and the radio and navigation network now had sufficient transmitters and navaids to make a flight from India to China seem more like one from St. Louis to New York. The ICD also went so far as to see that "attractive feminine agents" checked passengers aboard flights at larger terminals and made a point of attending to such amenities as back-rests, portable air coolers, and portable seat tables for passengers to use to eat or play games. Unfortunately, though, the division surgeon deemed in-flight meal service inadvisable, fearing the food would spoil in the warm climate.[72]

Tunner was also working to get the accident rate under control. He had seen improvement toward the end of 1944, but the first three months of 1945 looked like a return to rates experienced under Hardin's command. Smith was angry with the trend and in early March demanded that Tunner get the problem under control, even if it meant a reduction in Hump tonnage. To get a better grasp of the problem, a month later Tunner trimmed his April tonnage forecast from 48,000 tons to 42,000 in a move that drew ire in the other direction. Upset by the reduction, Stratemeyer, still the ranking air officer in the India-Burma Command, was confronted by Gen. Ira Eaker, the AAF's new deputy commander who had likely been persuaded by Chennault that the ICD was being too careful in avoiding accidents and not aggressive enough in hauling cargo. Stratemeyer wrote George, citing the ICD's accident rate of only one crash per 400 sorties and reminding him that this was much lower than the loss rate of bombers—which was closer to one crash per 150 sorties in April 1945.[73] Stratemeyer claimed that the Hump was "the most exacting and difficult air route in the world" and was more of a combat mission than any of hundreds of other ATC runs that dotted the globe. Thus, he told George (and Smith and Tunner), ATC needed to "modify . . . policies concerning flying accidents for hump making them consistent with a combat [mission]" and take a more aggressive posture in operations.[74]

Tonnage did improve, along with the accident rate, though by now China's position was reduced to an appendage of Allied strategy. Roosevelt died in April, and Truman shared little of his predecessor's unique warmth toward the Asian ally or FDR's hope for China's role in the postwar world. Wedemeyer's Beta Plan to capture Fort Bayard never came to fruition, and the PAC-AID shipments to the coast were no longer held at a premium, even in the midst of U.S. plans to invade the Japanese home islands. Still, by July more flights were traveling between India and China than anywhere else in ATC. The ICD's fleet had grown to almost 750 aircraft and numbered over 4,400 pilots, an organization roughly the size of American Airlines in 2006. The division was also supplemented by tactical units (B-25 and B-24 squadrons), which were available to conduct airlift duties due to an absence of targets in China, though Tunner found the bomber pilots to be poor Hump fliers. Many of these crews groused about the mission, with one recalling, "It is easily evident that there is nothing inspiring in 'Hump' flying."[75]

To prove the mettle of his outfit, Tunner called for a massive push on August 1, the AAF's official "birthday," and so challenged the division to see how much it could carry in a single twenty-four-hour period. Gravely Point notified ICD headquarters in mid-July of the "celebration," and after a few meetings Tunner and his staff decided a "working celebration" would be best. Plans were set in motion to maximize cargo throughput at the beginning of the month, with divisionwide furor beginning as a slow rumble. Individual pilots turned it into a game by betting on the odds of how much would be carried. Ground crews got into the contest as well: so confident was Chanyi air base that it posed a challenge to the other Chinese terminals in a theaterwide radio message, "Put up or shut up. 1342 [Chanyi Base Unit] has 1,000 dollars which says that we will have the lowest turn-around time on all types aircraft for Army Air Forces' birthday 1 August. Total pool of 4,000 dollars is objective. Any takers." No other base took the bet even when the odds were raised to four-to-one. The effort began on July 31 at 7 P.M. with a few isolated thunderstorms cropping up and delaying the excitement at some fields. Halfway through the day, base-to-base taunting began, with the China Wing telegramming the Assam Wing, "Get the rest of your personnel out of bed and start them working. Send over more aircraft. We can use the business. The boredom is terrific," to which Assam replied, "This is a routine day for Assam Wing. Why can't China Wing turn our ships around like this every day[?]"[76] Banter aside, there was no way the division could have sustained that rate of cargo as the day's operations took on a "surge" mentality, delivering 5,327 tons in the single twenty-four-hour period, exceeding half of Roosevelt's *monthly* goal of 1943 in a *single day*. In doing so, Tunner demonstrated the seemingly limitless capability of the airlift, now operating with a full-grown infrastructure and limited only by the available number of planes and aircrews.

The headline of the August 14 *Hump Express* announced, "Japan War Ends:

Terms Accepted." Two atomic bombs along with a Soviet invasion of Manchukuo led to Japanese capitulation, though this did not bring an immediate end to the Hump. The division would begin scaling down but by necessity would play a major role in Allied demobilization. And just as Chinese troop movements were a regular feature of the war's last year, they would continue to be into September 1945 in the rush to accept the surrender of Japanese armies scattered throughout China. If the Japanese surrender meant the end of the war for the Americans, it simply marked a transition for Chiang and his government, now focused completely on the problem that had consumed him prior to the Marco Polo Bridge incident in July 1937, that of dispensing with the Communists.

THE END OF THE HUMP

The news of the Japanese surrender changed little for the India-China Division. Day-to-day flights continued, albeit at a slower pace due to Tunner's operational choice that placed safety before tonnage. Instrument flight rules became mandatory for all sorties to ensure adequate spacing and reduce the risk of a midair collision, and pilots flew no more than one hundred hours per month.[1] Most flights were accomplished by two-engine C-46s while the older C-87s were used only during the daytime and C-54s were used even more sparingly. In addition, only experienced pilots flew passenger missions, though this rule proved unhelpful in the face of the division's last crash of the war, a C-54 loaded with forty U.S. servicemen from Chabua en route to Karachi on November 3. The plane was reported missing after being many hours overdue; it was not found until another plane spotted its wreckage in Bhutan two weeks later. Investigators speculated that the pilots may have intentionally flown off course to treat their passengers to a "sight-seeing trip of Mt. Everest." The accident investigator noted that "a holiday spirit prevailed among all passengers facing the possibility of an early arrival in the U.S.," encouraging the tragic diversion.[2]

CLOSING THE HUMP

Division morale spiraled downward with air and ground crews obsessed on when they would return to the United States. Tunner vainly tried to arrest this trend with homegrown entertainment in the form of "one act plays, musical dramas, minstrel shows, dramatic stunts, play reading, Vaudeville acts, and amateur nights," but the average airman was concerned only with getting home. Family members in the United States increased the pressure by asking congressmen why their sons, husbands, or sweethearts were being kept overseas. Making matters worse were reports that earlier restraints on allowable cargo were being relaxed; in mid-October Congressman John J. Cochran of Missouri contacted Hap Arnold to inform him of the contents of a letter from a constituent who was an ICD aircrew member and who claimed, "The cargo that has been going into China these past three weeks is of the type that I refuse to fly and risk my life for. They consist of: Shrubbery (for the China General's house), baled cotton, women's sanitary napkins, prophylactics, beer, ping pong tables, talcum powder, cocktail tables, [and] tent pegs. . . . Those [American] fellows in China don't want all those things. All they want is to go home like the rest of us. By the way, last week I took over a load of two-by-fours." Cochran closed his letter with the veiled threat that Arnold should be grateful the "letter did not get into the hands of someone who likes to criticize," or else it would have been read "on the Floor" (i.e., of the House).[3]

Problems and abuses aside, the ICD played a critical role in initial demobilization plans, serving as the chief means to get India- and China-based troops to port cities for shipment home. The Hope Project moved 14,000 men from Chabua to Karachi in September while maintaining regular shipments to support troops still in China.[4] Americans in China were flown to coastal cities for shipment home across the Pacific, as Tunner's "airline" played the key role in CBI demobilization while still delivering almost 40,000 tons of supplies to China in September and 8,000 tons in October. The Hump was formally scheduled to close on November 15, though Tunner relinquished command in late October and returned to the United States because his wife was undergoing major surgery for brain cancer. He was replaced for the Hump's last month by Brig. Gen. Charles W. Lawrence, a bomber group commander.[5]

Concurrent with the frenzied U.S. demobilization effort was the larger strategic matter of the Japanese surrender in China, something that posed an immediate threat to Chiang's leadership. Wedemeyer had been goading Chiang since July to make preparations for Japan's surrender and was dismayed by the generalissimo's seeming carelessness for this eventuality. Writing to Marshall on August 1, Wedemeyer stated: "Frankly, if peace should come within the next few weeks we will be woefully unprepared in China. On the American side we could handle our own unilateral personnel and property interests but many of our activities are inextricably tied in with the Chinese, and, if peace comes suddenly, it is reasonable to expect widespread confusion and disorder. The Chinese have no plan for rehabilitation, prevention of epidemics, restoration of utilities, establishment of balanced economy and redisposition of millions of refugees."[6]

Wedemeyer's concerns were real—epidemics, the economy, and refugees were all domestic matters requiring the generalissimo's attention—but they were not Chiang's highest priority. His most immediate problem had to do with the looming power vacuum that would result from the surrender of Japanese forces in the northeast: he had no loyal forces in the area to assume control, making the situation all the more problematic because the Communists were well placed to accept the Japanese surrender (see figure 36).

On August 11 Chiang asked Wedemeyer for a U.S. army of occupation to secure China's coastal cities and for airlift support to move GMD troops to these cities. No such occupying force could be quickly deployed to China, but the repositioning of Chinese troops was possible. The War Department gave Wedemeyer permission to help the Nationalists with whatever airlift requirements they had to get into position to accept the Japanese surrender, with the one caveat that "the American government would not support the Chinese government in civil war."[7] But with four Communist armies under Zhu De marching north to link up with the Soviets (who invaded Manchukuo on August 8), securing roads, railroads, and bridges in preparation to move their forces to Nanjing, Beijing, and Shanghai, any airlift of GMD forces to these areas would be a de facto source of friction. Chiang ordered Zhu to halt his "abrupt and illegal actions," telling him "never again to take independent action," to which the Communist general replied by calling Chiang a "Fascist chieftain" who treated "enemies as friends and friends as enemies."[8] The Yalta and Potsdam agreements both claimed that Chiang's government was to accept the surrender, but this was only a political declaration. It was up to U.S. airlift assets in India and China to make it a reality.

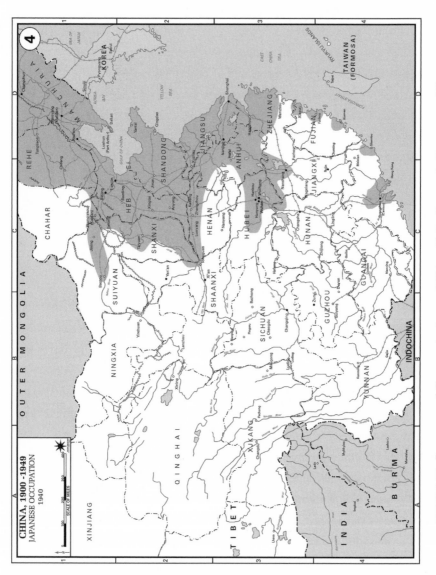

FIGURE 36. Japanese and Communist Areas of China, 1949. *Courtesy the Department of History, U.S. Military Academy.*

Like the Grubworm and Rooster movements earlier in the year, both the ICD and Tenth Air Force troop carrier units were tasked with four major troop deployments between September 6 and October 27. The movements, code-named "Cannon," "Egg," "Charlie," and "Baker," involved the transport of the Ninety-fourth, Sixth, and Ninety-second Armies from central and south-central China to Shanghai, Nanjing, and Beijing. The first of these—the Cannon project—was run exclusively by ICD and posed the greatest logistical challenge. Airplanes based at Tezgaon (in modern-day Bangladesh) were to pick up soldiers in Liuzhou (in Guangxi Province), 1,200 miles to the east, and move them to Shanghai, another 900 miles to the northeast. The problem was complicated by the fact that there were no opportunities for refueling or repairs once the planes left Tezgaon. Tunner summarized the problem by recalling, "Suppose, for example, that our planes were based in Los Angeles, that thirty thousand Chinese were to be flown from Atlanta to Boston—and that there was not a drop of gasoline nor one item of equipment or aircraft parts east of the Rockies. That would just about size up the situation."[9] To accomplish the mission C-54s from Col. Andrew Cannon's (the mission's namesake) Bengal Wing were loaded to maximum capacity with drums of aviation fuel and flown to Liuzhou. There they off-loaded the fuel and on-loaded eighty to eighty-five Nationalist soldiers (along with the required fuel) to make the round-trip flight to Shanghai. Back at Liuzhou the planes again refueled and returned to Tezgaon to repeat the cycle until all of the Ninety-four Amy's 26,000 troops were moved. The Cannon project took eighteen days, and when all four movements were done, a total of 107,000 Chinese soldiers had been moved from China's interior into a position that allowed Chiang to re-assert his rule over the part of China from which he had fled eight years earlier.[10] Without the airlift, it would have taken his armies weeks (and possibly months) to get to northeast China, arriving well after Zhu De's forces controlled Beijing, Nanjing, and Shanghai. Air transport surmounted Chiang's immediate need, and it also allowed him to strategically reposition his forces through much of 1946, evidenced by the fact that at the time of the Japanese surrender, the Nationalists controlled only 15 percent of the country, geographically speaking, but in a year their influence had spread to over 80 percent. The GMD, in the words of one observer, had "to show initiative, strength, and cohesions, while overcoming the corruption and lack of discipline that had spread during the last phase of the anti-

Japanese war."[11] The presence of U.S. air transport went far in helping Chiang extend his reach; in the words of Tang Tsou, it "swung the balance in favor of the Nationalist government and averted an imminent Communist victory."[12]

CHIANG'S POST-V-J DAY REALIGNMENT

A critical factor in determining to what extent—if at all—the United States might have prevented a Chinese surrender to the Japanese centers on the true nature of Chiang Kaishek's wartime relationship with the Japanese, something still veiled in a fair amount to mystery. Chiang was publicly defiant toward Japan after the Xian Incident in December 1936, but prior to Xian, Chiang had viewed the Japanese as less troublesome than Mao's Communists.[13] Once the "China Incident" began in the summer of 1937 and up through the Pacific War, Chiang's rhetoric was consistently anti-Japanese, as were his responses to Japanese peace offers, never budging on his demand that Manchukuo be returned to China.[14] What is murkier, though, is the degree to which he communicated with the Japanese off the record. Dai Li, the Himmler-esque head of the Juntong secret service (and a man whom Chiang trusted implicitly), was in regular radio contact with Zhou Fohai, who in 1944 replaced Wang Jingwei, the president of China's collaborationist puppet government in Nanjing.[15] Zhou supposedly consulted with Chiang (through Dai) on a number of matters, some of them picayune, as in 1943 when he asked the generalissimo who should be chosen as the next mayor of Shanghai.[16] Now, the mere existence of this dialogue between Nanjing (and, by extension, Tokyo) and Chongqing does not necessarily indicate a level of agreement or collusion; the Juntong had earlier adopted the strategy of *quxian jiuguo* ("saving the nation through devious ways") by openly working with enemy intelligence services in an effort to infiltrate the hundreds of spy networks among the Chinese (both Nationalist and collaborationist) and Japanese.[17] But what this level of communication between collaborationist Nanjing and Chongqing does suggest is that Chiang, while formally rebuffing the Japanese government, was likely at the same time employing covert modes of communication with Tokyo, recognizing that the Japanese could do much to help him maintain a monopoly on Nationalist power, especially in provinces where his control was more tenuous.

In contrast to the questions surrounding Chiang's wartime dialogue with the Japanese is the matter of his relationship with them immediately following the

FIGURE 37. Gen. Okamura Yasuji. *Courtesy U.S. Army Center of Military History.*

war, something known with more clarity. In December 1944 John Paton Davies wrote, "Chiang's greatest hope for domestic reascendency [*sic*] lies in cooperation with the Japanese-sponsored Chinese puppets," a true enough statement that would be borne out after the surrender in September 1945.[18] But what Davies did not anticipate was the mind-boggling post-surrender level of cooperation between the Chinese and Japanese, starting with the CEA's commander, Gen. Okamura Yasuji, who did not return home after the war but instead remained in China as a senior military advisor for the generalissimo. Okamura was imprisoned after signing Japan's surrender in Nanjing on September 9 but was released soon after by Chiang—for whom he worked as an advisor during the civil war with the Communists. In a bit of twisted irony, Okamura's post on Chiang's staff allowed him to escape the war-crime trials that many of his peers were undergoing in Tokyo, Nanjing, Manila, and Djakarta while he—the architect of the "Three Alls" campaign ("Kill all, burn all, destroy all") of 1940—remained comfortably in Nanjing. In January 1949 he was officially cleared of all wrongdoing by a (Nationalist) Shanghai court, news that infuriated Mao, who vowed to bring Okamura to trial. Okamura returned home to Japan at the beginning of 1949 and continued to voice his support for Chiang's government, now in Taiwan.[19]

Okamura was not the only Japanese soldier to remain in China after 1945 at the request of the Nationalists. In November 1946 Wedemeyer complained to Chiang that his troops were moving too slowly in disarming the Japanese in Beijing, where an estimated 70,000 Japanese soldiers were still garrisoned.[20] Three months later sources reported that 80,000 Japanese soldiers were still fighting alongside Chiang's armies in eastern and northwestern Manchuria and were being supplied from GMD depots more generously than their Nationalist counterparts, costing Nanjing two billion Chinese dollars a month. It was not uncommon for Japanese soldiers to exchange their uniforms for civilian clothes following the surrender in order to blend into the Chinese population; if they were experienced NCOs, the GMD offered them commissions in the Chinese army and they then became part of Chiang's officer corps. Additionally, warlord (and nominal Chiang-ally) Yan Xishan amassed an entire Japanese army, hired to protect his home province of Shanxi from Communist forces, which they did successfully for almost four years. It was this army that kept Yan's provincial capital of Taiyuan—also the site of a huge Nationalist arsenal—from the Communists until 1949.[21]

The motives for Japanese soldiers to remain in China were varied. For some the shame of returning home after being defeated was too humiliating. For others there was the fear of being unable to find jobs or food in Japan. As in the case of Okamura, there was the fear of an Allied military tribunal that might lead to incarceration or the death penalty. There were also those who were staunch Japanese militarists and viewed continued duty in China as an opportunity to rebuild some of Japan's prewar might. Shanxi was rich in both coal and iron, and Yan Xishan was willing to trade these resources with his Japanese commanders if they would protect the province from the Communists. Yan's ultimate goal was eventual independence from the rest of China; in return the Japanese would be allowed to use the province's rich resources to rebuild Japan's military.[22] Such possibilities were not outlandish, as Yan himself, a great admirer of Japanese military prowess, was a graduate of the Japanese Military Academy. In 1946 he allowed the Japanese to establish a military academy in Taiyuan, and one day while he was inspecting its soldiers, one of his Chinese generals led the formation in a series of cheers, shouting, "Long live the Republic of China," which after a short time morphed into "Long live the Empire of Japan." One observer remarked that this was the first time "Long live the Empire of Japan" had been openly exclaimed, all the more poignant because it was done by a blended formation of Japanese and Chinese soldiers.[23] Yan's Japanese force would be among the last to surrender to the Communists, doing so in April 1949 with their commander, Gen. Imamura Hosaku, first committing suicide by swallowing a cyanide pill.[24]

In the December 1944 memo cited above, John Paton Davies wonders if Chiang had at that time already established a mutual nonaggression treaty with the Japanese. There is no firm evidence to substantiate the claim—and it is likely that there was no such formal agreement, even secretly maintained. But Okamura's advisory position and the presence of Japanese troops in Nationalist armies so soon after September 1945 displays a level of permeability among the various parties up to—and well after—the end of the Pacific War while also showing that Chiang was determined to make the necessary political moves to maintain his position of power in China. In the mid-1930s he made liberal use of Soviet aid to strengthen his military while systematically trying to stamp out the faction that threatened him most, the CCP. Domestically, he successfully evaded claims of appeasing Tokyo for the five years between the annexation of Manchuria and Xian, but at the start of 1937 it was, politically speaking, too dangerous to turn a blind eye to Japanese encroachment. He now began taking a hard line toward Tokyo, which served to precipitate the "incident" in July. The first fifteen months of the War of Resistance had gone badly for Chiang, but the Japanese—though in control of most of China's coast and a ready supply of rich resources—had fared little better, with Tokyo unable to find a way to extricate itself from the continent on desirable terms by 1941. Then, with the start of the Pacific War in December, Chiang knew the Americans would deal appropriately with Japan, but he could also use the situation to his advantage and play off the United States' peculiar affinity for China to improve his own stock, both domestically and internationally. Finally, when that war was finished, he could return to his original conflict with the Communists, and do so in league with his former opponent—the Japanese—with a clear conscience. So, when the United States displayed a willingness to demonstrate its fidelity to its Asian ally by flying supplies through one of the world's most volatile weather systems and highest terrain, he was happy to oblige.

CONCLUDING OBSERVATIONS

Broadly speaking, did the airlift keep China in the war? On its face, the answer is no. The supplies delivered over the Himalayas—though at tremendous cost—did not keep Chiang from surrendering, as there was likely nothing that would have brought him to that point during his war with Japan. Tokyo offered terms from 1940 to 1945, some of them fairly attractive, but Chiang remained steadfast, not because he was motivated by an iron character but rather because he needed only to be patient. When the news of Japan's attack on Pearl Harbor reached Chongqing on December 8, 1941, cheers erupted from the city—and from the generalissimo—not because of malice toward the Americans but because now he believed it was only a matter of time until the Japanese were defeated—by the Americans.[25]

That said, the question of whether the Hump "kept China in the war" is still useful, as it can be answered either yes or no depending on how it is qualified. If "keeping China" means providing sufficient military aid to the GMD so as to prevent its capitulation, then the answer is still no; it did not keep China in the war, as the supplies delivered to the Nationalists in 1944 and 1945 were scant. This was the time of China's greatest military peril—under Ichi-go's onslaught—and also the time of the airlift's greatest increase, with only 5 percent of all tonnage being consigned to the Nationalists. The rest went to Chennault's Fourteenth Air Force, Stilwell's (and Wedemeyer's) U.S.-trained Chinese divisions (constituting only a minute fraction of the larger Nationalist army), or the Twentieth Air Force's B-29s (see figure 38). Chiang regularly asked for more aid, but the tonnage rarely went directly to him. True, Hump supplies did support air and ground campaigns in China, but neither of these were decisive in the sense that they alone staved off Japanese advances that prevented China from tottering and falling to defeat. The largest consignee of Hump tonnage throughout the war was the Fourteenth Air Force, whose damage reports were frequently exaggerated, as in the case of

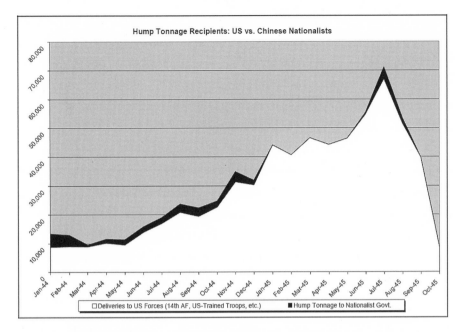

FIGURE 38. Total Hump Tonnage vs. Tonnage to Nationalist Government, January 1944–October 1945. *Source:* U.S. Strategic Bombing Survey, Military Analysis Division, *The Air Transport Command in the War against Japan.*

its attacks against Japanese locomotives. A lack of photographic reconnaissance meant pilots who strafed locomotives made their own damage claims, oftentimes reporting targets destroyed because they saw an inordinate amount of steam coming from attacked locomotive. But as was found in Europe, locomotives were difficult to damage by strafing and nearly impossible to destroy. In actuality, the real impact of Chennault's air force was felt not against railroads or shipping (riverine or seagoing), but in the area of battlefield interdiction—when it was used in concert with Chinese ground offensives, which were few and far between.[26]

Conversely, if "keeping China" means using the airlift—as James McHugh observed—as a vehicle to display the United States' loyalty to China, then it succeeded. Less than a month after the attack on Pearl Harbor, Roosevelt felt it necessary to include China in the "Grand Alliance," making Chiang one of the "Big Four." Roosevelt's chief motive behind this decision—which Churchill opposed—was his sense of China's role in the postwar world, implying an element of insincerity in the way FDR shaped the alliance. But apart from Joseph Stilwell's advisory position and Chennault's AVG, there was little substance to the alliance. Thus, in early 1942 the alliance was nothing more than an agreement on paper, and worth little more, adding no troops and few airplanes to the theater. But once it was shown that cargo planes could ferry supplies from India to China—however meager those first loads were—the airlift took on a new meaning, now able to support Stilwell's and Chennault's plans for China.

Chiang quickly recognized this, attaching as he did cries for more Hump tonnage to warnings of an impending Chinese surrender, realizing too that U.S. responsiveness to his calls could only boost his domestic stature. Then with the achievement of the 10,000-ton goal in December 1943, the airlift began to appropriate a mythic status irrespective of who was getting the tonnage or what was being hauled. All that mattered was that the loads kept on coming and that they continued to increase—which they did with great success. By design, all alliances are characterized by the array of contributions the different parties bring to the relationship. The Americans offered war matériel and advice (solicited or otherwise), and the Chinese offered a geographical proximity to the enemy while serving as a grand diversion for the Japanese—with the Hump airlift serving as the nexus of this alliance. In this manner, the Hump was the military operation that sustained the alliance, one that held special importance, as it placed Japan between the looming American threat to the east and an intractable war in the west.

Edward Drea observes that it is paradoxical that only the Japanese have published a unified history of the war in Asia that adequately ties together all its disparate theaters. This fact is unsurprising, though, as they alone were occupied with fighting the Chinese in China, the Soviets in Northeast Asia, the U.S. Navy in the Pacific, the Americans and Australians in the Southwest Pacific, and the British Empire in Southeast Asia and India.[27] It was the Japanese who were forced to cancel an invasion of Sichuan Province because of U.S. successes at Guadalcanal, and it was the Japanese who had to temper Ichi-go's momentum due to the continual threat of a Soviet invasion of Manchukuo. But it was also the Japanese who understood the importance of the Hump's role in the war, providing "camphor injections" that sustained the "material and spiritual" needs of Chongqing. Thus, the airlift became the object of a concerted air campaign in 1943 (Tsuzigiri) and a ground offensive in 1944 (U-Go). The airlift also served as the lifeline for Chennault's (and to a lesser extent, LeMay's) bombers, a threat the Japanese tried to remove with Ichi-go, though only with temporary success. Unable to cut this airborne line of communication, the airlift continued unabated, undergoing a shift at the beginning of 1944. It was then, in the aftermath of the Cairo Conference, that growing U.S. cynicism toward China's constant pleas for aid served to transform the airlift from an operation designed to morally sustain China into a major feature of the United States' final drive against the Japanese home islands. Like Aesop's boy who cried wolf, Chiang's calls for more tonnage by 1944 fell on deaf ears, though Hump tonnage skyrocketed because the airlift's infrastructure was now in place and because U.S. plans now called for the use of China as a western lodgment for the final offensive against Japan. Despite the shift in motives, the Hump still continued to display the resolve of the Sino-U.S. alliance, however fractured that alliance was in reality.

All of this played out through the development of the five themes outlined in the introductory chapter: airlift as an expression of airpower, the Hump as a dramatic feat of aerial logistics, the impact of the Hump in both theater and global war strategy, airlift as an expression of the "national-ness" of airpower, and airlift as the means for facilitating a paradigm shift in global logistics.

First, airlift is seen as a legitimate expression of airpower. Airpower is typically associated with the kinetic effects of the air weapon, often measured bomb tonnages dropped or enemy aircraft destroyed. In one example, the Anglo-American Combined Bomber Offensive (1943–1945) was designed to cripple Hitler's war-making capability both by the pinpoint targeting of key chokepoints in Germany's "industrial web" or by demoralizing its workforce by area bombing attacks like the raid on Hamburg, appropriately named Operation Gomorrah. In such instances, the goal of the attacks was the attainment of victory through the destruction of the enemy. But the nonkinetic nature of the airlift is no less an expression of airpower, as it is bent not on the destruction of the opponent but on the succor of friendly forces, like Chennault's Fourteenth Air Force or Stilwell's Y-force. Just because airlift's impact is felt indirectly does not mean it should be overlooked as a valid expression of airpower, one that in this case was important to the maintenance of the Sino-U.S. alliance, if not in deed, then at least in word.

Second, the airlift was a feat of aerial logistics that had no precedent before or during the war. Airlifts had been attempted as early as World War I, such as when the British unsuccessfully tried to resupply of the garrison at Kut al-Amara in Mesopotamia. Later, in World War II, the German attempt to sustain ground forces at Demyansk and Stalingrad are famous as bold (yet failed) attempts at resupply that required tremendous daring on the part of the transport crews who flew those missions. But in these cases the needs were acute, associated with a particular tactical or operational problem, like encirclement of Paulus's Sixth Army. By contrast, the Hump addressed a chronic need. No other aerial resupply effort went to such lengths to create an airfield and airway infrastructure designed solely to facilitate the flow of supplies to China, nor would such an effort be matched until nearly three years after the war when the Americans used the airlift to break the Soviet siege of Berlin.

As an aerial achievement, the Hump was also remarkable on the individual level—that of the aircrews that flew its missions. The environment required an uncommon degree of flying skill and airmanship, qualities that many of the Hump's fliers lacked by virtue of their hasty training or minimal experience. Many of these men completed their primary and secondary pilot training and were dispatched to India without ever having flown the type of airplane they would then be forced to fly over the world's most difficult terrain and in its worst weather. They rarely had the satisfaction seeing the fruits of their labor and in fact had to struggle with personal cynicism, provoked by witnessing the squandering of supplies they had risked life and limb to deliver. It was this characteristic of the operation—one that required much personal courage while delivering questionable results—that places it among few equivalents in the history of aerial warfare.

Third, the Hump impacted—and was impacted by—the United States' global and theater strategy in the CBI. Globally, transports were a scarce resource in 1942 and 1943, meaning Roosevelt and the Joint Chiefs had to prioritize how to best use these planes. Consolidated B-24 bombers could easily be converted into C-87 transports, but such a move would reduce the United States' bomb-dropping capability in Europe. Additionally, Eisenhower needed transports for the invasion of Italy, but this in turn would reduce the number of planes available to fly the Hump. Later in the war the Hump would also play a part in enabling Matterhorn, the first sustained bombing campaign against Japan, while also delivering China-based PAC-AID supplies to support the U.S. invasion of the Japanese home islands.

The Hump also shaped the way the Americans fought in the CBI theater, dictated by who received its supplies and in turn fostering the "air-versus-ground" debate that colored U.S. military strategy in the theater, with Chennault doggedly advocating an air strategy and Stilwell equally adamant in favor of a ground campaign. In reality, though, time has only served to increase the perceived polarity of their respective positions. Stilwell, an infantry officer, understood—and respected—what airpower could do, though he was skeptical that it could stop a major Japanese ground offensive that could (and did in Guizhou Province) overrun that air arm's network of bases. Chennault likewise understood the need for a solid contingent of troops, but he tended to overstate airpower's capabilities, just as he overstated many of his convictions (even to his own detriment) as an ACTS instructor in the late 1930s, promising too much from airpower and yet delivering too little. Ironically, though, Stilwell's greatest contribution to the war in the CBI was the recapture of Myitkyina; this allowed the Hump to be flown at a lower altitude by the larger C-54 that was coincidentally becoming available for greater use on the Hump. Stilwell's plan to reform China by reforming its army stood on shaky cultural assumptions and was too grand—it was based on his belief that he could infuse "a Puritan spirit" (as his political officer referred to it) and a New England Protestant work ethic in the Chinese and make them fight the Japanese in Burma.[28] In some ways Chennault and Stilwell were similar, both visionaries who felt they could glean a hearty return from a modest investment—Chennault with a handful of planes and Stilwell with a handful of U.S.-trained Chinese divisions. Friction arose when the theater's meager supplies could be used to support only one of these avenues, with those supplies arriving almost exclusively by air over the Himalayas.

Fourth, the Hump displayed something of the "national-ness" of airpower. Airpower is much more than simply airplanes and pilots. It also includes an industry capable of designing airplanes, an "air-minded" culture that produces pilots to fly those planes, and the technological infrastructure—like airfields and airways—needed to govern and direct the use of airplanes. The free-market characteristic of U.S. commercial aviation worked in favor of military air transport simply because companies like Douglas and Curtiss-Wright benefited from the fact that C-47s, C-46s, and C-54s could be used in both wartime and peacetime. The prewar U.S. population was embracing air travel as a speedier replacement for railroads or ships, creating a crop of commercial pilots who could just as easily haul passengers from St. Louis to Washington as they could haul parts from Detroit to Charleston. To manage the flow of the increasing number of airplanes and airlines in the late 1930s, Americans began building a communication and navigation structure that could then, with the start of the Hump airlift, be replicated over the Himalayas. It is here, in the blending of industry, culture, and technological infrastructure, that the Americans were unique among all the war's belligerents: they alone constructed a worldwide system of military air transport capable of ferrying supplies halfway around the globe in only a few days.

Fifth, the Hump reflects the paradigm shift in logistics that took place during the war, with air transport challenging—and even supplanting—land transport as the most effective and efficient mode of supply. From January 1943 to October 1945 the airlift delivered 80 percent of all supplies carried to China (see figure 39), dwarfing deliveries over the Stilwell Road and through the four-inch and six-inch pipelines that paralleled the road. From one vantage point, this came as no surprise because the airlift had been in operation since 1942, while the Stilwell Road did not open until January 1945, delivering 5,231 tons in its first month and jumping to an impressive 32,807 tons just four months later. But June 1945 marked the road's peak output, with tonnage slipping to 23,370 in July and 15,866 in August. Overland transport could never come close to matching what was being flown across the Hump.

Additionally, because many of the trucks driven from Ledo to Kunming were left in China to make up for China's lack of indigenous trucks, road tonnages always included the weight of the trucks themselves, an enormously significant fact: vehicle weight alone accounted for 76 percent of road cargo tonnage in May 1945 and increased the following month to hover at roughly 90 percent of the weight of all overland cargo delivered to China during the summer of 1945.[29] Trucks were critical to the flow of supplies within China. Without them, Hump deliveries stacked up at terminals like Kunming. But the fact of the matter remains that the air transports delivered so much more net tonnage than either the road or the pipeline that it signaled a remarkable shift military logistics. Assuming that three-quarters of all Stilwell Road tonnage was vehicle weight (a conservative figure that likely was higher), this reduces the road's deliverable cargo considerably,

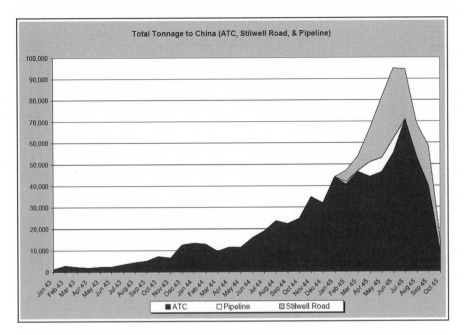

FIGURE 39. Tonnages via ATC, Stilwell Road, and Pipeline, January 1943–October 1945. *Source:* U.S. Strategic Bombing Survey, Military Analysis Division, *Air Operations in China, Burma, India,* pp. 42–43.

as seen in comparing figures 39 and 40. What makes the comparative performance of air and land transport all the more significant is that—at least to Joseph Stilwell—the airlift was only a stopgap measure designed to deliver supplies until a more conventional and durable LOC was built. But contrary to his assumption, it proved easier to build airlift bases and cross northern Burma by air rather than by land, pointing to a clear departure from the orthodox idea that land transport was inherently more enduring and efficient than air transport.

POSTSCRIPT: THE HUMP'S LEGACY

What was the Hump's impact beyond the confines of World War II? First, others who have written on the airlift rightfully point to its role in shaping U.S. military transport considerations in such a way as to make the Berlin Airlift a conceptual possibility. Tunner commanded that airlift in 1948–1949, and a solid number of Hump veterans saw service in the operation that was really the first air campaign

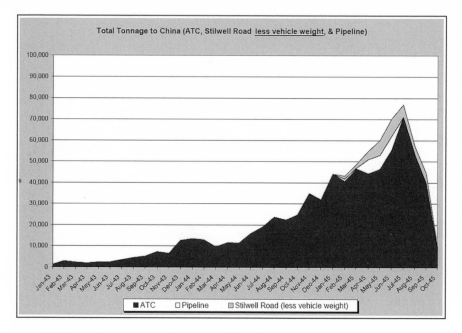

FIGURE 40. Tonnages via ATC, Stilwell Road (less vehicle weight), and Pipeline, January 1943–October 1945. *Source:* U.S. Strategic Bombing Survey, Military Analysis Division, *Air Operations in China, Burma, India,* pp. 42–43; ATC Statistical Control Officer, "Comparative Statistics," May–August 1945, September 5, 1945, 312.3081-4, AFHRA.

of the Cold War. Oft-overlooked factors, such as an orderly sequencing of traffic, the efficient loading and unloading of cargo, and the rapid inspection and repair of airplanes were as vital to that airlift as they were to the Hump's successes in 1945–all factors learned in the skies between India and China. The airlift to keep Berlin supplied was established in a few short months, thanks to many of the lessons learned on the Hump. This was not by accident, as Tunner managed to scrape together some of his staff from India to help manage operations in Germany. To run day-to-day operations, he recruited Col. Robert "Red" Forman, his chief pilot in India. Maj. Edward Guibert, who had managed cargo traffic on the Hump; Lt. Col. Manuel Fernandez, who had run communications; and Capt. Jules Prevost (a disciple of Col. Robert White, the man who brought PLM to the Hump)–all were selected by Tunner as his staff in Germany, superimposing the same operational template on the Berlin Airlift as was used in China.[30] This transfer of experience was no small matter, either: compared with the Hump, the Berlin Airlift delivered a million more tons of cargo in about one-quarter of the time, albeit over significantly shorter distances, allowing the Americans to win their first battle of the Cold War.

The second legacy of the Hump must be looked at from the vantage point of the broader perspective of U.S. air transport. Air Transport Command was a worldwide airline of which the Hump was only a part. Yet the Hump constituted the largest single part of that command by the end of the war. As such, it significantly contributed to a fundamental shift in conceptualizing logistics as air transport became a viable competitor with ground and sea logistics, albeit with its own strengths and weaknesses. It could never compete with the tonnage potential of shipping, trucking, or rail, but it also had no competitor when it came to its speed, range, and geographical indifference. These strengths, blended with the powerful commercial strain present in the United States, translated into a leap forward in U.S. air travel after the war. The AAF bought thousands of transports during the war—over 1,000 C-54s, 3,000 C-46s, and 10,000 C-47s.[31] In addition to the airplanes were the thousands of men who were now trained as pilots and pursuing jobs in an expanding postwar airline industry, easing the transition to civilian life, thanks to AAF programs that gave them training in civilian flight rules and procedures while still on active duty.[32] A glut of planes and pilots on the market meshed well with a growing sense that airplanes were to become another standard option for the traveling public, like the automobile at the turn of the century or the railroad a half century earlier. This "air-mindedness" was a major byproduct of the war: air travel among Americans leaped from eight million air miles in 1945 to twelve million one year later and to seventeen million at the start of 1950.[33]

A third legacy of the airlift is one that persists today as an important point of contact in contemporary Sino-U.S. relations. Following World War II, a number of monuments were erected by Chinese to commemorate the contribution of U.S. airmen during the war. The Communist victory in 1949 saw many of these destroyed for their inconsistency with the party-line narrative that denigrated the U.S.-GMD alliance during the war. Over the past two decades, though, China has witnessed a marked shift in perspective that now emphasizes the United States' role in the larger "anti-Fascist war," downplaying its wartime relations with Chiang Kaishek and instead reasserting the value of the "Flying Tigers" who flew the Hump route.[34] Monuments have been rebuilt, museums established, and new exhibits unveiled, all commemorating the resupply effort.[35] The George Bush Presidential Library and Museum, on the campus of Texas A&M University, contains an exhibit donated by the Chinese government in honor of James R. Fox, a CNAC pilot who died flying the Hump. The Chinese People's Anti-Japanese War Memorial Hall in Wanping County near Beijing (at the site of the Marco Polo Bridge incident) contains an elaborate exhibit dedicated to the Hump's flyers. And in 2003 the *Washington Post* conducted an interview with Wen Jiabao, the premier of the State Council of the People's Republic of China, who began his comments remarking on two historical points of contact between China and the United States. The first was China's involvement in supplying workers to build the transcontinental railroad; the second was the Hump:

> *I also remember very well that from May 1942 to September 1945 a group of young American pilots from the famous Flying Tiger squadron flew the Hump Route to support China during the war against fascism. The Hump Route was famous for its danger and in those years more than 500 planes crashed, claiming the lives of more than 1,500 Chinese and American pilots. That route was also known as the "aluminum trail" for the wreckage of crashed planes glittering in the sunlight. However, that route is a testimony to the cooperation between the Chinese and the Americans.*[36]

Today Chinese schoolchildren learn about the Americans who flew the *tuofeng hangxian,* or "camelback air route," as a part of their primary education, while most Americans have no knowledge whatsoever that such an operation ever took place. Perhaps, in some extended way, it is because the airlift was always more important for its moral effect than its physical impact. It is also remembered, not because of what it carried, but because it was tried, found to be difficult, and accomplished nonetheless.

NOTES

INTRODUCTION

1. Originally the term "Hump" referred only to the southerly Himalayan mountain range crossed during flights between India and China. As the war progressed, the Hump became synonymous with that airlift itself, serving as shorthand for both the airlift's location and operation. I retain that shorthand throughout this work.

2. The best estimate on the precise amount of tonnage delivered to China from India by U.S. military air transport is 738,987 short tons (all tonnage in this work is expressed in short tons of 2,000 pounds unless otherwise noted). This figure is derived from the totals found in USAAF, ATC, Historical Officer, *Air Transportation to China under the 10th Air Force;* and U.S. Strategic Bombing Survey, Military Analysis Division, *Air Transport Command.* Note also that the Burma and Ledo Roads would eventually connect and be renamed the Stilwell Road in January 1945.

3. The best single-volume survey of the Hump is Koenig's *Over the Hump,* part of Ballantine's Illustrated History of the Violent Century series. Koenig packs a wealth of information (and photos) into the book's 150 pages, covering the Hump's history from the beginning to end. He rightly emphasizes the early part of the lift, as it is the operation's growth up to the summer of 1944 that is the most significant part of the story. His sources are all secondary (books printed in English), so they leave out the Chinese and Japanese perspectives. The most prominent memoir is Tunner's *Over the Hump,* covering the final year of the operation from his vantage point as the India-China Wing commander. Tunner was pivotal in bringing the era of "big business" to the lift, as he built on Thomas Hardin's work to boost the lift to phenomenal heights. *Over the Hump* is helpful, too, in that it covers the Berlin Airlift (which Tunner eventually commanded), the conceptual

offspring of the Hump. The chief weakness of the work is that it covers only the tail end of the operation and is furthermore written as a work of advocacy, thus lacking a critical dimension. A good complement to Tunner is Spencer's *Flying the Hump*. Spencer was a Hump pilot who served toward the midpoint of the campaign, and his memoirs are useful primarily in showing just how challenging it was to fly the Hump, especially as inexperienced flyers were tossed into missions in the world's deadliest terrain and weather. In discussing the Hump as part of the broader air war in World War II, Craven and Cate's *Army Air Forces* still remains a standard reference. Volume 1 contains a chapter titled "Commitments to China," which briefly covers the U.S. airpower history of the China-Burma-India theater up to the creation of the Tenth Air Force. Volume 7 is more specific, with a major section titled "Air Transport" as well as the 38-page chapter "Airline to China."

4. I use the pinyin system of romanization throughout this work with the exception of direct quotes from period sources and in the case of prominent figures like Chiang Kaishek (in lieu of Jiang Jieshi) and T. V. Soong (in lieu of Song Ziwen). In the case of Chiang I have also chosen to adopt the pinyin convention that drops the hyphen from his surname.

5. One of the earliest examples of this interplay came on June 26, 1942, when Chiang was notified that U.S. B-17 bombers and A-24 attack aircraft assigned for service in China had been redirected by the U.S. Army Chief of Staff, Gen. George Marshall, to fly to Egypt to help British forces that were being threatened by Rommel's Afrika Korps. When Chiang was informed of Marshall's decision, he went on to question the United States' sincerity toward China, sardonically stating, "I am unhappy about this development. The China Theater of War is lightly regarded. Naturally I wish to know whether America and Britain consider it as one of the Allied Theaters." Three days later Chiang issued three demands as a way of testing the sincerity of FDR's rhetoric, requesting, among other things, 5,000 tons per month of tonnage over the Hump. Romanus and Sunderland, *Stilwell's Mission*, pp. 169–72.

6. The clearest example of this is seen in a report titled *Summary of Spring Diversions*, issued by ATC in the spring of 1944, explaining why its trans-Himalayan tonnage had dropped (it was at this time that Hump transports were diverted from the India-China route to support British troops in their effort to blunt the Japanese U-Go ground offensive from Burma into western India). As

will be covered in later chapters, had ATC not gotten involved in supporting the British (who were at one point completely cut off from all ground lines of supply), it is conceivable that the Japanese advance would have overrun the ATC bases in Assam, India, stopping Hump flights altogether.

7. Dallek, *Franklin D. Roosevelt,* p. 29.

8. Schaller, *U.S. Crusade in China,* pp. 90–91.

9. Dallek, *Franklin D. Roosevelt,* p. 329.

10. Chiang was featured on *Time's* cover a total of ten times between 1927 and 1955, including the issue of January 3, 1938, in which he and his wife were 1937's "Couple of the Year," the only pair ever to garner such a designation by the magazine. For a detailed study of Luce's impact on the United States' popular perception of China, see Jespersen, *American Images of China.*

11. Quoted in Elleman, *Modern Chinese Warfare,* p. 194.

12. Zeng Guofan, the military general and court official who played a prominent part in suppressing China's bloody Taiping Rebellion and restoring some prominence of the Qing in the late Imperial period figures largely here. As a statesman, he noticed that the United States in the late 1850s was "respectful and compliant towards China" and looked for ways to lure them into a closer relationship with the Chinese to serve as a counterweight to the "more crafty" British and French. Li Hongzhang carried this mindset forward into the 1870s and sought to use the United States—a burgeoning power that had just successfully emerged from its own civil war—over and against the Japanese, Koreans, and Vietnamese (French) between 1879 and 1895. Hunt, *Making of a Special Relationship,* pp. 58–60, 115–42. Chiang Kaishek read Zeng's works while studying in Japan in his late twenties, praising Zeng as an important figure in unifying modern China. For more on examples of *yiwu* in modern Chinese foreign relations, see Paine, *Imperial Rivals,* and Brady, "'Treat Insiders and Outsiders Differently': The Use of Control of Foreigners in the PRC," *China Quarterly* 164 (Dec. 2000): 943–64.

13. USAAF, Office of Statistical Control, *Army Air Forces Statistical Digest,* p. 135. Other aircraft totals were 1,832 bombers, 2,170 fighters, 475 reconnaissance, 7,340 trainers, and 226 communications aircraft.

14. Cleveland lists the more prominent of these men in *Air Transport at War,* pp. 55–56.

15. Arnold also went on to suggest that the Hump airlift be civilianized. In July 1942 he wired Stilwell and suggested that the China National Aviation Corporation (CNAC), a company jointly owned by the Chinese government and by Pan Am airlines, take control of the airlift. Arnold felt that a private air transport company could do a better job—and not siphon off the relatively few transports available for duty in the CBI. Stilwell understandably disliked the idea, wanting to have complete control of the airlift assets available in his theater, control he would lose if the mission was civilianized. USAAF, ATC, Historical Officer, *Air Transportation to China,* p. 13.

16. In 1940 J. Parker Van Zandt delivered a lecture at Norwich University titled "European Air Transport on the Eve of War–1939" in which he compared the various European airline companies with each other and then with the U.S. Van Zandt's published lecture is chock-full of numbers and tables, showing the United States' dominance in commercial aviation. He notes that in 1937 the twenty principal European companies flew a combined total of 50 million miles, carrying one million passengers, while the top eighteen U.S. companies flew 77 million miles and carried 1.25 million passengers.

17. I am indebted to Dr. Roger Miller, Air Force Historical Studies Office, for his helpful discussion on this topic.

18. La Farge, *Eagle in the Egg,* pp. 84–85.

19. William Koenig follows this same general outline. See Koenig, *Over the Hump,* pp. 151–52.

CHAPTER 1

1. Quoted in Fenby, *Chiang Kai-shek,* p. 290.

2. Drea, *In the Service of the Emperor,* p. 29.

3. Dorn, *Sino-Japanese War,* pp. 146–58, provides the most detailed history of the battle in English. Dorn—who could never be accused being too generous toward the Chinese in his writings—concludes his account by stating, "For the first time since their attempted invasions of Korea under Hideyoshi had been disastrously repulsed in 1592–98, the Japanese had been forced to swallow the bitter pill of a major defeat at the hands of a despised opponent" (p. 157). Tai'erzhuang was a great victory for the Chinese, though it would stand as one of their few of the entire war.

4. Drea, *In the Service of the Emperor,* pp. 30–31.

5. Hatori, "Struggle over the Control," p. 3. Professor Hatori teaches at the Japanese National Defense Academy.

6. A metric ton is equal to 1,000 kilograms, or approximately 2,200 pounds.

7. Hattori, *Complete History,* 1:58, 6–17. According to recently declassified documents, Hattori was a key figure in a failed coup to overthrow the Japanese government and assassinate Prime Minister Shigeru Yoshida in 1952 ("Papers Tie U.S. to 1950s Japan Coup Plot," *China Daily,* March 10, 2007). Hattori's history is fairly balanced, despite the hawkish tendencies displayed by this plot.

8. Hattori, *Complete History,* 1:61.

9. Japanese Monograph 71, *Army Operations in China,* p. 15. Nearly two hundred monographs were written following the war under the Supreme Commander for the Allied Powers to the Japanese Government. The monographs were written by former officers of the Japanese Army and Navy and were translated by the Intelligence Service Group of Far East Command. In the absence of many destroyed orders, plans, and journals, they are considered accurate and reliable with respect to the larger contours of the war's narrative (and as used in this work) but must be used with caution on points of detail.

10. Between 1937 and 1941 the Soviets supplied the Chinese with 904 aircraft, 31,600 bombs, 82 tanks, 1,140 artillery pieces, 2 million shells, 9,720 machine guns, 50,000 rifles, and 180 million rounds of ammunition. Garver, *Chinese-Soviet Relations,* pp. 37–41. For a personal account of Soviet aid, see Kalyagin, *Along Alien Roads.*

11. Kalyagin, *Along Alien Roads,* p. 3.

12. Peattie, *Sunburst,* pp. 113–14.

13. Chennault, *Way of a Fighter,* p. 62.

14. Kalyagin, *Along Alien Roads,* p. 4.

15. For the best works on these two battles, see Coox, *Anatomy of a Small War,* and his *Nomonhan.*

16. Animal hides were used for leather goods or for winter clothing; pig bristles were used to make brushes for either horses or soldiers; tungsten was used to harden metals for either artillery shells or armor plating; antimony was used to harden lead in the production of either bullets or tracers. Eugene A. Avallone and Theodore Baumeister III, eds., *Marks' Standard Handbook for Mechanical*

Engineers, 9th ed. (New York: McGraw-Hill, 1987), pp. 6–33, 6–35, 6–87, 6–89, 6–99.

17. Garver, *Chinese-Soviet Relations,* p. 48.

18. Chuikov, *Mission to China,* pp. xxxii–xxxiv, 83.

19. Ibid., pp. xxxii–xxxiv.

20. McHugh, "The Burma Road," Dec. 31, 1938, McHugh Papers, reel 1, Personal Correspondence and Military Reports, 1935–1946. For McHugh's report of bureaucratic complications of the Burma Road, also see his "Conditions on the Burma Road," Aug. 30, 1941, reel 2, Personal Correspondence, 1937–1946.

21. It is worth noting that in 1945 the average tonnage carried across Stilwell Road—the merger of the U.S.-built Ledo Road and the older Burma Road—stood at about 18,000 tons per month between February and September, 1945. This marks the road's peak efficiency, as it was under strict control of the U.S. Army; even so, the monthly tonnage includes necessary fuel and supplies for the drivers and road maintainers. Romanus and Sunderland, *Time Runs Out,* p. 14.

22. U.S. Strategic Bombing Survey, Military Analysis Division, *Air Operations in China,* p. 57.

23. Quoted in Tarling, *A Sudden Rampage,* p. 55.

24. Ibid.

25. Churchill, *Their Finest Hour,* pp. 497–98.

26. Hattori, *Complete History,* 1:68.

27. Ibid., 2:98. According to Hattori, the IGHQ thought that initially the Chinese would be emboldened by a wider war that included the British and Americans but that this sentiment would wane as Chinese aid evaporated. Hattori goes on to state that the Japanese incursion into Burma "would also result in halting the transportation or aid over the Burma Road, owing to the southward advance of Japanese forces; and in stopping the aid to Chiang's activities from Chinese merchants in the Southern Area, following the successful conclusion of our military conquest of that area. These factors would aggravate the financial and economic difficulties, which would substantially reduce the power of resistance and while casing a gradual loss of fighting power, they would also have a grave effect on the spirit or resistance, not only of the general public but among the leading members of the Chungking regime. As a result, the increasing num-

ber of warlords who are not absolutely loyal to Chiang would switch sides to the Nanking Regime and, ultimately, cause a split in the united front of the Chungking regime, weakening the power of the Chiang Government."

28. See Chuikov's memoir for a detailed discussion of the return of Soviet advisors to the USSR.

29. As early as 1937 the U.S. Treasury Department agreed to buy up to $50 million of Chinese yuan at an agreed-upon rate in an effort to stabilize China's currency. This was repeated in April 1941. The first of many credits were offered in the amount of $18.9 million in 1936 and 1937. See U.S. Department of State, *China White Paper,* pp. 30–33.

30. Liang, *Sino-German Connection,* and Kirby, *Germany and Republican China.*

31. A Soviet historian records that a total of 3,665 Soviet military "specialists" saw service in China. Kalyagin, *Along Alien Roads,* p. 9.

32. Doolittle, of the famed "Doolittle raid" on Japan in April 1942, was a demonstration pilot for the Curtiss Airplane Company in the early 1930s; it was his demonstration of the Curtiss Hawk at the Shanghai Air Show in May 1932 that prompted the Chinese to buy that fighter over the other competitor, the Italian Fiat C.R. 32. Robert E. Van Patten, "Before the Flying Tigers," *Air Force Magazine,* June 1999, p. 6. See also William M. Leary Jr., "Wings for China: The Jouett Mission, 1932–1935," *Pacific Historical Review* 38 (1969): 447–62, and Xu Guangqiu, "American-British Aircraft Competition in South China, 1926–1936," *Modern Asian Studies* 35 (2001): 157–93.

33. The best biography of Chennault is Byrd, *Chennault;* see also Ford, *Flying Tigers.* Chennault's autobiography, *Way of a Fighter,* gives a glimpse of his passionate and caustic character but contains a number of factual errors.

34. "Resume of the Economic and Political Situation in China and Suggestions for Action," U.S. Department of State, *FRUS: Diplomatic Papers, 1941,* 5:622–25.

35. Schaller, *U.S. Crusade in China,* p. 49.

36. Ibid.

37. Ibid., pp. 54–55. Newman's *Owen Lattimore* is the most current and complete biography of Lattimore.

38. The precursor to AMMISCA was a temporary military mission, led

by Brig. Gen. Henry B. Clagett, that spent May 1941 in Chongqing attempting to assess the Nationalists' precise needs. Clagett was the commander of the Philippine Department Air Force (Romanus and Sunderland, *Stilwell's Mission,* p. 27). Clagett's mission was more technical that Currie's, as it attempted to determine precise air power needs. His team spent most of its time in Kunming and Chengdu and was most interested in seeing how airfields in the south (at Kunming and Guiyang) could be improved. The fact that the Americans showed interest in the northerly Soviet fields near Lanzhou led chief Soviet military advisor Vasili Chuikov to remark that the United States must have intended to "facilitate joint [ground and air force] operations with Chinese ground forces against Japanese staging points further south." To Marshal Chuikov, "This confirmed in our view that the Japanese were preparing for a move into Southeast Asia and beyond." See Chuikov, *Mission to China,* p. 144.

39. Schaller, *U.S. Crusade in China,* pp. 56–57.

40. Ibid., pp. 57–58. See Leighton and Coakley, *Global Logistics,* 1:83, on Currie's role with the CDS.

41. "Secretary of State to Consul General at Hankow, Feb 10, 1938," U.S. Department of State, *FRUS: Diplomatic Papers, 1938,* 3:78–80. See also Schaller, *U.S. Crusade in China,* pp. 40–41.

42. Quoted in Kalyagin, *Along Alien Roads,* p. 132.

43. "Chiang to Soong, 25 Nov. 41," U.S. Department of State, *FRUS: Diplomatic Papers, 1941,* 4:660–61.

44. McHugh to Currie, Apr. 14, 1941, McHugh Papers, reel 2, Personal Correspondence, 1937–1946.

45. Chuikov, *Mission to China,* p. 145.

46. Stilwell had a knack for foreign languages. He taught French and Spanish at West Point from 1906 to 1910, and after World War I the army's Military Intelligence Division selected him as its first candidate to learn Chinese (despite being overage for the program). The army sent him to Berkeley to learn Chinese in a program that he felt was inadequate because it did not sufficiently immerse its students in the new language. It was not until his first tour in China in the early 1920s that he got a solid grasp of Chinese. See Tuchman, *Stilwell,* pp. 61–67).

47. Stilwell was rough and aggressive in character, and this translated to the way he preferred to use his troops—sometimes to the point of abuse. In the sum-

mer of 1944 Stilwell was determined to retake northern Burma. At one point, after successfully recapturing the town of Myitkyina, his force was encircled by the Japanese. He ordered a breakout and a forced march of his best infantry unit, the 5307th Composite Unit (provisional), better known as "Merrill's Marauders," after its commander, Frank Merrill. Stilwell's breakout order was seen as unnecessary, but the hard-charging general was determined not to be denied his prize. The forced march decimated the already disease-ridden Marauders, leaving only a fraction of their original numbers combat-effective. So badly had Stilwell treated them that their commander issued a formal complaint, which Stilwell was able to squelch by sending them back to the United States. One member of the Marauders loathingly remembers of Stilwell, "I had him in my rifle sights. No one woulda known it wasn't a Jap who got the son-of-a-bitch." Quoted in Masters, *Road Past Mandalay,* p. 244.

48. Audio recording of memorandum, "General Drum on China Mission," Jan. 5, 1942, NARA II, RG 493, Central Decimal Files 463.8a.

49. War Department to Drum, Jan. 5, 1942, NARA II, RG 18, Central Decimal Files, Oct. 1942–44, Foreign Files 300-A to 300-D, Box 914.

50. Ibid.

51. Quoted in Tuchman, *Stilwell,* pp. 240–41.

52. Quoted in ibid., p. 241.

53. Marshall to Stilwell, "Instructions as U.S. Army Representative in China," Feb. 2, 1942, Formation of China-Burma-India Theater, NARA II, RG 493, Box 1. The origin of Stilwell's label for Chiang is unclear. Most assume it referred to the generalissimo's physical appearance, with his clean-shaved scalp. More likely, though, "Peanut" was probably Chiang's code name in War Department secret message traffic, as it was not uncommon for such names to be either humorous or derisive. For example, Naval Intelligence secret correspondence referred to Chiang as "Cock," Gen. He Yingqin (Chiang's Chinese chief of staff) as "Cuckoo," William Henry Donald (the Australian journalist and the generalissimo's confidant) as "Duck," and Madame Chiang as "Crane" (McHugh Papers, Military Reports, 1935–1946). It is likely that Stilwell adopted the code name for Chiang for permanent use in his private diary, especially as his candor was boundless, referring once to President Roosevelt as "'Piece-of-Pie' Frank" (Stilwell, Original Diaries, entry for Apr. 30, 1943, Stilwell Papers).

54. *Miandian gonglüe zou zhan* [The Burma Offensive], trans. Zeng Qinggui (Taipei: Guofangbu Shizheng Bianyi Ju, 1997), pp. 105–336, as cited in Van de Ven, *War and Nationalism in China,* pp. 21–23.

55. The Japanese bombing of Rangoon succeeded in stopping most work at the port. Many were prodded back to work, but this did not stop the overall exodus from the city that saw nearly 70,000 leave by boat in January, and between 100,000 and 200,000 escape up the Chittagong River toward Mandalay. British general H. Alexander's decision to withdraw his force along the same route slowed down the fleeing refugees, who eventually numbered between 400,000 and 500,000; deaths are estimated to be as many as 50,000. Tarling, *A Sudden Rampage,* pp. 99–100. On the bombing of Rangoon, see A. D. Harvey, "Army Air Force and Navy Air Force: Japanese Aviation and the Opening Phases of the War in the Far East," *War in History* 6 (1999): 174–204.

56. Van de Ven, *War and Nationalism in China,* p. 22. Long Yun, the so-called "the king of Yunnan," ruled the province from 1927 to 1945. Politically, he always supported the war against Japan, but he also closely guarded his own provincial interests against GMD encroachment by establishing his own regional banks exempt from central oversight and taxation; he also refused to pass on to Chongqing the regionally collected sales tax, using the money instead to build fourteen of his own regiments. This was significant from the U.S. perspective because the provincial capital of Yunnan was Kunming, the Chinese terminus of the Hump airlift. The steady influx of U.S. aid gave birth to a lucrative local economy, and Long was careful to see that the GMD got as little of the proceeds as possible. To secure his own power, Long kept in close contact with neighboring warlords and even established a secret telegram code with Communist leaders Zhou Enlai and Zhu De. He was deeply suspicious of Chiang and proved to be a continual thorn in the generalissimo's side throughout the war. Hsiung and Levine, *China's Bitter Victory,* pp. 60–62. For a detailed discussion of Long Yun and his relationship with the central government, see Lloyd Eastman's essay, "Regional Politics and the Central Government: Yunnan and Chungking," in Sih, ed., *Nationalist China,* pp. 329–62. Bai Chongxi was another regional warlord (over Guangxi Province) who then became a skilled Nationalist general during the war. Stilwell insisted that Chiang give Bai a place of real authority within the army, but the generalissimo refused because of Bai's regional loyalties and

his pedigree of rebellion against the GMD before the war. Fairbank and Feuer-werker, eds., *Republican China,* p. 579, and Romanus and Sunderland, *Stilwell's Command Problems,* p. 411.

57. Prewar Memo on Defense of Kunming from Japanese Attack, NARA II, RG 18, Central Decimal Files, Oct. 1942–44, World War II, Entry 300, Box 933, File 450-A. See also Bartsch, *December 8, 1941.*

58. Arnold, *Global Mission,* pp. 278–79.

59. Ibid., p. 302. Arnold's membership on the Joint Staff is a point worthy of note. Prior to the war's start, he was not considered anything more than the head of the Air Corps, a position that meant he was the army's chief airman and nothing more. It was here, at the Arcadia Conference in Washington (held December 22, 1941, to January 14, 1942), that Arnold first was treated as a member of the Joint Staff, a consideration that C. R. Smith attributed to the British. Smith, a man very close to Arnold, claimed that the British wanted a U.S. airman to serve on the Combined Chiefs of Staff opposite Air Chief Marshal Charles "Peter" Portal, thus elevating Arnold's stature to a position on the staff. Arnold himself records a U.S.-only joint staff meeting with Roosevelt immediately prior to Arcadia, stating that it was here that the president first addressed him as "Hap," convincing Arnold that he was finally "in" with the administration. C. R. Smith, interview, Apr. 8, 1970, Washington, D.C., microfilm no. 43827, AFHRA; and Daso, *Hap Arnold,* pp. 170–71.

60. EAC stayed in business as a Sino-German venture until August 1941, when the company was taken over completely by the Nationalist government following China's severing of diplomatic ties with Germany.

61. Leary, *Dragon's Wings,* pp. 118–21. The U.S. State Department got involved, condemning the attack, but backed off when the Japanese claimed they suspected the plane of conducting enemy activities, despite its obvious CNAC markings.

62. Ibid., p. 131. Carrying freight is different from carrying passengers. It requires a different aircraft configuration (removing the seats) and the infrastructure on the ground to manage the loading and off-loading of cargo; hauling freight was more challenging of the two modes.

63. In the end Bond spent nearly twenty years in China, arriving in Shanghai in March 1931 and returning to the United States after the fall of the Nationalist

government on mainland China. His oldest son, Langhorne Bond, was a lawyer and eventually became the head of the Federal Aviation Administration (FAA) in the United States. Bond and Ellis, *Wings for an Embattled China,* p. 13.

64. In July 1940 T. V. Soong asked U.S. Secretary of the Treasury Henry Morgenthau for $20 million of Lend-Lease aid specifically earmarked for CNAC. Leary, *Dragon's Wings,* p. 134.

65. Once the Pacific War began, CNAC was continually requesting more airplanes from the United States under the provisions of Lend-Lease, though it was not until the summer of 1943 that this request could be seriously entertained by the transport-lacking Air Corps

66. Leary, *Dragon's Wings,* p. 135.

67. Ma Yufu, *Tuo feng kong yun,* pp. 15–16. Xia's route of flight was probably not as far north as the later Hump flights would be; the presence of Japanese fighters in northern Burma by the summer of 1942 forced pilots to fly a more northerly track over higher terrain to stay out of range of this threat.

68. The War Department was reorganized along functional lines in June 1941, placing the Army Air Corps (AAC) within the larger Army Air Forces (AAF).

69. Leary, *Dragon's Wings,* p. 154.

70. Craven and Cate, *Army Air Forces,* 7:4; see also Roger G. Miller, "Air Transport on the Eve of Pearl Harbor," *Air Power History,* Summer 1998, 45.

71. USAAF, ATC, Historical Division, Office of the Assistant Chief of Staff, *History of Air Transport Command,* p. 188.

72. C. R. Smith, interview, Apr. 8, 1970, Washington, D.C., microfilm no. 43827, AFHRA.

73. Following the war Smith admitted that Arnold wanted to keep George as the titular head of Air Transport Command only temporarily, with Smith running the daily operations. Once Smith got comfortable with the army's mode of operations, George would go back to a combat command, with Smith running the entire command. But by Smith's own admission, he thought that even after many months of service he would "have a hell of a hard time fitting in some of these things with the Army," a euphemism for the often-rigid bureaucracy of the military, and so George and Smith both remained in their respective positions for most of the remainder of the war. Ibid.

74. William H. Tunner, interview by James C. Hasdorff, Oct. 5–6, 1976, Ware Neck, Va., p. 24, K239.0512–911, AFHRA.

75. Surprisingly, Smith has no dedicated biography, the closest being Serling's *Eagle,* which contains a wealth of Smith anecdotes. Smith's papers are housed at the American Airlines C. R. Smith Museum in Fort Worth, Texas.

76. On February 6 Roosevelt authorized Arnold to send "50 to 75 planes in operation . . . the exact number which will go on the China run depends on number they will be able to handle with facilities available." A month later this became the ABC Ferry Command. USAAF, ATC, Historical Officer, *Air Transportation to China under the 10th Air Force.*

77. See Bartsch, *December 8, 1941,* pp. 410–24.

78. USAAF, ATC, Historical Officer, *Air Transportation to China under the 10th Air Force.*

79. Brereton, *Brereton Diaries,* p. 111.

80. USAAF, Assistant Chief of Air Staff, Intelligence, Historical Division, *The Tenth Air Force, 1942,* p. 32. The command changed names several times over a relatively short period of time. Initially called the Air Corps Ferrying Command in May 1941, it was renamed the Army Air Forces Ferry Command in March 1942, then redubbed Air Transport Command later in the summer of 1942. AFHRA Factsheet, "Military Airlift Command," http://www.afhra.af.mil/factsheets/factsheet.asp?id=12476 (accessed June 2010).

CHAPTER 2

1. Brewer, ed., *China Airlift,* 1:30, 37.

2. Kensley Robert Thompson (Hump pilot), interview by author, Sept. 30, 2005, Memphis, Tenn.

3. Lydia Rossi, wife of Flying Tiger pilot Dick Rossi, recalls this event, which took place during the first two weeks of September 2005; see http://www.flyingtigersavg.com/china_trip.htm (accessed June 2010).

4. "Northwest Goes East," *Time,* Jan. 1, 1945.

5. The minimum instrument altitude is just that–the lowest an aircraft could fly on instruments only (the pilot being unable to see outside of the cockpit) and remain at least 1,000 feet above any terrain obstructions within twenty-five nautical miles of the route of flight.

6. McKeown to Hunter, Sept. 18, 1942, *Air Transportation to China under the 10th Air Force.*

7. Ibid. The "hood" McKeown refers to is just that—a cloth hood that keeps the pilot's eyes shielded from looking outside the aircraft, forcing him to rely only on his instruments, while the other pilot visually keeps the airplane clear of obstacles.

8. See Fuller, *Thor's Legions,* pp. 107–20 for a history of weather forecasting in the CBI during the war.

9. Quoted in Donovan Webster, "The Impossible Mission of 1943," *Best Life,* February 2006, 12.

10. Carey et al., *East Asia,* pp. 3–1–3–5.

11. Weather Division, AAF Headquarters, "Forecasting and Related Problems in China," p. 4.

12. Flight path information is taken from two sources: USAAF, ATC, ICD, Historical Section, "A History of the India-China Wing, June through December 1943," p. 512, and USAAF, ATC, Historical Officer, *Air Transportation to China under the 10th Air Force.* All elevation data is taken from current Tactical Pilotage Charts (TPCs), H-10A (Edition A, March 1980), H-10B (Edition 2, June 1988), H-10C (Edition 2, January 1990), and H-10D (Edition 3, October 1984), produced by the Defense Mapping Agency Aerospace Center, St. Louis, Mo.

13. C. R. Smith to Hal George, Dec. 1, 1943, Box 04040601, ICD-ATC Reports and Letters, AMCHO.

14. Harold Alexander, "A Plan for the Increase of Air Cargo Capacity from India into China during 1943," Jan. 7, 1943, Box 04040603, ICD Forecasts and Organization, AMCHO.

15. "War Zone Familiarization Guide," Headquarters 1 Troop Carrier Command, Aug. 28, 1944, p. 45, NARA II, RG 18, Bulky Files, Entry 300, Box 1037, Oct. 1942–May 1944.

16. Ibid., p. 57.

17. Spencer, *Flying the Hump,* p. 112. Matterhorn B-29s flying the Hump were as a matter of routine assigned altitudes of 20,000 feet for eastbound flights and 22,000 feet for westbound flights. This was done to keep them clear of lower-flying traffic, not because the terrain dictated such altitudes. USAAF, ATC, ICD,

Historical Section, "History of the India-China Division, Air Transport Command, 1944," 2:567.

18. This difference is based on the assumption that mountain elevations have changed little in the past six decades and is found by comparing the Defense Mapping Agency's Tactical Pilotage Chart H-10C (Edition 2, January 1990) with an original Hump pilot's chart, "ICW-ATC Flight Chart, July 1944," Feb. 22, 1943–June 30, 1944, 312.073–4, AFHRA. A copy of this Hump chart is reproduced in color in Ethell and Downie, *Flying the Hump,* pp. 70–71. The mountain peak in question is located at approximately 27°06′N, 100°11′E.

19. The 3rd Photo Mapping Squadron, composed of B-25s and B-24s, was the unit detailed on this mission. NARA II, RG 165, Operations Division File 13, Entry 418, Box 1568.

20. "Summary of Project 7A; AAL help w/ Project 7," Box 04040606, AMCHO.

21. The other commodity useless to a pilot is "runway behind you."

22. Col. Harold R. Harris to Brig. Gen. Earl Hoag, Nov. 29, 1943, Box 04040607, AMCHO. For more on the training program at Reno, see Craven and Cate, *Army Air Forces,* 6:677.

23. Brig. Gen. Earl Hoag to Col. Harold R. Harris, Dec. 30, 1943, Box 04040601, ICD-ATC Reports and Letters, AMCHO.

24. Spencer, *Flying the Hump,* p. 77.

25. Weather Division, AAF Headquarters, "Forecasting and Related Problems in China," p. 3.

26. Severe icing is defined as a condition whereby the ice accumulates on the aircraft faster that deicing equipment is able to remove it.

27. Also called "knots," a frequent unit of measurement when referring to all things aeronautical; a nautical mile is 6,076 feet, as opposed to a normal statute mile, which is 5,280 feet, which means that 100 knots is equivalent to 115 miles per hour.

28. India-China Division, Historical Section, "A History of the India China Wing for the Period June through December 1943," pp. 513–524.

29. Weather Division, AAF Headquarters, "Studies on Local Forecasting, Kunming, China," p. 3.

30. *South Asia,* pp. 2–11.

31. USAAF, ATC, ICD, Historical Section, "A History of the India-China Wing, June through December 1943," p. 521.

32. Ibid., p. 516.

33. Hanks, *Saga of CNAC #53,* pp. 35–47.

34. Supply and Service to Arnold, "Aluminum Containers–India China Wing, ATC," Mar. 25, 1944, NARA II, RG 18, Central Decimal Files, Oct. 1942–1944, Entry 300, Box 916, Folder 400-B.

35. This annual average is based on rainfall statistics collected over seventy-five years. "National Intelligence Survey, India and Pakistan: Weather and Climate," p. 134. William Langhorne Bond was at this meeting with Arnold and told the AAF chief that none of his CNAC pilots had ever seen rains that extreme. This was no doubt true as well, for CNAC flights would not have taken pilots to that part of India. Bond, *Wings for an Embattled China,* p. 316.

36. "National Intelligence Survey, India and Pakistan: Weather and Climate," p. 131.

37. Japanese Monograph No. 56, *Southeast Area Air Operations Record,* p. 18.

38. A wing deicing boot was a rubber bladder that ran along the leading edge of a wing and intermittently inflated with air, mechanically breaking any ice buildup off that part of the airplane. The boots were effective, but only when they worked; hot and dry temperatures on the ground in India took its toll on the rubber, causing it to dry and crack, rendering the boots useless in flight.

39. Craven and Cate, *Army Air Forces,* 7:30.

40. USAAF, Office of Statistical Control, *Army Air Forces Statistical Digest,* p. 28.

41. Ibid., p. 81.

42. Craven and Cate, *Army Air Forces,* 7:31.

43. Ibid.

44. Wendell C. and John B. Tombaugh, *Fulton County Indiana Handbook, Service Men, World War II, 1945* (Rochester, Ind.: Tombaugh House, 2001). See also http://www.fulco.lib.in.us/Genealogy/Tombaugh/Family%20Books/Html/Tombaugh%20History.htm (accessed June 2010).

45. Craven and Cate, *Army Air Forces,* 7:32. See also ibid., 6:572, on how trainees were selected for the type of aircraft they would fly after graduation,

being a combination of factors to include "the student's aptitude, his physicals measurements, and preference."

46. The peacetime pilot training program lasted twelve months but was trimmed to seven by May 1940 with the threat of war. Training was further reduced to twenty-seven weeks after Pearl Harbor. Ibid., 6:566.

47. Quoted in ibid., 7:36.

48. Morzik, *German Air Forces Airlift Operations,* pp. 1–2.

49. Quoted in Cameron, *Training to Fly,* p. 400.

50. Marshall to FDR, "Memorandum for the President, India-China Transport," July 15, 1943, NARA II, RG 165, General Correspondence, 1942–45, Entry 418, Box 1580.

51. A letter from ATC Headquarters to General Arnold dated July 14, 1943, on the status of the airlift to China stated that one-third (89 out of 277) of the new pilots sent to India were "found to be only trained in single engine equipment." This meant that ATC would have to institute a pilot training program in the theater to provide them the extra thirty to fifty hours of instructional time in multi-engine aircraft, an added burden on the theater's flying commitment. ATC to General Arnold, "Transportation Supplies to China," July 15, 1943, NARA II, RG 18, Entry 300, Box 915, Folder 400-A.

52. True to Arnold, July 12, 1943, Box 04040508, ICD Documents, AMCHO.

53. Smith to George, Dec. 5, 1943, Box 04004601, ICD-ATC Reports and Letters, AMCHO.

54. "Notes on Colonel Mountain's Report on Temporary Duty in India-China Wing during July and August, 1943," Box 04040508, ICD Documents, AMCHO.

55. "Caged" refers to keeping the instrument lock in place so that it will not spin or tumble unnecessarily; this was done only while the aircraft was parked on the ground.

56. Quoted in Cameron, *Training to Fly,* p. 398.

57. Ibid., p. 400.

58. Quoted in ibid., p. 403.

59. Tunner to Douglas, Mar. 10, 1945, Box 0404601, ICD-ATC Reports and Letters, AMCHO.

60. Kenneth K. Goldstein, "Unit History of 492nd Bombardment Squadron, July 1945," NARA II, RG 493, Box 645. Ironically, though the Hump took such a heavy toll on the unit, its pilots scorned the transport missions, with the unit historian recording, "It is easily evident that there is nothing inspiring in 'Hump' flying. That fact alone cuts off half the incentive necessary for an 'Eager Beaver' squadron. As one of the linemen said, 'We shoulda stood wid bombing.' How right."

61. "'Hump' Cargo Flights End," *New York Times,* Nov. 17, 1945, p. 3.

62. Consolidated also built a "tanker" version of the C-87, called the C-109, which had internal fuel tanks exclusively for carrying fuel.

63. USAAF, Headquarters, *Pilot Training Manual for the Skytrain,* AAF Manual 51–129–2, Aug. 1945, provided to author courtesy of the National Museum of the U.S. Air Force, Dayton, Ohio.

64. Pearcy, *Dakota at War,* p. 14.

65. Eisenhower, *Crusade in Europe,* pp. 163–64.

66. Eveland, "The Evacuation of Burma." Eveland's claim of carrying seventy-four passengers in a cargo compartment that was roughly half the area of a racquetball court is probably not an exaggeration. During the evacuation of Saigon in 1975 a C-130A—an aircraft about the size of a Boeing 737, designed to carry no more than 100 passengers—is reported to have flown with nearly 350 passengers on board. Such heroics did not stop with fixed-wing aircraft. Two HH-53 rescue helicopters (rated for a crew of three and twenty-three fully equipped troops) each carried at least 120 evacuees in a single trip, most of whom were women and children, but still serving as examples of operating aircraft well beyond their design limits. John F. Guilmartin, personal communication, Dec. 2006.

67. "Service ceiling" is defined as the maximum altitude an airplane can reach and still maintain a slight climb of 100 feet per minute. See U.S. Army Air Forces, "Pilot's Flight Operating Instructions, C-47 Airplane," Technical Order 01–40NC-1, Nov. 1, 1942, p. 50, National Museum of the U.S. Air Force, Dayton, Ohio.

68. It is impossible to say with precision how many accidents were caused by pilots' failure to use their oxygen, but it was likely more than a few. As will be discussed later, Hap Arnold's crew got lost over the Hump because they failed

to use their oxygen. Even as late as the spring of 1945, Hump commanders had to mandate the use of oxygen for crews in unit regulations (USAAF, ATC, ICD, Headquarters, "Weekly Summary, 21–28 April 1945," Apr. 30, 1945). William Tunner also records how uncomfortable it was to fly with a mask (*Over the Hump,* p. 48).

69. Herbert L. Matthews, "Peaks in Himalayas Awesome from Air," *New York Times,* Dec. 30, 1942, p. 5. CNAC pilot Joseph Genovese records a similar high-altitude flight in which he was carrying a full load of passengers, all but three of whom were passed out, and was flying at his aircraft's maximum altitude of 21,000 feet to avoid ice buildup on the wings. Genovese, *We Flew without Guns,* pp. 1–16.

70. Davis, Martin, and Whittle, *Curtiss C-46 Commando,* p. 17. The C-46A–the variant used most in 1943–had a maximum military overload takeoff weight of 49,600 pounds and an equipped empty weight of 30,669 pounds when carrying cargo. Accounting for a fuel load of 8,400 pounds, this left 10,531 pounds for crew and cargo.

71. "Memo to Air Staff on Necessary C-46 Modifications," Oct. 11, 1943, NARA II, RG 18, Central Decimal Files, Oct. 1943–May 1944, Box 1253, Folder 452.1, Transports. As of October 11, 1943, 130 C-46s had been sent to India for Hump service. Of that number, 2 were lost en route to the theater (it took over seventy hours of flying to make it from California to India), and 29 were lost in the theater due to various factors not related to the enemy.

72. HQ AAF to General George, "C-46 Operations (in Cold Weather)," Oct. 9, 1943, NARA II, RG 18, Central Decimal Files, Entry 294, Box 744, File 452.1-G.

73. "Estimated Requirement to Meet July and September Objectives India-China Air Transport Operations," May 23, 1943, NARA II, RG 18, Bulky Files, Oct. 1942–44, World War II, Entry 300, Box 1036.

74. Air Transport Command, "Public Relations Weekly Report for 11 September, 1943," Box 04040508, ICD Documents, AMCHO.

75. USAAF, Headquarters, Record Sheet, "C-56 Airplanes and Engine Failure at High Altitude, Especially on the 'Over-hump,'" Oct. 19, 1943, NARA II, RG 18, Central Decimal Files, Entry 300, Box 917, Folder 452.1-A.

76. Chief Pilot Report to ICD Commanders on C-46 Operations, "Herbert O. Fisher's Report on Activities of C-46's in CBI Theater," Aug. 12, 1945, Box 04030604, ATC Documents, AMCHO.

77. C-46s had problems with carburetor deicing equipment as late as the first quarter of 1945, when leaky lines that supplied alcohol to the carburetor started engine fires (USAAF, ATC, ICD, Historical Section, "History of the India-China Division, January–November 1945," 312.01, AFHRA, p. 335).

78. "TWA–Pilot's Narrative Report–Special Flight Army C-46 Aircraft," May 27, 1943, Box 04040508, ICD Documents, AMCHO.

79. Both the official AAF history and General Tunner's memoirs state that the C-54 was "altitude limited" but do not elaborate further. According to the aircraft's technical data, it was clearly shows it being able to climb to altitudes of over 20,000 feet, even with a full load of cargo ("Flight Operation Instruction Chart" in *Pilot's Handbook for C-54A,* June 25, 1944, AN 01–40NM-1, pp. 135, 140), but aircraft performance with three engines put the plane too close to the mountains along the northerly "high" Hump.

80. Tests flown in 1943 showed the plane's Pratt & Whitney Twin-Wasp R-2000 engines would cut out in heavy icing. Knight to Hoag, "Comparison of C-87 and C-54 Type Transports," Dec. 4, 1943, India-China Wing Reference Data, 312.197–2, AFHRA.

81. USAAF, ATC, ICD, Historical Section, "History of the India-China Division, January–November 1945," 312.01, AFHRA, p. 362.

82. The C-87–the transport version of the Consolidated B-24 bomber–was a jury-rigged transport as well, with one out of twelve B-24s being converted to this role during the first half of the war until the designed transport fleet became large enough. "War Production Board Cargo Airplane Requirements, Nov. 2, 1942," NARA II, RG 18, Central Decimal Files, Box 1251, Folder 452.1, Trainers to Transports.

83. C. R. Smith to H. H. Arnold, "Economic Aspects of the Commercial Use of Converted Military Aircraft," May 27, 1944, Box 04030604, ATC Documents, AMCHO. In the same memo Smith also suggests that the AAF try to get the CAA to allow Douglass to up the load limits on its DC-3 and DC-4. CAA safety restrictions limited the DC-3's takeoff weight to 24,400–25,200 pounds,

and Smith wanted to help the commercial aviation sector by getting this limit raised to 29,000–31,000 pounds, the maximum used by the AAF for the C-47.

84. O. P. Echols to Assistant Secretary of War for Air, "Construction of Long-Range Transports by Lockheed Aircraft for Pan American Airways," Jan. 22, 1943, NARA II, RG 18, Central Decimal Files, Oct 1942–44, Entry 294, Box 745, Folder 452.1-O. The Lockheed aircraft he referred to eventually became the C-121 Constellation.

85. Between January 1944 and August 1945 ATC carried a total of 1,404,661 tons (a figure including both passengers and cargo). Over the same period, what would become the India-China Wing (and later the India-China Division) of ATC carried 632,938 tons, almost 45 percent of the command's total tonnage. USAAF, Office of Statistical Control, *Army Air Forces Statistical Digest*, pp. 302, 307.

CHAPTER 3

1. Leighton and Coakley, *Global Logistics*, 1:206–207.

2. U.S. Department of State, *FRUS: Diplomatic Papers, 1942, China*, p. 13.

3. USAAF, Office of Statistical Control, *Army Air Forces Statistical Digest*, p. 183.

4. Ibid., pp. 127–32.

5. "Outline of CBI History, 1941–1945," p. 11, 825.01C, AFHRA; Weinberg, *A World at Arms*, pp. 328–29. Gerhard Weinberg points out that if the Japanese had succeeded in taking Madagascar in the spring of 1942, they could have threatened supplies lines to Egypt, the Soviet Union (across Iran), and India, making the Hump airlift a moot point.

6. Audio recording of memo by Joseph T. McNarney, "1st Special Bombing Mission (China)," Apr. 16, 1942, NARA II, Central Decimal Files 463.3a. The Chinese ended up getting none of the bombers; all of the planes would be destroyed or captured by the Japanese after the attack. See Glines, *Doolittle Raid*.

7. OPD to Marshall, cited in Matloff and Snell, *Strategic Planning for Coalition Warfare*, p. 203.

8. The AAF received 2,807 air transports from factories in the thirty-six months between January 1940 and December 1942. By the war's end in August 1945—just thirty-two months later—it would receive a total of 24,059 transport

aircraft. USAAF, Office of Statistical Control, *Army Air Forces Statistical Digest,* p. 112).

9. "Maj. Naiden Army Golf Champ," *Washington Post,* June 20, 1927, p. 13; "Funeral Services Scheduled Today for Gen. Patrick," *Washington Post,* Jan. 31, 1942, p. 18.

10. Earl Naiden Biography, 167.74, AFHRA.

11. This estimate was reasonable, based on the assumption that at least 75 percent of the fleet (fifty-six total) was flyable at a given time, with each airplane able to make thirty-three trips from Dinjan to Myitkyina in a month (roughly one trip per day), carrying a full load of four tons.

12. Naiden's report exaggerated the amount of rainfall in the Dinjan area, claiming the airfield got 150 inches over the five months of the monsoon, but the weather station at Dibrigarh, located fifteen miles west of Dinjan, averaged only 85 inches of rain from May through September ("National Intelligence Survey, India and Pakistan: Weather and Climate," p. 130).

13. Weinberg, *A World at Arms,* p. 324.

14. Naiden's report was candid and realistic and has been unfairly criticized by the AAF official history as being an indication of a "defeatist" attitude (Craven and Cate, *Army Air Forces,* 7:119–20), a charge laid by Frank D. Sinclair, a technical advisor to the Douglas Aircraft Company who made a trip to China in September to assess the reasons for the airlift's poor production. Sinclair's first reason for the Hump's problems was the "defeatist attitude" of the Tenth Air Force regarding feasibility of successfully carrying 10,000 tons per month. Sinclair's report goes on to list in detail a number of reliable observations concerning the airlift's failure, but it should be noted that he was first an employee of the China Defense Supply Company, the intermediary organization based in Washington that coordinated requests and receipt of Chinese Lend-Lease equipment. Sinclair's report was clearly intended to provoke a response from both the War Department and State Department to generate more aid for China. See USAAF, ATC, Historical Officer, *Air Transportation to China under the 10th Air Force.*

15. Fragments of this history can be found in Scott, *God Is My Co-pilot,* pp. 50–89, and Henry Byroade, interview by Niel M. Johnson, Sept. 19, 1988, Potomac, Md., Oral History Interviews, Harry S. Truman Library and Museum, Independence, Mo.

16. "U.S. Bomber Lands Supplies," *New York Times,* Feb 7, 1939, p. 13; Drew Pearson, "The Washington Merry-Go-Round," *Washington Post,* Sept. 20, 1942, p. B4; "Caleb Haynes, 71, Retired General," *New York Times,* Apr. 7, 1966, p. 36.

17. *History of the India-China Ferry under the Tenth Air Force,* p. 5.

18. USAAF, ATC, Historical Officer, *Air Transportation to China under the 10th Air Force.*

19. U.S. Department of State, *FRUS: Diplomatic Papers, 1942, China,* p. 44.

20. USAAF, ATC, Historical Officer, *Air Transportation to China under the 10th Air Force.*

21. Shores, Cull, and Izawa, *Bloody Shambles,* 2:369.

22. *History of the India-China Ferry under the Tenth Air Force,* p. 4.

23. Leo E. Veins, "Myitkyina–The Dunkirk of Burma, 1942," 1989, author's files.

24. Hull to Marshall, May 9, 1942, NARA II, RG 165, Entry 418, Box 1240.

25. USAAF, ATC, Historical Officer, *Air Transportation to China under the 10th Air Force.*

26. Audio recording of memos between Arnold and acting Chief of Staff McNarney on the diversion of B-24s for the Hump airlift, May 12–17, 1942, NARA II, Central Decimal File 463.4a.

27. Stilwell to Adjutant General, May 21, 1942, AMMISCA Weekly Reports, NARA II, RG 493, Entry 1.

28. Shores, *Bloody Shambles,* pp. 14–15.

29. Carter and Mueller, *Air Force Combat Chronology.*

30. Charles H. Corbett, "Conditions in Chekiang and Kiangsi," *Far Eastern Survey* 12 (May 1943): 95–99.

31. Japanese Monograph No. 71, *Army Operations in China,* pp. 116–17.

32. Weinberg, *A World at Arms,* pp. 332–39.

33. Hsiung Shihfei to Marshall, June 3, 1942, NARA II, RG 165, Entry 418, Box 1240.

34. Memo by Stanley K. Hornbeck, U.S. Department of State, *FRUS: Diplomatic Papers, 1942, China,* pp. 49–51.

35. Roosevelt was keenly set on using aircraft production as a strategic deterrent against the Axis with the war in Europe under way since September 1939; to this end, he was more concerned with the production of whole aircraft

and not the parts that actually helped sustain a functional air arm. See Under-wood, *Wings of Democracy.*

36. Cairncross, *Planning in Wartime,* p. 178, and Craven and Cate, *Army Air Forces,* 6:347–48.

37. "R-1830 Engines in Transports," July 27, 1942, NARA II, RG 165, Entry 418, Box 1455. There was a hope that the P-66 engines would actually perform better than those designed for the C-47, as the former had a two-stage impeller that helped it to perform better at high altitudes. This was problematic for the regular R-1830, which had to be operated over 65 percent to maintain the Hump route's required altitude, reducing engine life and the mean time between main-tenance cycles. See USAAF, ATC, Historical Officer, *Air Transportation to China under the 10th Air Force.*

38. *History of the India-China Ferry under the Tenth Air Force,* p. 7.

39. For a solid operational history of the war in 1942 in North Africa, see Murray & Millett, *A War To Be Won,* pp. 262–73; and Weinberg, *A World at Arms,* pp. 348–63.

40. USAAF, Assistant Chief of Air Staff, Intelligence, Historical Division, *The Tenth Air Force, 1942,* p. 58.

41. USAAF, Assistant Chief of Air Staff, Intelligence, Historical Division, "Ninth Air Force in the Western Desert Campaign to 23 January 1943," AAF Historical Studies 30, Feb. 1945, 0467604, AFHRA, pp. 10–11; USAAF, Assis-tant Chief of Air Staff, Intelligence, Historical Division, *The Tenth Air Force, 1942,* pp. 47–48.

42. Quoted in Romanus and Sunderland, *Stilwell's Mission,* pp. 169–71.

43. Ibid., p. 170.

44. Hull to Gauss, July 4, 1942, U.S. Department of State, *FRUS: Diplomatic Papers, 1942, China,* p. 98.

45. Stilwell to Adjutant General, July 1, 1942, AMMISCA Weekly Reports, NARA II, RG 493, Entry 1.

46. Hsiung to Marshall, June 3, 1942, NARA II, RG 165, Entry 418, Box 1240.

47. McHugh, "Navy Department Intelligence Report," Oct. 5, 1942, McHugh Papers, reel 2, Military Reports, 1935–1946.

48. Ibid.

49. Australian journalist Rhodes Farmer recorded an interview in which Chiang claimed, "Wherever I go is the Government and the centre of resistance," then boldly declared, "I am the state." Quoted in Fenby, *Chiang Kai-shek,* pp. 326–27.

50. McHugh, "Navy Department Intelligence Report," Oct. 5, 1942, McHugh Papers, reel 2, Military Reports, 1935–1946.

51. It should be remembered that the Nationalist Army was a heterogeneous organization composed mostly of regional units of varying capabilities and loyalties, numbering just over 3,500,000 men. At the center of this army was the Central Army (Zhongyang Jun), which numbered about 300,000 and whose officer leadership mostly came from military academies like Whampoa, where Chiang was the commandant in the 1920s. The Central Army officers tended to be fiercely loyal to Chiang, making McHugh's observation all the more significant. Eastman et al., *Nationalist Era in China,* p. 137. In contrast to those loyal to Chiang were those who grew increasingly wary of his leadership during the war. One example of this was seen in the failed "Young Generals Coup" in late 1943, discovered by Dai Li while Chiang was in Cairo. See Schaller, *U.S. Crusade in China,* p. 455.

52. McHugh, "Navy Department Intelligence Report," Oct. 5, 1942, McHugh Papers, reel 2, Military Reports, 1935–1946. McHugh was not an overzealous airpower advocate. If the United States was unable or unwilling to launch his suggested air offensive against Japan from China, then he advocated a more robust application of direct U.S. Navy power to turn the "tide of the war in the Far East."

53. Ibid.

54. McHugh to Knox, July 1, 1942, McHugh Papers, reel 1, Personal Correspondence, 1937–1946.

55. McHugh to Knox, July 9, 1942, ibid.

56. "Outline of CBI History, 1941–1945," p. VI-5, 825.01C, AFHRA. Jepson also served as Brereton's personal secretary during his deployment to Cairo; see Peggy Preston, "Capital Visitor Cites Yank Influence in India," *Washington Post,* Feb. 27, 1944, p. S2.

57. Handy to AMMISCA, July 25, 1942, NARA II, RG 165, Central Decimal File 580.82, Entry 418, Box 1580; see also USAAF, ATC, Historical Officer, *Air Transportation to China under the 10th Air Force.*

58. Quoted in USAAF, ATC, Historical Officer, *Air Transportation to China under the 10th Air Force,* pp. 13–17.

59. Audio copy of memorandum from Marshall to Combined Chiefs of Staff, Aug. 14, 1942, NARA II, Central Decimal Files, 463.6.

60. "Northwest Route to China through Russia," Jan. 4, 1943, NARA II, RG 165, Entry 418, Box 1580.

61. Hornbeck memorandum, Aug. 17, 1942, U.S. Department of State, *FRUS: Diplomatic Papers, 1942, China,* p. 138.

62. Craven and Cate, *Army Air Forces,* 1:340.

63. Greenough, *Prosperity and Misery in Modern Bengal,* pp. 144–45.

64. USAAF, Assistant Chief of Air Staff, Intelligence, Historical Division, *The Tenth Air Force, 1942,* p. 78.

65. USAAF, ATC, Historical Officer, *Air Transportation to China under the 10th Air Force.*

66. Quinn, *Aluminum Trail,* p. 3.

67. McKeown to Croil, Sept. 18, 1942, in USAAF, ATC, Historical Officer, *Air Transportation to China under the 10th Air Force.*

68. Robert Kashower (CNAC pilot), interview by Allen E. Settle, Feb. 24, 1943, Natal, Brazil, Box 04040508, ICD Documents, AMCHO.

69. Spencer, *Flying the Hump,* p. 127.

70. Quinn, *Aluminum Trail,* p. 7.

71. "India-China Air Trail Now Flown at Night," *New York Times,* Sept. 13, 1942, p. 26.

72. Evans and Peattie, *Kaigun,* pp. 342–43.

73. Francillon, *Japanese Aircraft of the Pacific War,* p. 33.

74. Ibid., pp. 206–14. Japanese air bases in Burma were located at Toungoo, Meitila, Swebo, Magwe, Akyab, Moulmein, Maubin, Mingaladon, and Pegu. There was also a base at Chiang Mai in northern Thailand (see Shores, *Bloody Shambles,* pp. 425–428 for a brief overview of IJAAF units and bases). The Ki-43 was armed with two machine guns mounted in the engine cowling, either two 7.7mm guns or a single 7.7mm accompanied by a 12.6mm gun.

75. Alvin D. Coox, "The Rise and Fall of the Imperial Japanese Air Force," *Aerospace Historian* 27 (June 1980): 75.

76. Shores, *Bloody Shambles,* pp. 29–30.

77. *History of the India-China Ferry under the Tenth Air Force,* p. 8, AFHRA; Shores, *Bloody Shambles,* p. 29.

78. For a memoir of a soldier who manned a radio warning post, see Phillips, *KC8 Burma.* KC8 was overrun by the Japanese in the spring of 1943 ("Loss of Important Stations in Radio Warning Net," Apr. 17, 1943, Box 04040605, AMCHO). According to intelligence gathered by the 51st Fighter Group, the Japanese rarely flew at night in Burma (AAF Informational Intelligence Summary, Mar. 4, 1943, NARA II, RG 18, Central Decimal Files, Bulky Files, Box 38); see also "51st TFW Story," p. 13, K-WG-51-Hi, AFHRA. Radar could not be used for enemy aircraft detection due to the rugged terrain to the east ("Use of Radar in Upper Assam," Mar. 1943, RG 18, Central Decimal Files, Oct. 1942–44, Entry 300, Box 916, Folder 410-A).

79. Alexander to George, July 4, 1943, ICD Documents, Box 04040508, ICD Documents, AMCHO.

80. Audio copy of message, Chiang Kaishek to Roosevelt, Nov. 24, 1942, NARA II, Central Decimal Files 463.7.

81. Smith to Arnold, "India-China Ferry Operation," Oct. 13, 1942, in USAAF, ATC, Historical Officer, *Air Transportation to China under the 10th Air Force.* Bissell instead advocated a circuitous 4,000-mile route that began in New Delhi. Byrd, *Chennault,* p. 157; for Bissell's attitude, see Claire Chennault, interview by L. G. Heston et al., Apr. 5, 1948, Washington, D.C., 105.5–13, AFHRA.

82. Craven and Cate, *Army Air Forces,* 7:19.

CHAPTER 4

1. Official U.S. Air Force biography of Brig. Gen. Edward H. Alexander (current as of December 1954), available at http://www.af.mil/information/bios/bio.asp?bioID=4496 (accessed June 2007); Air Staff Intelligence Historical Division, "Administrative History of the Ferry Command, 29 May–30 June 1942," 0467624, AFHRA; Edward H. Alexander, interview by Murray Green, Dec. 26, 1970, Pompano Beach, Fla., microfilm no. 43817, AFHRA.

2. Tunner, *Over the Hump,* p. 61.

3. Sources are sketchy as to how many airplanes the ICW had when ATC took over the airlift on December 1. According to one letter (Alexander to George, Feb. 13, 1943, Box 04040508, ICD Documents, AMCHO), the ICW had forty-four C-47s (or C-47 variants) and ten C-87s assigned as well as sixteen C-47s "attached" or on loan from the Tenth Air Force, totaling seventy aircraft. Between the date of this memo and the day ATC took over the lift on December 1, three C-47s were lost (Quinn, *Aluminum Trail,* pp. 8–9).

4. Alexander to George, Jan. 4, 1943, Box 04040508, ICD Documents, AMCHO.

5. Stilwell to Alexander, "Movement of Cargo and Passengers," Dec. 15, 1943, Box 04040603, ICD Forecasts and Organization, AMCHO. It is also noteworthy that Stilwell never once made a disparaging remark about Alexander in his diary entries of 1942 and 1943, significant by virtue of the fact that Stilwell's candor was most transparent in his private diaries; he ostensibly used them as a cathartic "outlet" and never hesitated to heap scorn on those who had given him even the slightest trouble. Original and transcribed copies of Stilwell's diaries are part of the Stilwell Papers at the Hoover Institution, Stanford University.

6. Love to Alexander, Feb. 27, 1943, Box 04040601, ICD-ATC Reports and Letters, AMCHO. For a consideration of the relationship between the Tenth Air Force and the ICW from Bissell's perspective, see "History of AAF Activities on the Continent of Asia, December 1941–May 1946," vol. 2, 825.01C, AFHRA.

7. Bissell was difficult to get along with and was not well regarded by many of his contemporaries in India and China in 1942 and 1943. Chennault had continual problems with him while his own China Air Task Force (an AAF evolution of the AVG) was part of Bissell's Tenth Air Force until becoming the Fourteenth Air Force in March 1943. When AVG pilots were given the opportunity to join the AAF in the summer of 1942, only four took the offer; many of them claimed they turned it down simply because Bissell had taken the approach of threatening the fliers by declaring, "If you don't accept induction [into the Air Corps] here in China I will personally see that someone from the Draft Board meets you at the bottom of the boarding ladder [of the ship back to the United States]. You will end up as enlisted men, not as pilots." Most of the AVG pilots later agreed that the intent of Bissell's speech was to purposely see that none of the pilots volunteered for active duty, something that would make Chennault—a man seen by many in

the War Department as something of a renegade—"fall flat on his ass." Typical of fighter pilots, the AVG flyers got a small amount of revenge when they taught Chinese refueling crews that "Piss on Bissell" was a friendly U.S. greeting, such that the local fuel truck driver would greet arriving airplanes "with a smile and a thumbs-up sign, cheerily shouting, "Piss on Bissell." Shilling, *Destiny,* pp. 189–90. The failure of the AAF to embrace the AVG is consistent with the (then) Air Service's poor treatment of the Lafayette Escadrille in World War I after the United States formally entered the war. See Flammer, *Vivid Air.*

8. Carter and Mueller, *Air Force Combat Chronology,* "1 January 1943" to "31 March 1943."

9. These included Karachi (March 29), Chabua (April 2), Sookerating (April 2), and Jorhat (April 9) in India, and Yangkai (March 16) and Kunming (5 April) in China. Army Airways Communications Service, History Office, *History of the Army Airways Communications Service,* pp. 627–28.

10. A good contemporary guide to D/F navigation published for World War II–era pilots can be found in McIntosh, *Radio Navigation for Pilots.*

11. The actual cargo delivered in July and December 1943 was 3,451 and 12,590 tons respectively. U.S. Strategic Bombing Survey, Military Analysis Division, *Air Transport Command in the War against Japan.*

12. Barry Watts outlines the roots of this Newtonian or Laplacian (named for French mathematician and astronomer Simon Pierre de Laplace) mentality so pervasive in the interwar years (and afterward) in *Foundations of US Air Doctrine.*

13. "Plans for Cargo Aircraft Allocations for the India-China Wing for 1943," Feb. 1, 1943, Box 04040603, ICD Forecasts and Organization, AMCHO. The monthly rate of 50,000 tons *was* eventually met—but only eighteen months later in June 1945.

14. Weinberg, *A World at Arms,* pp. 437–38.

15. Quoted in Dallek, *Franklin D. Roosevelt,* p. 355.

16. For the fullest treatment of the motives and specifics of Chennault's claims, see Byrd, *Chennault,* pp. 172–76.

17. U.S. Department of State, *FRUS: Conferences at Washington and Casablanca,* p. 597.

18. USAAF, Office of Statistical Control, *Army Air Forces Statistical Digest,* p. 112.

19. Arnold order on staff use of transports, Dec. 17, 1942, NARA II, RG 18, Central Decimal Files, Box 1251, Folder 452.1, Trainers and Transports.

20. U.S. Department of State, *FRUS: Conferences at Washington and Casablanca,* pp. 597, 632.

21. Arnold applauds Bissell in his diary, giving the Tenth Air Force commander accolades for doing enough "detail work" so as to recognize that a request by Chennault for medium bombers was unsound because there was no way for getting the planes the necessary 100-octane fuel for China operation. John W. Huston, ed., *American Airpower Comes of Age,* 1:491–92.

22. Arnold, *Global Mission,* pp. 415–20.

23. Ibid., p. 427.

24. Ibid., p. 461.

25. Arnold memorandum, "Aid to Chinese Air Force," Feb. 7, 1943, NARA II, RG 18, Central Decimal File, Oct. 1942–1944, Entry 300, Box 915, Folder 400-A.

26. Arnold memorandum, "Operations of Heavy Bombers in China," Feb. 7, 1943, ibid. See also Haynes and Feuer, *General Chennault's Secret Weapon;* Craven and Cate, *Army Air Forces,* 4:518–29.

27. Arnold memorandum, "Air Transport Command Operations India to China," Feb. 7, 1943, NARA II, RG 18, Central Decimal File, Oct. 1942–44, Entry 300, Box 915, Folder 400-A.

28. "Americans Crash in Burma Jungle; Surgeon Parachutes to Their Aid," *New York Times,* Aug. 9, 1943, p. 1. In the 1950s Flickinger became a leading flight surgeon for the early space program and sat on the board that selected the first seven Mercury astronauts. He retired from the air force as a brigadier general, a rare achievement for a military physician.

29. Alexander to Love, Feb. 13, 1943, Box 04040601, ICD-ATC Reports and Letters, AMCHO.

30. Alexander to George, Jan. 20 and Feb. 13, 1943, Box 04040508, ICD Documents, AMCHO.

31. USAAF, ATC, ICD, Historical Section, *Medical History of the India-China Division of Air Transport Command,* p. 57.

32. Ibid., pp. 59–60.

33. Ibid.

34. Ibid., pp. 60–61.

35. Ibid., p. 58.

36. Ibid., p. 59.

37. Ibid., pp. 64–65.

38. "Medical Report on Air Transport Command, Mohanbari, India," June 20, 1944, NARA II, RG 18, Central Decimal File, Oct 1942–44, Entry 300, Box 915, Folder 300-G.

39. Wells, *Courage and Air Warfare,* p. 70. It is also noteworthy that the annual rate of those diagnosed with neuropsychiatric disorders in the CBI was 24.3 per 1,000, very close to the ICW average. U.S. Army Medical Department, *Medical Statistics in World War II* (Washington, D.C.: Government Printing Office, 1975), pp. 43–45.

40. Arnold to Alexander, Mar. 4, 1943, NARA II, RG 18, Central Decimal Files, Entry 300, Box 918, Folder Misc. A. Arnold also promised in the same memo ten C-87s per month, starting June 15 until fifty were in place.

41. The chairman of the JCS, Adm. William Leahy, sent Marshall and Arnold a memo on Feb. 24 notifying them of the details of a meeting he had just had with the president, with FDR telling him he had been misinformed about the details of the support the 308th would need to accomplish its mission, saying he was under the "understanding that one bombing plane [used as a transport] could carry on one trip sufficient gas and munitions to make four bombing expeditions against enemy targets." There is no hint as to what gave FDR this impression, though Chennault is the most likely candidate. Leahy to Marshall and Arnold, Feb. 24, 1943, NARA II, RG 18, Central Decimal Files, Entry 300, Box 917, Folder 452.1-A.

42. On Arnold's impression of Chennault's logistical abilities, see Huston, ed., *American Air Power Comes of Age,* 1:513.

43. Marshall to Roosevelt, Feb. 27, 1943, NARA II, RG 18, Central Decimal Files, Entry 300, Box 917, Folder 452.1-A.

44. Air Technical Service Command Historical Office, "Case History of C-46 Airplane Project," Aug. 1945, NARA II, RG 18, AAF Office of the Assistant Chief of the Air Staff, Matériel and Services (A-4), Entry 22, Box 12. Wright personally assured Arnold that fifty airplanes had been modified for overseas use, but a later investigation revealed that none of the fifty planes had been fully modi-

fied and that only a few of them had been partially modified. There is no record as to why Wright told Arnold the planes were ready when they were not.

45. USAAF, Office of Statistical Control, *Army Air Forces Statistical Digest,* p. 134.

46. Alexander to George, Jan. 20 and Feb. 13, 1943, Box 04040508, ICD Documents, AMCHO.

47. Alexander to Arnold, April 4, 1943, NARA II, RG 18, Central Decimal Files, Entry 300, Box 918, Folder Misc. A.

48. Edward H. Alexander, interview by Murray Green, Dec. 26, 1970, Pompano Beach, Fla., microfilm no. 43817, AFHRA.

49. Smith to Arnold, Apr. 8, 1943, NARA II, RG 18, Central Decimal File, Entry 300, Box 918, Folder Misc. A.

50. The minutes of an airfield meeting held at Chabua on May 9 listed the top three "bottlenecks" in airfield construction: the lack of rail transportation for stone (the current railroad could deliver only 2,500 tons of stone a day, although 250,000 tons were needed to build the seven runways); the availability of stone to crush for runway subsurfaces; and the lack of labor (which needed to be raised from 35 percent to 55 percent. ICW Airfield Meeting Minutes, Chabua, May 9, 1943, Box 04040508, ICD Documents, AMCHO.

51. Alexander to Arnold, "India-China Air Freight Operations," Apr. 19, 1943, Box 04040606, AMCHO.

52. Arnold to Dill, "Airdromes in Assam," Apr. 30, 1943, NARA II, RG 18, Central Decimal Files, Entry 300, Box 918, Folder Misc. A.

53. Daso, *Hap Arnold,* p. 183.

54. U.S. Department of State, *FRUS, Conferences at Washington and Quebec, 1943,* p. 301.

55. Chennault advocated a fire-bombing campaign against Japan and so was in step with the AAF's strategic bombing concept for that enemy. The Plans Division of the Air Staff was studying the possibility of such a campaign as early as May 1943 as a precursor to what would become Curtis LeMay's controversial air effort against the Japanese two years later. Office of the Assistant Chief of the Air Staff, Intelligence, "Japan Incendiary Attack Data, Oct. 1943," NARA II, RG 165, General Records (1942–44), Top-Secret General Correspondence,

Entry 419, Box 43. For Chennault's plan see Chennault, "Plan for Operations in China," Apr. 30, 1943, NARA II, RG 165, Entry 419, Box 57, Case No. 124.

56. Audio recording of meeting minutes between Stilwell and Chennault, Apr. 30, 1943, NARA II, Central Decimal Files 463.3a. For Stilwell's plan see "General Stilwell's Plan of May 21, 1943," NARA II, RG 165, Entry 419, Box 57, Case No. 144. For Stilwell's concerns that increased Hump deliveries might promote idleness in Chinese armies, see Alexander to George, "1943 Program for the India-China Wing," Mar. 24, 1943, NARA II, RG 18, Central Decimal File, Oct. 1942–44, Foreign Files, Entry 300, Box 914. The black market in Nationalist China was prolific enough to force the U.S. military to pay its China-based troops in U.S. currency rather than Chinese national currency, when the official exchange rate might be ten to twelve time less than the black market exchange rate. For China's black market, see Walter Rundell Jr., "Currency Control by the United States Army in World War II: Foundation for Failure," *Pacific Historical Review* 30 (Nov. 1961): 381–99, and Young, *China's Wartime Finance and Inflation,* pp. 306–307.

57. Tuchman, *Stilwell,* pp. 367–68.

58. Byrd, *Chennault,* p. 191; Chennault, *Way of a Fighter,* pp. 225–26.

59. Hattori, *Complete History,* 2:160–61; Japanese Monograph No. 76, *Air Operations in the China Area,* pp. 118, 126–28. Sichuan was a major food-producing province and the Imperial General Headquarters wanted to launch a ground offensive here throughout most of 1943 to increase the pressure on Chiang's government in Chongqing but was unable to do so due to Pacific commitments.

60. Churchill, *Hinge of Fate,* p. 786.

61. U.S. Department of State, *FRUS: Conferences at Washington and Quebec, 1943,* pp. 52–61.

62. Wavell was much too generous with his estimate; the actual average was 2,350 tons monthly from February to April 1943.

63. U.S. Department of State, *FRUS: Conferences at Washington and Quebec, 1943,* p. 62.

64. Ibid., pp. 62–65; Stilwell, Original Diaries, entry for May 14, 1943, Stilwell Papers.

65. U.S. Department of State, *FRUS: Conferences at Washington and Quebec, 1943,* p. 72–76.

66. Ibid., pp. 77–85.

67. Churchill, *Hinge of Fate,* pp. 785–86.

CHAPTER 5

1. Hump veteran Edwin Lee White's colorful memoir of the early Hump revolves around the attainment of this goal and is titled *Ten Thousand Tons by Christmas.*

2. Lowest-priority items went by barge, whose six-week trip equaled the six weeks it took the freight to get from the port at Charleston, South Carolina, to the port at Calcutta. The railroad was faster but switched from a regular to a meter gauge at Santahar, requiring a lengthy off-loading and loading of cargo–done by hand. Making matters worse, the Assam rail cars were designed to carry tea and so were prone to breakdowns when overloaded with heavy equipment. The rail cars also had three river crossings that forced the engine and cars to separate into segments of only a few cars to be loaded onto a rail ferry and then recoupled once the crossing was complete. Smith to George, "Trip Report," Dec. 23, 1943, Box 04040601, ICD-ATC Reports and Letters, AMCHO. When cargo arrived in China, it still had to be parsed out to its correct point of delivery, meaning that in the worse case supplies took nearly a half year to make the complete trip from start to finish. Smith to Arnold, "Review of Operation–India-China," Feb. 11, 1944, NARA II, RG 18, Entry 300, Box 914, Folder 300-D.

3. Barney M. Giles (Asst. Chief of the Air Staff) to Marshall, "India-China Air Transport Wing," May 23, 1943, NARA II, RG 165, Entry 418, Box 1580, Folder OPD 580.82 CTO. The archival copy of this document is stamped "not used," and while it may not have been passed to Marshall, it accurately represents ATC and ICW needs on the heels of FDR's tonnage directive.

4. USAAF, ATC, ICD, Historical Section, "A History of the India-China Wing, June through December 1943," p. 39.

5. These three airlines were American (fleet size: 74), United (62), and TWA (40). The fifteen largest commercial airline companies in the United States had a combined fleet of 322 airplanes at the start of 1942. R. E. G. Davies, *A History of the World's Airlines,* p. 136.

6. USAAF, Office of Statistical Control, *Army Air Forces Statistical Digest,* p. 303.

7. George to Arnold, June 6, 1943, Box 04040508, ICD Documents, AMCHO.

8. Alexander to George, July 11, 1943, ibid.

9. F. G. Atkinson to Asst. Chief of Staff, Plans, "Resume of Action Taken on Securing Flight Personnel for Project 7," June 1, 1943, in USAAF, ATC, ICD, Historical Section, "A History of the India-China Wing, June through December 1943," p. 458.

10. Love to Arnold, July 14, 1943, NARA II, RG 18, Entry 300, Box 915, Folder 400-A.

11. USAAF, ATC, ICD, Historical Section, "A History of the India-China Wing, June through December 1943," p. 452.

12. J. M. McDonnell to George, July 15, 1943, Box 04040605, AMCHO.

13. American Airlines, Inc., "Project 7-A Summary," Box 04040606, ibid. During their four months in India the American Airlines detachment averaged 94 tons per airplane per month, making a total of 499 trips over the Hump and carrying 2,110 tons. The ICW tonnage per plane per month statistics are derived from data in Alexander's weekly reports of August 6 and August 13, in which he outlines the specific number of planes he was able to use exclusively for Hump operations. While it is true that the American Airlines crews flew only C-87s and not the lighter-loaded C-47s that were still being used by the ICW, the commercial crews nonetheless made more out of their trips than the military crews. Alexander to George, Aug. 6 and 13, 1943, Box 04040508, ICD Documents, AMCHO. For the only published book with information on Project 7-A, see Mangan, *To the Four Winds.*

14. Notes on India-China Wing, Aug. 12 1943, NARA II, RG 18, Entry 300, Box 934, Folder 580-A; Love to Arnold, "Progress Report India-China Wing, Air Transport Command," Oct. 9, 1943, ibid., Box 914, Adjutant General Records.

15. Alexander to George, July 4, 1943, Box 04040508, ICD Documents, AMCHO.

16. Henry Byroade, "Notes on Airdrome Construction and Cargo Availability for India-China Freight Line," NARA II, RG 165, Entry 418, Box 1580; Smith to Sullivan, July 19, 1943, NARA II, RG 18, Entry 300, Box 934, File 580-A. Immediately after the war Byroade served as an aide to Marshall during the latter's mission to China. Later in his State Department career he served as

the U.S. ambassador to Egypt (1955–56), South Africa (1956–59), Afghanistan (1959–62), Burma (1963–1968), the Philippines (1969–73), and Pakistan (1973–77); his papers are maintained at the Harry S. Truman Library and Museum in Independence, Mo.

17. Alexander to George, Aug. 6, 1943, Box 04040508, ICD Documents, AMCHO. As an interesting aside, the Japanese also complained about similar difficulties—but for perhaps different reasons—with Colonel Nonaka, the director of operations for the IJA Third Air Force, stating that "although Thailand and Indo-China area were our allies, we had a hard time acquiring grounds and levying labor there." Japanese Monograph No. 56, *Southeast Area Air Operations Record,* p. 21.

18. Alexander to George, July 4, 1943, Box 04040508, ICD Documents, AMCHO.

19. Love to Arnold, "Transportation of Supplies to China," July 14, 1943, NARA II, RG 18, Entry 300, Box 915, Folder 400-A.

20. F. G. Atkinson (ATC Personnel) to Hoag, Nov. 2, 1943, Box 04040607, AMCHO.

21. John J. Sbrega, "Anglo-American Relations and the Selection of Mountbatten as Supreme Allied Commander, South East Asia," *Military Affairs* 46 (Oct. 1982): 139–45.

22. Van de Ven, *War and Nationalism,* p. 28.

23. Arnold to Stilwell, Aug. 28, 1943, and Arnold to Chennault, Aug. 28, 1943, NARA II, RG 493, Box 21, SEAC Files.

24. Lewis, *Eddie Rickenbacke,* pp. 472–77.

25. USAAF, Assistant Chief of Air Staff, Intelligence, Historical Division, *Fourteenth Air Force,* p. 39.

26. The rudder lock mechanically secured that flight surface to keep it from being damaged from gusty winds while parked on the ground. Flying with it locked would be akin to riding a bicycle with the handlebars locked in place.

27. Altmayer to Hoag, "Survey of ICW-ATC," Oct. 28, 1943, 312.152–1, AFHRA.

28. "Notes on Col. Mountain's Report on Temporary Duty in India-China Wing during July and August, 1943," Box 04040508, ICD Documents, AMCHO.

29. Alexander to George, July 4, 1943, ibid.

30. Love to George, Sept. 2, 1943, Box 04040601, ICD-ATC Reports and Letters, AMCHO.

31. Serling, *Eagle,* pp. 47–48.

32. Hardin biographical information provided to the author by the University of Texas at Dallas, which houses the small collection of Hardin's papers. Hardin is also mentioned (though not by name) in Miller, *A Preliminary to War,* p. 1.

33. Love to George, Sept. 2, 1943, Box 04040601, ICD-ATC Reports and Letters, AMCHO; Tunner intimates in his published memoirs that Alexander was demoted after leaving the ICW (*Over the Hump,* p. 51).

34. White, *Ten Thousand Tons by Christmas,* p. 132.

35. Ibid., pp. 138–39.

36. Smith to George, "ICW Trip Report," Dec. 5, 1943, Box 04040601, ICD-ATC Reports and Letters, AMCHO.

37. Ibid.

38. Roosevelt to Chiang, July 16, 1943, NARA II, RG 18, AAF Central Decimal File Oct. 1942–44, Foreign Files, Entry 300, Box 914.

39. Soong to Roosevelt, July 3, 1943, ibid., Box 915, Folder 400-A.

40. Roosevelt to Marshall, Oct. 15, 1943, NARA II, RG 18, AAF Central Decimal File Oct. 1942–44, Foreign Files, Box 914.

41. "Plot to Slay U.S. Fliers in China Bared," *Washington Post,* Sept. 21, 1943, p. 3.

42. Japanese Monograph No. 64, *Burma Air Operations Record,* p. 11

43. Quinn, p. 19; George to Arnold, August 13, 1943, Box 04040508, ICD Documents, AMCHO.

44. Shores, *Bloody Shambles,* p. 104; Quinn, p. 36.

45. Quinn, *Aluminum Trail,* pp. 40–41.

46. Shores, *Bloody Shambles,* p. 108; Chennault, *Way of a Fighter,* p. 249; Dunlop, *Behind Japanese Lines,* pp. 225–26.

47. USAAF, ATC, ICD, Historical Section, "A History of the India-China Wing, June through December 1943," pp. 454–45; Craven and Cate, *Army Air Forces,* 4:532–34; C. R. Smith refers to the November 25 attack on Shinchiku, stating, "The Japs are sore as hell and have broadcast that they are going to wipe out

Kunming" because it was the Hump delivery base that supplied the U.S. attackers (Smith to George, Dec. 1, 1943, Box 04040601, ICD-ATC Reports and Letters, AMCHO).

48. Japanese Monograph No. 64, *Burma Air Operations Record,* p. 19.

49. Katayama, "Logistical Activities of the Japanese Imperial Army."

50. Combined Intelligence Committee, "The Contribution of China to Allied Strategy," July 5, 1943, NARA II, RG 165, Entry 419, Box 57.

51. Green, *Fighters,* pp. 70–75.

52. Quinn, *Aluminum Trail,* pp. 46–47.

53. Hoag to Harris, Dec. 30, 1943, Box 04040601, ICD-ATC Reports and Letters, AMCHO.

54. Sapozhnikov, *China Theater,* pp. 134–35.

55. Barrett and Shyu, eds., *Chinese Collaboration with Japan,* pp. 68–69. See also U.S. Department of State, *FRUS: Diplomatic Papers, 1943, China,* pp. 89, 167.

56. Atcheson to Hull, Sept. 11, 1943; NARA II, RG 49, Box 21, SEAC Files (Data Regarding Asiatic Theater). George Atcheson Jr. was trying to generate political momentum in Chongqing with the intention of having Chinese troops fight in Burma. He advised Hull to have Roosevelt send Chiang a message encouraging such action, as "a message from the President to Chiang might be very helpful as giving Chiang both armor and ammunition with which to take the necessary action" in the face of resistant Guomindang organs or government. Atcheson continued, "Such messages (in comparatively mild form) might be able to effect that [the decision to fight in Burma] in the occasion of the formal gathering of Chinese leading statesmen and Generals in whose hands rest the direction of China's war effort in partnership with the United States and other allies."

57. Atcheson to Hull, Aug. 12, 1943, U.S. Department of State, *FRUS: Diplomatic Papers: 1943, China,* pp. 86–87.

58. Barrett and Shyu, eds., *Chinese Collaboration with Japan,* p. 66–68, 73; Soong to Roosevelt, Nov. 28, 1940, U.S. Department of State, *FRUS: Diplomatic Papers, 1940,* 4:698–700.

59. Japanese Monograph No. 71, *Army Operations in China,* p. 158.

60. Sapozhnikov, *China Theater,* p. 82.

61. See John Carter Vincent's assessment of this in his telegram to Cordell

Hull, April 24, 1943, U.S. Department of State, *FRUS: Diplomatic Papers, 1943, China*, pp. 50–51.

62. Hull to Roosevelt, Nov. 29, 1943, U.S. Department of State, *FRUS, Conferences at Cairo and Tehran*, pp. 620–21.

63. Dallek, *Franklin D. Roosevelt*, p. 427; see also Sainsbury, *Turning Point*, for an in-depth study of both conferences.

64. General Frank Dorn, a reliable source and Stilwell's aide at the time, records a private conversation between the two soon after the Cairo Conference wherein the CBI commander stated that Roosevelt implied that, if Chiang proved to be too great an obstacle in the theater, Stilwell should "get rid of him." Dorn, who had a longstanding, close relationship with Stilwell, recalls Stilwell stating, "The Big Boy's fed up with Chiang and his tantrums, and said so. In fact he told me in that Olympian manner of his: 'If you can't get along with Chiang and can't replace him, get rid of him once and for all. You know what I mean. Put in someone you can manage.'" Dorn then hatched a plan that involved the Hump, whereby the crew carrying the generalissimo on a trip over the mountains would fake catastrophic engine failure that would force all the plane's passengers to parachute to safety. Chiang's parachute would have been sabotaged before the flight, causing him to jump unsuspectingly to his death. Dorn, *Walkout*, pp. 75–79.

65. Meeting of the CCS, Nov. 24, 1943, U.S. Department of State, *FRUS, Conferences at Cairo and Tehran*, p. 342.

66. Roosevelt to Churchill, Dec. 5, 1943. The only copy of the telegram to Chiang comes by way of a draft the president wanted to send to Chiang with Churchill's approval. U.S. Department of State, *FRUS, Conferences at Cairo and Tehran*, p. 803.

67. Romanus and Sunderland, *Stillwell's Command Problems*, pp. 74–75.

68. USAAF, ATC, ICD, Historical Section, "A History of the India-China Wing, June through December 1943," p. 81; according to this unit history, none of November's major accidents were a result of being shot down, but Quinn records a C-46 attacked on November 24 while flying from Kunming to Sookerating (p. 57).

69. Minutes of the President's Meeting with the JCS, Nov. 19, 1943, U.S. Department of State, *FRUS, Conferences at Cairo and Tehran*, p. 258.

70. White, *Ten Thousand Tons,* p. 223.

71. One often-overlooked problem with night flying during this period in the Hump's history was the lack of radio frequencies for use at nighttime. Daytime frequencies were often unusable at night, and with the ICW now flying much of its schedule after dark, there was no way for air traffic control to communicate with aircraft, causing expected problems; see Flynn to Arnold, "Special Night Frequencies for India-China Area," Dec. 6, 1943, NARA II, RG 18, Entry 300, Box 919, Folder Misc. B; see also White p. 231.

72. Smith to George, Dec. 1, 1943, Box 04040601, ICD-ATC Reports and Letters, AMCHO.

73. Altmayer to Hardin, "Survey of ICW-ATC," Oct. 28, 1943, 312.152–1, AFHRA.

74. Quoted in Craven and Cate, *Army Air Forces,* 7:129–30.

75. Report by the U.S. Joint Administrative Committee, Aug, 18, 1943, U.S. Department of State, *FRUS, Conferences at Washington and Quebec,* pp. 973–75.

76. Memo for Asst. Chief of Air Staff Plans, "History of Project 8," Jan. 17, 1944, and Nowland to Hoag, "Project 8," Sept. 23, 1943, Box 04040607, AMCHO.

77. USAAF, ATC, ICD, Historical Section, "A History of the India-China Wing, June through December 1943." pp. 83, 303–304.

78. White, *Ten Thousand Tons,* p. 234.

79. Ibid.

80. George to Arnold, Jan. 17, 1944, Box 04040607, AMCHO.

81. Stratemeyer to George, [mid-Jan.] 1944, ibid.

CHAPTER 6

1. Smith to Arnold, "Trip Report," Feb. 11, 1944, NARA II, RG 18, Entry 300, Box 914, Folder 300-D.

2. Stilwell to Stratemeyer, "Development of Present ATC Route to China," Feb. 27, 1944, Box 04040508, ICD Documents, AMCHO.

3. Hardin to Baker, Jun. 17, 1944, in USAAF, ATC, ICD, Historical Section, "History of the India-China Division, Air Transport Command, 1944," 1:43.

4. Somervell to Marshall, Jan. 24, 1944, NARA II, RG 165, Entry 419, Box 86, OPD 400-TS, no. 122.

5. Hoag to Wheeler, "Labor Shortage in Assam," Jan. 25, 1944, Box 04040508, ICD Documents, AMCHO.

6. Hardin to George, "Need for Colored Troops for Cargo-Handling and Service Duties," Apr. 4, 1944, NARA II, RG 18, Entry 300, Box 915, Folder 300-F. As an aside, Hardin could make such requests for African Americans on the India side of the Hump, but not for the Chinese side, because the United States feared that the use of "colored" troops in China would prompt Chinese complaints that the United States was sending only low-quality troops to China. As Ulysses Lee points out, the surplus of unskilled labor in China rendered moot the need for more workers, but even so, "While the Chinese are not race-conscious, their Government is ready to exploit politically any action which can be distorted to appear discriminatory. They will undoubtedly complain of any Negro combat troops sent to China as second rate and will seek to make a political issue of the matter." To avoid this accusation, OPD decreed in June 1942 that no African Americans would serve in China so there would never be the hint that the United States took a low view of its Chinese ally. See Lee, *Employment of Negro Troops,* p. 436.

7. Hardin to Hoag, Nov. 18, 1943, Earl S. Hoag Papers, 168.7002, AFHRA.

8. USAAF, ATC, ICD, Historical Section, "History of the India-China Division, Air Transport Command, 1945," p. 122.

9. See McIntosh, *Radio Range for Flying.* AACS experimented with broadcasting copies of popular U.S. radio shows over the airways in place of the Morse signals: "When the music comes in hot and sweet the boys know they're on the beam." "Jazz Outmodes Dot-Dash Keeping Fliers on Beam," *New York Times,* Sept. 18, 1944, p. 8.

10. "Chabua Range Approach," author's files.

11. Historical Report, 1349th Base Unit (Jiwani), cited in USAAF, ATC, ICD, Historical Section, "History of the India-China Division, Air Transport Command, 1944," 2:565. The sheer number of U.S. pilots trained during the war undoubtedly had something to do with the contrasting instrument proficiency of the Americans and British, with over 193,000 Americans graduating from advanced pilot training between July 1939 and August 1945 (USAAF, Office of Statistical Control, *Army Air Forces Statistical Digest,* p. 64, table 47).

12. Historical report, 1349th Base Unit (Jiwani), cited in USAAF, ATC,

ICD, Historical Section, "History of the India-China Division, Air Transport Command, 1944," 2:565.

13. George to Smith, Nov. 15, 1943, Box 04040601, ICD-ATC Reports and Letters, AMCHO.

14. George to Hoag, "Rotation of Air Crew Personnel," Nov. 10, 1943, Earl S. Hoag Papers, 168.7002, AFHRA.

15. Cole (ATC Personnel) to George, "India-China Aircrew Rotation," Mar. 31, 1945, Box 04040607, AMCHO.

16. Hardin to George, "Air Crew Member Rotation," Aug. 22, 1944, ibid.

17. Davidson (Tenth Air Force) to Arnold, Dec. 10, 1943, NARA II, RG 18, Entry 300, Box 914, Folder 300-D.

18. Hattori, *Complete History*, 3:186–87.

19. Quoted in Allen, *Burma,* p. 154.

20. Martin Wolfe, a veteran of many of TCC's operations in Europe, records an anecdote illustrating the TCC crews' low opinion of ATC crews. "The tendency to confuse troop carrier with the Air Transport Command, a branch of the Air Forces that did not drop paratroopers nor tug gliders into combat. The most humiliating case of such confusion involves Dwight Eisenhower himself. On August 10, 1944, he was addressing a parade of 101st Airborne Division soldiers during an awards ceremony. Referring to the fact that both airborne troopers and plane crews now would be under FAAA [First Allied Airborne Army] commanders, Eisenhower said, 'It's through this [combined] command that we hope all the airborne troops and the Air Transport Command will become brothers. . . . I am proud of you and what the Air Transport Command has done.'" Wolfe, *Green Light!* p. 440.

21. The shortest of these alternate routes was a circuitous 2,320-mile route from Lalminir Hat, India, to Lanzhou, China (via Darjeeling, Lhasa, Jekundo, and Sining) that could support 37 tons per aircraft per month. The worse-case diversion was a 9,800-mile route from Fairbanks, Alaska, to Lanzhou (via Yakutsk) that could sustain only 9 tons per aircraft per month. Given these figures, a diverted Hump using 250 airplanes would be reduced to 9,250 tons (at best) and 2,250 tons at worst. Philipp to Asst. Chief of Staff for Plans, "The Strategic Withdrawal of ATC Operations from the CBI Theater," Box 04040508, ICD Documents, AMCHO.

22. ICW Historical Report, "Diversions from Hump Operations," Feb.–June 1944, 312.308, AFHRA.

23. Slim, *Defeat into Victory,* pp. 245–69.

24. Harries and Harries, *Soldiers of the Sun,* pp. 409, 414.

25. ICW Historical Report, "Diversions from Hump Operations," Feb.–June 1944, 312.308, AFHRA.

26. Quoted in USAAF, ATC, ICD, Historical Section, "History of the India-China Division, Air Transport Command, 1944,"1:249.

27. Leighton and Coakley, *Global Logistics,* 2:524. It was from this need that Hap Arnold created "Combat Cargo," specially designated troop carrier units with the capability to rapidly relocate from one base—often close to enemy lines—to another, depending on where they were needed.

28. Ibid., 2:516–17.

29. Quoted in ibid., p. 517.

30. Handy to Somervell, "Expansion of India as a Base of Operations," Apr. 19, 1944, NARA II, RG 165, Entry 419, Box 57, Case 351.

31. Romanus and Sunderland, *Stilwell's Command Problems,* p. 160.

32. Chiang to Roosevelt, Mar. 27, 1944, cited in Romanus and Sunderland, *Stilwell's Command Problems,* p. 308; Slim also records this Japanese sentiment in *Defeat into Victory,* p. 245.

33. He Yingjin to Marshall, Apr. 21, 1944, cited in Romanus and Sunderland, *Stilwell's Command Problems,* p. 314.

34. ICW Historical Report, "Diversions from Hump Operations," Feb.–June 1944, 312.308, AFHRA.

35. Ch'i, *Nationalist China at War,* pp. 71–72.

36. Ch'i Hsi-sheng asserts that the Fourteenth Air Force's attack on Hsinchu (Shinchiku) airfield on Formosa "prompted Japanese military planners to contemplate a large-scale operation against China" because the U.S. raid "was a clear signal that China-based air attacks against Japan's homeland were only a matter of time" (quoted in Hsiung and Levine, *China's Bitter Victory,* pp. 162–63). Ronald Spector similarly claims that Ichi-go was "intended to stop 14th Air force attacks on their supply lines by depriving Chennault of his air bases in eastern China" and was also "directed against the more serious threat of raids by the new American superbombers" (Spector, *Eagle against the Sun,* p. 365). Bruce Elle-

man follows this appraisal but mistakenly claims that Ichi-go was prompted by an Allied bombing attack on Kyushu on June 15, 1944, an air raid that occurred nearly two months *after* the start of the Japanese offensive (Elleman, *Modern Chinese Warfare,* p. 211).

37. Ch'i, *Nationalist China at War,* pp. 71–72. Japanese agents in Calcutta reported to Tokyo in April that that city was preparing for the arrival of the B-29s, certainly giving more weight to the desire to attack U.S. airfields but not serving as the invasion's main objective (USAAF, ATC, ICD, Historical Section, "History of the India-China Division, Air Transport Command, 1944," 3:807).

38. Katayama, "Logistical Activities of the Japanese Imperial Army." Mark Peattie points out that fuel shortages became so acute in Japan later in 1944 that experiments were being conducted to see if aviation fuel could be extracted from pine roots (*Sunburst,* pp. 194–95).

39. Ch'i corroborates both Japanese and Chinese sources to come up with what are fairly reliable casualty figures; both Chinese and Japanese historians frankly admit the poor performance by the Nationalist troops (Ch'i, *Nationalist China at War,* pp. 74–76, p. 255 n. 158).

40. Ibid., p. 76.

41. Katayama, "Logistical Activities of the Japanese Imperial Army."

42. Ibid.

43. Ch'i, *Nationalist China at War,* p. 77.

44. Katayama, "Logistical Activities of the Japanese Imperial Army."

45. Hardin to George, May 9, 1944, Box 04040508, ICD Documents, AMCHO; Hardin to Chief of Air Staff, May 17, 1944, NARA II, RG 18, Entry 300, Box 919, Folder Misc. C.

46. MacArthur also made a case to have the Twentieth come under his control as the theater commander of the Southwest Pacific.

47. The Twentieth Air Force was comprised of the 20th and 21st Bomber Commands, each of which contained four groups of twenty-eight B-29s.

48. Craven and Cate, *Army Air Forces,* 5:94.

49. Smith to Hardin, May 18, 1944, Box 04040601, ICD-ATC Reports and Letters, AMCHO.

50. Ibid.

51. "XXth Bomber Command Digest of Operations," Dec. 31, 1944, NARA II, RG 18, Entry 10, Box 27.

52. LeMay and Kantor, *Mission with LeMay,* pp. 321–22.

53. All the workers were drawn from surrounding counties; the work began in January and ended in April. Chiang worked through the local Sichuanese government, with payment being made in rice. The job was compulsory, a problem because it kept farmers away from their fields during planting season, with some escaping the rigors under the watchful eye of troops who served as a local police force for the job. According to historian Li Xiaowei and author of *Chao bao dui* (Superfortress Team), many were uninspired by the promise that the bombers held, being forced to work through the Spring Festival. Li Xiaowei, interview by author, Aug. 12, 2006, Chengdu, China. Li is the author of a three-volume work, published in 2007, on the Chengdu-based B-29s.

54. Japanese Monograph No. 76, *Air Operations in the China Area,* p. 184. It is likely the Japanese did attack the field, though it is unlikely that any B-29s were destroyed. The sensitive nature of their mission and the visibility afforded them by the War Department would have left a trail of memos and letters concerning an alleged attack of this magnitude.

55. USAAF, ATC, ICD, Historical Section, "History of the India-China Division, Air Transport Command, 1944," 1:37–38. By comparison, the U.S. commercial air carrier Southwest Airlines had a fleet of 484 airplanes at the end of 2006.

56. General Xue Yue, the commander of the 9th War Area, repeatedly asked Chiang (and the United States) for weapons while fighting the Japanese in the summer of 1944, but Chiang refused. He never completely trusted Xue because of his role in the Xian Incident in 1936 and his tepid allegiance to the generalissimo.

57. USAAF, ATC, ICD, Historical Section, "History of the India-China Division, Air Transport Command, 1944," 1:31; Hardin to George, May 9, 1944, Box 04040508, ICD Documents, AMCHO.

58. ATC press clipping, Hump Files, Box 04040508, ICD Documents, AMCHO.

59. Stilwell, Original Diaries, entry for Sept. 9, 1944, Stilwell Papers.

60. Handy to Arnold, "Operations of U.S. Air Units from Chinese Bases," May 19, 1944, NARA II, RG 165, Entry 419, Box 57, Case 375.

61. Barrett and Shyu, *China in the Anti-Japanese War,* pp. 70–71; Boyle, *China and Japan at War,* pp. 313–14.

CHAPTER 7

1. Frank, *Downfall,* pp. 31, 36.

2. Craven and Cate, *Army Air Forces,* 7:140–51.

3. Leighton and Coakley, *Global Logistics,* 2:622.

4. Van de Ven, *War and Nationalism in China,* p. 57.

5. Ibid., p. 60. The preponderance of sources on Stilwell's recall could fill a historiographical essay. Several noteworthy ones are: Stilwell, *Stilwell Papers* (pp. 323–49), Tuchman, *Stilwell,* (pp. 483–509), and Romanus and Sunderland, *Stilwell's Command Problems* (pp. 436–72). Van de Ven provides a revisionist view in *War and Nationalism in China* (pp. 56–63), claiming that election-year politics also factored into Roosevelt's calculations in Stilwell's recall.

6. See Romanus and Sunderland, *Time Runs Out,* pp. 231–62; also Taylor to Wedemeyer, "Alpha Plan," Nov. 1944, NARA II, RG 493, Box 11, Folder Alpha Plan, USFCT, Notes and Memos.

7. Ch'i, *Nationalist China at War,* pp. 77–79; Leighton and Coakley, *Global Logistics,* 2:525–30.

8. Craven and Cate, *Army Air Forces,* 2:683.

9. Japanese sources called the Hankow operation "highly effective" on the part of the Americans, especially as Japanese fighters were diverted to cover the city after the attack, drawing off protection from other Japanese strong points (Romanus and Sunderland, *Time Runs Out,* p. 174). The attack was the first daytime incendiary raid, with the much smaller nighttime incendiary attack having been launched against Nagasaki four months earlier. Werrell, *Blankets of Fir,* pp. 105, 109.

10. Assistant Chief of Air Staff, Intelligence, "Japan Incendiary Attack Data," Oct. 1943, NARA II, RG 165, Entry 419, Box 43; "XXth Bomber Command Digest of Operations," Dec. 31, 1944, NARA II, RG 18, Entry 10, Box 27.

11. A turbosupercharger is an accessory attached to the engine; it uses an

exhaust-gas-driven turbine to drive a compressor that delivers pressurized air to the engines, something needed for high-altitude flight.

12. Knight to Hoag, "Comparison of C-87 and C-54 Type Transports," Dec. 4, 1943, India-China Wing Reference Data, 312.197–2, AFHRA.

13. The C-54's susceptibility to icing kept it off the Hump until the low route was established, but even without this problem, only 98 of the wartime production total of 1,089 C-54s were available by the end of 1943 (USAAF, Office of Statistical Control, *Army Air Forces Statistical Digest,* p. 118). The pilot's manual for the C-54A lists it as having either the Pratt & Whitney Twin-Wasp R-2000–3 or 7 engine. Both had built-in, two-stage blowers for high-altitude flight, but this was not the same as a turbosupercharger. As high-altitude flight is an advantage only for aircraft equipped with jet engines, the DC-4/C-54 had little need to fly that high and so was not designed as such, though this characteristic proved problematic in the Hump's high terrain.

14. Office of the Assistant Chief of Air Staff, Matériel, Maintenance, and Distribution, memorandum, Mar. 24, 1944, NARA II, RG 18, Entry 294, Box 745, Folder 452.1-J.

15. William H. Tunner, interview by James C. Hasdorff, Oct. 5–6, 1976, p. 38, K239.0512–911, AFHRA.

16. Tunner, *Over the Hump,* p. 51.

17. USAAF, ATC, ICD, Historical Section, *Medical History of the India-China Division;* "History of the U.S. Army Medical Department in Delhi, India," Oct. 9, 1945, NARA II, RG 493, Box 656; "A History of Preventative Medicine in the United States Army Forces of the India-Burma Theater, 1942 to 1945," Dec. 8, 1945, NARA II, RG 493, Box 655.

18. "History of the U.S. Army Medical Department in Delhi, India," Oct. 9, 1945, pp. 35–36, NARA II, RG 493, Box 656.

19. Ibid., p. 15.

20. Green to Tunner, "Dissatisfaction of Negro Troops in This Command," Aug. 13, 1945, and Rust to Green, "Dissatisfaction of Negro Troops in This Command," Aug. 17, 1945, Box 04040607, India-China Files, AMCHO.

21. George to Arnold, "Aircraft Accident Rate, India-China Operations," Aug. 31, 1944, NARA II, RG 18, Bulky Files, Entry 300, Box 1037.

22. Wisman to Tunner, "Herbert O. Fisher's Report on Activities of C-46's in CBI Theater," Aug. 12, 1945, Box 04040604, AMCHO.

23. Tunner to Smith, Jan. 3, 1945, Box 04040607, AMCHO.

24. Tunner, *Over the Hump,* p. 57.

25. A selection of issues of the *Hump Express* is available at http://cbi-theater-9.home.comcast.net/~cbi-theater-9/hump_express/humpexpress .html (accessed June 2010).

26. For a lively contrast between the "organization man" business culture of the 1940s, 1950s, and 1960s, see Frank, *Conquest of Cool.*

27. Leighton and Coakley, *Global Logistics,* 2:527.

28. Ch'i, *Nationalist China at War,* p. 79.

29. Hatori, "Struggle over the Control."

30. Fuller, *Shokan,* pp. 141–42.

31. Ch'i, *Nationalist China at War,* p. 79; Romanus and Sunderland, *Time Runs Out,* pp. 49–51, 55–56, 164–65.

32. Memorandum to Marshall, "Air Lift of Chinese Troops for Defense of Kunming Area," Nov. 24, 1954, NARA II, RG 165, Entry 419, Box 89.

33. Romanus and Sunderland, *Time Runs Out,* pp. 144–45.

34. Ibid., pp. 61–62.

35. Romanus and Sunderland state that Chiang did not want to move these Xian-based troops, but OPD documents record that he wanted to move many more than Wedemeyer proposed. It is likely that Wedemeyer had a difficult time reading the generalissimo's manners (especially as all conversations were conducted through an interpreter). There was no shortage of Nationalist troops in the Xian war area, so the U.S. offer of airlift gave Chiang the perfect opportunity to reposition loyal troops to the south to serve as a counter against Xue Yue's forces, who were of questionable loyalty. See ibid., pp. 61–62, and the War Department memorandum titled "Brief of Transportations Problem of Chinese Troops for the Defense of the Kunming Area," Nov. 24, 1944, NARA II, RG 165, Entry 419, Box 89.

36. USAAF, ATC, ICD, Historical Section, "History of the India-China Division, Air Transport Command, 1944," 1:237–42.

37. "Operation Grubworm Historical Data," Jan. 29, 1945, 830.04–2, AFHRA.

38. John Hunter Boyle cites a popular rumor that the Japanese had arranged a deal with Chiang whereby they would not press into western China so long as the generalissimo promised to stop all future resistance to Japanese advances elsewhere. There is no firm evidence for this claim, though it was not beyond the generalissimo's scruples, especially if he sensed his star was rising in the face of a Japanese decline in China (*China and Japan at War,* p. 320).

39. Romanus and Sunderland, *Time Runs Out,* p. 50.

40. Davies memorandum, "General Political Comments," Jan. 5, 1945, U.S. Department of State, *FRUS: Diplomatic Papers, 1945,* 7:159–60.

41. Tunner to George, "Weekly Summary (30 September–7 October 1944)," Oct. 9, 1944, Box 04040508, ICD Documents, AMCHO.

42. Drew Pearson, "Washington Merry-Go-Round," *Washington Post,* Nov. 26, 1943, p. 13.

43. "U.S. Fliers Rushed China Army to Gap," *New York Times,* Jan. 21, 1945, p. 7.

44. "Operation Grubworm Historical Data," Jan. 29, 1945, 830.04–2, AFHRA.

45. USAAF, ATC, ICD, Headquarters, "Weekly Summary, Jan. 7–13, 1945"; "North China Troops Moved by ICD," *Hump Express,* Jan. 25, 1945, p. 1; USAAF, ATC, ICD, Historical Section, *A History of Hump Operations, January 1 to March 31, 1945,* pp. 74–92. See also "Chronological List of Aircraft Crashes on Hump Route," 312.3912–2, AFHRA.

46. "Smugglers Infest Air Run to China," *New York Times,* Dec. 16, 1945, p. 3; "Convict Yanks as India-China Air Smugglers," *Chicago Daily Tribune,* Dec. 16, 1944, p. 1. The same story appeared a week later in *Time* as "Smuggling over the Hump," Dec. 25, 1944.

47. Tunner to Sultan, Jan. 13, 1945, in USAAF, ATC, ICD, Historical Section, "History of the India-China Division, Air Transport Command, 1944," vol. 3, appendix.

48. Hoag to Alexander, Nov. 5, 1943, Earl S. Hoag Papers, 168.7002, AFHRA.

49. "Conclusive Chapter of 1340th AAF Base Unit History for Nov. 1944," in USAAF, ATC, ICD, Historical Section, "History of the India-China Division, Air Transport Command, 1944," vol. 3, appendix.

50. USAAF, ATC, ICD, Historical Section, "History of the India-China Division, Air Transport Command, 1944," 3:894.

51. Ibid., 3:894–931.

52. Ibid., 3:912.

53. Ibid.

54. Ibid., 3:892–93.

55. USAAF, ATC, ICD, Historical Section, "History of the India-China Division, Air Transport Command, 1945," p. 325.

56. Ibid., pp. 324, 330.

57. William H. Tunner, interview by James C. Hasdorff, Oct. 5–6, 1976, pp. 46–49, K239.0512–911, AFHRA; USAAF, ATC, ICD, Historical Section, "History of the India-China Division, Air Transport Command, 1945" (Jan.–Mar.), pp. 199–224, 325–26; see also Tunner, *Over the Hump,* pp. 93–96.

58. Tunner to George, "Rotation of Air Crew Personnel," Sept. 29, 1944, Box 04040607, AMCHO.

59. Tunner to Douglas, Mar. 10, 1945, Box 04040601, ICD-ATC Reports and Letters, AMCHO.

60. Tunner to George, June 28, 1945, ibid.

61. Smith to Tunner, "India China Rotation," May 14, 1945, Box 04040607, ibid.

62. Leighton and Coakley, *Global Logistics,* 2:622–23.

63. USAAF, Office of Statistical Control, "Tonnage into China," Aug. 3, 1945, NARA II, RG 18, Entry 10, Box 10.

64. Romanus and Sunderland, *Time Runs Out,* p. 344; USAAF, ATC, ICD, Historical Section, "History of the India-China Division, Air Transport Command, 1945" (Jan.–Nov.), p. 85.

65. Romanus and Sunderland, *Time Runs Out,* p. 337.

66. Supplies Flown to China Communists," *Hump Express,* Feb. 1, 1945, p. 1.

67. See Yu, *OSS in China.* The OSS proposed equipping 25,000 Communist guerillas, something Chiang would agree to only if they were placed under his command.

68. Barrett and Shyu, eds., *Chinese Collaboration with Japan,* p. 71–72. Miao Bin's offer was likely genuine, as Chiang's best option late in the war was to work with the puppet government in the hopes it would act as an intermediary between

him and the Japanese, vital especially after the Japanese had been defeated by the Americans in the Pacific. Because of this, John Paton Davies postulated that the generalissimo did not mind if some of his generals were captured by the Japanese, as they would be incorporated into Nanjing's forces that—as Chiang assumed—would eventually be reabsorbed back into his own army. John Paton Davies, "The Generalissimo's Dilemmas," U.S. Department of State, *FRUS: Diplomatic Papers, 1944,* 6:724–27.

69. USAAF, ATC, ICD, Historical Section, "History of the India-China Division, Air Transport Command, 1945" (Jan.–Nov.), pp. 189–96; Romanus and Sunderland, *Time Runs Out,* pp. 276–85; "Chihkiang Loss Is Blow to Japanese Hopes," *Hump Express,* June 7, 1945, p. 1.

70. USAAF, ATC, ICD, Historical Section, "History of the India-China Division, Air Transport Command, 1945" (Jan.–Nov.), pp. 468–75.

71. Ibid., pp. 177–78; Romanus and Sunderland, *Time Runs Out,* p. 66.

72. USAAF, ATC, ICD, Headquarters, "Weekly Summary," June 11 and July 9, 1945.

73. The AAF's April 1945 combat aircraft loss rate in Europe of one per 250 sorties is calculated by comparing the number of sorties (120,897) and number of aircraft (825) from USAAF, Office of Statistical Control, *Army Air Forces Statistical Digest,* pp. 220, 254, tables 118, 158.

74. Stratemeyer to George (radio), Apr. 19, 1945, Box 04040601, ICD-ATC Reports and Letters, AMCHO. Eaker had recently been named Arnold's deputy and was touring the Pacific and Asia in preparation for that position. On April 14 he met with Chennault in Kunming, where the subject of the Fourteenth Air Force's dependence on the Hump was likely discussed. (Eaker and Chennault—both originally fighter pilots—worked together at ACTS in the 1930s, and the former transitioned to bombers before the war.) The Fourteenth Air Force, with its dependence on Hump tonnage, felt the pinch of reduction in early spring due to diversionary missions like troop movements. Chennault also had a record of using unofficial channels (seen at its height in this direct correspondence with Roosevelt) to request more tonnage, as in May 1944, in the midst of Ichi-Go, when he wrote James McHugh in Washington and asked him to pull strings in Washington to get more tonnage. Similarly, it is likely that he convinced Eaker that the ICD lacked the necessary ethos of a combat command (Chennault had

little patience for the prudence of ATC operations), with Chennault asking Eaker to pressure ATC and Tunner (with whom Chennault did not have a good relationship) for more supplies. Chennault to McHugh, May 28, 1944, McHugh Papers, reel 2, Personal Correspondence. See also Parton, *"Air Force Spoken Here,"* pp. 97, 98, 436–37.

75. As mentioned in chapter 2, it was easy for these combat pilots to look down their noses at the ICD crews, but the flying–though different–was no less hazardous; "492nd Bomb Squadron History, July 1945," NARA II, RG 493, Records of the U.S. Army Forces of the CBI Theater of Operations, Historical Section, Historical Records, Box 645.

76. USAAF, ATC, ICD, Historical Section, "History of the India-China Division, Air Transport Command, 1945" (Jan.–Nov.), pp. 58–59.

CHAPTER 8

1. Planes flying under instrument flight rules (IFR), as opposed to visual flight rules (VFR), are under the constant control of air traffic control agencies, reducing (hypothetically) the risk of a midair collision.

2. USAAF, ATC, ICD, Historical Section, "History of the India-China Division, Air Transport Command, 1945" (Jan.–Nov.), pp. 100–103; Quinn, *Aluminum Trail,* pp. 473–74.

3. Cochran to Arnold, Oct. 16, 1945, Records of the Assistant Chief of the Air Staff, 145.95, AFHRA.

4. USAAF, ATC, ICD, Historical Section, "History of the India-China Division, Air Transport Command, 1945" (Jan.–Nov.), pp. 142–45.

5. William H. Tunner, interview by James C. Hasdorff, Oct. 5–6, 1976, p. 67, K239.0512–911, AFHRA; "Gen. Tunner Leaves ICD, Goes to US," *Hump Express,* Nov. 8, 1945, p. 1.

6. Quoted in Romanus and Sunderland, *Time Runs Out,* p. 390.

7. Feis, *China Tangle,* p. 337.

8. Quoted in Tsou, *America's Failure in China,* pp. 304–307.

9. Tunner, *Over the Hump,* p. 139.

10. For a detailed account of these movements see Plating, "Cannon, Egg, Charlie, and Baker: Airlift Links between World War II and the Chinese Civil War," *Air Power History* 53, no. 3 (Fall 2006): 4–13.

11. Westad, *Decisive Encounters*, p. 69.

12. Tsou, *America's Failure in China*, p. 305.

13. For a summary of Chiang's pre-1937 posture toward Japan, see Parks M. Coble Jr., "Chiang Kai-shek and the Anti-Japanese Movement in China: Zou Tao-fen and the National Salvation Association, 1931–1937," *Journal of Asian Studies* 44 (Feb. 1985): 293–310.

14. Barrett and Shyu, *Chinese Collaboration with Japan*, pp. 72–76.

15. For the best biography of Dai Li, see Wakeman, *Spymaster*.

16. Boyle, *China and Japan at War*, pp. 322–25.

17. Wakeman, *Spymaster*, p. 314.

18. Davies memorandum, "The Generalissimo's Dilemma," U.S. Department of State, *FRUS: Diplomatic Papers, 1944*, 6:724–27.

19. Boyle, *China and Japan at War*, p. 331.

20. Donald G. Gillin and Charles Etter, "Staying On: Japanese Soldiers and Civilians in China, 1945–1949," *Journal of Asian Studies* 42 (May 1983): 497–518.

21. Ibid., p. 500.

22. Ibid., p. 506.

23. Boyle, *China and Japan at War*, p. 330.

24. In the November 22, 1948, issue of *Life* magazine, Yan was pictured heroically displaying a box of cyanide pills intended for him and his family, but he found a way around their use by fleeing to Taiwan at the end of 1949 and reconciling his differences with Chiang. Boyle, *China and Japan at War*, p. 331.

25. Fenby, *Chiang Kai-shek*, p. 369.

26. Joe G. Taylor, *Air Interdiction in China in World War II*, USAF Historical Study No. 132 (Maxwell Air Force Base, Ala.: USAF Historical Division, Research Studies Institute, Air University, September 1956), AFHRA.

27. Drea, *In the Service of the Emperor*, p. xi. Here Drea refers to the 102-volume official history *Senshi Sosho*.

28. Davies to Gauss, "The Stilwell Mission," Mar. 9, 1943, U.S. Department of State, *FRUS: Diplomatic Papers, 1943, China*, p. 29.

29. U.S. Strategic Bombing Survey, Military Analysis Division, *Air Operations in China*, pp. 42–43; percentages of vehicle-to-cargo weight were derived from ICD-ATC Statistical Control Officer, "Comparative Statistics," Sept. 5, 1945, 312.3081–4, May–Aug 1945, AFHRA.

30. Tunner, *Over the Hump,* p. 163.

31. USAAF, Office of Statistical Control, *Army Air Forces Statistical Digest,* p. 118, table 76.

32. In the summer of 1945 the division established a Civil Aeronautics Authority (CAA, the precursor to the Federal Aviation Administration, or FAA) school at Tezgaon to get its pilots certified with commercial qualifications as well as its mechanics certified by CAA standards. USAAF, ATC, ICD, Headquarters, "Weekly Summary, June 30–July 7, 1945," July 9, 1945.

33. Davies, *A History of the World's Airlines,* pp. 238–40, 244.

34. The Chinese popularly regard the Hump pilots as part of the Flying Tigers.

35. The Beijing Aviation Association commissioned a monument in Nanjing in 1991 to commemorate the "Aviation Martyrs of the Second World War." It was dedicated in 1995. On the outskirts of Kunming is another monument dedicated specifically to the airmen who flew the Hump.

36. Leonard Downie Jr., "Interview with Premier Wen Jiabao," *Washington Post,* Nov. 23, 2003, available at http://www.washingtonpost.com/ac2/wp-dyn ?pagename=article&node=&contentId=A6641–2003Nov22&notFound=true (accessed June 2010).

BIBLIOGRAPHY

PRIVATE PAPERS

McHugh, James M., Papers. No. 2770. Division of Rare and Manuscript Collections. Cornell University Library.

Stilwell, Joseph Warren, Papers. Original Diaries, 1900–1946. Hoover Institution. Stanford University. Available at http://www.hoover.org/library-and-archives/collections/east-asia/featured-collections/joseph-stilwell.

OFFICIAL RECORDS

Three repositories hold much of the official correspondence, reports, and files surrounding the Hump airlift: the National Archives in College Park, Maryland (NARA II); the Air Force Historical Research Agency (AFHRA) in Montgomery, Alabama (at Maxwell Air Force Base); and the Air Mobility Command History Office (AMCHO) in Belleville, Illinois (at Scott Air Force Base). Records of the Army Air Forces (Record Group 18), Records of the War Department General and Special Staffs (RG 165), and Records of the U.S. Army Forces in the China-Burma-India Theaters of Operation (RG 493) are abundant archives, but finding aids are very broad. AFHRA's collection is easily searchable, thanks to its computer-based finding aid, and it hold a greater collection of small unit histories and personal papers that help flesh out the history of the Hump. Lastly, the AMCHO contains the largest single collection of documents on Air Transport Command during the war; though there are no dedicated finding aids, the materials are all located in one place and easy to sift through.

The Hump Pilot's Association (HPA) has designated the Museum of Aviation at Robins Air Force Base in Warner Robins, Georgia, to serve as its unofficial repository (the same museum has a large collection of American Volunteer Group artifacts). The HPA officially disbanded at the end of 2005 due to the advanced age of many of its members and thus dwindling membership. Upon the closing of the organization's main office in Amarillo, Texas, most of its holdings were sent to the museum in Georgia.

The National Museum of the U.S. Air Force (formerly the Air Force Museum) at Wright-Patterson Air Force Base, Ohio, has a small collection of letters and documents as well as technical manuals for nearly every aircraft in the air force inventory, past and present.

Carey, Donald E., Melody L. Higdon, Robert S. Lilianstrom, and Charles D. Surls. *East Asia: A Climatological Study.* Vol. 1, *Continental.* AFCCC TN-97/002. Scott Air Force Base, Air Force Combat Climatology Center, September 1997.

Hattori, Takushiro. *The Complete History of the Greater East Asia War.* 4 vols. Tokyo: Masu Publishing, 1953.

"History of the India-China Ferry under the Tenth Air Force, March–November 1942." 830.04–4. AFHRA.

"National Intelligence Survey, India and Pakistan: Weather and Climate." NIS 35 and 36, Section 23. Scott Air Force Base, Air Force Combat Climatology Center, December 1996.

South Asia, A Climatological Study. Vol. 2, *Continental South Asia.* AFCCC/TN-02/002. Scott Air Force Base, Air Force Combat Climatology Center, May 1, 2002.

Taylor, Joe G. *Air Interdiction in China in World War II.* USAF Historical Studies 132. USAF Historical Division, Research Studies Institute, Air University, Maxwell Air Force Base, September 1956. 0467604. AFHRA.

U.S. Army Air Forces [USAAF]. Air Force Communications Command. *AACS at Work: A Report Prepared with the View of Presenting a Comprehensive Picture of World-wide Operations and Activities of the Army Airways Communications System.* Washington, D.C., 1943.

———. Air Transport Command [ATC]. Historical Division. Office of the Assistant Chief of Staff. *History of Air Transport Command, Ferrying Command Operations, December 7, 1941–June 30, 1942.* ATC Headquarters, 1946. Box 27010201, Document Collection of Early Air Transport, 1922–1942. AMCHO.

———. ATC. Historical Officer. *Air Transportation to China under the 10th Air Force, April–November 1942*. 312.04–3. AFHRA.

———. ATC. India-China Division [ICD]. Headquarters. "Weekly Summary." October 1944–August 1945. 312.114. AFHRA.

———. ATC. ICD. Historical Section. "History of Hump Operations, January–March 1945." 1945. AFHRA.

———. ATC. ICD. Historical Section. *A History of Hump Operations, January 1 to March 31, 1945*. 312.04–2. AFHRA.

———. ATC. ICD. Historical Section. "History of the India-China Division, Air Transport Command, 1944." 3 vols. 1945. 168.7158–289. AFHRA.

———. ATC. ICD. Historical Section. "History of the India-China Division, Air Transport Command, 1945." 1945. 312.01. AFHRA.

———. ATC. ICD. Historical Section. "A History of the India-China Wing, June through December 1943." 312.01. AFHRA.

———. ATC. ICD. Historical Section. *Medical History of the India-China Division of Air Transport Command, December 1942 to December 1945*. Division Headquarters, Calcutta, India. AFHRA.

———. Army Airways Communications Service. History Office. *History of the Army Airways Communications Service, November 1938–September 1945*. September 1945. AFHRA.

———. Assistant Chief of Air Staff. Intelligence, Historical Division. *The Fourteenth Air Force to 1 October 1943* (Short Title: *AAFRH-9*). Washington, D.C: AAF Historical Office, July 1945. 0487693. AFHRA.

———. Assistant Chief of Air Staff. Intelligence, Historical Division. *The Tenth Air Force, 1942*. AAF Historical Studies 12. August 1944. IRIS 0467604. AFHRA.

———. Assistant Chief of Air Staff. Intelligence, Historical Division. *The Tenth Air Force, 1 January–10 March 1943* (Short Title: *AAFRH-4*). U. S. Air Force Historical Study 104. Washington, D.C, November 1944.

———. Office of Statistical Control. *Army Air Forces Statistical Digest: World War II*. Headquarters, U.S. Army Air Forces, December 1945. Available at http://www.afhra.af.mil/timelines/index.asp (accessed June 2010).

History of the India-China Ferry under the Tenth Air Force, March to November 1942. 1943. 830.04–4. AFHRA.

U.S. Department of the Army. Office of Military History. *Guide to Japanese Monographs and Japanese Studies on Manchuria, 1945–1960.* Washington, D.C: 1962.

U.S. Department of State. *The China White Paper, August 1949: United States Relations with China.* Stanford, Calif.: Stanford University Press, 1967.

———. *Foreign Relations of the United States [FRUS]: The Conferences at Cairo and Tehran, 1943.* Washington, D.C., 1961. The *FRUS* series is available at http://digicoll.library.wisc.edu/FRUS/ (accessed June 2010).

———. *FRUS: The Conferences at Washington, 1941–1942, and Casablanca, 1943.* Washington, D.C., 1968.

———. *FRUS: Conferences at Washington and Quebec, 1943.* Washington, D.C., 1970.

———. *FRUS: Diplomatic Papers, 1938.* Vol. 3, *The Far East.* Washington, D.C., 1954.

———. *FRUS: Diplomatic Papers, 1940.* Vol. 4, *The Far East.* Washington, D.C., 1955.

———. *FRUS: Diplomatic Papers, 1941.* Vol. 4, *The Far East.* Washington, D.C., 1956.

———. *FRUS: Diplomatic Papers, 1941.* Vol. 5, *The Far East.* Washington, D.C., 1956.

———. *FRUS: Diplomatic Papers, 1942, China.* Washington, D.C., 1956.

———. *FRUS: Diplomatic Papers, 1943, China.* Washington, D.C., 1957.

———. *FRUS: Diplomatic Papers, 1944.* Vol. 6, *China.* Washington, D.C., 1967.

———. *FRUS: Diplomatic Papers, 1945.* Vol. 7, *The Far East, China.* Washington, D.C., 1969.

U.S. Strategic Bombing Survey. Basic Materials Division. *Coals and Metals in Japan's War Economy.* USSBS Reports, no. 036. Washington, D.C., 1947.

———. Military Analysis Division. *Air Operations in China, Burma, India–World War II.* USSBS Reports, no. 067. Washington, D.C., March 1947.

———. Military Analysis Division. *The Air Transport Command in the War against Japan.* USSBS Reports, no. 068. Washington, D.C., December 1946.

———. Overall Economic Effects Division. *The War against Japanese Transportation 1941–1945.* USSBS Reports, no. 054. Washington, D.C., 1947.

Van Slyke, Lyman P. *The Chinese Communist Movement: A Report of the United States War Department, July 1945.* Stanford: Stanford University Press, 1968.

Weather Division, AAF Headquarters. "Forecasting and Related Problems in

China." Air Weather Service Technical Report 105–32. December 1944. Scott Air Force Base, Air Force Combat Climatology Center, 1997.

————. "Studies on Local Forecasting: Kunming, China." Weather Division Report 600–111. Scott Air Force Base, Air Force Combat Climatology Center, October 1944.

BOOKS, ARTICLES, AND MONOGRAPHS

Ackroyd-Kelly, Ian Howard. "A Military Geography of the Japanese Invasion of China." Master's thesis, University of North Carolina, 1972.

Alexander, Jack. "Just Call Me C. R." *Saturday Evening Post,* Feb. 1941, 2.

Allen, Louis. *Burma: The Longest War, 1941–45.* New York: St. Martin's Press, 1984.

American Airlines. *The Education of an Airline: Here, There, Anywhere; How an Airline Became a Lifeline Round the World; The Story, Up to October, 1944, of American Airlines' War Assignments Including Its Global Operations under Contract to the Air Transport Command.* New York: American Airlines, Inc., 1944.

Anders, Leslie. *The Ledo Road: General Joseph W. Stilwell's Highway to China.* Norman: University of Oklahoma Press, 1965.

Arnold, Henry Harley. *Global Mission.* Blue Ridge Summit, Pa.: TAB Books, 1989.

Bagby, Wesley Marvin. *The Eagle-Dragon Alliance: America's Relations with China in World War II.* London: Associated University Presses, 1992.

Barrett, David P., and Lawrence N. Shyu. *China in the Anti-Japanese War, 1937–1945: Politics, Culture, and Society.* New York: Peter Lang, 2001.

————, eds. *Chinese Collaboration with Japan, 1932–1945: The Limits of Accommodation.* Stanford, Calif.: Stanford University Press, 2001.

Bartsch, William H. *December 8, 1941: MacArthur's Pearl Harbor.* College Station: Texas A&M University Press, 2003.

Bates, Charles C., and John F. Fuller. *America's Weather Warriors, 1814–1985.* College Station: Texas A&M University Press, 1986.

Belden, Jack. *China Shakes the World.* New York: Harper, 1949.

Bianco, Lucien. *Origins of the Chinese Revolution, 1915–1949.* Stanford, Calif.: Stanford University Press, 1971.

Bilstein, Roger E. *Airlift and Airborne Operations in World War II.* Washington, D.C.: Air Force History and Museums Program, 1998.

Bond, W. Langhorne, and James E. Ellis. *Wings for an Embattled China*. Bethlehem, Pa: Lehigh University Press, 2001.

Bowers, Ray L. *Tactical Airlift*. Washington, D.C: Office of Air Force History, 1984.

Boyle, John Hunter. *China and Japan at War, 1937–1945: The Politics of Collaboration*. Stanford, Calif.: Stanford University Press, 1972.

Brady, Anne-Marie. "'Treat Insiders and Outsiders Differently': The Use of Control of Foreigners in the PRC." *China Quarterly* 164 (Dec. 2000): 943–64.

Brereton, Lewis H. *The Brereton Diaries: The War in the Air in the Pacific, Middle East, and Europe, 3 October 1941–8 May 1945*. New York: Morrow, 1946.

Brewer, James F., ed. *China Airlift–The Hump: China's Aerial Lifeline and the Beginning of the China-Burma-India Hump Pilots Association*. 3 vols. Dallas: Taylor, 1979–92.

Brook, Timothy. *Collaboration: Japanese Agents and Local Elites in Wartime China*. Cambridge, Mass.: Harvard University Press, 2005.

Byrd, Martha. *Chennault: Giving Wings to the Tiger*. Tuscaloosa: University of Alabama Press, 1987.

Cairncross, Alec. *Planning in Wartime: Aircraft Production in Britain, Germany, and the U.S.A*. New York: St. Martin's Press, 1991.

Cameron, Rebecca Hancock. *Training to Fly: Military Flight Training, 1907–1945*. Washington, D.C.: Air Force History and Museums Programs, 1999.

Carter, Carolle J. *Mission to Yenan: American Liaison with the Chinese Communists, 1944–1947*. Lexington: University Press of Kentucky, 1997.

Carter, Kit C., and Robert Mueller. *Air Force Combat Chronology, 1941–1945*. Washington, D.C.: Center for Air Force History, 1991.

Cave, Hugh B. *Wings across the World: The Story of the Air Transport Command*. New York: Dodd, Mead & Company, 1945.

Chassin, Lionel Max. *The Communist Conquest of China: A History of the Civil War, 1945–1949*. Cambridge, Mass.: Harvard University Press, 1965.

Chen, Yung-fa. *Making Revolution: The Communist Movement in Eastern and Central China, 1937–1945*. Berkeley: University of California Press, 1986.

Chennault, Claire Lee. *Way of a Fighter: The Memoirs of Claire Lee Chennault*. Edited by Robert B. Hotz. New York: G. P. Putnam's Sons, 1949.

Cherepanov, Aleksandr Ivanovich. *As Military Adviser in China*. Moscow: Progress, 1982.

Chesneaux, Jean, and Lucien Bianco. *Popular Movements and Secret Societies in China, 1840–1950*. Stanford, Calif.: Stanford University Press, 1972.

Ch'i Hsi-sheng. *Nationalist China at War: Military Defeats and Political Collapse, 1937–45*. Ann Arbor: University of Michigan Press, 1982.

———. *Warlord Politics in China, 1916–1928*. Stanford, Calif.: Stanford University Press, 1976.

Christie, Carl A., and F. J. Hatch. *Ocean Bridge: The History of RAF Ferry Command*. Toronto: University of Toronto Press, 1997.

Chuikov, V. I. *Mission to China: Memoirs of a Military Adviser to Chiang Kaishek*. Translated by David P. Barrett. Norwalk, Conn.: EastBridge, 2004.

Churchill, Winston. *The Hinge of Fate*. Boston: Houghton Mifflin, 1950.

———. *Their Finest Hour*. Boston: Houghton Mifflin, 1949.

Cleveland, Reginald McIntosh. *Air Transport at War*. New York: Harper & Bros., 1946.

Coble, Parks M. "Chiang Kai-shek and the Anti-Japanese Movement in China: Zou Tao-fen and the National Salvation Association, 1931–1937." *Journal of Asian Studies* 44 (Feb. 1985): 293–310.

Coble, Parks M. *Facing Japan: Chinese Politics and Japanese Imperialism, 1931–1937*. Cambridge, Mass.: Harvard University Press, 1991.

Collier, Richard. *Bridge across the Sky: The Berlin Blockade and Airlift, 1948–1949*. New York: McGraw-Hill, 1978.

Constein, Carl Frey. *Born to Fly the Hump: A WWII Memoir*. Bloomington, Ind.: 1stBooks, 2001.

———. *Tales of the Himalayas: Letters from WWII Airmen Who Flew the Hump and from Other Veterans of the CBI*. Bloomington, Ind.: 1stBooks, 2002.

Coox, Alvin D. *The Anatomy of a Small War: The Soviet-Japanese Struggle for Changkufeng-Khasan, 1938*. Westport, Conn.: Greenwood Press, 1977.

———. *Nomonhan: Japan against Russia, 1939*. Stanford, Calif.: Stanford University Press, 1985.

———. "The Rise and Fall of the Imperial Japanese Air Force." *Aerospace Historian* 27 (June 1980): 75–86.

Corbett, Charles H. "Conditions in Chekiang and Kiangsi." *Far Eastern Survey* 12 (May 1943): 95–99.

Corum, James S. *The Luftwaffe: Creating the Operational Air War, 1918–1940*. Lawrence: University Press of Kansas, 1997.

———, and Richard Muller. *The Luftwaffe's Way of War: German Air Force Doctrine, 1911–1945*. Baltimore, Md.: Nautical & Aviation Publishing, 1998.

Crackel, Theodore J. *A History of the Civil Reserve Air Fleet*. Washington, D.C.: Air Force History and Museums Program, 1998.

Craft, Stephen G. *V. K. Wellington Koo and the Emergence of Modern China*. Lexington: University Press of Kentucky, 2003.

Craven, Wesley Frank, and James Lea Cate. 7 vols. *The Army Air Forces in World War II*. Chicago: University of Chicago Press, 1948–58.

Curtis, Lettice. *The Forgotten Pilots: A Story of the Air Transport Auxiliary, 1939–45*. Henley-on-Thames, Eng.: Foulis, 1971.

Dallek, Robert. *Franklin D. Roosevelt and American Foreign Policy, 1932–1945*. New York: Oxford University Press, 1979.

Daso, Dik A. *Hap Arnold and the Evolution of American Airpower*. Washington, D.C.: Smithsonian Institution Press, 2000.

Davies, John Paton. *Dragon by the Tail: American, British, Japanese, and Russian Encounters with China and One Another*. New York: Norton, 1972.

Davies, R. E. G. *Airlines of Asia since 1920*. London: Putnam, 1997.

———. *Airlines of the United States since 1914*. Washington, D.C.: Smithsonian Institution Press, 1998.

———. *Fallacies and Fantasies of Air Transport History*. McLean, Va.: Paladwr, 1994.

———. *A History of the World's Airlines*. London: Oxford University Press, 1964.

———. *Lufthansa: An Airline and its Aircraft*. New York: Orion Books, 1989.

———. *Rebels and Reformers of the Airways*. Washington, D.C.: Smithsonian Institution Press, 1987.

———, and Mike Machat. *TWA: An Airline and Its Aircraft*. McLean, Va.: Paladwr, 2000.

Davis, John M., Harold G. Martin, and John A. Whittle. *The Curtiss C-46 Commando*. Essex, England: Air-Britain, 1978.

Davis, Larry. *C-47 Skytrain in Action*. Carrollton, Tex.: Squadron/Signal Publications, 1995.

Donovan, Frank Robert. *Bridge in the Sky.* New York: D. McKay, 1968.

Dorn, Frank. *The Sino-Japanese War, 1937–41: From Marco Polo Bridge to Pearl Harbor.* New York: Macmillan, 1974.

————. *Walkout: With Stilwell in Burma.* New York: Crowell, 1971.

Drea, Edward J. *In the Service of the Emperor: Essays on the Imperial Japanese Army.* Lincoln: University of Nebraska Press, 1998.

————. *MacArthur's ULTRA: Codebreaking and the War against Japan, 1942–1945.* Lawrence: University Press of Kansas, 1992.

Dreyer, Edward L. *China at War, 1901–1949.* New York: Longman, 1995.

Dunlop, Richard. *Behind Japanese Lines: With the OSS in Burma.* Chicago: Rand McNally, 1979.

Eastman, Lloyd Eric, Jerome Ch'en, Suzanne Pepper, and Lyman P. Van Slyke. *The Nationalist Era in China 1927–1949.* Cambridge, Mass.: Cambridge University Press, 1991.

————. *Seeds of Destruction: Nationalist China in War and Revolution, 1937–1949.* Stanford, Calif.: Stanford University Press, 1984.

Eisenhower, Dwight D. *Crusade in Europe.* Garden City, N.Y.: Doubleday, 1948.

Elleman, Bruce A. *Modern Chinese Warfare, 1795–1989.* London: Routledge, 2001.

Esherick, Joseph. *The Origins of the Boxer Uprising.* Berkeley: University of California Press, 1987.

Ethell, Jeffrey L., and Don Downie. *Flying the Hump: In Original World War II Color.* St. Paul, Minn.: Motorbooks, 2002.

Evans, David C., and Mark R. Peattie. *Kaigun: Strategy, Tactics, and Technology in the Imperial Japanese Navy, 1887–1941.* Annapolis, Md.: Naval Institute Press, 1997.

Eveland, Wayne. "The Evacuation of Burma." *The Clipper* (newsletter of the Pan Am Historical Foundation), no. 7, available at the Pan Am Historical Foundation's website, http://www.panam.com/cgi-bin/_textdisplay_0.asp?display=BURMAEVAC&refer=315867946&call=M (accessed June 2010).

Fairbank, John K., and Albert Feuerwerker, eds. *Republican China 1912–1949.* Vol. 13, pt. 2 of *The Cambridge History of China.* Denis Twitchett and John K. Fairbank, gen. eds. Cambridge, Eng.: Cambridge University Press, 1986.

Feis, Herbert. *The China Tangle: The American Effort in China from Pearl Harbor to the Marshall Mission.* Princeton, N.J.: Princeton University Press, 1953.

Fenby, Jonathan. *Chiang Kai-shek: China's Generalissimo and the Nation He Lost*. New York: Carroll & Graf, 2004.

Feng, Chongyi, and David S. G. Goodman. *North China at War: The Social Ecology of Revolution, 1937–1945*. Lanham, Md.: Rowman & Littlefield, 2000.

Fenn, Charles. *At the Dragon's Gate: With the OSS in the Far East*. Annapolis, Md.: Naval Institute Press, 2004.

Feuerwerker, Albert, Rhoads Murphey, and Mary Wright. *Approaches to Modern Chinese History*. Berkeley: University of California Press, 1967.

Flammer, Philip M. *The Vivid Air: The Lafayette Escadrille*. Athens: University of Georgia Press, 1981.

Ford, Daniel. *Flying Tigers: Claire Chennault and the American Volunteer Group*. Washington, D.C.: Smithsonian Institution Press, 1991.

Francillon, René J. *Japanese Aircraft of the Pacific War*. Annapolis, Md.: Naval Institute Press, 1987.

Frank, Richard B. *Downfall: The End of the Imperial Japanese Empire*. New York: Random House, 1999.

Frank, Thomas. *The Conquest of Cool: Business Culture, Counterculture, and the Rise of Hip Consumerism*. Chicago: University of Chicago Press, 1998.

Frillmann, Paul, and Graham Peck. *China: The Remembered Life*. Boston: Houghton Mifflin, 1968.

Fuller, John F. *Thor's Legions: Weather Support to the U.S. Air Force and Army, 1937–1987*. Boston: American Meteorological Society, 1990.

Fuller, Richard. *Shokan: Hirohito's Samurai*. New York: Sterling Publishing, 1992.

Garver, John W. *Chinese-Soviet Relations, 1937–1945: The Diplomacy of Chinese Nationalism*. New York: Oxford University Press, 1988.

Genovese, J. *We Flew without Guns*. Philadelphia: John C. Winston, 1945.

Gillin, Donald G., and Charles Etter. "Staying On: Japanese Soldiers and Civilians in China, 1945–1949." *Journal of Asian Studies* 42 (May 1983): 497–518.

Glines, Carroll V. *The Doolittle Raid: America's Daring First Strike against Japan*. Atglen, Pa.: Schiffer, 1991.

Green, William. *Fighters*. Vol. 3 of *War Planes of the Second World War*. New York: Hanover House, 1961.

Greenough, Paul R. *Prosperity and Misery in Modern Bengal: The Famine of 1943–1944*. New York: Oxford University Press, 1982.

Hall, J. C. S. *The Yunnan Provincial Faction, 1927–1937.* Canberra: Australian National University Press, 1976.

Hanks, Fletcher. *Saga of CNAC #53.* Bloomington, Ind.: AuthorHouse, 2004.

Harries, Meirion, and Sue Harries. *Soldiers of the Sun: The Rise and Fall of the Imperial Japanese Army.* New York: Random House, 1991.

Harvey, A. D. "Army Air Force and Navy Air Force: Japanese Aviation and the Opening Phases of the War in the Far East." *War in History* 6 (1999): 174–204.

Hatori, Toshimichi. "Struggle over the Control of the Chang [*sic*] Kaishek Supply Route." Conference paper based on Japanese-language sources and presented in 1999. Author's files.

Haydock, Michael D. *City under Siege: The Berlin Blockade and Airlift, 1948–1949.* Washington, D.C.: Brassey's, 1999.

Haynes, Elmer E., and A. B. Feuer. *General Chennault's Secret Weapon: The B-24 in China.* Westport, Conn.: Praeger, 1992.

Hines, Jay E. *History of Foreign Training at ATC, 1941–1976.* Randolph Air Force Base, Tex.: History and Research Division, Office of the Chief of Staff, Headquarters, Air Training Command, 1977.

Hsiung, James Chieh, and Steven I. Levine. *China's Bitter Victory: The War with Japan, 1937–1945.* Armonk, N.Y.: M. E. Sharpe, 1992.

Hsu Long-hsuen and Chang Mingkai. *History of the Sino-Japanese War, 1937–1945.* Translated by Wen Ha-Hsiun. Taipei: Chung Wu, 1972.

Hugill, Peter J. *World Trade since 1431: Geography, Technology, and Capitalism.* Baltimore, Md.: Johns Hopkins University Press, 1993.

Hunt, Michael H. *The Making of a Special Relationship: The United States and China to 1914.* New York: Columbia University Press, 1983.

Huston, John W., ed. *American Airpower Comes of Age: General Henry H. "Hap" Arnold's World War II Diaries.* 2 vols. Maxwell Air Force Base, Ala.: Air University Press, 2002.

Japanese Monograph No. 56, *Southeast Asia Air Operations Record, Phase II, July 1942–June 1944.*

Japanese Monograph No. 58. *Burma Operations Record, Phase II, 1943–1944* (edited 1952).

Japanese Monograph No. 64. *Burma Air Operations Record, January 1942–August 1945.*

Japanese Monograph No. 71. *Army Operations in China, December 1941–December 1943*. Edited 1956.

Japanese Monograph No. 72. *Army Operations in China, January 1944–August 1945*.

Japanese Monograph No. 76. *Air Operations in the China Area, July 1937–August 1945*.

Jespersen, Christopher T. *American Images of China: 1931–1949*. Stanford, Calif.: Stanford University Press, 1996.

Jessen, Morten. *The Junkers Ju 52: The Luftwaffe's Workhorse*. London: Stackpole Books, 2002.

Johnston, Alastair I. *Cultural Realism: Strategic Culture and Grand Strategy in Chinese History*. Princeton, N.J.: Princeton University Press, 1995.

Kalyagin, Aleksandr Ya. *Along Alien Roads*. Translated by Steven I. Levine. Occasional Papers of the East Asian Institute. New York: East Asian Institute, Columbia University, 1983.

Kan, Michael M. *One Heart Full of China*. New York: Carlton Press, 1968.

Katayama, Hirohito. "The Logistical Activities of the Japanese Imperial Army in the Ichi-go Operation." Tokyo, n.d. Author's files.

King, Steven C. *Flying the Hump to China*. Bloomington, Ind.: AuthorHouse, 2004.

Kirby, William C. *Germany and Republican China*. Stanford, Calif.: Stanford University Press, 1984.

Koenig, William J. *Over the Hump: Airlift to China*. Ballantine's Illustrated History of the Violent Century, Campaign Book 23. New York: Ballantine Books, 1972.

La Farge, Oliver. *The Eagle in the Egg*. Boston: Houghton Mifflin, 1949.

Leary, William M. *The Dragon's Wings: The China National Aviation Corporation and the Development of Commercial Aviation in China*. Athens: University of Georgia Press, 1976.

———. "Wings for China: The Jouett Mission, 1932–1935." *Pacific Historical Review* 38 (1969): 447–62.

Lee, Ulysses. *The Employment of Negro Troops*. Washington, D.C.: Center of Military History, 1966.

Leighton, Richard M., and Robert W. Coakley. *Global Logistics and Strategy*. 2 vols. 1955–68. Reprint, Washington, D.C.: Office of the Chief of Military History, U.S. Army, 1995.

LeMay, Curtis E., and MacKinlay Kantor. *Mission with LeMay: My Story.* Garden City, N.Y.: Doubleday, 1965.

Lewis, W. David. *Eddie Rickenbacker: An American Hero in the Twentieth Century.* Baltimore, Md.: Johns Hopkins University Press, 2005.

Li Xiaowei. *Chao bao dui* [Superfortress Team]. 3 vols. Hong Kong: Tin Ma Book Company, 2007.

Liang Hsi-huey. *The Sino-German Connection: Alexander Von Falkenhausen between China and Germany, 1900–1941.* Assen, Netherlands: Van Gorcum, 1978.

Liu Xiaotong. *Tuo feng kong yun* [Camelback Airline]. Beijing: China Inland Publishers, 2005.

Liu, F. F. *A Military History of Modern China, 1924–1949.* Princeton, N.J.: Princeton University Press, 1956.

Ma Yufu. *Tuo feng kong yun* [Hump Air Transport]. Beijing: China Intercontinental Press, 2003.

McIntosh, Colin Hugh. *Radio Navigation for Pilots.* New York: McGraw-Hill, 1943.

———. *Radio Range Flying.* Chicago: Ringer Press, 1941.

Maguire, Jon A. *Gooney Birds & Ferry Tales: The 27th Air Transport Group in World War II.* Atglen, Pa.: Schiffer, 1998.

Mangan, James M. *To the Four Winds: A History of the Flight Operations of American Airlines Personnel for the Air Transport Command, 1942–1945, Including Project 7A.* Paducah, Ky.: Turner, 1990.

Marks, Lionel S., and Eugene A. Baumeister. *Marks' Standard Handbook for Mechanical Engineers.* New York: McGraw-Hill, 1996.

Martin, John G. *It Began at Imphal: The Combat Cargo Story.* Manhattan, Kans.: Sunflower University Press, 1988.

Martin, John G. *Through Hell's Gate to Shanghai: History of the 10th Combat Cargo Squadron, 3rd Combat Cargo Group, C.B.I. Theater, 1944–1946.* Ashland, Ky.: J. G. Martin, 1983.

Masters, John. *Bugles and a Tiger: A Volume of Autobiography.* New York: Viking, 1956.

———. *The Road Past Mandalay: A Personal Narrative.* New York: Bantam, 1963.

Matloff, Maurice, and Edwin Marion Snell. *Strategic Planning for Coalition Warfare, 1941–1942.* Washington, D.C.: Office of the Chief of Military History, Department of the Army, 1953.

Melby, John F. *The Mandate of Heaven: Record of a Civil War.* Garden City, N.Y.: Anchor Books, 1971.

Miller, Charles E. *Airlift Doctrine.* Maxwell Air Force Base, Ala.: Air University Press, 1988.

Miller, Roger G. "Air Transport on the Eve of Pearl Harbor." *Air Power History* 45, no. 2 (Summer 1998): 26–37.

———. *A Preliminary to War: The 1st Aero Squadron and the Mexican Punitive Expedition of 1916.* Washington, D.C.: Air Force History and Museums Program, 2003. Available at http://handle.dtic.mil/100.2/ADA440092 (accessed June 2010).

Moreira, Peter. *Hemingway on the China Front: His WWII Spy Mission with Martha Gellhorn.* Washington, D.C.: Potomac Books, 2006.

Morzik, Fritz. *German Air Force Airlift Operations.* Introduction by Telford Taylor. USAF Historical Studies 167. New York: Arno Press, 1961.

Murray, Williamson, and Allan R. Millett. *A War To Be Won: Fighting the Second World War.* Cambridge, Mass.: Belknap Press of Harvard University Press, 2000.

Newman, Robert P. *Owen Lattimore and the "Loss" of China.* Berkeley: University of California Press, 1992.

Paine, S. C. M. *Imperial Rivals: China, Russia, and their Disputed Frontier.* Armonk, N.Y.: M. E. Sharpe, 1996.

Parton, James. *"Air Force Spoken Here": General Ira Eaker and the Command of the Air.* Montgomery, Ala.: Air University Press, 2000.

Pearcy, Arthur. *Dakota at War.* London: I. Allan, 1982.

Peattie, Mark R. *Sunburst: The Rise of the Japanese Naval Air Power, 1909–1941.* Annapolis, Md.: Naval Institute Press, 2001.

Pepper, Suzanne. *Civil War in China: The Political Struggle, 1945–1949.* Berkeley: University of California Press, 1978.

Phillips, Bob. *KC8 Burma: CBI Air Warning Team, 1941–1942.* Manhattan, Kans.: Sunflower University Press, 1992.

Proctor, Raymond L. *Hitler's Luftwaffe in the Spanish Civil War.* Westport, Conn.: Greenwood, 1983.

Quinn, Chick Marrs. *The Aluminum Trail: China-Burma-India, World War II, 1942–1945: How & Where They Died.* Privately printed, 1989.

Rasor, Eugene L. *The China-Burma-India Campaign, 1931–1945: Historiography and Annotated Bibliography.* Westport, Conn.: Greenwood, 1998.

Richards, Denis. *Portal of Hungerford: The Life of Marshal of the Royal Air Force, Viscount Portal of Hungerford.* London: Heinemann, 1977.

Romanus, Charles F., and Riley Sunderland. *Stilwell's Command Problems.* Washington, D.C.: Office the Chief of Military History, 1956.

———. *Stilwell's Mission to China.* Washington D.C.: Office of the Chief of Military History, 1953.

———. *Time Runs Out in CBI.* Washington, D.C.: Office of the Chief of Military History, 1959.

Rundell, Walter, "Currency Control by the United States Army in World War II: Foundation for Failure." *Pacific Historical Review* 30 (Nov. 1961): 381–99.

Sainsbury, Keith. *The Turning Point: Roosevelt, Stalin, Churchill, and Chiang-Kai-Shek, 1943: The Moscow, Cairo, and Teheran Conferences.* Oxford, Eng.: Oxford University Press, 1985.

Sapozhnikov, Boris G. *The China Theatre in World War II, 1939–1945.* Moscow: Progress Publishers, 1985.

Sbrega, John J. "Anglo-American Relations and the Selection of Mountbatten as Supreme Allied Commander, South East Asia." *Military Affairs* 46 (Oct. 1982): 139–45.

Schaller, Michael. *The U.S. Crusade in China, 1938–1945.* New York: Columbia University Press, 1979.

Schofield, Victoria. *Wavell: Soldier & Statesman.* London: John Murray, 2006.

Scott, Robert Lee. *God Is My Co-Pilot.* New York: Scribner, 1943.

Serling, Robert J. *Eagle: The Story of American Airlines.* New York: St. Martin's, 1985.

Sheridan, James E. *Chinese Warlord: The Career of Feng Yü-Hsiang.* Stanford, Calif.: Stanford University Press, 1966.

Shilling, Erik, *Destiny: A Flying Tiger's Rendezvous with Fate.* Privately printed, 1993.

Shores, Christopher F. *Bloody Shambles.* Vol. 3, *The Air War for Burma, 1942–1945.* London: Grub Street, 2005.

———, Brian Cull, and Yasuho Izawa. *Bloody Shambles.* 2 vols. London: Grub Street; 1992–93.

Shores, Louis. *Highways in the Sky: The Story of the AACS.* New York: Barnes & Noble, 1947.

Sih, Paul K. T., ed. *Nationalist China during the Sino-Japanese War, 1937–1945.* Hicksville, N.Y.: Exposition Press, 1977.

Sinclair, William Boyd. *Confusion beyond Imagination: China-Burma-India in World War II.* Coeur d'Alene, Idaho: J. F. Whitley, 1986.

Slim, William Joseph. *Defeat into Victory.* New York: D. McKay, 1961.

Smith, C. R. *"A.A.": American Airlines since 1926.* New York: Newcomen Society in North America, 1954.

———. *Air Transportation and National Defense.* Washington, D.C.: Library of Congress, 1947.

———. *Government Policy for Air Transportation.* Dallas: American Airlines, Inc., 1954.

———. *Safety in Air Transportation over the Years.* New York: Wings Club, 1971.

———. *The Turbine Engine and Air Transportation.* Syracuse, N.Y., 1953.

Smith, Felix. *China Pilot: Flying for Chiang and Chennault.* Washington, D.C.: Brassey's, 1995.

Smith, Henry Ladd. *Airways: The History of Commercial Aviation in the United States.* Washington, D.C.: Smithsonian Institution Press, 1991.

Snow, Edgar. *Red Star over China.* New York: Grove Press, 1968.

Solinger, Dorothy J. *Regional Government and Political Integration in Southwest China, 1949–1954: A Case Study.* Berkeley: University of California Press, 1977.

Spector, Ronald H. *Eagle against the Sun: The American War with Japan.* New York: Free Press, 1985.

Spencer, Otha Cleo. *Flying the Hump: Memories of an Air War.* College Station: Texas A&M University Press, 1992.

Stilwell, Joseph Warren. *The Stilwell Papers.* Edited by Theodore H. White. New York: W. Sloane Associates, 1948.

Strickland, Patricia. *The Putt-Putt Air Force: The Story of the Civilian Pilot Training Program and the War Training Service (1939–1944).* Washington, D.C.: Department of Transportation, Federal Aviation Administration, Aviation Education Staff, 1970.

Sweeting, C. G. *Hitler's Squadron: The Fuehrer's Personal Aircraft and Transport Unit, 1933–45.* Washington, D.C.: Brassey's, 2001.

Tarling, Nicholas. *A Sudden Rampage: The Japanese Occupation of Southeast Asia, 1941–1945.* Honolulu: University of Hawaii Press, 2001.

Taylor, John William Ransom, and Kenneth Munson. *Air Transport before the Second World War*. London: New English Library, 1975.

Tennien, Mark A. *Chungking Listening Post*. New York: Creative Age Press, 1945.

Thorne, Bliss K. *The Hump: The Great Military Airlift of World War II*. Philadelphia: Lippincott, 1965.

Tsou, Tang. *America's Failure in China, 1941–50*. Chicago: University of Chicago Press, 1963.

Tuchman, Barbara W. *Stilwell and the American Experience in China, 1911–45*. New York: Macmillan, 1970.

Tunner, William H. *Over the Hump*. 1965. Reprint, Washington, D.C.: Office of Air Force History, 1985.

Underwood, Jeffery S. *The Wings of Democracy: The Influence of Air Power on the Roosevelt Administration, 1933–1941*. College Station: Texas A&M University Press, 1991.

Van de Ven, Hans J. *War and Nationalism in China, 1925–1945*. London: RoutledgeCurzon, 2003.

———. *Warfare in Chinese History*. Leiden, Netherlands: Brill, 2000.

Van Patten, Robert E. "Before the Flying Tigers." *Air Force Magazine* 82, no. 6 (June 1999). Available at http://www.airforce-magazine.com/Magazine Archive/Pages/1999/June%201999/0699before.aspx (accessed Jun. 2010).

Van Zandt, J. Parker. *European Air Transport on the Eve of War–1939: A Lecture Delivered by J. Parker Van Zandt, PH. D*. Northfield, Vt.: Norwich University, 1940.

Wachtel, Joachim. *The History of Lufthansa*. Cologne: Lufthansa German Airlines Public Relations, 1975.

Wakeman, Frederic E. *The Fall of Imperial China*. New York: Free Press, 1975.

———. *Spymaster: Dai Li and the Chinese Secret Service*. Berkeley: University of California Press, 2003.

Waldron, Arthur. *From War to Nationalism: China's Turning Point, 1924–1925*. Cambridge, Eng.: Cambridge University Press, 1995.

Watts, Barry D. *The Foundations of US Air Doctrine: The Problem of Friction in War*. Maxwell Air Force Base, Ala.: Air University Press, 1984.

Weaver, Herbert, and Marvin Rapp. *The Tenth Air Force, 1942*. Manhattan, Kans.: Sunflower University Press, 1997.

Wedemeyer, Albert C. *Wedemeyer Reports!* New York: Holt, 1958.

———, and Keith E. Eiler. *Wedemeyer on War and Peace.* Stanford, Calif.: Hoover Institution, Stanford University, 1987.

Weinberg, Gerhard L. *A World at Arms: A Global History of World War II.* Cambridge, Eng.: Cambridge University Press, 1994.

Weinstein, Allen, and Alexander Vassiliev. *The Haunted Wood: Soviet Espionage in America—The Stalin Era.* New York: Random House, 1999.

Wells, Mark K. *Courage and Air Warfare: The Allied Aircrew Experience in the Second World War.* London: Frank Cass, 1995.

Werrell, Kenneth. *Blankets of Fire: U.S. Bombers over Japan during World War II.* Washington, D.C.: Smithsonian Institution Press, 1996.

West, Levon, and Ivan Dmitri. *Flight to Everywhere.* New York: McGraw-Hill, 1944.

Westad, Odd Arne. *Cold War and Revolution: Soviet-American Rivalry and the Origins of the Chinese Civil War, 1944–1946.* New York: Columbia University Press, 1993.

———. *Decisive Encounters: The Chinese Civil War, 1946–1950.* Stanford, Calif.: Stanford University Press, 2003.

White, Edwin Lee. *Ten Thousand Tons by Christmas.* St. Petersburg, Fla.: Valkyrie Press, 1984.

White, Gerald A., Jr. *The Great Snafu Fleet.* Philadelphia: Xlibris, 2000.

White, Theodore H., and Annalee Jacoby. *Thunder Out of China.* New York: W. Sloane Associates, 1946.

Wolfe, Martin. *Green Light! Men of the 81st Troop Carrier Squadron Tell Their Story.* Philadelphia: University of Pennsylvania Press, 1989.

Wragg, David W. *Airlift: A History of Military Air Transport.* Novato, Calif.: Presidio Press, 1987.

Xu Guangqiu. "American-British Aircraft Competition in South China, 1926–1936." *Modern Asian Studies* 35 (2001): 157–93.

———. *War Wings: The United States and Chinese Military Aviation, 1929–1949.* Westport, Conn.: Greenwood, 2001.

Young, Arthur N. *China and the Helping Hand, 1937–1945.* Cambridge: Harvard University Press, 1963.

———. *China's Wartime Finance and Inflation, 1937–1945.* Cambridge, Mass.: Harvard University Press, 1965.

Yu Maochun. *The Dragon's War: Allied Operations and the Fate of China, 1937–1947.* Annapolis, Md.: Naval Institute Press, 2006.

————. *OSS in China: Prelude to Cold War.* New Haven, Conn.: Yale University Press, 1996.

Zhang Chengjun and Liu Jianye. *Zhongguo kang Ri zhan zheng hua shi* [Illustrated History of China's War of Resistance against Japan]. Beijing: Foreign Languages Press, 2000.

INDEX

1st Ferry Group, 61–62, 85, 97

20th Bomber Command, 187–90, 199–200, 209, 221

AACS. *See* Army Airways Communication Service

ABC Ferry Command, 40–42, 261

accidents, 9, 64, 69–70, 137, 158–59, 187, 205–206, 224, 246, 266; accident rate, 142, 202, 205–206, 220, 226

advisors to China, foreign, 12, 25, 27, 38, 198, 235

African Americans, 110, 135, 160, 166–67, 170, 204–205, 289

aid to China: AMMISCA, 28, 31–32; from Germany, 25; psychological impact, 30, 85, 114; from the US, 5–6, 9, 27–28, 30, 84–85, 92, 193, 196–97, 238, 241; from USSR, 20–21, 25, 28; withheld from Chinese commanders, 196–97. *See also* Chiang Kaishek, requests for aid

air attacks, Japanese, 18, 33, 129

Air Corps, 9–10, 25–26, 39, 62, 105, 259–60, 276

Air Corps Training Command, 137

aircraft: assigned to Hump, 116, 161; available for Hump, 85, 138; Japanese, 33, 274; Japanese, fighters, 37, 47, 52, 81, 100, 148, 151, 177, 260, 294; maintenance, 10, 81, 140; production, 201, 271; transport (general), 37, 39, 78

aircraft crashes, 53, 167

aircrew morale. *See* morale, aircrew

airdrop, 174–75

airfields: construction, 9, 40, 97, 107, 125–26, 139, 280; general problems, 38, 43, 57–58, 101, 106, 135; Japanese attacks, 77, 79, 83, 99–101, 125, 132, 292

airlift: as airpower, 6–7; of animals, 21, 211–12, 224; efficiency, 97, 163; German, 86; of ground troops, 177, 212, 214, 224, 299; as a national characteristic, 9–10

airline pilots, 45–46, 61, 64, 97, 176, 214

Air Staff, 136–37, 161, 166, 267, 279–80, 282, 300

air traffic control, 140, 167–71, 176, 288, 298

Air Transport Command, 4, 12, 41–42, 85, 102–104, 110–11, 121, 247; airline expertise, 42; Hump expansion, 162; movement of Chinese troops, 13, 209–10, 224; organization, 103, 260; origins, 39–41, 60, 102–103, 106; pilots, 62, 117–18, 176, 214, 216, 265; post-World War II, 13; supplement Troop Carrier Command, 176–77; supporting Matterhorn, 187, 189, 191

Alexander, Edward H., 25, 105–106, 116–17, 216, 276; aircrew welfare, 108, 116–17, 120, 139; airfield construction, 126; leadership problems, 142–43; night fly-